Current Controversies and Issues in Personality

Third Edition

Lawrence A. Pervin
Rutgers University

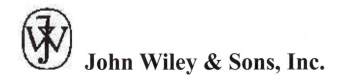

John Wiley & Sons, Inc.

ACQUISITIONS EDITOR	Helen McInnis
MARKETING MANAGER	Sue Lyons
PRODUCTION EDITOR	Brienna Berger/Kelly Tavares
COVER DESIGNER	Maddy Lesure

This book was set in 10/12 Times New Roman, and printed and bound by Courier Corp. The cover was printed by Phoenix Color.

ISBN 0-471-41563-4

Printed in the United States of America
10 9 8 7 6 5 4 3 2

PREFACE

Theory and research in the area of personality psychology rarely is dull. Not only do the issues generally "touch home," but often they involve matters of social and political importance. The chapters in this book cover the major issues confronting psychologists currently interested in personality theory and research. The emphasis is on the current and controversial. Theoretical positions are considered but only in the light of their conflicting positions on a variety of issues. Along with this emphasis on the current and controversial there is an effort to present the issues within their broader social context; that is, to demonstrate that often issues become controversial because they are linked to broader questions of values and beliefs within the surrounding society. Thus, issues arise and change not only because of advances in the field but also because of changes within society generally.

The second edition of *Current Controversies* appeared in 1984. A decade-and-a-half later, we find some issues remain, but a number of new ones have emerged as well. Issues such as the person-situation controversy, the nature-nurture controversy, and why people do and do not change remain. For the first time the issue of a balance between evolutionary and cultural views appears, as does the issue of the relation between the disciplines of psychology and biology—the mind-body issue.

My appreciation to Richard Contrada and Carolyn Morf for their comments on chapters in this book. Sections of this book have been taken or adapted from my book *The Science of Personality*.

Lawrence A. Pervin
Princeton, N.J.
June 2001

CONTENTS

CHAPTER 1

The Enterprise of Personality Research: How Should It Be Conducted?

General Theme

This chapter considers three approaches to research individual case studies, correlational, and experimental. It is suggested that the three approaches often differ in the types of personality-relevant data that are obtained and in their association with various personality theories. In other words, there is a link among research approach, data obtained, and theory. An issue for the field is that of convergence or agreement among findings obtained from different data sources (e.g., self-report, physiological, observations of overt behavior). Future research will profit from methodological pluralism and the demonstration of convergence among findings from different data sources.

> *From this panorama of methods our principal conclusion can be that there is no "one and only" method for the study of personality. All methods have their value, most of them being adapted to the exploration of one special aspect of the problem. The wise investigator will not place his faith in any one exclusively, but will use several to cover more ground, and at the same time to check the findings of each method against those of another.*
>
> *Allport, 1937, p. 398*

> *The story generated by our historical perspective carries a major lesson for the current situation in personality research. The lesson is that methodological pluralism prevails and should be fostered in the field of personality research.*
>
> Craik, 1986, p. 49

When I was a graduate student in personality/clinical psychology, I was struck with the contrast between two points of view, what might even be seen as two different cultures. There existed a battle between the *academicians* and the *clinicians* as to how people were to be studied and understood. On the one hand, the academicians, those who worked primarily in the context of an academic department in a university, emphasized the importance of scientific understanding—empirical rigor, systematic understanding, clear statement and testing of hypotheses, replicability of observations, and statistical tests of significance. On the other hand, the clinicians, those who worked primarily in the context of a clinical setting in a hospital or outpatient clinic, emphasized the importance of case studies and clinical observation—individuals, studied in depth and in their entirety, in real-life situations. Whereas the former looked up to the creative empiricist, the latter looked up to the insights of the sensitive clinician.

At times, rather than respecting what each had to offer to an understanding of personality functioning, the approach of one or the other would be denigrated. For example, the academicians described the clinicians as "crystal ball gazers" as they continued to make use of tests such as the Rorschach inkblot test despite the research literature that challenged its reliability and validity. At the same time, the clinicians suggested that "the academicians wouldn't know a real person if they saw one," removed as they were from what really went on in people as they struggled with inner conflicts and adaptation to real-world difficulties. At times the conflict was exacerbated by a difference in theoretical view, the academicians being committed to one or another form of learning theory (e.g., Hull's S-R theory or Skinnerian theory) and the clinicians being committed to psychoanalytic theory. However, the differences went beyond such a theoretical contrast to the heart of how people were to be understood.

A similar polarization of views is noted by the eminent neuroscientist Eric Kandel in relation to his training in psychiatry during the early 1960s. He captures the split in terms of what was at the time a much-quoted remark: "There are those who care about people and there are those who care about research" (1998, p. 458). In today's somewhat popularized terms it was almost as if the academicians functioned primarily with the left side of the brain and the clinicians with the right side of the brain.

The gap between the academicians and the clinicians posed quite a dilemma for beginning students of the field, who were trying to find out what the field was about, who they were in relation to it, and whether they had any chance for a future as a psychologist—academician or clinician. I suspect that the division is less intense now than it was almost half a century ago but that the issue remains. Thus, the first chapter in this book of current controversies and issues in the field considers the alternative strategies personality psychologists have used to uncover the mystery of human psychological functioning.

The Three Disciplines of Psychology

Aware of the contrasting academician and clinician points of view, it was of interest to me to subsequently learn of a historical tension in the field of psychology as to how the scientific enterprise should be conducted. In a presidential address to the American Psychological Association, "The Two Disciplines of Scientific Psychology," Cronbach (1957) described two streams of "method, thought, and affiliation," the *experimental* and the *correlational*, that divided psychologists. In the experimental approach the goal is to produce consistent variation in behavior as a result of treatments or manipulations of the independent variables. The experimenter changes conditions to observe consequences but, most critically, it is the consequences that are uniform for all, or at least most, subjects that are of interest. The approach has the virtues of permitting tight control over variables, rigorous tests of hypotheses, and confident statements about causation. In its extreme form, Cronbach described it as follows:

> Individual differences have been an annoyance rather than a challenge to the experimenter. His goal is to control behavior, and variation within treatments is proof that he has not succeeded. Individual variation is cast into that outer darkness known as "error variance." For reasons both statistical and philosophical, error variance is to be reduced by any possible device. You turn to animals of a cheap and short-lived species, so that you can use subjects with controlled heredity and controlled experience. You select human subjects drawn from a narrow subculture. You decorticate your subject by cutting neurons or by giving him an environment so meaningless that his unique responses disappear. You increase the number of cases to obtain stable averages, or you reduce N to 1, as Skinner does. But whatever your device, your goal in the experimental tradition is to get those embarrassing differential variables out of sight.

(Cronbach, 1957, p. 674)

In contrast with the experimental approach, where treatments (situations) are varied and individual differences are minimized, the correlational approach takes existing individual differences to be the crux of the matter and regards treatment or situational factors as a source of annoyance. What cannot be completely controlled by the experimental psychologist, the effects of natural events, the simultaneous operation of multiple factors, the diversity of human responses to the same situation, are the very phenomena of interest to the correlational psychologist. Thus, according to Cronbach, "the correlational psychologist is in love with just those variables the experimenter left home to forget. He regards individual and group variations as important effects of biological and social causes. All organisms adapt to their environments, but not equally well. His question is: What present characteristics of the organism determine its mode and degree of adaptation?" (1957, p. 674).

> *Individual differences have been an annoyance rather than a challenge to the experimenter . . . the correlational psychologist is in love with just those variables the experimenter left home to forget.*
>
> *Cronbach, 1957, p. 674*

Cronbach was not the first psychologist to draw attention to differing views among psychologists concerning conduct of the scientific enterprise. In 1939, the president of the American Psychological Association distinguished between the *experimental* attitude and the *clinical* attitude, the former emphasizing control over variables and the latter discovery of the totality of the individual (Dashiell, 1939). The experimental attitude was described by Dashiell as one of science, enabling one, through careful experimentation, to gain control over variables and to understand the conditions under which phenomena occur. In contrast with this, Dashiell described the clinical attitude as one of speculation, wherein the peculiar makeup of the individual person is the primary subject matter. Whereas the former seeks to isolate the factors that influence the *typical* person, the latter seeks to isolate the *individual*. According to Dashiell such differences in focus and approach were not primarily issues of subject matter, but rather of attitude, viewpoint, and ultimate aim.

Nor was Cronbach the last psychologist to draw attention to these differing approaches. In 1982, Hogan, a leading personality psychologist, noted the existence of two distinct traditions, each typified by a specific subject matter, methodology, and theoretical orientation. In the one tradition, there is an emphasis on experimental methodology, single aspects of human performance, and what is true for people generally. In the other tradition, there is an emphasis on clinical case study or questionnaire research, individual differences, and relationships among the parts. And, shortly thereafter, Kimble (1984) described the *two cultures* of psychology—the scientific and humanistic. The two cultures were contrasted in terms such as the following: observation versus intuition, laboratory versus field study and case history, manipulation of variables versus naturalistic observation, observation versus self-report, *nomothetic* (i.e., what is true for the group as a whole) versus *idiographic* (i.e., what is true for the individual), and elementalism (i.e., parts) versus holism (i.e., properties of the whole).

Recognizing these differences in approach and the potential contributions of each approach to an understanding of psychological functioning, periodic calls have been made for a rapprochement, perhaps even a collaborative effort, among the disciplines. Indeed, Dashiell's (1939) focus was on a possible rapprochement in psychology and Cronbach (1957) called for a united discipline: "It is not enough for each discipline to borrow from the other. Correlational psychology studies only variance among organisms; experimental psychology studies only the variance among treatments. A united discipline will study both of these, but it will also be concerned with the otherwise neglected interaction between organismic and treatment variables" (p. 681). Despite such calls for harmony and integration, the disciplines remain.

In sum, we have evidence of a historical tendency in psychology research generally, and personality research in particular, to follow one of three traditions—*experimental, correlational,* or *clinical*. Although such differences need not logically lead to differences in *what* is studied, in fact they tend to be associated with differences in subject matter focus as well as in research methodology. Thus, historically personality researchers have tended to fall on one or the other side of three basic orientations: (1) "making things happen" in research (experimental) versus the "studying what has occurred" (correlational); (2) all persons (experimental) versus the single individual (clinical); and (3) one or a few aspects of the person versus the total individual. Discussion of the disciplines of scientific psychology makes it clear that although psychologists share common goals, they have preferences and biases concerning *how* the scientific enterprise should be conducted. Despite the general objectivity of science, research is a human enterprise. Furthermore, as we shall see in the next section, different research strategies are linked with different kinds of data, and thereby frequently to different theoretical points of view. The observations of one approach may fit better with the focus of one or another theory of personality, and the phenomena emphasized by different theories of personality may be investigated more or less readily by each approach to research.

Three Research Traditions in Personality Psychology: Clinical, Correlational, and Experimental

In this section we will consider the three research traditions in personality psychology, the links between these three traditions and theoretical perspectives, and, perhaps most important of all, the question of agreement among observations obtained from each of the approaches to research.

The Clinical, Case Study Approach to Personality Research

Clinical, case study research involves the systematic, in-depth study of individuals. Historically much of traditional personality theory was based on clinical research. Thus, for example, Freud's psychoanalytic theory, Carl Rogers' humanistic theory, and George Kelly's personal construct theory all were based primarily on clinical observations. According to Kelly, we are all scientists in our efforts to understand and predict the behavior of others based on some construction we have of human functioning. This construction, or lay theory of personality, is based on our observations of the behavior of others. In this sense, the clinical method goes back to the very beginnings of the development of our species as developers of theories of mind. The Old Testament, for example, includes descriptions of the personalities of individuals and the reasons for their behavior. From the time of the Greek civilization, there were efforts to relate individual differences in personality (temperament) to the functioning of the body, a view in principle not that different from current biological views of personality. Historically, philosophers have been concerned with the fundamental nature of humans and the reasons for human action, and many psychology departments in universities evolved out of philosophy departments.

In terms of more systematic clinical efforts, consider the work of the French physician Jean Charcot (1825–1893) at a neurological clinic in Paris. Charcot was interested in understanding the problems of hysterical patients who came to his clinic, individuals who, for example, had paralyses that did not make anatomical sense, problems with seeing despite a healthy visual apparatus, periods of fainting of unknown cause, and inexplicable amnesias or gaps in memory. Charcot began to study these patients, to classify their symptoms, and to treat them, largely through the use of hypnosis. Could one rule out the possibility of physical, organic difficulties? Yes. Could one conclude that they were faking their difficulties? No.

Charcot also trained other physicians, three of whom went on to make their own important observations and are part of the history of personality. One student was Pierre Janet (1859–1947), who succeeded Charcot as director of the neurological clinic and continued Charcot's study of hysterical disorders and his work with hypnosis. Janet attempted to systematize the clinical observations of hysteria and relate them to concepts in psychology. Janet found that patients under hypnosis could recall experiences completely forgotten under normal awake conditions. Suggestions from him to hypnotized patients could often be therapeutic to them in their awake state, even if they had no recall of the suggestions. Thus, Janet was led to the view that there is a splitting of consciousness in hysteria; that is, Janet's clinical observations led him to posit the existence in hysterics of two or more streams of mental functioning that are split off from one another rather than being united as in normal functioning. It was as if the individual could have ideas, "fixed ideas," that were dissociated from one another. Because of this dissociation, conscious awareness and control of the fixed ideas were not possible. It was the existence of these dissociated or split-off parts of consciousness that led to the symptoms of hysteria. Thus, the symptom, such as the paralyzed hand, was under the control of a split-off fixed idea rather than under the voluntary control of the rest of the personality. Although Janet's dissociation theory of hysteria and mental processes was neglected for a long period of time, it has now regained considerable interest from cognitive psychologists interested in unconscious processes (Kihlstrom, 1990).

Another student of Charcot's was the American Morton Prince (1854–1929). Prince is of particular importance to the field of personality for two reasons. First, his book *The Dissociation of Personality* (1906) contained case descriptions of multiple personalities, or individuals within whom two or more distinct and separate personalities exist, often with some personalities being unaware of the existence of other personalities. His detailed case presentation of the treatment of Miss Beauchamp provided many important observations concerning the functioning of multiple personalities. It was the forerunner of such later famous cases as *The Three Faces of Eve* (Thigpen & Cleckley, 1954) and Sybil (Schreiber, 1973).

A second reason for the importance of Morton Prince was his establishment of the Harvard Psychological Clinic in 1927. Here Prince continued his research and provided the climate for clinical research by other psychologists. One such psychologist was Henry Murray (1883–1988), author of the monumental *Explorations in Personality* (1938) and forefather of a generation of personality psychologists interested in the intensive study of the individual. As Prince's successor as director of the Harvard Psychological Clinic, Murray played an important role in furthering efforts to study individuals intensively through the combination of clinical and other methods of investigation.

The third Charcot pupil of note was Sigmund Freud (1856–1939). Many would argue that it is Freud's clinical observations, rather than his theoretical formulations, that show his true genius. As someone who has practiced as a clinician for over 30 years, I share this point of view—the greatness of Freud was in his observations and descriptions of aspects of personality functioning ignored by some and also challenged by many to this day.

What is it that Freud did? Stripped away from the complexities of theory, Freud listened to people. He listened not just for a few minutes but for an hour or so at a time and for weeks, months, and years with the same individual. During this time he encouraged his patients to let their minds wander and to follow but one rule, to say everything that came to mind and withhold nothing. It was Freud's genius to take seriously, and attempt to understand, just these thoughts and feelings, and to encourage individuals to join in this endeavor with him. In its essence, psychoanalysis is a clinical method for investigating the wishes and fears that people have, a method for investigating their memories of the past and the sense they make of these memories in relation to their current functioning, a method for investigating memories of their childhood and how these memories color their relationships in the present, a method for investigating their struggles to cope with painful feelings such as anxiety and shame, and a method for investigating their reluctance to share many thoughts and feelings with others, at times even with themselves. Stripped of abstract and metaphorical terms such as *id, ego, superego,* and *Oedipus complex,* psychoanalysis is about the drama of life played out in each of us, about the inexplicable symptoms we develop and senseless things we find ourselves doing, about why some of us are driven to succeed and others cannot allow themselves success, about how we can both crave intimacy and also be afraid of it.

As is well known, Freud's observations and his theories have been challenged from the time of their initial presentation to today. Not only do we have psychoanalysts who question the "scientific truth" of what patients recall in psychoanalysis (Spence, 1982, 1987) but those who question the very nature of the observations themselves. In particular, there is the question of the extent to which Freud and all psychoanalysts influence the data they observe, either through subtle or not so subtle forms of suggestion (Crews, 1993; Esterson, 1993; Powell & Boer, 1994). In other words, for all of the brilliance of Freud and his efforts at careful observation and description, there are many who still ask: Where are the data? Although some suggest that observations drawn from patients in analysis are adequate grounds for testing concepts, others suggest that clinical data remain suspect and are an inadequate basis for testing theory (Grunbaum, 1993). In the words of Eysenck, a frequent and passionate critic of psychoanalysis, "we can no more test Freudian hypotheses on the couch than we can adjudicate between the rival hypotheses of Newton and Einstein by going to sleep under the apple tree" (1953, p. 229). Thus, it is here that we run into the nub of the problem with many forms of clinical data—unless the observations can be confirmed by others, in systematic and specified ways, they are useless from a scientific standpoint.

No other method allows the depth of observations of a single Personality offered by the psychoanalytic method. . . . Clinical observation casts a broad net for observing psychologically meaningful phenomena, particularly in the "context of discovery" . . .

Westen & Gabbard, 1999, p. 83

While the precise nature of Freud's clinical material remains a matter of conjecture, it is evident that much of it was elicited by means of a highly directive and coercive technique . . .

Esterson, 1998, p. 7

It would be unfortunate, even tragic, if the rich insights that have come from psychoanalysis were to be lost. . . . Insights from individual cases can be powerful. But clinical insights, especially those based on individual cases, need to be supported by independent and objective methods.

Kandel, 1998, p. 467

The Correlational Approach to Personality Research

Correlational research typically involves the use of statistical methods to establish the association, or correlation, between measures on which individuals have been found to differ. In other words, the correlational approach emphasizes individual differences and the effort to establish relationships among those differences on various personality characteristics. About the same time that Charcot was conducting clinical studies of hysteria, Sir Francis Galton was involved with studies that would lead him to be called the "founder of individual psychology" (Boring, 1950). A half-cousin of Darwin's, Galton was influenced by Darwin's discoveries and his theory of evolution. Thus, he set out to study differences in humans and whether those differences were due to heredity. With a background in meteorology, he believed that quantitative measurement was a necessary characteristic of a truly scientific endeavor. His early work was on the question of whether genius and eminence tend to run in families. Through the use of defined criteria for rating such accomplishments, and the careful biographical study of families of men of accomplishment, Galton found a strong relationship between the biological closeness of two men and the probability of their both being eminent. His resulting emphasis on "nature" over "nurture" formed the basis for the nature-nurture controversy, to be considered in Chapter 5.

Following this research, Galton set up a laboratory to measure individuals on a great variety of characteristics. Over the course of time he measured thousands of individuals on a variety of physical and psychological characteristics. In this research he used tests, ratings, and questionnaires. To establish relationships among the data, he developed the concept of the correlation coefficient or the quantitative measure of the association between two sets of data. Galton's work on the measurement of mental abilities was further pursued by another British psychologist, Charles Spearman (1863–1945). Inspired by Galton's work, Spearman set out to determine whether there was something that might be called general intelligence or whether individual differences in intelligence were due to differences in multiple, independent, separate abilities. To do this, he gave many different tests of mental ability to hundreds of people and conducted correlation tests to determine whether those high on one ability also tended to be high on other abilities. His answer to the question concerning intelligence was that there is a general intelligence or *g* factor. In this work he also created the statistical procedure known as *factor analysis*, through which one finds commonalities, called *factors*, in a large mass of data. The question for personality researchers is whether there are basic groups of characteristics, or factors, on which people differ. If we measure people on lots of personality characteristics, do the many differences really boil down to a few groupings, and, if so, what are they?

The development of factor analysis has been fundamental to the correlational approach to personality. Beginning with the 1940s, personality research has witnessed extensive use of ratings and questionnaires as sources of personality data, the use of factor analysis as a statistical technique, and the concept of the trait as a fundamental unit of personality. This combination of a statistical technique (factor analysis), particular kinds of data (ratings and questionnaires), and a concept (the trait), has exerted a powerful influence on the field. It is here that we see the emphasis on measurement and individual differences noted as fundamental to the correlational approach to personality. It is here that we can see at least partial fulfillment of Allport's prediction in 1937 that Galton's view "seems destined to dominate the psychology of personality during the twentieth century" (Allport, 1937, p. 97).

This combination of the use of ratings and questionnaires, factor analysis, and the trait concept is seen in the influential early work of trait psychologists such as Raymond B. Cattell (1905–1998) and Hans J. Eysenck (1916–1997). It also is seen in the more contemporary research associated with the *Big Five* (Goldberg, 1993) and the *Five-Factor Theory* (McCrae & Costa, 1999) approaches to personality.

At its core, the correlational approach to personality seeks to define the basic structure of personality, what Cattell viewed as personality's basic table of the elements. Although there is diversity among researchers within the correlational tradition, with various researchers studying different concepts, using different kinds of data, and using different statistical procedures for data analysis, the defining characteristics are the use of questionnaire data and the statistical method of factor analysis. Ultimately, then, the value of this approach will be defined by the extent to which personality psychologists agree that self-report data, particularly in the form of questionnaires, can form the foundation for a science of personality and agree that the factors derived from using the method of factor analysis make sense as basic units of personality. At the present time many personality psychologists are encouraged by the progress being made. However, agreement by no means exists among all personality psychologists concerning the utility of factor analysis as a method for discovering the basic units of personality. Many would agree with Allport's early suggestion that the factors identified through factor analysis "resemble sausage meat that has failed to pass the pure food and health inspection" (1958, p. 251). In addition, as we will now consider in some depth, many personality psychologists suggest that the field places excessive emphasis on self-report, questionnaire data.

The Place of Self-Report Data in the Science of Personality. Self-report data are used by personality psychologists of all theoretical orientations. However, particularly in the form of questionnaires, they play a central role in contemporary trait theory. Given the role of such data in contemporary research, an in-depth evaluation of this method seems in order.

Unfortunately, self-reports are fallible sources of data . . .

Schwartz, 1999, p. 93

Self-report indexes seem to possess great validity.

Howard, 1990, p. 294

The facts important to personality psychologists go beyond those that can be gathered by questionnaires . . . . Psychologists want and need to know what people actually do, think, and feel in the various contexts of their lives.

Funder, 2001, p. 213

The arguments against the utility of self-report data include the psychoanalytic emphasis on defenses, problems of distortions due to self-serving and self-presentational biases, errors due to problems of information processing such as memory distortions and errors in keeping track of large amounts of data about one's own behavior, and lack of agreement with other (e.g., physiological) data (Greenwald & Banaji, 1995; Holtzman & Kagan, 1995; Wilson, 1994). Self-report data also are extremely sensitive to the wording of items: "Unfortunately, self-reports are fallible sources of data, and minor changes in question wording, question format, or question context can result in major changes in the obtained results" (Schwarz, 1999, p. 93).

At the same time, these measures also have their supporters (Hogan & Nicholson, 1988). At times one finds strange bedfellows among the supporters. Thus, although for different reasons and emphasizing different kinds of self-report data, both social cognitive and trait theorists find merit in them. Social cognitive theorists, such as Bandura (1986), suggest that self-report data are useful when questions are directed at phenomena to which the subject has attended and which do not tax memory resources. Thus, for example, Bandura (1986, 1999) is a strong proponent of the utility of self-efficacy belief measures (i.e., measures of individual beliefs concerning their ability to master tasks in specific situations). On the other hand, as we will shortly consider in greater detail, trait psychologists (Funder 1989, 1993; McCrae & Costa, 1990) suggest that by and large people are pretty accurate judges of their own behavior and personality functioning.

Agreement between self-report data and other personality measures seems particularly problematic when they involve global, memory-dependent judgments as opposed to situation-specific, momentary assessments. The problem of lack of agreement between global self-report data and other measures can be seen in studies of subjective reports of coping. Years of research on how individuals cope with stress led Richard Lazarus and his colleagues to develop a questionnaire measure of individual differences in preferred coping method—the *Ways of Coping Scale* (Folkman, et. al, 1986; Lazarus, 1993). Individuals are asked to think about specific events in their lives and to indicate the extent to which they respond in one or another way. The use of each of eight coping strategies is assessed, with a central distinction made between problem-focused forms of coping (e.g., efforts to alter the situation) and emotion-focused forms of coping (e.g., emotional distancing, escape-avoidance, seeking social support).

Although the scale has been extensively used in stress and adaptation research, with many interesting findings suggesting that both situational and personality factors influence choice of coping method, it also has come under considerable attack. In an article entitled "The Mismeasure of Coping by Checklist," Coyne and Gotlib (1996) suggested that "as they are currently employed, conventional checklists render an incomplete and distorted portrait of coping" (p. 959). Recent studies comparing responses to the Ways of Coping Scale to momentary sampling of responses to stressful situations suggests poor correspondence between the two. That is, retrospective reports of coping, such as obtained on the Ways of Coping Scale, do not correspond well with day-to-day reports of coping (Stone et al., 1998). The conclusion drawn from such research is that "with the passage of time, many people do not, and perhaps cannot, provide highly accurate summaries of how they coped with a stressor" (Smith, Leffingwell, & Ptacek, 1999, p. 1059). More generally, it is suggested that "self-report assessments of trait coping are poor measures of the trait component of momentary coping and very poor predictors of coping in specific situations" (Schwartz, et. al, 1999, p. 360).

As noted, the use of self-report measures is not without its proponents, particularly among supporters of the trait point of view. This could not be otherwise since so much of current trait theory is the result of analysis of responses to questionnaires, either in terms of self-ratings or ratings of individuals by peers, spouses, or parents. Thus, the issue of validity of self-report, questionnaire responses is central to the entire trait approach to personality. The suggested soundness of this approach is well-stated in the following:

> Most personality assessment relies on the use of questionnaires. Respondents are typically presented with a series of items and asked to indicate whether or to what extent each item accurately describes their personality. Questionnaires are also used to gather informant ratings of personality traits. In both cases, the method assumes that respondents understand the procedure and are both willing and able to provide reasonably accurate responses. Usually respondents are. The accumulated construct validity of all personality questionnaires is compelling evidence of the soundness of this method of measurement.

> *(Piedmont, et. al., 2000, p. 582)*

In other words, it is suggested that respondents have insight into their own personality and are prepared to answer in nondefensive ways. Validity scales, often used to identify subjects who may be responding in a biased or defensive manner, are viewed as unnecessary.

Supporters of self-report, questionnaire measures of traits place particular emphasis on self-other agreement as evidence for the validity of such measures. For example, consider the following:

> Self-other agreement—that is, the convergence between self- and other-ratings on the same trait—is a centrally important issue in personality research. Personologists traditionally have used peer judgments as key evidence in the validation of self-ratings. . . . Evidence regarding self-other agreement played a crucial role in establishing the reality of traits. It is now well established that substantial self-other agreement—reflecting correlations of .40 and higher—can be demonstrated across a broad range of traits.

> *(Watson, Hubbard, & Wiese, 2000, p. 546)*

At the same time, others caution that self-other agreement need not reflect accuracy—they can both be wrong!

What is the nature of self-other agreement that establishes the reality of traits? Here we may consider two questions: First, is the level of self-other agreement such that we can conclude that the same person is being rated or perceived in both cases? Second, is self-other agreement an adequate basis for establishing accuracy of report and trait reality? An excellent study by Funder, Kolar, and Blackman (1995) brings to the forefront some of the issues relevant to these two questions. In this study, self-reports of college students on the Big Five (i.e., *Neuroticism, Extraversion, Openness to Experience, Agreeableness, Conscientiousness*) were compared with reports of parents, college friends, and hometown friends. Interjudge agreement on the general order of correlations in the .40s was found, consistent with other reports in the literature (Funder, 1980; John & Robins, 1994). Agreement as a result of context overlap, communication, and self-observer similarity were ruled out as *the* basis for agreement. The self-observer correlations were judged to be sufficiently high, and the influence of context sufficiently small, to arrive at the following conclusion: "The results also show that judges who see the target in different contexts agree with *each other* about what the target is like, although those who know the target in the same context agree even better. It seems that the parents, hometown acquaintances, and college acquaintances all know the target as more or less the same person" (Funder, Kolar, & Blackman, 1995, p. 661, italics in the original).

Do such correlations indicate that actors and observers more or less know the same person? First, one can question whether correlations on the order of .4 represent "high" levels of agreement. Second, it is important to note that the magnitude of self-observer agreement varies depending on the trait considered. More observable traits, such as Extraversion, result in better agreement among raters than less observable traits, such as Neuroticism. Clearly the availability of cues for making trait judgments is a key ingredient in determining agreement among observers. Third, there is variability among observer correlations. For example, the correlations on the Neuroticism trait factor, obtained from ratings on the NEO-PI (a standard questionnaire measure of basic trait dimensions), were .50 for self-parents, .34 for self-college friend, and .22 for self-hometown friend. In addition to the importance of the trait being considered and observers making the ratings, agreement varies depending on qualities of the self-rater. For example, narcissistic individuals are prone to distort representations of themselves, resulting in lower self-other agreement than is true for nonnarcissistic individuals (Gosling, et. al, 1998).

Another point to consider is that self-observer agreement decreases as the personality characteristic considered becomes more specific. For example, self-observer correlations on the NEO-PI for the trait score (factor) for Neuroticism were higher than those for more specific components (scales) of Anxiety and Hostility, and self-observer correlations for the trait score for Extraversion were higher than those for the more specific components (scales) of Assertiveness and Activity. In addition, where judges rated targets on even more specific personality items, the mean self-observer correlation across 100 items was .16 and the mean observer-observer correlation across the 100 items was .20. Although lower reliabilities for the more specific measures may account for some of the decrease in size of the correlations, it also is possible that specificity of detail of personality functioning is the more critical ingredient.

Finally, context makes a difference. The mean same-context (college-college friends, mom and dad, hometown-hometown friends) correlation for the Big Five was .50, while that for the different context (parents-college, parents-hometown, college-hometown) was .29. Agreement between judges in different contexts generally was significant (14 of 15 correlations), but on average about 60 percent of the degree of agreement found among judges from the same context. The conclusion drawn by the authors from these data, while supportive of the overall emphasis on self-observer agreement, makes the point that context does make a difference: "These results indicate that judges who know a target in the same context agree better about his or her personality than do judges who know him or her in different contexts. However, this point should not overshadow the finding that judges from different contexts also tend to agree with each other. Viewing the target in the same context, although surely helpful, is not a *necessary* component of interjudge agreement" (Funder, Kolar, & Blackman, 1995, p. 660, italics in the original).

In sum, although Funder and his colleagues interpreted the results of this important study as supportive of self-other agreement, and thereby as supportive of the reality of traits, at least five variables seem to influence the magnitude of such agreement—availability of cues for the trait being rated, nature of the observer, qualities of the self-rater, specificity of the trait, and similarity of context of observation or basis on which the personality ratings are being made. At that, not all psychologists would agree with the assessment of the literature in general. Thus, although Funder and his colleagues conclude that "parents, hometown acquaintances, and college acquaintances all know the target as more or less the same person", (1995, p. 661), Kazdin (1994) concludes that "research to date has shown that scores obtained from different informants may not correlate with each other" (p. 262).

Does evidence that people often perceive themselves as others do mean that they perceive themselves accurately and that self-report data can be a foundation for a science of personality? Kenny (1994) has conducted considerable research on the question of agreement and accuracy in social perception. He suggests that the data "strongly support the conclusion that people do indeed see themselves as others do" (p. 189) but also suggests that "self-ratings carry a great deal of excess baggage; that is, they measure other things besides how the person truly is" (p. 202) and that the data "should lead researchers to question seriously the orientation that views personality as the study of self-report inventories" (p. 194). One may note here as well the finding of Swann and Gill (1997) that confidence in perception of the other in no way corresponds with greater accuracy. In other words, there is no reason to believe that limiting ratings to those in which there is high confidence would enhance accuracy.

Evidence regarding self-other agreement played a crucial role in establishing the reality of traits.

Watson, Hubbard, & Wiese, 2000, p. 546

So a perceiver who agrees with the self may be adopting the same mistaken view of the self. Researchers should, therefore, avoid using self-ratings as a criterion in accuracy research.

Kenny, 1994, p. 134

Further insight into the question of the accuracy of self-report data can be obtained from consideration of another excellent study by Funder and his colleagues (Spain, Eaton, & Funder, 2000). This study compared the relative accuracy of self versus other judgments of personality. Subjects rated themselves on the traits of Neuroticism and Extraversion and nominated acquaintances who knew them well to make ratings of them on these traits as well. These ratings were used to predict to daily emotional experiences of the subjects and to laboratory behavior expressive of the two traits. The criterion of daily emotional expression was assessed in terms of self-ratings of emotions four times a day for eight days. Laboratory behavior was assessed by observers of the subjects interacting with a new acquaintance. These observers were trained in the use of an objective coding scheme for behaviors expressive of the traits of Neuroticism and Extraversion.

Would subject self-ratings better predict emotional experience and laboratory behavior expressive of the traits of Neuroticism and Extraversion than ratings by acquaintances; that is, do people know themselves better than others do? Is the individual a better judge of his or her personality than others who know him or her well? The data using emotional experience as the criterion suggested that this is the case. For both Neuroticism and Extraversion, self-ratings correlated more highly with ratings of emotions than did ratings by acquaintances. However, a cautionary note in the interpretation of the data is in order; that is, the personality self-ratings may have been more accurate than the other-ratings because the criterion itself involved self-ratings (i.e., self-ratings of daily emotional experience). In regard to the laboratory behavior criterion, the data were more complex. Here self-ratings did a better job than other-ratings in predicting a composite score of Extraversion behavior but the predictions for specific behaviors (e.g., Is talkative; Seems likable) were quite low and statistically nonsignificant. In regard to laboratory behavior expressive of Neuroticism, neither self-ratings nor other-ratings were predictive of composite scores or specific behaviors (e.g., Expresses insecurity; Acts irritated). Thus, although many personality psychologists suggest that both self-ratings and other-ratings can be used to assess personality but that subjects know themselves best, the data are less than conclusive in this regard. Accuracy, defined in terms of the prediction of behavior, would appear to remain a problem for both self and other, at least in terms of the prediction of specific behaviors in specific situations.

I must confess that I have a particular point of view here, one that questions the degree to which self-observer agreement data support the validity of trait concepts and measures, and also that more generally questions our reliance in personality research on self-report measures (Pervin, 1999). In response to concerns I expressed in relation to the reported self-observer agreements, Funder (personal communication) asked: "What would be high enough self-observer correlations if these aren't? What other interesting relations between variables can you name where the relationships are as great?" These are reasonable questions, which makes the point that this is an issue in the field! Clearly part of the issue is how to interpret a correlation of a specific magnitude. Thus, whereas some interpret a correlation of .4 as reflecting good or high agreement, others consider it to represent moderate agreement and some as reflective of a lack of concordance (Tiffany, 1990). And, whereas some consider such correlations as evidence for the validity of the trait concept, others are not persuaded by the data.

A global evaluation of the merit of self-report measures of personality probably is impossible, their accuracy and utility being related to the variable being considered, the goals of the investigator, the measure of accuracy used, the degree of defensiveness of the individual, the observability of the trait being assessed, and so on. Clearly trait psychologists, as well as others, are sufficiently impressed with the self-observer agreement data and predictive utility of questionnaires in predicting job performance to feel comfortable basing much of their research enterprise on such measures (Hogan & Ones, 1997). On the other hand, others point to the lack of agreement between self and observer ratings, the lack of agreement between ratings made by different observers of the same person, and the problematic relationship between self-ratings and other personality measures (e.g., fantasy measures, physiological measures, objective measures of daily behavior) as the basis for questioning an exclusive, or even major, reliance on self-report measures. The boundaries of the utility of such measures remain to be determined. No scientific field can advance in the absence of methods for measuring relevant variables. Current advances in the life sciences are based in good part on technological advances that provide for the identification and measurement of phenomena previously inaccessible. Where the value of self-report data will stand as methodological advances occur in the field of personality remains to be seen.

The Experimental Approach to Personality Research

Experimental research involves the systematic manipulation of variables to establish causal relationships. Such manipulation does not occur in the clinical and correlational approaches. In contrast to the clinical emphasis on the individual, the experimental approach typically involves the study of many subjects. In contrast to the correlational approach, with its emphasis on individual differences, the experimental approach emphasizes general laws of psychological functioning that apply to all people. In contrast to both clinical and correlational research, there is direct experimental control over the variables of interest to the investigator.

At about the same time that Charcot was conducting his clinical investigations in France, and Galton was conducting his studies in England, Wilhelm Wundt (1832–1920) was establishing the first laboratory of experimental psychology in Germany. Whereas Galton has been described as the founder of individual psychology, Wundt has been described as the "founder of general psychology" (Boring, 1950, p. 487). Trained in chemistry and physiology, Wundt stressed the place of psychology as a science—an experimental science with procedures similar to those followed in the natural sciences. Wundt defined psychology as the science of immediate experience and investigated the effects of changes in stimuli (e.g., lights, sounds) on the intensity and quality of subjects' experiences.

Experimental research always has been a fundamental part of the scientific enterprise of psychology, dating back to early work using nonsense syllables to study memory, to Pavlov's research on classical conditioning, to the influential learning theories of Hull and Skinner during the period between the 1940s and 1960s. The work of Pavlov, Hull, and Skinner was broadly influential in psychology, including the area of personality. Since the cognitive revolution in the 1960s, many problems of importance to personality psychologists have been studied through the application of principles and procedures borrowed from experimental cognitive psychology. In particular, we can note such areas as the study of unconscious processes, the self, and motivation (Pervin, 1990). Although we have not seen the development of comprehensive theories of personality such as those that grew out of clinical approaches, or the development of a "consensual" view such as the five-factor model from the correlational approach, we have seen the development of social cognitive and information-processing approaches to personality (Bandura, 1999; Mischel & Shoda, 1999).

The psychologists associated with these cognitive approaches to personality depart radically from the principles and procedures emphasized by the early experimental learning psychologists such as Hull and Skinner. They make use of concepts of internal processes, such as goals, and often are eclectic in their methods of research, including at times the use of questionnaires. Generally they emphasize the study of human subjects rather than animals, sometimes in the natural environment rather than in the laboratory. What binds them together, however, and allows us to include them within the experimental tradition, is their emphasis on links with experimental psychology and the use of systematic research to establish general principles of personality functioning. Although accepting of the use of clinical material for suggesting hypotheses to be investigated, they reject the clinical approach as the fundamental basis for a science of personality. And, although accepting of the use of self-report in some research, they reject a primary emphasis on questionnaires and the use of personality concepts derived from correlational approaches such as factor analysis.

Although in many ways the experimental approach represents the scientific ideal, it is limited in the nature of the situations that can be presented to subjects. That is, often questions are raised concerning the ecological validity or generalizability of findings from the laboratory to the natural environment (Lewis, 1995). A tale of research by Epstein (1997) is interesting in this regard. Epstein was interested in anxiety in the natural setting and studied the responses of individuals learning to parachute jump. Excited by the results found, he was led to examine his findings under the more controlled conditions of the laboratory. Instead of the threat of a parachute jump, the threat of an electric shock was used. Instead of variation in experience in parachute jumping, there was variation in amount of exposure to the experimental shock condition. To his surprise, and consternation, he was unable to replicate his earlier findings. The robust results observed in the natural setting were virtually washed out by what were regarded as minor, inconsequential details of the experimental setting. One of the lessons Epstein reported that he had learned in over forty years of personality research was that laboratory results are less robust, replicable, and generalizable than many suspect.

In brief, the psychological laboratory has generally produced psychological truths, rather than trivialities.

Anderson, Lindsay, & Bushman, 1999, p. 3

In other words, there is good reason to suspect that many laboratory findings are less replicable and generalizable than is generally recognized.

Epstein, 1997, p. 11

For many personality psychologists, the most troubling aspect of the experimental approach is the limitation on studying the richness of relationships among the elements of an individual's personality. In limiting investigation to a few well-controlled variables, the experimental approach misses what is a fundamental aspect of personality functioning, the functioning of the parts in the context of a total system. Thus, even after defining cause-effect relationships among specific variables, the personality psychologist is left with the task of considering how all the pieces fit together, that is, of determining how the personality as a whole functions. After breaking down personality into the pieces, we are left with the task of putting Humpty-Dumpty back together again.

Linkages Among Theory, Content, and Research Method

I have highlighted aspects of the three traditions of research. The importance of these three traditions is not just the differing methodologies but, as suggested, their implications for the kinds of phenomena studied and the theoretical views that they lead to and are derived from. That is, there is a feedback loop among theory, data, and research method such that alternative personality theories tend to be associated with particular kinds of data and methods for studying specific phenomena. As suggested above, and considered in detail elsewhere (Pervin & John, 2000), the following relationships among theory, content, and research method can be considered: 1) psychoanalysis—fantasies and unconscious processes, conflict and defense—clinical case studies; 2) trait theory—dispositions, traits—questionnaires and ratings, correlations and factor analysis; 3) social cognitive theory—cognitive representations of self and goals, discriminations among situations—experiments in laboratory situations. This is not to suggest that every research in the personality literature will follow this pattern but rather that a strong tendency exists for these relationships among theory, phenomena of interest, and method of investigation.

The existence of such relationships is perhaps most clearly seen in the comments offered by representatives of each orientation concerning approaches supported by other points of view. For example, Cattell (1959), as noted a leader in the development of trait theory and early user of factor analysis to discover the basic units of personality, distinguished among three methods in the study of personality: bivariate, clinical, and multivariate. Cattell described the bivariate method as following the classical experimental design of the physical sciences. He felt that this represented a simplistic and piecemeal approach to personality, and thereby was inadequate to handle the complexity of interactions among variables that is characteristic of human personality functioning. Cattell felt that the clinical method had the advantage that researchers could study important behaviors as they occur and look for lawfulness in the functioning of the total organism but relied too much on intuition to assess variables and memory to keep track of relationships: "The clinician has his heart in the right place, but perhaps we may say that he remains a little fuzzy in the head" (Cattell, 1959, p.45). Which leaves, of course, Cattell's favoring of the multivariate method, which he viewed as having the scientific rigor and quantitative analyses characteristic of the bivariate method as well as the study of important phenomena and consideration of many variables characteristic of the clinical method. Thus, Cattell relied on the factor analysis of questionnaire data to arrive at sixteen factors or trait dimensions as the basic building blocks of personality. To his enormous credit, Cattell explored relationships among factors derived from such different sources of data as objective life events, ratings by observers and peers, self-reports, and objective-test (laboratory) data. Unfortunately, despite years of effort to match factors derived from these different data sources, no direct one-to-one mapping of factors was possible, an important point to which we shall return shortly.

Of course, clinicians, particularly of a psychoanalytic orientation, have their own well-known criticisms of both experimental-laboratory and correlational-questionnaire investigations. Early on, Freud expressed his lack of enthusiasm for laboratory investigations, even those investigations that confirmed what he felt were already apparent from his clinical observations. Subsequent reviews of the lack of experimental support for various psychoanalytic concepts (e.g., defenses) are rejected by clinicans for their inability to reproduce the circumstances under which the relevant phenomena are said to occur (Cramer, 1991; Vaillant, 1992). Similar skepticism is expressed by psychologists sympathetic to the psychoanalytic view in relation to the value of self-report measures of psychological well-being: "Countless scales exist to assess one or another facet of mental health. In general these scales are straightforward. Items tend to be transparent in intent and investigators tend to accept scale scores at face value. . . . In contrast, psychoanalytic thinkers (and depth psychologists more generally) are often unwilling to accept self-report data at face value. They take seriously the notion of unconscious processes and unconscious defenses and assume that psychological distress is often covert, experienced and expressed only indirectly. From this perspective, many people who report psychological health may not be healthy at all" (Shedler, Mayman, & Manis, 1993, p. 1117). The psychologists expressing this view go on to present evidence suggesting that many people who look healthy on standard mental health scales are not psychologically healthy and, because of the defensive processes involved, suffer from physiological costs that put them at risk for medical illness.

The clinician has his heart in the right place, but perhaps we may say that he remains a little fuzzy in the head.

Cattell, 1959, p. 45

. . . psychoanalytic thinkers (and depth psychologists more generally) are unwilling to accept self-report data at face value. . . . From this perspective, many people who report psychological health many not be healthy at all.

Shedler, Mayman, & Manis, 1993, p. 1117

Henry Murray, who with Christiana Morgan developed the *Thematic Appercep-tion Test*, was critical of the singular use of questionnaires since he felt that they could not tap into the phenomena of interest to depth psychologists: "Children perceive inaccurately, are very little conscious of their inner states and retain fallacious recollections of occurrences. Many adults are hardly better" (1938, p. 15). To his enormous credit, Murray attempted to capture the comprehensiveness of the clinical approach and the rigor of the experimental approach in his monumental *Explorations in Personality* (1938), to this day one of the finest pieces of personality research. His description of this effort is interesting in relation to the issues under consideration: "In short, then, we might say that our work is the natural child of the deep, significant, metaphorical, provocative and questionable speculations of psychoanalysis and the precise, systematic, statistical, trivial and artificial methods of academic psychology. Our hope is that we have inherited more of the virtues than the vices of our parents" (1938, pp. 33–34).

The person-situation controversy, to be considered in depth in a later chapter (Chapter 3), is interesting in relation to the issue of linkages among theory, data, and methodological approach. Briefly, Mischel (1968) sparked the controversy by attacking traditional personality theory (e.g., trait theory) for the suggestion of broad consistencies in behavior across situations and use of questionnaires. According to him, from a social cognitive perspective, people discriminate among situations and therefore behavior is more situation specific than suggested by trait theorists. In accord with this, he suggests that questionnaires assessing broad dispositions are of little predictive value.

A 1986 special issue of the *Journal of Personality* was devoted to the examination of research methods in personality psychology, particularly in the light of such issues. In an introductory chapter to the issue, West (1986) notes that experimental research conducted in the laboratory has had a privileged status as the method of choice for investigating personality issues. However, he goes on to suggest that such research has its own limitations, including lack of external or ecological validity. In relation to the person-situation issue, and of particular importance in relation to the linkage being suggested among theory, method, and data, he suggests that "several known conditions which facilitate finding strong trait-behavior relationships are contrary to the basic premises of the typical laboratory investigation. Creating environments in which situational constraint is low so that trait-behavior relationships will be maximized is antithetical to maintaining good experimental control. Allowing subjects to choose and/or modify situations, another method of enhancing trait-behavior relationships, is antithetical to maintaining random assignment to treatment conditions" (1986, p.5). In other words, West (1986) suggests that the experimental, laboratory methodology, the methodology emphasized by social cognitive psychologists, does not provide for observing the relationships emphasized by trait psychologists.

In the same journal issue, Moskowitz (1986) notes that methods such as self-reports and ratings by knowledgeable informants (e.g., peers) have their strong proponents, and that whereas those emphasizing person factors assume at least some validity in global judgments associated with such methods, those emphasizing situationist views focus on errors in human judgments and prefer the direct measurement of specific behaviors. According to her, proponents of each method have a different tolerance for the threats to validity associated with alternative methods. She also suggests that different methods may be more or less appropriate for the investigation of different phenomena.

In sum, there is considerable evidence of a linkage among theory, research method, and data such that proponents of one theoretical point of view are led to the investigation of some phenomena rather than other phenomena, emphasize the strengths of the research method associated with that point of view and the weaknesses of alternative research methods, and are drawn to conclusions concerning personality functioning that may differ from those drawn from the utilization of alternative research methods.

Convergence Among Data from Alternative Research Methods

We now come to a question fundamental to the science of personality psychology: To what extent do the measures from the various research traditions converge or agree with one another? It is one thing to suggest that different methods are best suited to study and measure different concepts. It is another thing to find that different data sources lead to different measures of the same concept. In an important article concerning this issue, Kagan (1988) suggested that "there is often a minimal correlation, or none at all, between an empirical index of a concept like anxiety based on overt behavior, cognitive functioning, symptoms or physiology, on the one hand, and one based on answers in an interview or on a questionnaire" (p. 614). Because of the extensive use of self-report measures in contemporary personality research, Kagan (1988) takes these to particular task. However, it also is the case that he does not claim that one source of data automatically is more valid than another. Thus, the fundamental issue is the questionable convergence of data from different sources.

For those who doubt the seriousness of the problem, consider the following: (1) clinical work with patients and experimental research on memory suggest different conclusions concerning the accuracy of recovered memories (Kluft, 1997; Loftus, 1997); (2) survey data and controlled clinical trials of alternative methods of psychotherapy come to different conclusions concerning the utility of self-report data and the comparative efficacy of various forms of therapy (Jacobson & Christensen, 1996; Seligman, 1995); (3) self-report data of level of anxiety and physiological measures do not necessarily agree, particularly in cases of defensive subjects (Newton & Contrada, 1992; Newton, Haviland, & Contrada, 1996); (4) self-reported attachment style correlates poorly with interview-based measures (Davila, Burge, & Hammen, 1997); (5) self-ratings, parent ratings, and teacher ratings of attachment show poor correspondence with one another and differing relationships to measures of psychological disturbance in children (Kazdin, 1994); (6) job performance measures show poor agreement with ratings of performance and tests of job knowledge

(Wagner, 1997); (7) self-reports of eating behavior and exercise show poor agreement with diary measures of diet and activity (Lichtman, et al., 1992).

Results such as these suggest a serious problem in considering data from different methods. They do not indicate that one or another data source is best, or at least best for measuring specific concepts. Rather they suggest a general problem in convergence. Surveying the field, Sechrest (1986) suggests that there are few prescriptions for choices between methods that can be made with any confidence. He offers the following distressing but perhaps sobering thought: "The results we find will depend on the investigator involved, on the method being employed, and on the topic being researched. But the results will also depend on interactions between those variables. Some investigators will employ some methods more skillfully or insightfully than others, some investigators will have better understanding of certain topics, and some topics will be better approached by some methods" (p. 330). Of particular import in relation to the issues under consideration in this chapter is the suggestion that some topics will be better approached by some methods, bringing to the fore again the relations among theory, concept, and research method.

Summary and Conclusions

From this panorama of methods our principal conclusion can be that there is no "one and only" method for the study of personality. All methods have their value, most of them being adapted to the exploration of one special aspect of the problem. . . . . Each method has its unique supporters. Unfortunately, enthusiasm for one method often blinds the investigator to the others. . . . Each is said to be the last word, making use of any other method unnecessary. This is foolish. For some problems one method of attack is best, for others, different methods. The wise investigator will not place his faith in any one exclusively, but will use several to cover more ground, and at the same time to check the findings of each method against those of another.

Allport, 1937, p. 398

In this chapter we have considered the issue of disciplines or research traditions in psychology. Each of these traditions has its strengths and limitations. However, proponents of one or another research tradition tend to emphasize its strengths and the limitations of the other traditions. Furthermore, it has been suggested that in the field of personality psychology there are connections among theory, research method, and phenomena investigated. Although evidence of overlap can be found, in general the three major theoretical orientations in the field (i.e., psychoanalytic theory, trait theory, social cognitive theory) differ in the phenomena emphasized and methods used to investigate these phenomena. This presents somewhat of a problem for comparison of theories, both in terms of general issues and specific issues (e.g., the person-situation controversy). The problem is further complicated by the frequent lack of convergence among data from different sources, either in terms of different methods (e.g., self-report, overt behavior, task performance, physiological response) or different observers (e.g., self, peer, interviewer). Thus, although self-report data constitute a major proportion of the data reported in the major personality journals, their status as a valid measure of the constructs of interest to personality psychologists remains controversial.

So where does this leave us? Craik (1986), reviewing the history of personality research methods, called for methodological pluralism: "The inherent agenda of personality research encompasses each and every one of these sources of information about persons" (p. 49). Some time ago, Henry Murray (1938), in what was noted as one of the finest pieces of personality research ever conducted, attempted such methodological pluralism. The same subjects were studied intensively through the use of a variety of research methods—self-report, interview, fantasy measures, laboratory, miniature real-life situations, and so forth. The personality psychologists participating in the research project, many of whom went on to become outstanding contributors to the field, then discussed the various data and attempted a cohesive, integrated, holistic picture of the individual. In Murray's words, "to know a subject well one must see him many times, and observe or hear about his behavior in many varied situations, when exposed to different treatment by different types of people" (p. 13).

Would a similar effort be of value today? My own view is that such an effort would be of tremendous value, particularly if it involved the collaborative effort of individuals representing different theoretical points of view and different research traditions. As I have suggested for some time (Pervin, 1970; Pervin & John, 2000), it makes sense to consider the possibility that each theoretical perspective and each method of personality assessment picks up an important part of personality functioning. That is, there is something to fantasy measures and psychoanalytic observations, to questionnaire measures and trait theory, to laboratory investigations and observations of daily behavior in the natural environment and social cognitive theory. The task for us as personality psychologists, then, is to use methodological pluralism and, perhaps, conceptual pluralism to determine the best means of integrating these various pictures of the person. One way in which this might be done is to have representatives of different theoretical orientations study the same individuals and then meet to discuss and attempt an integration of their varying data and perspectives.

Is such a collaborative effort possible? Unfortunately, probably not. Murray was able to accomplish this by force of his personality, by his fascination with multiple aspects of personality functioning and respect for various research traditions, and his ability to obtain significant research funding. He also was of sufficient independence, financially and personally, that he could undertake a high-risk project. It is hard to find such a combination of ingredients in one person today, and the spirit or *zeitgeist* of the field is not supportive of such a development. Thus, until such an effort is undertaken, or a new paradigm is developed that makes the current ap-

CHAPTER 2

What Units Shall We Use? Traits, Motives, And Cognitions

General Theme

Historically the major units emphasized by personality psychologists have been traits, motives, and cognitions. For the most part, each unit has been emphasized and studied by different groups of investigators. After considering illustrative research relevant to each unit, and evaluating each unit, the question of the relations among the units is considered. It is suggested that the challenge for the future of the field is to establish how thoughts, feelings, motives, and behaviors relate to one another as parts of an organized, dynamic personality system.

> *What units shall we use? That was the question Gordon Allport (1937) asked more than half a century ago and it remains the most urgent and* crucial challenge that personality psychologists still face now.
>
> *Mischel & Shoda, 1999, p. 197*

Every science makes use of conceptual units that provide the basis for theory and investigation in the field—for example, the periodic table of the elements in chemistry, the parts of the body in anatomy, and the units of matter in physics.

What are the units of the science of personality? When you think about your self, what is it that is basic to you? What is it that were it to change would mean that you no longer are you—thoughts, feelings, behaviors? This question, as noted asked by Allport as early as 1937, is still with us today and will be the focus of this chapter. Allport listed ten basic units: intellectual capacities, temperament traits, unconscious motives, social attitudes, cognitive styles and schema (ways of viewing the world), interests and values, expressive traits, stylistic traits, pathological trends, and factorial clusters of traits derived from factor analysis (Allport, 1958). Allport noted that we are not always able to directly observe the units of interest, such as unconscious motives or some traits. This inability, of course, is not unique to personality research since many sciences include units that cannot be directly observed or initially even measured. Such units may be employed where they help to explain in a theoretically meaningful way phenomena that otherwise would remain inexplicable.

The personality psychologist David McClelland considered the issue of basic units in his 1951 personality text. Three units received particular emphasis—traits, schema, and motives (McClelland, 1951). Although containing fewer items than Allport's list, McClelland's units actually are quite similar since virtually all of Allport's units could be included in the three categories suggested by McClelland.

How similar are the units of personality studied today and how far have we come in our observations and measurements in regard to these units? How do the units relate to one another and how far do they seem to take us in our efforts to understand personality—the organized, system aspects of the functioning of the person that provide for individual differences? To answer the first question, it can be suggested that the basic units of research in the field of personality today remain very similar to those noted by Allport and McClelland, particularly if we include emotions within the motivation category, as McClelland did. Thus, in this chapter we consider traits, cognitions-schemas, and motives as basic units of personality. We also consider questions relating to each conceptual unit as well as the question of relations among the three units of personality. Are traits, motives, and cognitions all necessary units of personality? Are they sufficient as fundamental units of personality? Can these units be integrated into a comprehensive theory of personality or do they express such different models of personality functioning that if one is emphasized, another must go? These are some of the questions addressed in this chapter that relate to fundamental issues that divide personality psychologists today.

Trait Units of Personality

As noted in Chapter 1, the use of trait terms to describe individual differences probably started with the earliest efforts to categorize people. The emphasis on the trait concept as a fundamental unit of personality also dates back to the beginnings of personality as a distinct part of psychology. Thus, in his groundbreaking book on personality, Allport (1937) suggested that traits were the fundamental units of personality. Another book on personality written in the same year similarly suggested that "traits are the units of personality" (Stagner, 1937, p. 12). Since that time the trait concept has gone through periods of popularity and disfavor among personality psychologists, but it always has remained an important part of the field. Even though traits have never been totally accepted as the basic units of personality, there have always been leaders in the field who believe them to be so.

Although trait psychologists do not always agree on to how to define and measure a trait, they do agree on two points: (1) Traits refer to regularities or broad behavioral consistencies in the conduct of people. As such, traits represent basic categories of individual differences in functioning. Thus, to describe someone as outgoing is to describe a general characteristic and to distinguish that person from others who are characterized as being shy. (2) As descriptions of such broad differences in functioning, traits are useful as the basic units of personality. Following from this, the task for personality psychologists is to discover the basic traits of personality, develop ways to measure them, explore how traits develop, and then determine whether the concept offers a satisfactory explanation for individual differences in functioning in a wide variety of contexts.

Early Trait Psychologists: Allport, Cattell, and Eysenck

We can consider the evolution of the trait concept in personality by dividing its history into two periods (Pervin & John, 2000). In the first period, continuing roughly through the 1960s and the beginning of the person-situation controversy, (to be considered in Chapter 3), the major figures were Gordon Allport, Raymond B. Cattell, and Hans J. Eysenck. In the second period, following the turmoil of the person-situation controversy and developing into a dominant position in the field, the major views are represented in the *Big Five* model of Lewis Goldberg and the *Five-Factor Model* of Paul T. Costa, Jr. and Robert R. McCrae.

Allport, Cattell, and Eysenck can be grouped together because of common emphasis on the trait concept during the same historical period. However, there were major differences among them. Perhaps of the greatest significance was the difference in view of the utility of factor analysis as a method for discovering basic traits. Whereas Cattell and Eysenck were deeply committed to this method, Allport was fundamentally critical of it, suggesting that factors identified through the method "resemble sausage meat that has failed to pass the pure food and health inspection" (1958, p. 251). Others were equally critical of the method, suggesting that it is comparable to putting people through a centrifuge and expecting the "basic stuff" to come out (Lykken, 1971; Tomkins, 1962). However, Cattell and Eysenck continued to persevere in the utilization of the method. *Persevere* would appear to be a particularly apt description since, in the precomputer days, much of the factor-analytic work had to be done by hand or calculator (John, 1990; John & Srivastava, 1999).

A second difference among the three early trait psychologists concerns their view of the relation between trait units and other personality units. Whereas Eysenck discounted the utility of motive and cognitive units, both Allport and Cattell struggled with the question of the relation between trait and motive units. Allport's position on the issue is somewhat unclear since at times he seemed to suggest that one or the other was the more basic unit. What is clear is that he felt that the motive concept was necessary because trait concepts were insufficiently dynamic (Pervin, 1993). Cattell's position was clear in that he distinguished among *ability traits, temperament traits,* and *dynamic traits*: "Psychologists have been accustomed to define three modalities of traits, namely, cognitive or ability traits, temperament or stylistic traits, and dynamic traits. In common-sense terms, the ability trait has to do with how well a person handles difficulties, the temperament trait has to do with the general style and tempo with which he carries out whatever he does, and the dynamic trait is concerned with why and how he is moved to do what he does" (1965, p. 165). Thus, although he used the term *trait* for all three units of personality, Cattell essentially divided personality into the trait, motive, and cognitive units already noted in this chapter.

The three early trait psychologists also differed in the level of preferred analysis of traits, ranging from a molecular level of analysis of many traits to a molar level of analysis of a few global traits. Allport, with his concern for the uniqueness of the person and the complex organization of personality, preferred the analysis of many traits, including traits unique to the individual. Cattell, on the other hand, used factor analysis to find traits at a more molecular level, as in his *Sixteen Personality Factor Inventory.* Finally, although Eysenck described personality as organized hierarchically (i.e., specific responses, habitual responses, traits, and superfactors), his major emphasis was on three basic dimensions—*Introversion-Extraversion, Neuroticism,* and *Psychoticism.*

In addition to their common emphasis on traits as basic conceptual units, it should be noted that all three recognized the importance of the situation in determining specific actions. Allport, as much a social psychologist as a personality psychologist, recognized the importance of the situation in explaining why a person does not behave the same way all the time: "Traits are often aroused in one situation and not in another" (1937, p. 331). Cattell recognized the importance of situational variability of individual behavior through his emphasis on the concepts of *states* (i.e., emotional and mood changes, such as anxiety or depression, that are partly determined by the provocative power of specific situations) and *role* (i.e., behaviors closely linked to customs and mores defining appropriate behavior in a specific situation). Eysenck suggested that although it made no sense to talk of traits in the absence of recognition of situational influences, the consistency of individual differences in behavior across situations gave testimony to the validity of the trait concept.

Each of the three early trait psychologists made noteworthy contributions to the field. Allport played a major role in establishing the field of personality and displayed great wisdom in discussing issues of fundamental concern to personality psychologists. On a personal note, I was a student of Allport's in graduate school and, because of my psychoanalytic bent, felt that Allport had only a superficial understanding of what personality is about. Whatever the merit of that view, with time I have grown to appreciate the wisdom with which he addressed so many major issues. Cattell not only played a major role in the factor analysis of trait terms used in language but also made noteworthy attempts to study the equivalence of traits assessed through different methods (e.g., questionnaire responses, ratings by others, and behavior in the laboratory) and to study the influence of genetic and environmental variables during the unfolding of personality over time. Finally, Eysenck's three factor dimensions of personality are among the most reliably found units of personality and his emphasis on the biological basis of these trait dimensions was prescient of what is today a major thrust of the field.

Current Trait Theory: The Big Five and Five-Factor Models

A consensus about the major trait dimensions of personality has begun to emerge among contemporary trait psychologists. Sometimes described under the rubric of the *Big Five* (Goldberg, 1993; Saucier & Goldberg, 1996) and sometimes under the rubric of the *Five-Factor Model* (FFM) (McCrae & Costa, 1999), the following trait dimensions are emphasized: *Neuroticism, Extraversion, Openness to Experience, Agreeableness,* and *Conscientiousness.* The distinction between the two models is subtle, the former relying more exclusively on the analysis of trait terms in language (i.e., the lexical approach) and constituting less a theory of personality functioning than the latter. In addition, the former is associated with a trait-rating measure while the latter is associated with a questionnaire—the NEO-PI-R (1992). However, scores on the two measures show good agreement with one another and most psychologists use the terms interchangeably to refer to the emphasis on the five basic dimensions.

What is striking about proponents of the model is the extent to which they view the field of personality as now defined by these basic trait dimensions and their associated measures. From the standpoint of many contemporary trait psychologists, the basic structural units of personality have been discovered and what remains to be done is to build on this foundation. When I once suggested to a proponent of this view that alternative conceptions of personality were possible, such as those emphasizing motivational and cognitive units, his answer was that such units could be added on to the trait model but that traits remained the basic structural units of personality. This view has been carried forth by McCrae and Costa (1999) in their effort to extend the five-factor model into a comprehensive theory of personality. Thus, although they continue to suggest that "much of what psychologists mean by the term personality is summarized by the FFM" (p. 139), they also emphasize such concepts as personal strivings, dynamic processes, and the self-concept as necessary parts of a comprehensive theory of personality.

*Taken together, they (the Big Five) provide a good answer
to the question of personality structure.*

Digman, 1990, p. 436

*The five-factor model of personality has brought order to
the competing systems of personality structure by showing
that most traits can be understood in terms of the basic dimensions of Neuroticism, Extraversion, Openness, Agreeableness, and Conscientiousness.*

McCrae & Costa, 1990, p. 176

*Just as cartographers eventually settled on a standard sys-
tem with north-south and east-west axes, so personality* researchers must settle on a standard set of locations for the
Big Five dimensions.

Goldberg, 1993, p. 30

In sum, many trait psychologists feel that Cattell's wish to use factor analysis to
determine psychology's periodic table of the elements is well on its way to being
accomplished. Accordingly, the claim is that "the five-factor model of personality is
largely sufficient for characterizing normal and abnormal personality functioning"
(Widiger, 1993, p. 82) and that "personality psychologists who continue to employ
their preferred measure without locating it within the five-factor model can only be
likened to geographers who issue reports of new lands but refuse to locate them on a
map for others to find" (Ozer & Reise, 1994, p. 361).

What is the basis for such strong sentiments on the part of contemporary trait
psychologists? Cattell (1979) cited five kinds of evidence as useful in establishing
traits as fundamental units of personality: (1.) the results of factor analyses of different kinds of data; (2.) similar results across cultures; (3.) similar results across age
groups; (4.) utility in the prediction of behavior in the natural environment; and (5.)
evidence of significant genetic contributions to many traits. Such an accumulation of
evidence would certainly be impressive and represent a record of accomplishment
unheard of in the history of personality research. Yet, it is these as well as other
forms of evidence that trait psychologists cite in support of their point of view. Consider, for example, the following:

1. *Universality.* The same basic factors are found in the factor analysis of trait
    terms in languages used around the world (Church, 2000; Goldberg, 1993;
    McCrae & Costa, 1997; Saucier & Goldberg, 1996). Although some language
    groups have yet to be studied, and the studies to date mainly emphasize Indo-
    European languages, for the most part the Big Five factors have been replicated

in studies conducted in languages other than English and in countries other than the United States or in Europe.

2. *Heritability.* There is evidence of an inherited or genetic contribution to each of the five basic trait dimensions (Loehlin, 1992; Riemann, Angleitner, & Strelau, 1997). According to the results of twin and adoption studies, "for almost every behavioral trait so far investigated, from reaction time to religiosity, an important fraction of the variation among people turns out to be associated with genetic variation. This fact need no longer be subject to debate" (Bouchard, et. al., 1990, p. 226). Recent estimates of the overall percentage of variation in personality traits due to genetic determinants is 40 percent.

3. *Evolutionary significance.* Trait terms are believed to have emerged in language to help people categorize behaviors fundamental to the human condition. In addition, these traits are believed to have emerged to solve adaptive tasks (e.g., extraversion and emotional stability are important for mate selection and conscientiousness and agreeableness are important in relation to group cohesion and survival) (A. H. Buss, 1997; D. M. Buss, 1997, 1999).

4. *Cross-species representation.* There is evidence of cross-species representation of these dimensions, particularly for the Extraversion, Neuroticism, and Agreeableness factors and particularly for species closer to humans in evolutionary development (e.g., chimpanzees) (Gosling & John, 1999). Evidence of cross-species representation of the major factors supports the view that they are not just human constructions and that they are of evolutionary significance.

5. *Self-other agreement.* As noted in Chapter 1, there is evidence that self-ratings show good agreement with ratings made by peers and other observers (Funder & Colvin, 1997; Funder, Kolar, & Blackman, 1995; Riemann, Angleitner, & Strelau, 1997).

6. *Longitudinal stability.* There is evidence of the longitudinal stability of trait scores, particularly once individuals have reached early adulthood (Caspi, 2000; Costa & McCrae, 1997; McCrae et al., 2000). In other words, as a minimum adult traits are seen as "relatively enduring" (Caspi & Roberts, 1999) and some would argue that trait continuities are such that "the child is father of the man" (Caspi, 2000, p. 158).

7. *Biological foundations.* There are suggestive relationships between basic trait dimensions and neurophysiological structures (Pickering & Gray, 1999; Zuckerman, 1995; reviewed in Pervin & John, 2000, Chapter 9). These relationships remain suggestive at this time and clearly multiple genes and multiple biological processes contribute to the expression of any single trait. However, recent work suggests that Eysenck showed considerable foresight in his emphasis on the biological underpinnings of the basic trait dimensions.

8. *Predictive utility.* There is evidence that scores on basic trait dimensions can be used to predict behavior across situations and to make personnel employment decisions (Hogan, 1991). According to one review, "when personality research

is organized in terms of the Big Five factors, personality is consistently related to job performance criteria" (Hogan & Ones, 1997, p. 850).

9. *Psychopathology.* There is evidence that the five basic trait dimensions can be used to diagnose individuals with psychological disorders, perhaps to a better extent than the categorical model currently in use (Costa & Widiger, 1994; Widiger, 1993; Widiger & Sankis, 2000). In the words of one expert in the field, "the five-factor model of personality is largely sufficient for characterizing normal and abnormal personality functioning" (Widiger, 1993, p. 82).

Critique of Current Trait Theory

As is clear from the above list of supportive evidence, the five-factor model has led to considerable research, in varied domains of personality functioning, and an impressive array of supportive findings. At the same time, it is not without its critics (Block, 1995; McAdams, 1992; Pervin, 1994). In part, these criticisms stem from what are perceived to be overzealous and excessively extreme statements on the part of some trait theorists. For example, statements equating personality theory with trait theory ignore other points of view (e.g., social cognitive theory, psychoanalytic theory) and statements suggesting that "personality traits, like temperaments, are endogenous dispositions that follow intrinsic paths of development essentially independent of environmental influences" (McCrae, et al., 2000, p. 173) needlessly return us to the "nature-nurture" debate (see Chapter 5). In part, these criticisms stem from the view that trait theory, as posited by the five-factor model, is inadequate to capture the depth of personality characteristic of the individual. In the words of McAdams (1992), it is the psychology of the stranger. Beyond such broad criticisms, however, are questions raised in relation to virtually every one of the above points listed as supportive of current trait theory. For example, consider the following as representative in this regard:

1. *The method.* A variety of questions have been raised concerning the method of factor analysis for deriving the structure of personality. For example, Epstein (1996) suggests that "there is no reason to assume, as those who endorse the FFM have, that factor analysis can determine the most fundamental and useful dimensions of personality theory, any more than it would be able to do so in any other discipline" (p. 437). In addition, Block (1995) suggests that many studies find the same five basic dimensions because the items used bias the results in this direction. In addition, he suggests that the five factors are not independent of one another (e.g., *Neuroticism* and *Extraversion* routinely correlate negatively with one another) and the placement of subscales (i.e., facets) under each of the five major factors is problematic. In terms of the latter, this suggests that the more specific components of each of the basic factors do not necessarily fall into place in the way predicted by the model.

> *Serious uncertainties have arisen in regard to the claimed 5-factor structure and the substantive meanings of the factors.*
>
> *Block, 1995, p. 187*

> *The five-factor model (FFM) of personality offers a structural organization of personality traits in terms of 5 broad factors. J. Block's critique of the FFM failed to recognize the utility of a trait taxonomy and the intent of research designed to test the 5-factor hypothesis.*
>
> *Costa & McCrae, 1995, p. 216*

> *Unfortunately, Block's brilliant critique is terribly biased...it attempts to explain away the extensive evidence for the Big Five model...it omits a good deal of crucial evidence favorable to the Big Five model. . .*
>
> *Goldberg & Saucier, 1995, p. 221*

> *There is no disagreement among us regarding the usefulness of a common conceptual scheme that is both parsimonious and comprehensive; we differ in the faith we invest in the method of factor analysis and whether the five factors so decisively proposed sufficiently achieve the desired goal.*
>
> *Block, 1995, p. 226*

2. *Universality.* Although impressive linkages have been established among trait factors found in languages throughout the world, even proponents of the model suggest that "strong conclusions about the linguistic universality of the lexically derived Big Five would be premature" (John & Srivastava, 1999, p.109). There is evidence of unique factors found in some languages and that the same trait terms can have different meanings in different cultures.

3. *Longitudinal stability.* There is considerable disagreement concerning the degree of longitudinal stability found in personality with some suggesting that there is considerable plasticity or potential for change in all aspects of personality functioning (Lewis, 1999, 2001) (Chapter 5). What seems clear is that there is greater evidence for stability in adulthood than in childhood, and greater evidence for stability over short periods of time than over extended periods of time (Roberts & Del Vecchio, 2000). Even where evidence of stability in adulthood exists, stability may be due to self- maintaining behaviors on the part of the per-

son and stability-inducing elements in the environment rather than to an inherent fixed quality to personality traits.

4. *Prediction.* Questions continue to be raised concerning the degree to which behavior is stable across situations (Mischel & Shoda, 1999) and the extent to which valid predictions can be made about occupational performance on the basis of scores on trait inventories (Hough, 1997; Hough & Oswald, 2000). The most consistent factor associated with job performance across occupational categories appears to be that of *Conscientiousness.* Even here trait scores correlate better with supervisor ratings of performance than with objective criteria.

It is ironic that, at a time when other subfields of psychology are becoming contextualized and discarding global personal structures for more particularized ones, much of the field of personality is seeking causes of human behavior in omnibus conglomerate traits severed from the social realities of everyday life.

Bandura, 1999, pp. 160–161

---

5. *Heritability.* Extreme statements concerning the role of genes in personality functioning ignore the role of environmental influences. Evidence that parental influences on personality development differ for children in the same family still indicate the importance of environmental variables as does evidence of peer influences and chance events (Maccoby, 2000) (Chapter 5).

6. *Where is the individual?* In addition to the suggestion that knowledge of a person's standing on the Big Five hardly constitutes knowing him or her as a person, there is the question of the extent to which these dimensions are the ones found in analysis of individuals. The Big Five factors are derived from the analysis of trait ratings across subjects. However, this amalgamation of data from large numbers of subjects may not reflect the data from many, perhaps even most, individual subjects. In other words, these factors may represent what is common to subjects but not what is characteristic of any one subject. As aptly put by Caprara and Cervone (2000), "if we examine the physiology of each and every individual, we will find a circulatory system. To support the psychological claim [that the Big Five constructs apply at the individual level as well as at the group level], one must be able to examine the psychology of each and every individual and find the factors" (p. 77).

7. *Is that all there is?* Individuals supportive of the trait point of view have raised the question of whether there are factors that yet remain to be determined. For example, research suggests the need for addition of such factors as *spirituality-religiosity* (MacDonald, 2000; Paunonen & Jackson, 2000), *conventionality, manipulativeness,* and *seductiveness*: "We are led to the conclusion that there are plenty of dimensions of behavior beyond the Big Five" (Paunonen & Jack-

son, 2000, p. 821). Whether such additional dimensions will be found to have the same characteristics of the Big Five (e.g., universality, self-peer agreement, etc.) remains to be determined.

In addition to these specific criticisms, three additional general criticisms can be noted.

8. *Agreement among trait conceptions.* Although it is suggested that a consensus is emerging around the Big Five, in fact there is disagreement among trait theorists concerning the trait concept and the number of basic trait dimensions (Pervin, 1996). Concerning the trait concept, whereas some trait theorists confine the concept to overt behavior, others include within it thoughts, feelings, and latent propensities or predispositions to respond. In other words, are traits defined exclusively by overt behavior or by other criteria as well? If the latter, by which other criteria? Tests used to measure traits typically include items from diverse areas of personality functioning, including internal thoughts and feelings that would be difficult or impossible for an observer to know about unless disclosed by the person (e.g., "Frightening thoughts sometimes come into my head.").

9. *Description or explanation?* Are traits descriptions of behavioral regularities or explanations of observed regularities? Are they "real" or are they convenient means of communication, more folk concepts that scientific concepts? Trait theorists differ in terms of these questions (Pervin, 1994). If traits are only descriptive, then isn't it circular to say that someone is sociable and active because they are extroverted—a point made by Eysenck (1992)? If traits are explanatory, what do we need to know to understand how they develop and their interplay with one another and other aspects of personality to account for behavior?

10. *Static or dynamic?* A problem in relation to trait theory is that it presents a static model of personality functioning (Pervin, 1994). That is, how do trait psychologists account for uncharacteristic, atypical pieces of behavior—the model child who suddenly commits a violent crime, the moral person who lives a secret life of deceit and immorality, the person destined for success who becomes a failure, and the person destined for trouble who becomes a success? According to a dynamic perspective, behavior expresses the dynamic interplay among many elements (e.g., motives) and seemingly different manifestations can be expressive of differing combinations of the same dynamic elements. More recent statements of the five-factor model have attempted to add dynamic processes to the model (McCrae & Costa, 1999). However, these are not well integrated into the overall conceptualization of personality.

Dispositional-trait approaches are vulnerable to the criticism that they do not adequately consider, or even address, the psychological processes and dynamics that underlie behavioral dispositions.

Mischel & Shoda, 1999, p. 198

In sum, traits have a long history in the field of personality and recent advances are noteworthy. At the same time, controversy remains concerning specific aspects of the trait model as well as the overall conceptualization.

Motive Units Of Personality

Traditionally, the concept of motivation has been used to address three questions: (1) What *activates* the organism? (2) Why does the organism *select* or choose one response over another, one direction of activity over another? For example, given a choice between food and water, why does a dog choose one or the other? Or, given a choice between becoming a business executive or a college professor, why does a person choose one or the other? (3) Given the same stimulus, why does the organism sometimes *respond* one way and sometimes another? Why does a dog sometimes seem very interested in food and sometimes not at all? Or, why is a person sometimes interested in being with people and at other times interested in being alone?

These are the *activation, selection-direction*, and *preparedness of response* aspects of motivation: what activates the organism, why one or another direction is chosen, and why differential responses are given at various times to the same stimulus. The concept of motivation suggests that there are internal qualities that play an important role in the activation and regulation of behavior. From the standpoint of personality psychology, the concept of motivation suggests that these internal qualities act upon other aspects of the person's functioning. Thus, motives are seen as influencing cognition and action, thinking and behavior. Given individual differences in motives, our motives and ways of expressing them play an important role in giving a particular stamp to us as persons. In other words, our motives are an important part of our personality, both in and of themselves as well as in relation to their influence on other parts of the personality.

In its most basic terms, the concept of motivation addresses the question of *why*—why we behave as we do. Put this way, it might seem obvious that we need such a concept. Yet, this is not necessarily the case. Although motivation has generally been an area of keen interest on the part of psychologists, there have been times when its utility as a scientific concept has been questioned (Pervin, 1983). During the 1950s and 1960s, there was a noticeable decline in interest in the concept. This had to do with both the demise of interest in the concept of drive and the cognitive revolution. The decline in interest in motivation, and shift toward a cognitive model, was so great that in the 1970s the editors of the distinguished *Nebraska Symposium on Motivation* series considered dropping the term *motivation* from the title. A concerned motivation theorist was led to ask: "Where, in cognitive theory, are the strong urges and the `hot' emotions or passions that have been central to our thinking in respect to motivation and emotion for so long?" (Cofer, 1981, p. 52).

There seems to be increasing evidence over the years that the motivational concept as such has reached the end of its usefulness as a scientific construct.

Jones, 1962, p. viii

*If there is a cornerstone in the science of human behavior,
it must be the field of motivation. Motivational theories ask
a fundamental question, namely: What moves a person.
They are concerned with the prime forces at work in human nature and human culture.*

Ryan, 1998, p. 114

The name of the series was not changed, more for practical than conceptual reasons—libraries had standing orders for the series and a change in name threatened
these standing orders. Thus, it is interesting that the 1990 edition of the *Nebraska
Symposium* indicates that it has returned to its roots and will again confront the concept of motivation directly (Dienstbier, 1990). After a drought of around twenty
years, interest in motivation has returned. The issues it addresses could not be dealt
with by other approaches. Just as the learning theorist Tolman was criticized for
leaving his rats "left in thought" (Guthrie, 1952), without an explanation for what
activated, energized, and directed them, so the cognitive models of the early cognitive revolution threatened to leave humans left in thought. Motivation is back, both
as a concept of interest in its own right as well as an important influence on how we
process information concerning the world. In the words of a recent reviewer of the
literature: "Motivation has always been central to personality psychology, although
interest in motivational concepts has waxed and waned over the past 50 years...today
theorists and researchers are more willing to invoke motivational concepts into their
descriptive and explanatory models" (Emmons, 1997, p. 486*)*.

Pitchfork-Drive, Carrot-Incentive, and Cognitive Theories of Motivation

Most, although not all, theories of personality include a theory of motivation. Some
theories postulate one motive, others a few basic motives, and some a hierarchy of
motives. The cognitive personality theorist George Kelly (1958), while rejecting the
need for a concept of motivation, offered a system for categorizing the various theoretical models:

Motivational theories can be divided into two types, push theories and pull theories. Under
push theories we find such terms as drive, motive, or even stimulus. Pull theories use such
constructs as purpose, value, or need. In terms of a well-known metaphor, these are the pitchfork theories on the one hand and the carrot theories on the other. But our theory is neither of
these. Since we prefer to look at the nature of the animal himself, ours is probably best called a
jackass theory.

(Kelly, 1958, p. 50)

To a certain extent, all categorizations of theories of motivation are somewhat arbitrary since there generally is some overlap among the theories and differences within a category. However, Kelly's categories do make some sense even if, as we shall see, his own theory was hardly that of a jackass. In fact, despite his rejection of the concept of motivation, Kelly had a quite interesting cognitive theory of motivation.

Pitchfork-Drive Theories of Motivation, Perhaps the best example of pitchfork theories of motivation are those associated with *drive* states and tension reduction. Traditional drive theories suggest that an internal stimulus drives the organism. The drive typically is associated with a biological state, such as hunger or thirst, that creates a state of tension in the organism. In its simplest form, being without food produces a physiological deficit and tension state associated with the hunger drive, whereas being without water produces a physiological deficit and tension state associated with the thirst drive. These states of tension are associated with displeasure or pain, whereas the process of tension reduction is associated with positive reinforcement or pleasure. Thus, drive theories typically are tension-reduction models of motivation. They also can be considered *hedonic* or pleasure-oriented theories of motivation in that they emphasize the organism's efforts to seek pleasure and avoid pain.

Freud's theory of motivation is an example of a drive, tension-reduction, hedonic theory. According to Freud, the source of all energy lies in states of excitation within the body that seek expression or tension reduction. These states of excitation are called instincts or drives and represent constant, inescapable forces. The instincts (drives) are characterized by a source, an aim, and an object. As noted, the source of the instincts is in bodily states of excitation or tension. The aim of all instincts is tension reduction, which is associated with pleasure. The object of the instinct is the way in which it is satisfied or the way in which the tension is released and reduced.

Psychoanalysis is known as a dynamic theory of personality. The dynamics of personality involve the motivational forces in the individual and the interplay among those forces. For example, motives can be integrated or in conflict with one another. Of particular importance are conflicts between the wish to express the drives and the fears of harm from within (e.g., guilt, shame) or from the external world. A person may wish to express sexual desires but may feel guilty or fear criticism and rejection from others. Or, the person may wish to express anger but feel ashamed of feeling angry or fear retribution from others. Drive or tension-reduction theories of motivation were popular in psychology through the 1950s. The concept of drive played an important role in Hull's (1943) stimulus-response (S-R) learning theory and in Dollard and Miller's (1950) effort to translate psychoanalytic theory into S-R terms. S-R theory emphasized the importance of *primary drives,* such as pain and hunger, and *secondary drives* or drives that are acquired on the basis of their association with the satisfaction of primary drives. Even what appeared to be cognitive theories were based on a tension-reduction model. For example, Festinger's (1957) theory of cognitive dissonance suggested that when two or more cognitions are inconsistent or in conflict with one another (e.g., "I smoke." "I want to be healthy." "Smoking is bad for your health."), a state of dissonance or tension exists. This leads to a motivation to reduce the state of tension created by the cognitive dissonance.

Drive, tension-reduction models of motivation came under attack during the 1950s and 1960s because not all motivated behavior seemed to be based on physiological needs or tension-reduction. White's (1959) critique was particularly influential, bringing together the evidence suggesting that humans, as well as other species, often seek tension as well as avoid tension. He suggested that rather than seeking tension reduction, people are motivated toward gaining competence or the ability to deal effectively with the environment. Challenging data, critiques such as those by White, and the cognitive revolution were the death knell for drive theories. Unfortunately, with the demise of the drive concept there was, as noted, a decline in interest in the entire field of motivation.

Carrot-Incentive Theories of Motivation. Incentive theories emphasize the motivational pull of incentives, that is, the motivational pull of end points anticipated by the organism. It is not so much that the organism is being pushed as that it is being pulled toward something. An end point associated with pleasure has the quality of a "carrot" or incentive that pulls the organism toward it. An end point associated with pain pulls the organism in another direction, away from the pain. Although different in this sense from drive, tension-reduction models, it should be clear that incentive theories of motivation still emphasize the importance of striving for pleasure and avoiding pain. In this sense they too are hedonic theories of motivation.

Incentive theories of motivation go back some time in the field of psychology. McDougall (1930) was so struck with the directed, goal-seeking quality of behavior that he announced himself to be a purposive psychologist. He rejected a mechanistic, reflex, stimulus-determined view of behavior in favor of an emphasis on active strivings toward anticipated goals: "We foresee a particular event as a possibility; we desire to see this possibility realized, we take action in accordance with our desire, and we seem to guide the course of events in such a way that the foreseen and desired event results" (1930, p. 5). It was the persistent, variable, but goal-directed quality of behavior that led McDougall to characterize it as *purposive*.

Other theorists also emphasized the purposive, goal-directed quality of behavior (Lewin, 1935; Tolman, 1932). Yet, these views fell into decline for three reasons. First, they seemed very mentalistic (i.e., emphasizing what was going on in the mind rather than observable behavior) and teleological. Teleology refers to the direction of functioning toward some end point. For example, we may seek to have a specific career or a particular family life or to live a moral life. For some psychologists, this was taken to mean that future events determine present events. Such a view, of course, was rejected by psychologists. Behavior can be governed only by the present, which can include, however, one's images of the future. Despite this argument, purposive views were rejected. Second, the S-R view was so powerful as to dominate the field and relegate other positions, such as the purposive view, to a minor status. Third, as noted, with the demise of drive theory and the beginning of the cognitive revolution, there was a general decline in interest in motivation. Purposive theories of motivation experienced the same fate as other theories of motivation even though they included a strong cognitive element—the anticipation or mental representation of the future.

Interestingly enough, developments in the area of cognition eventually led the field back to a strong interest in goal-directed behavior. During the 1940s, there were major advances in cybernetics—the study of how complex machines can be directed in their functioning toward some target or end point (Wiener, 1948). Consider, for example, a home thermostat that turns the heat or air-conditioning on and off to maintain a steady temperature or end point. Or, consider an antiaircraft gun automatically guided by radar toward a moving plane. Today, these machines have become so complex that at times their functioning is indistinguishable from that guided by humans, so that as passengers on a plane we are not aware that the plane is being landed mechanically.

In addition, there was the development of computers in the 1950s. Computer models of human functioning suggested that people use broad principles to guide behavior toward goals (Newell, Shaw, & Simon, 1958). Then, in 1960, a very influential book, entitled *Plans and the Structure of Behavior*, suggested a model of functioning whereby people kept a standard or end point in mind and then kept adjusting their behavior to meet that standard (Miller, Galanter, & Pribram, 1960). What the authors suggested was that we consider how an ordinary day is put together. The structure of an ordinary day includes plans for what needs to be done and what is expected to happen; that is, the day has an organized, patterned, goal-directed quality. They suggested that the person's goals are represented by images of end points or targets that direct the person's behavior, just as is true of a thermostat or radar-directed antiaircraft gun. Plans are developed to achieve the goal and actions are tested against the mental representation of the end point to see whether we are remaining on course and getting closer to the goal. For example, someone might organize her day around an important business meeting, taking care to make sure that the staff is ready, the necessary documents have been put together, and the presentation rehearsed. Or, someone might organize his day around an important athletic event, taking care to eat specific foods, have adequate rest, take adequate time to warm up, and make plans for a party following the anticipated success.

What was striking about this development was that it became legitimate to think in terms of purposive, future-oriented, goal-directed behavior. Behavior was not being directed by the future but by some mental representation of the future. If machines could function in terms of some standard or end point, why not humans? However, what was left out of this model was how goals get established and how we select among goals or desired outcomes. Although providing for purposive behavior, the model remained cognitive in nature and lacked the power of a motivational force. To a certain extent, the person was left in thought just as Guthrie (1935, 1952) suggested was true of Tolman's rats. Over time, developments in the cognitive revolution moved from a focus on "cold cognition," or purely cognitive processes, to a focus on "hot cognition," or the relation of emotion and motivation to cognition. Associated with this has been an interest in goal theories of motivation. Today, the concept of *goal*, in one or another form, has become a major part of motivation and personality theory (Austin & Vancouver, 1996; Carver & Scheier, 1982; Emmons,

1997; Higgins, 1997; Little, 1999; Pervin, 1989). It is expressed in various concepts such as *life tasks* (Cantor, 1990), *personal strivings* (Emmons, 1997), *personal projects* (Little, 1999), *current concerns* (Klinger, 1977), *possible selves* (Markus & Ruvolo, 1989), *standards* (Bandura, 1999; Higgins, 1999), and *goals* (Austin & Vancouver, 1996; Ford, 1992; Locke & Latham, 1990; Mischel & Shoda, 1999; Pervin, 1983, 1989). What is common to these concepts is an emphasis on purposive, goal-directed behavior, that is, the view that the person's behavior is organized around the pursuit of desired end points or goals.

How does goal theory relate to personality? First, goal theory returns the concept of motivation to center stage as an area of concern for personality psychologists. It suggests that in order to understand human behavior, in particular its patterned, organized, and directed quality, we must consider its motivation. The concept of a goal and the view of humans as organized goal systems are suggested as useful motivational perspectives. Second, there are individual differences in the kinds of goals that people pursue. Of particular importance in recent research is the contrast between the pursuit of *approach* goals as opposed to *avoidance* goals (Elliot & Sheldon, 1997), or, similarly, between a focus on *promotion* as opposed to *prevention* of outcomes (Higgins, 1997; Shah & Higgins, 1997). For example, individuals may strive to be creative in their work (i.e., approach, promotion) or to avoid being a failure (i.e., avoidance, prevention). Third, there are individual differences in the ways that people pursue their goals, that is, in the strategies and plans they use in goal-system functioning. Fourth, there are individual differences in the complexity of organization of goal systems and in the degree of conflict as opposed to integration within the goal system (Emmons, 1997). Illustrative goal conflicts might be the wish for intimacy and the fear of rejection or the wish to compete and the fear of failure.

Cognitive Theories of Motivation, As noted, both drive and incentive theories of motivation are hedonic in their emphasis on the gaining of pleasure (e.g., approach goals) and the avoidance of pain (e.g., avoidance goals). In contrast with them, cognitive theories emphasize purely cognitive processes. For example, the self psychologist Prescott Lecky (1945) emphasized the person's motivation to maintain the unity, organization, or consistency of the self. Although this may seem similar to Festinger's emphasis on the need for cognitive consistency, Lecky did not associate any tension or noxious state with the lack of consistency. We are motivated to maintain consistency because that is the way we function. Pleasure may be a byproduct of such achievement of consistency, but it is not the motivating force. More recently, Swann (1997) has emphasized the need for self-verification, that is, the need to confirm the way we see ourselves even if such confirmation is damaging to our self-esteem. Such a cognitive need for self-verification is contrasted with the affective need for self-enhancement. Thus, although the term *need* may be used by some cognitive theorists, there is not an emphasis on tension reduction or drive principles. Rather the emphasis is on the search for cognitive clarity and cognitive consistency because that is the nature of the beast.

Here we can return to Kelly (1955) and his theory of personal constructs. According to Kelly, we do not need the concept of motivation to account for why people are active—it is in the nature of the organism to be active. Nor do we need a concept of drive or need to account for the direction of activity. According to Kelly, people act like scientists, that is, they seek to make better and better predictions over a wider range of phenomena. In sum, according to Kelly the person chooses the course of action that promises the greatest further development of his or her construct system. In our daily functioning we seek to make better predictions concerning our own behavior and that of others.

Note that although the term *seek* is used in relation to the functioning of the construct system, it is not being used in the sense of seeking some end point (goal) associated with positive value. Once more, it is just in the nature of the cognitive functioning of the organism that this occurs. According to Kelly, we seek better predictions because that is what we are about—jackasses, scientists, or whatever. We do not seek better predictions to satisfy our drives or to better obtain some incentive. Nor do we seek consistency to reduce cognitive dissonance and the tension created by it. Rather we seek consistency and dissonance-free cognitions so as to make better predictions. No further assumptions are necessary.

In sum, cognitive theories of motivation emphasize movement toward cognitive clarity and consistency. In strictly cognitive theories there is no emphasis on reward, tension-reduction, or pleasure associated with goal attainment as is true for "pitchfork" and "carrot" theories of motivation.

Critique of the Motive Unit

As indicated, interest in the concept of motivation has waxed and waned over the years. Currently there is considerable interest in the concept and in how motives direct thought and action. However, here are many challenges facing psychologists who emphasize the importance of this concept. Questions such as the following can be considered: Where do motives come from? Are there basic, universal human motives or is the range of possible motives virtually unlimited? How are we to measure motives? Evidence suggests that self-report and fantasy measures of motivation do not agree with one another and show different relationships with other variables. Which is the "true" measure of the motive?

Where Do Motives Come From? The origins of motives is a question neglected by many interested in motivational concepts such as goals (Pervin, 1989). Most psychologists who emphasize the concept of goals suggest that affect, or emotion, is important in relation to goals. However, beyond this there appear to be two points of view, one suggesting that approaching a goal is associated with positive affect and the other suggesting that the goal itself is associated with positive affect (i.e., approach motivation) or negative affect (i.e., avoidance motivation). According to the former, we can experience emotion associated with the anticipation of achieving the desired goal or avoiding the unwanted end-point. There is both the excitement of anticipation of attaining the desired, pleasurable goal and the dread of anticipation of being unable to avoid the goal associated with pain. The intensity of each becomes greater as we come closer to the goal (Carver & Scheier, 1990). According to the latter, approach goals take on their motivational power because they are associated with positive emotion (pleasure) and avoidance goals take on their motivational power because they are associated with negative emotion (pain)—a hedonic view of motivation in which emotions are the basis for pleasure and pain (Pervin, 1983). According to this view some goals are intrinsically associated with pleasure or pain while other goals are acquired on the basis of their association with pleasure or pain. Because of the flexibility of our system functioning and the development of an advanced cognitive system, we are able to associate pleasure or pain with a wide array of events, objects, and people as well as with memories, thoughts, images, symbols, and fantasies. Thus, what can become a goal, what we seek to approach or avoid, is virtually unlimited. In both views, affect is key to the motivational concept. However, this is a neglected area of research.

Are There Universal Motives? Are there basic, universal motives? If so, which? How would we recognize them? That is, which criteria would be used to evaluate whether a motive was universal? When asked about universal motives, students typically come up with candidates such as food, shelter, and clothing. These have to do with survival. Is *survival* itself a fundamental human motive, as suggested by some psychologists: "We argue that the most basic of all human motives is an instinctive desire for continued life, and that all more specific motives are ultimately rooted in this basic evolutionary adaptation" (Pyszczynski, Greenberg, & Solomon, 1997, p.1)? Is *self-actualization* a fundamental human motive, as suggested by human potential movement psychologists (Maslow,1968; Rogers, 1961)? What of the suggestion that there is a basic human need for *autonomy, competence,* and *relatedness* (Ryan, 1998)?

In a challenging theoretical article, Baumeister and Leary (1995) outlined nine criteria for a motive to be considered fundamental:

1. A fundamental human motive should operate in a wide variety of settings.

2. A fundamental human motive should have emotional, hedonic consequences.

3. A fundamental human motive should guide cognition.

4. Failure to satisfy a fundamental human motive should produce ill effects. That is, health, adjustment, or well-being require satisfaction of the motive.

5. A fundamental human motive should elicit goal-directed behavior designed to satisfy it with the potential for substitution of specific subgoals for other subgoals while retaining the commitment to the overall goal (e.g., retain the goal of having friendships although the specific friendships may vary from situation to situation or from time to time).

6. A fundamental human motive should be found in all societies and cultures.

7. A fundamental human motive should not be derived from another motive—it should show an evolutionary pattern and physiological mechanisms.

8.   A fundamental human motive should affect a wide variety of behaviors.

9.   A fundamental human motive should influence historical economic and political events. That is, a fundamental human motive should have implications that go beyond the individual to include broader social events and patterns.

These criteria are reasonable but would appear to be difficult to satisfy. Seemingly, one could think of exceptions to almost any suggested fundamental motive. The need to survive? But what of people who commit suicide and cultures in which martyrs are venerated? The need for sex? But what of people who remain abstinent? Baumeister and Leary (1995) suggest that a *need to belong,* that is, a need to form and maintain at least a minimum quantity of interpersonal relationships, is a fundamental human motive. They detail the ways in which such a need meets the nine suggested criteria. For example, they suggest that it is found in all cultures, that it has an evolutionary basis with both survival and reproductive benefits, that there is a tendency to experience pleasure from social relatedness and distress when deprived of social contact, and that the need to belong stimulates goal-directed thought and action designed to satisfy it. But what of shyness and the life of the hermit? Here it is suggested that it is the fear of rejection that leads to shyness and withdrawal from social contact and that the emotion of rejection expresses the distress associated with frustration of this fundamental motive. One can perhaps think of other counterexamples of the suggested basic human motive of a need to belong. Baumeister and Leary (1995) suggest that the evidence supports their view but the issue remains open for debate, as is true for other human motives suggested as basic by other theorists. Thus, the more general question of universal motives remains unanswered.

How Are Motives to Be Measured? Can self-report measures be used to assess motivation? Do unconscious motives exist and therefore, as Murray (1938) suggested, fantasy measures must be used to discover their existence? What happens when the two are compared? McClelland (1980; McClelland, Koestner, & Weinberger, 1989) strongly argued that self-report and fantasy measures of the same motive did not correlate well with one another and should be identified by different terms, the former to be called *self-attributed motives* and the latter to be called *implicit motives.* Self-attributed motives were viewed as similar to values and involved efforts to behave in line with one's self-concept and social norms. Implicit motives were viewed as being more important in influencing behavior in unconstrained situations (i.e., where behavior was not constrained by social reinforcers) and in influencing behavior over extended periods of time. These are meaningful contrasts and it makes sense that different methods of assessment are necessary to measure more and less conscious motives. However, which motives are best assessed with which measures and, perhaps most significantly, how unconscious goals are to be assessed remain issues to be addressed.

Unfortunately, the history of the field of motivation is that not only has interest in the concept in general waxed and waned but that this has been the case for specific motives as well—anxiety, achievement, self-actualization, power, intimacy, control, self-enhancement and self-esteem maintenance, and so on. In contrast with the emerging trait consensus around the Big Five, or something close to that, and around some measures of these traits, there is no such consensus emerging around the importance of a few motives and related measures of them. This remains true despite current enthusiasm for the motivation concept, particularly in relation to the concept of goals, and the view that such a concept is necessary to capture the dynamic aspect of personality functioning (Pervin, 1994).

Cognitive Units of Personality

> *Cognitive factors partly determine which environmental events are observed, what meaning is conferred on them, what emotional impact and motivating power they have, and how the information they convey is organized and preserved for future use.*
>
> *Bandura, 1999, p. 170*

Cognition refers to the processes we use to know the world—that is, to the processes we use to acquire, transform, and store information from the environment. As such, cognition includes the study of learning, perception, memory, language acquisition and utilization, and thinking. Cognitive units of personality involve both the kind of information that is received and the ways in which the information is processed; that is, both *content* and *process* aspects of cognition are important for understanding personality. The term *cognition* is not new to the field; it has been in use almost from the beginnings of psychology. Yet, what is referred to as the "cognitive revolution" began in roughly the 1960s (Boneau, 1992). Since that time, cognition has formed an increasingly important part of psychology generally, and personality in particular.

Cognitive Style

Much of the early work on cognition and personality, begun during the 1950s, focused on individual differences in *cognitive style*. The concept of cognitive style suggested that individuals have broad dispositional tendencies to perceive the world in particular ways. In other words, the concept of cognitive style suggested a trait-like quality to individual differences in cognition. For example, Herman Witkin (Witkin et al., 1962) developed the concept of *field dependent–field independent cognitive style*. According to this concept, individuals differ in the extent to which they perceive a part of the environment as independent of its surroundings. Such individual differences were defined by performance on perceptual tasks. Field-independent individuals are much more able than field-dependent subjects to perceive parts of the field independently of the surroundings. In a sense, they are able to see the forest from the trees. However, these individual differences in perception were found to be related to differential functioning in other areas as well. For example, relative to field-dependent people, field-independent people were found to be more active in their coping efforts, more able to control their impulses in a flexible manner, and less bothered by feelings of inferiority. Although there is no difference in general learning ability or memory between field-dependent and field-independent individuals, the former tend to learn social material better than the latter while the reverse is true for nonsocial material. Whereas field-dependent people favor careers involving working with people and human content (e.g., social worker, minister, social science teacher), field-independent individuals favor more abstract careers that involve lesser amounts of interpersonal contact (e.g., scientist, engineer, math teacher). In addition, cognitive style can be an important variable in students' selection of majors and performance in courses. Thus, field-independent subjects have been found to prefer and do better in courses requiring analytical skills (e.g., sciences, mathematics, engineering), while field-dependent subjects prefer and do better in areas that require involvement with people (e.g., social sciences, counseling, teaching).

Other concepts describing cognitive styles also were developed during this period. For example, there were *levelers* and *sharpeners,* referring to sensitivity to differences between objects; and *repressors* and *sensitizers*, referring to differences in sensitivity to feelings; and people who were *cognitively complex* and others who were *cognitively simple*, referring to differences in the complexity with which individuals structured their world. Today, one rarely hears of such differences in cognitive style. What has happened to these earlier concepts of cognitive style? For the most part, they have disappeared from the literature. One rarely sees reference to them in personality journals or personality texts. Most current psychology students probably never heard of them! Why did they disappear from the literature? First, as more research was done, inconsistent findings began to emerge. In addition, it often was hard to define ways in which similar-sounding cognitive styles were different from or related to one another. Of perhaps even greater significance, however, were questions raised concerning the generality of these cognitive styles, similar to questions raised concerning the generality of traits (Cantor & Kihlstrom, 1987). Individuals were not found to be as consistent from task to task, and from one area of personality functioning to another, as was suggested by the concept of cognitive style. In other words, whereas cognitive style theorists treated such individual differences as traits, questions were raised concerning the cross-situational generality of the differences. Thus, such concepts were replaced by others less stylistic in nature and more reflective of developments in the cognitive revolution.

Cantor and Kihlstrom's Social Intelligence

It is hard to overestimate the importance of the cognitive revolution. Prior to it, there were signs of an emerging cognitive emphasis in personality psychology. This was seen in the social learning theory of Julian Rotter (1954) and the personal construct theory of George Kelly (1955). Cantor and Kihlstrom (1989), in tracing the history of the "social cognitivists," give pride of first place in the development of social cognitive approaches to personality to Rotter. Whereas behaviorists such as Hull and Skinner defined the value of reinforcers in objective terms and disregarded cognitive processes, Rotter defined reinforcers in terms of their subjective value for the individual and emphasized the importance of subjective expectancies concerning the outcomes of events. These points of emphasis led to the development of an expectancy-value theory of personality functioning. Kelly, although rejecting the depiction of his theory as a cognitive theory of personality, emphasized the importance of understanding how people construe or interpret the world and defined personality in terms of the person's construct system. According to Cantor and Kihlstrom (1989), Kelly was the first major theorist to provide a thoroughly cognitive treatment of personality.

Personality has "gone social" and "gone cognitive"...

Cantor & Kihlstrom, 1981, p. xi

Currently, cognitive units are most clearly expressed in the personality theories of Albert Bandura (1999) and Walter Mischel (Mischel & Shoda, 1995, 1999). Before noting the place of cognition in their theories, however, let us briefly consider the *social intelligence* view of personality of Nancy Cantor and John Kihlstrom (1982, 1987, 1989), for it represents an early, explicit attempt to formulate a theory of personality linked to theory and data developed in laboratories studying cognitive processes. According to them, adaptive behavior is the natural domain for the study of personality, and adaptive behavior is expressed in intelligent action. Such action is expressed in action flexibly directed toward achieving goals and solving personal life tasks.

A couple of points are noteworthy in relation to other approaches to personality. First, in contrast with the trait emphasis on generalized dispositions and the earlier emphasis on generalized cognitive style, it is suggested that people develop knowledge and expertise that is task or domain specific. The "smart" person in one domain may be rather "dense" in another. Second, both standardized questionnaires and experimental laboratory situations are deemphasized as models for the assessment of personality relative to data closer to the naturalistic context of life tasks. The former are deemphasized because they distill personality into a few basic trait dimensions, the latter because they do not tap the actual adaptive functioning of individuals as they try to solve life tasks. Both are rejected because they do not assess the world of personal meanings. For the most part, self-report measures are emphasized since it is assumed that generally people are aware of their goals and strategies used to achieve them. At the same time, it is recognized that other measures, such as fantasy measures and direct observations of behavior, are used to assess the structure and dynamics of individual personality functioning.

Social Cognition: Expectancies, Beliefs, and Attributions

As noted, currently the importance of cognitive units is most clearly expressed in the theories of Bandura and Mischel. Bandura (1999) assigns a central role to cognitive processes in personality functioning. The capacity to represent people and events, to think about and plan constructive courses of action, and to reflect back upon one's thoughts and actions are fundamental to human personality functioning. The capacity for forethought means that one can establish goals, develop expectancies and plans, and regulate action. For Mischel (Mischel & Shoda, 1995, 1999), personality includes how the person construes the self, people, events, and situations. In addition, it includes expectancies and beliefs about the world and the outcomes for behavior in specific situations, and the cognitive strategies used to organize action and regulate one's own behavior.

Perhaps of greatest importance to cognitive personality psychologists is the concept of *schema*, referring to a cognitive structure that organizes information. As a way of interpreting and categorizing events in the world, the schema concept is similar to Kelly's construct. From a personality standpoint, individuals differ in the schema they form, in the relations among these schema, and in the ways in which they process information relevant to their schema. Of particular importance are schema we have for viewing ourselves and others. That is, individuals differ in the schema or concepts they use to define themselves and others. They also differ in their schema concerning their *possible selves* or selves that they might become (Markus & Ruvolo, 1989).

Of importance as well are individual differences in *beliefs*. Of particular importance are beliefs concerning the self, such as *self-efficacy beliefs* or the perceived ability to cope with specific situations (Bandura, 1999). Such beliefs involve judgments people make concerning their ability to meet specific demands in specific situations and to master specific tasks. According to this view, people do not have a self or self-esteem. Such concepts are too global and do not reflect the situational variability in the way we see ourselves and the specificity of self-evaluations. Such beliefs are important for personality functioning generally and pathological functioning in particular. Thus, for example, *maladaptive* and *irrational beliefs* concerning the self, the world, and the future are viewed as the basis of abnormal personality functioning (Beck, 1993; Ellis & Harper, 1975).

Another important cognitive unit is that of *attributions* or causal explanations given for events (Weiner & Graham, 1999). According to attributional models, people make causal explanations for events. Attribution theorists have suggested the following as dimensions along which attributions may differ: *controllabillity* (the extent to which events can be controlled), *stability* (whether events are stable or unstable), *malleability* (whether phenomena can be changed or are fixed), *internal-external* (whether events are caused by the self or forces external to the self), and *global-specific* (whether the causes are specific to the event or more general) (Dweck, 1999; Peterson & Park, 1998; Seligman, 1975; Weiner & Graham, 1999). Differences in causal explanations along such dimensions are viewed as having important implications for motivation and emotion. For example, successful outcomes attributed to ourselves lead to greater self-esteem than do such outcomes attributed to external causes such as an easy task or good luck. On the other hand, such attributions for unsuccessful, negative outcomes also lead to greater self-blame and lessening of self-worth. Attributions of controllability for personal failure are associated with emotions such as guilt, shame, and humiliation, whereas attributions associated with uncontrollability for personal failure do not lead to such self-criticism. Similarly, we hold others responsible for failures attributed to controllable causes and feel angry toward them. On the other hand, we feel sympathy toward those whose failures are seen as the result of circumstances beyond their control. If failure or illness is seen as the result of needlessly risky behavior, we may feel angry toward the person and stigmatize him or her; whereas if it is seen as the result of heredity or other circumstances beyond the person's control, we may feel sympathy and seek to be of assistance. In sum, the attributions we make determine whether we see the problem as one of sin (controllable) or sickness (uncontrollable) (Weiner, 1993).

In sum, although not excluding the importance of other units, in particular those of motivation and emotion, social cognitive personality psychologists focus attention on the person's constructions of the self and the world and the ways in which these constructions enter into efforts to solve life's tasks.

Critique of the Cognitive Model

Cantor and Kihlstrom (1989) suggest that "the major issue in personality is consistency" (p. 43). In sympathy with Bandura, Mischel, and other "cognitivists," they suggest that personality functioning is much more situation or domain-specific than suggested by trait psychologists. But let us hold off with this issue, for it will be the focus of our attention in the next chapter. Here let us consider two questions relevant to social cognitive models of personality:

1. To what extent do social cognitive models capture the "hot" aspects of personality functioning as well as the "cold" aspects of cognitive functioning?

2. To what extent do social cognitive models capture individual differences and the functioning of the person as a system as opposed to only general processes?

What About the "Hot" Aspects of Personality Functioning? Early developments in social cognitive theory focused on cognition to the near exclusion of an interest in emotion and motivation. Cantor and Kihlstrom (1982, 1989) were eager to indicate that as "cognitivists" they were not uninterested in emotions and motivations: "Ours is not a view of men and women as coldly calculating processors of information" (1982, p. 181). Indeed, they indicated that emotions and motives can affect cognitive processes. However, clearly emotions and motives were secondary to their emphasis on cognitive structures and processes. This was true for the early work of Bandura and Mischel as well. However, over time there has been a shift in this regard such that emotion and motivation are much more central concepts for these social cognitive psychologists. Mischel (Mischel & Shoda 1995, 1999) in particular has gone so far as to call the most recent form of his theory *CAPS*—cognitive affective personality system. Thus, although Kelly's personal construct theory and early social cognitive theories were criticized for their lack of attention to the importance of emotion and motivation in personality functioning, that is, to the "hot" aspects of personality functioning, such criticism is less relevant to more recent social cognitive theory.

What About Individual Differences and General Processes? The contrast between the individual differences focus of trait approaches to personality and the general processes focus of social cognitive approaches is drawn sharply by Cantor and Kihlstrom (1982). One can ask, then, about the extent to which cognitive units can be used to capture individual personalities. Cantor and Kihlstrom (1989) are critical of the somewhat superficial Big Five descriptions of people: "These broad trait dimensions might be considered 'blind date questions'—the basic information that we would want about a stranger with whom we have to interact" (p. 18). Do social cognitive descriptions of people go beyond such blind date questions? Social cognitive personality psychologists are concerned with individual differences. The differences of concern to them are the ways in which individuals construe the world about them and themselves, the goals they set for themselves and the strategies they use to achieve these goals, the expectations they have and the value they attach to various outcomes. In other words, a new set of person variables is suggested. In addition, it is suggested that individual functioning on these new person variables may be much more fluid and changing than the picture represented by trait psychologists.

Have the person variables suggested by social cognitive personality psychologists become a focus of individual differences research? Certainly individual differences in self-efficacy beliefs has been a major area of inquiry. The concept of goals has become a major area of research, although not necessarily derived exclusively, or even primarily, from social cognitive theory. Cantor (1990) has described individual differences in strategies used to solve adaptive tasks, particularly in making the transition to life as a college student. However, it would be hard to think of a specific social cognitive unit of personality that has been the subject of investigation to the extent to which has been true for the Big Five. In part this is because of the greater focus on general processes than on individual differences. In part this is because of the criticism of the use of standardized questionnaires that force subjects to use the investigator's constructs and that force subjects to disregard the contextual variability of their behavior. The bottom line, however, is that we have not been given illustrations of social cognitive descriptions of personality that go beyond blind date descriptions. Kelly (1955) illustrated the application of personal construct theory to individual cases but comparable presentations have been lacking on the part of more recent social cognitive theorists. In fact, the only social cognitive presentation of a person is that by Mischel (1999), and that is a fictitious person. Thus, although the cognitive units suggested by social cognitive psychologists seem promising as individual difference variables, how far they take us beyond the blind date remains to be determined.

For many personality psychologists it is the functioning of the person as a system that lies at the heart of the field (Pervin, 1999; Pervin & John, 2000). What does it mean to consider the person as a system? It means that individual behavior reflects the operation of many parts operating together rather than the operation of single units operating in isolation from one another. It means that any complex human behavior reflects the operation of many units—cognitive, motive, and so on. It means that the operation of these units and processes can be integrated with one another or in conflict with one another. We shall return to this issue in the final chapter but it is important to note here the challenge for any theory of personality to consider the system aspects of personality functioning. To the credit of recent social cognitive theory, there has been increased attention to this issue. Bandura (1999) frequently refers to the personality system and, as noted, in CAPS Mischel (1999) specifically focuses on the system aspects of personality functioning. At the same time, the fact that the concept of conflict does not appear in their presentations suggests that greater attention needs to be given to this aspect of personality. As undoubtedly is reflected in the above comments, the call here is for illustrations of the interplay among cognitive units and between these and other units in the lives of individual cases.

In sum, just as questions are raised concerning trait and motive units of personality, questions can be raised concerning cognitive units, in this case questions concerning the relation of cognitive units to emotion and motivation and the relevance of such units for the study of individual differences and the system aspects of personality functioning. Although significant progress has been made, developments in these areas remain challenges for the future for models of personality based on cognitive units and cognitive processes.

Relations Among the Units

Trait, motive, and cognitive units are not the only possible units for the study of personality. For example, emotion and emotion regulation is another area that is significant in relation to personality functioning (Gross, 1999; Izard, 1993; Malatesta, 1990). Emotion and motivation have been considered as traits and related to factor models of personality (Zuckerman, et. al., 1999). Emotion has been viewed as the basis for motivation (Pervin, 1983; Rolls, 2000) and increasingly seen as an influence on cognitive processes (Forgas & Vargas, 2000; Isen, 2000). However, the units considered in this chapter have been the major focus of attention of personality psychologists and thus will remain our focus in this concluding section.

What are the relations among the trait, motive, and cognitive units? First, there is the question of whether the units are distinct from one another, overlap with one another, or perhaps even duplicate one another. Second, if all are distinct and central to personality, there is the question of how they function in relation to one another. Considering the first question, traits and cognitive units have tended to be considered in isolation from one another. The one major exception to this is the trait of *Openness to Experience,* the most controversial of the Big Five (McCrae & Costa, 1997). One interpretation of this factor emphasizes cognitive abilities as expressed in trait adjectives such as *intelligent, perceptive, knowledgeable,* and *analytical.* However, McCrae and Costa (1997) argue for a much broader interpretation of this factor, one that includes motivational as well as cognitive components. Central to their conception of this factor is the need for new experience, that is, an active need to seek out the unfamiliar.

What is the current status of trait and motive concepts? Are they really the same concepts, albeit with different labels, or are they different? How much do they actually overlap? Are both required for understanding personality and behavior, or can we get along with only one?

Winter, et. al., 1998, pp. 230–250

The mixing of motivational and cognitive characteristics in the interpretation of the Openness to Experience factor brings us to the question of the relation between trait and motive units. Early on, both Allport (1937) and Murray (1938) distinguished between trait and motive concepts. Allport distinguished between stylistic, expressive traits and motivational traits. Murray suggested that although a motive might operate but once in a person's life, a trait referred to a recurrent action pattern. And, although a motive might rarely express itself in behavior, particularly in a direct form, it might still be an important part of the dynamic organization of the person's personality. Therefore, he suggested that psychologists who think of personality as traits and those who think of it as motives focus attention on different phenomena, use different methods to investigate personality, and end up with different explanations. A different view, however, was offered by Costa and McCrae (1988). Critical of Murray's alphabetical list of needs, they explored the relation between trait and motive (need) concepts by comparing scores on questionnaire measures of traits and motives. The motive questionnaire was based on Murray's classification of needs. They found that the motives could be organized within the framework of the five-factor model and concluded that "we need not develop separate taxonomies for traits and for needs, the five-factor model can accommodate both" (Costa & McCrae, 1988, p. 264). These results were for the most part replicated in a subsequent study comparing responses to the two questionnaire measures (Finch, Panter, & Caskie, 1999). In the latest presentation of a five-factor theory of personality, McCrae and Costa (1999) suggest that the five trait factors they emphasize are biologically based basic tendencies out of which are derived, among other things, personal strivings.

A different point of view is expressed by Winter, et al, (1998). Considering the status of trait and motive concepts, they suggest that the two concepts reflect two fundamentally different elements of personality—conceptually distinct, complementary concepts. Rather than being antagonistic rivals, they suggest that traits and motives interact. They propose that traits channel the behavioral expression of motives. That is, traits constitute the stylistic expression of motives, a view that is quite at odds with that expressed by Costa and McCrae. The view of traits and motives as distinct concepts is supported by the research of Roberts and Robins (2000), who found that motives (life goals) and traits could not be subsumed by one another and were best viewed as complementary units of analysis. They also suggested that individual differences in personality traits are predictive of the goals people choose to pursue in life.

Can these views be reconciled? Part of the problem appears to be in how a trait is defined, in particular whether it is defined in terms of overt behavior or is defined in much broader terms and as inclusive of thoughts, feelings, and motives as well as behavior. Trait psychologists themselves differ in this regard. If traits are defined as individual differences in temperament, as often is the case, then one can consider them to be biologically based tendencies which influence the development of motives and cognitive processes. If traits are defined as individual differences in expressive style, as reflected in overt behavior, then they may be seen as the characteristic expression of motives and, perhaps, cognitive processes. If traits are defined as inclusive of temperament, emotion, motives, and thoughts, as appears to be the case with McCrae and Costa, then the independent status of motive and cognitive concepts appears to be in question.

Relations between the remaining pair of concepts, motives and cognitions, appear to be somewhat more straightforward. Most psychologists would consider them distinct units that interact with one another. Thus, for example, there is evidence that cognitions, such as self-efficacy beliefs and attributions, have implications for motivation and that motives affect cognitive processes (Bandura, 1999; Dweck, 1999; Kunda, 1987). Goals are mental representations, thereby involving cognitive processes. Which goals we choose to pursue is influenced by our constructions of the world, about what is possible and what is probable. But the way in which we process information, where we focus our attention and which events we call forth from memory, is influenced by the goals operating at the time.

Can the trait, motive, and cognitive units be viewed as functioning in relation to one another? A recent article by Morf and Rhodewalt (2001) seeks to interpret narcissistic functioning within a framework that unites dispositional (trait) and social cognitive approaches to personality, two approaches which they note have been thought to be competing and mutually preemptive. According to the American Psychiatric Association, the central characteristics of narcissism are described as being a pervasive pattern of grandiosity, self-focus, and self-importance. According to Morf and Rhodewalt (2001), narcissists are individuals with grandiose but fragile self-conceptions. They are *motivated* to foster and protect this grandiose self-view. The core goal of their functioning is to constantly receive attention, affirmation, and admiration from others to corroborate the grandiose self-view. They have a need for uniqueness and seek power rather than intimacy. Basically these motives operate in the service of preserving their self-esteem. These motives affect *cognitive processes*. Thus, narcissists are sensitive to perceived threats to their self-esteem, have a distorted recall of their accomplishments, overestimate their positive qualities and underestimate their negative qualities, view themselves as superior to others, and attribute success to internal qualities and failure to external, situational conditions. Together, these cognitive and motivational processes lead to stable patterns of behavior. Thus, narcissists are characterized by the following *traits*: arrogance, hostility, dominance, derogation of others, lack of empathy, manipulative and exploitive, bragging, excuses for failure. In other words, the core goal of preserving the grandiose self-image leads the narcissist to behave in stable, trait-like ways. However, this does not mean that these behaviors will be expressed in all situations. They are most likely to be expressed where self-esteem is most at stake and potentially threatened. In sum, according to the authors it is possible to make use of these units in an integrative way. Such a formulation serves as a model for the kind of integrative efforts that may be made in the future.

Summary

In the first chapter we considered competing traditions of thought and research. It was suggested that specific conceptual units are associated with these competing traditions. In this chapter we have considered the major units emphasized by personality psychologists—traits, motives, and cognitive processes. For the most part, the units have been studied by different groups of investigators, each group committed to its own conceptual foundation. Findings supportive of the importance of the unit are obtained while competing lines of research are ignored or criticized. Thus, the strengths and limitations of each unit become apparent. Perhaps the most important question then becomes that of establishing relations among the units and formulating a framework which works out the interconnections among those that are distinctive. Psychologists committed to the motive and cognitive processes units appear to agree that these are distinct concepts and that they interactively influence one another. The status of the trait concept in relation to the motive and cognitive processes units is less clear, depending in part upon the definition given to the trait concept. Clearly cognition, motivation, behavior, and emotion are all central to personality functioning. At issue is which units should be emphasized and how their relationships should be defined. The greatest challenge for the future of the field is to establish not only the units of personality but the ways in which they function as parts of an organized system—at times integrated with one another and at times in conflict with one another, but always interacting with one another.

CHAPTER 3

Am I Me Or Am I The Situation? Where We Stand In Relation To The Person-Situation Controversy

General Theme

Throughout the history of the field there has been a tendency to emphasize internal, personality determinants or external, situational determinants of behavior. During the period 1968–1988, these differences were reflected in the person-situation controversy and the associated theoretical divide between trait psychologists and social cognitive psychologists. Some personality psychologists suggest that the controversy is now over and that a rapprochement between trait and social cognitive psychologists is both possible and necessary. However, there is evidence that the debate continues and that incompatibilities between the two theoretical perspectives will make a rapprochement difficult.

> *I am exactly the same person I was before, but my situation in life is different and I behave as differently as if I were another person.*
>
> *S. Krim, New York Times, November 18, 1974*

If we observe and reflect on our own behavior and our experience of ourselves behaving, we are struck by two conclusions. First, our behavior varies according to

55

the situation we are in. Not only do we behave differently in the classroom than at a party, but we notice differences according to whether we are at a party with strangers or with friends, whether the party is formal or informal, whether we are only with members of our own sex or we are in mixed company. Second, at the same time that we are behaving differently in these situations we regard ourselves as the same person. The fact that I dress one way in school and another way while gardening, that I behave somewhat differently at a large cocktail party than at a small gathering of friends, that I talk more as a teacher and listen more as a therapist, that I am quick-tempered in some situations and patient in other situations—these variations in my behavior do not interfere with the sense that there is one person, me, involved in all of them.

There is, then, the observation of both change and stability, of behaving differently and yet being the same person. Were my behavior to be the same in all situations, it would be perfectly predictable but I and others would wonder about why I was so rigid and why I behaved so inappropriately in some situations. On the other hand, if no consistency or pattern could be observed in my behavior, then I might wonder whether I wasn't being a "phony" much of the time or I would be bothered by feelings of depersonalization—so much change would leave me without a feeling of knowing who I am or, perhaps, without a feeling of being a person at all. Indeed, most of us have struggled with such questions from time to time, particularly in adolescence, when we focus our attention on forming an identity or when we behave in a way that is "out of character" for us and try to reconcile this behavior with what we otherwise know and believe about ourselves.

In sum, in observing our own behavior we are struck with aspects of ourselves that are different and yet the same, with a sense of stability in the face of constant variation. Such dual observations of ourselves are the norm and we are bothered when our behavior is so rigid that it is at times painfully inappropriate to the situation or so variable that we lose a sense of who we are.

The same conclusions apply to our observations of others. If I ask you to describe someone you know well, you would come up with a list of characteristics that you feel captured the personality of this individual. Yet, if you really know this person well you could undoubtedly describe situations in which his or her behavior was not in accord with the characteristics you listed. Thus, in both the perception of our own behavior and the perception of the behavior of others we see pattern and regularity in the face of diversity and variability, and we draw conclusions about "personality characteristics" while recognizing the importance of "situational" differences. Indeed, observations of our behavior over diverse situations might also apply to our behavior over a period of time. Our behavior certainly is different in childhood, adolescence, and adulthood, and yet generally there is at least some sense of continuity and stability as a person—the perception of continuity and sameness over time that Erikson describes as basic to a sense of identity. In light of these two conclusions—that is, we can recognize consistent personality characteristics while also recognizing the variability of behavior over time and across situations—we are drawn to the quote that began this chapter and to the issue that has been a source of controversy among personality psychologists. The author of this introductory quote served as an editor from 1961 to 1965 and tells us that during this period he generally was cool, rational, and reassuring and smiled compassionately at the temperament of his writers. In his own terms, he disciplined his own needs for approval because they were irrelevant. However, there was "another self that lived a separate life" that came out when Mr. Krim himself became an author. Then Mr. Krim became aggressive and anxious about the acceptance of his writing, found it hard to relax, was blunt and demanding rather than diplomatic, and was less able than previously to be objective or take an impersonal view. His confusion and insight were expressed as follows:

> What does it all mean? I often ask myself with some wonder as if I were a stranger to myself. I am the same man, I smoke the same foolish cigarettes, wear approximately the same clothes, respond to the same music and movies. It means, I'm afraid that the situation is more crucial than personality; at least that is so, or seems to be so, in my case. The situation you're in determines who you are...And yet, I tell you frankly that in my heart I'm exactly the same man who used to be reasonable, detached, smilingly helpful to those many egos so aggravated by their unfulfilled position in life and so much less fortunate than myself.

(S. Krim, New York Times, November 18, 1974)

Mr. Krim's confusion is similar to that of many, if not most, psychologists studying personality and probably has the same basis. He recognizes both stability and change in his behavior in relation to situations and recognizes the possible importance of both his personality and the situation in determining his behavior. Yet, he seeks to account for his behavior in terms of himself *or* the situation. Thus, he concludes, with some hesitance, that the situation determines who you are. Although he feels that he is the same man regardless of the idiosyncratic nature of the situation, such feelings do not match the governing characteristics of the situation. As we shall see, his framing of the question as a dichotomy between personality determinants and situation determinants is not unlike the dichotomy drawn by many psychologists. The battle and confusion within himself concerning which is more important, the person or the situation, is not unlike the battle and confusion between psychologists who emphasize the importance of person characteristics (e.g., traits, needs, motives) and psychologists who emphasize the importance of situation characteristics (e.g., stimuli, cues, rewards, and punishments) in regulating behavior. His conclusion that the situation is more important than the personality, though he may feel the same person regardless of the situation, is not unlike the position of psychologists who argue that behavior is situationally determined and that it is only we as observers who attribute behavior to personality characteristics and dispositions (Jones & Nisbett, 1971; Nisbett & Ross, 1980). Thus, the issue we are faced with is how do we assess and account for stability and change in behavior? Are the determinants of behavior in the person, in the situation, or where? Can we usefully speak of *factors inside the person* that affect behavior or should we focus our attention on *situational characteristics external to the person* and regard personality characteristics as virtual figments of our imagination—perhaps useful to us in going about our daily living, but of limited scientific value?

The Dichotomy Between Internal and External Determinants of Behavior

The issue of whether to focus attention on the person or on the situation can be viewed as an aspect of a broader issue—the relative significance of internal and external determinants of behavior. In some ways there is reason to believe that the emphasis on internal or external determinants of behavior involves broad philosophical commitments in addition to rational decisions based on scientific evidence. Historically there have been cultures that have viewed behavior as caused by forces inside the individual and other cultures that have viewed behavior as caused by forces external to the individual. Plato believed that people are molded by society whereas Aristotle believed that behavior reflects the inherent nature of the individual. Hippocrates believed that people could be characterized according to their temperament type, with temperaments being determined by the bodily functions or humors. Such a view of a relationship between bodily functioning or constitutional type and behavior found later expression in the views of Kretschmer and Sheldon. Such views can be contrasted with cultural views that place behavior under the control of the gods or spirits. Riesman (1950) described a change in American character from inner-directedness to outer-directedness, the former involving behavior governed by internalized goals and the latter involving behavior governed by the expectations and values of the surrounding peer group. Different societies see the causes and cures of illness as coming from within the individual or from forces in the outside world acting upon the individual.

Thus, we find an internal-external dimension to be relevant to broad philosophical views concerning human nature. What then about psychology in general and personality theory in particular? Allport (1955) found this issue of whether behavior is governed from within or from without, above all others, to divide psychologists. He attributed the differences to commitment to either a Leibnitzian tradition or a Lockean tradition. In the former tradition it is the organism that is important, and causes are seen as internal to the organism, whereas in the latter tradition the organism is seen as reactive to events external to it. European schools of psychology (e.g., Gestalt psychology, Freud's psychoanalysis) have tended to follow the Leibnitzian tradition, whereas British and American schools of psychology (e.g., associationism and behaviorism) have tended to follow the Lockean tradition. While virtually all psychologists would emphasize the importance of both internal and external determinants of behavior, or organism and environment, clear differences in emphasis and interpretation emerge as one considers the history of psychology, different fields within psychology, and different theories within a field. Obviously there is both individual and environment, person and situation, nature and nurture, yet the tendency has remained to emphasize one or another set of variables. Thus, for example, Freud's emphasis upon our being "lived" by unknown, internal forces can be contrasted with Skinner's suggestion that "a person does not act upon the world, the world acts upon him" (Skinner, 1971, p. 211).

> *Is it governed from without, or governed from within? Is it*
> *merely reactive or is it active? It is on this issue, above all*
> *others, that we find psychologists dividing.*
>
> *Allport, 1955, p. 6*

As we have seen, these alternative views can have ramifications in terms of what is looked at, how it is studied, and how personality is conceptualized. Although we are focusing attention on the study of personality, the differences noted are not limited to the study of personality. The relative importance of internal and external variables has been a particularly critical issue in the field of personality research but is by no means limited to that area of research.[1] The dilemma of Mr. Krim, and the debate among personality psychologists concerning the importance of person and situation determinants, can be seen as part of a broader question that runs throughout much of psychology and is fundamental to questions concerning the nature of people.

We can turn now to the intense debate over persons versus situations as determinants of behavior, for the light it sheds upon both internal and external determinants in general and upon the issue of person and situational influences in personality research in particular.

The Person-Situation Debate: 1968–1988

> *For the past two decades the person-situation debate has*
> *dominated personality psychology...it puts on trial the cen-*
> *tral assumption that internal dispositions have an impor-*
> *tant influence on behavior.*
>
> *Kenrick & Funder, 1988, p. 23*

During the 1940s and 1950s the field of personality tended to be dominated by internal theories. Freudian psychoanalysis exercised a strong influence on the issues that received attention, the kinds of assessment devices that were used, the research that was conducted, and the kind of training clinical psychologists received. The intensive study of individuals was pursued at the Harvard Psychological Clinic as well as elsewhere, and there was intense interest in the study of personality types—

---

[1] The issue under consideration also appears in the field of biology. Thus consider the following statement by a biologist: "... it seems to me that a fundamental division in biological thinking exists between people who are primarily interested in events inside the organism and those interested in events outside. . . . We have to remember that events inside the organism and outside form connected systems and that our separation is purely a matter of convenience. . . we have to relate external and internal events, and we need to be careful that our system of organizing knowledge does not interfere with this" (Bates, 1960, p. 549).

the anal character, the creative personality, the authoritarian personality. The study of the authoritarian personality was seen as a classic example of how a personality type could be defined and systematically studied in terms of the dynamics of functioning and the early determinants of character formation. The focus upon questions such as fascism, anti-Semitism, and authoritarianism was clearly a response to issues of concern to people during World War II. However, the formulation of an "authoritarian personality" was a response to the psychoanalytic influence. In fact, several investigators associated with this classic study had either been psychoanalyzed or had received training in psychoanalysis.[2] Even when learning theorists, such as Dollard and Miller, attempted to apply new principles to personality phenomena, they did so within a psychoanalytic framework. Thus, much of the genius of their book *Personality and Psychotherapy* (1950) was in the translation of psychoanalytic theory into the language of learning theory rather than in the breaking of new ground. The emphasis on the person, represented in psychoanalytic and in trait theory, and expressed in the use of projective techniques and personality trait inventories, was so strong that one psychologist was led to comment that "the persisting pattern which permeates everyday life of interpreting individual behavior in the light of personal factors (traits) rather than in the light of situation factors must be considered one of the fundamental sources of misunderstanding personality in our time. It is both the cause and the symptom of the crisis in our society" (Ichheiser, 1943, p. 152).

The Mischel Challenge: 1968

Partly out of frustration with the results of psychoanalytically based research and practice, and partly because of social-cultural changes, there began to grow an interest in an alternative way of looking at the phenomena of interest. Then in 1968 Walter Mischel came out with a book, *Personality and Assessment,* which focused attention on issues that were brewing in the field and that needed both articulation and the presentation of relevant data. Basically Mischel was critical of traditional personality theories (i.e., trait theory and psychodynamic theory) and of the assessment procedures associated with these theories. A major part of Mischel's criticism concerned the emphasis given by trait and dynamic personality theories to internal properties of the organism: "Traditional personality theories assume an internal structure-dynamic hierarchy in which various hypothesized aspects of the person stand in superordinate or subordinate relations to each other. . . . The implication in all hierarchical personality models is that some internal entities underlie others, and that their dynamic interrelations determine or produce the behavior that the person displays" (Mischel, 1968, p. 4).

The issue was being framed. Trait theory was criticized for its assumption that personality is made up of stable and enduring predispositions that exert fairly generalized effects on behavior. In other words, a connection was drawn between the emphasis on hierarchically arranged internal entities on the one hand and generalized

---

[2] By contrast, today we see little if any interest in the study of the "racist personality" or the "sexist character type."

ways of behaving on the other. Similarly, psychodynamic theory was criticized for its emphasis on internal entities and its associated emphasis on longitudinal and cross-situational stability: "Psychodynamic theory, like trait theory, assumes that the underlying personality is more or less stable regardless of the situation. According to the psychodynamic view, the individual develops during childhood a basic personality core that does not change much in its essentials" (Mischel, 1968, p. 6).

If hierarchically arranged internal entities and stable patterns of behaving over time and across situations were to be rejected, what was to be emphasized? Instead of emphasizing broad dispositions that manifest themselves stably and independently of stimulus conditions, Mischel suggested that changes in stimulus (external) conditions modify how people behave and therefore behavior is relatively situation-specific: "The principles that emerge from studies of the variables that control behavior in turn become the bases for developing theory, not about global traits and states, but about the manner in which behavior develops and changes in response to environmental stimulus changes" (Mischel, 1968, p. 10). Since behavior depends on stimuli, regularities in behavior are to be explained in terms of regularities in external events rather than in terms of internal characteristics. Personality consistency is dependent on stable environmental supports rather than upon stable response predispositions in people. One could now emphasize maintaining conditions in the environment rather than character structures or personality trait profiles. While this is an oversimplification of the issue, in a certain sense Freud, psychodynamic theory, and trait theory were out and Skinner, Bandura, and social learning theory were in.

> *While trait and state theories search for consistencies in people's behavior across situations, social behavior theory seeks order and regularity in the form of general rules that relate environmental changes to behavior changes (p. 150). . . . Behavior depends on stimulus conditions and is specific to the situation (p. 177).*
>
> *Mischel, 1968*

Mischel's critique of traditional personality theory and assessment can be summarized as follows:

1. With the possible exception of cognitive and intellectual ability functions, there is little evidence of longitudinal stability and cross-situational consistency in behavior.

2. Since behaviors that are often construed as stable personality trait indicators are actually dependent upon evoking and maintaining conditions in the environment, traditional dispositional theories can be called into question.

3. Since assessment devices based upon dispositional theories (e.g., projectives such as the Rorschach and TAT, and personality trait questionnaires such as the Cattell Sixteen Personality Factor Inventory) are of limited utility in predicting

behavior in a situation, the use of such assessment devices may also be called into question.

4. Trait terms are common in personality theory and in our everyday descriptions of others but they must represent something other than stable predispositions. The suggestion is made that traits represent verbal terms that are used to describe behavior but that do not mirror behavior—traits represent descriptive categories that trait researchers, and people generally, use to organize their worlds, but they do not reflect actual behavioral regularities or internal structures. We see such modes of making judgments about people, in extreme form, in stereotypes. Finally, there is evidence that we generally assume certain linkages among personality characteristics. Thus, for example, if a person is seen as extraverted, we also tend to see the person as spirited, exuberant, outgoing, lively, and perhaps venturesome, whereas if a person is seen as introverted, we also tend to see that person as quiet, timid, shy, and perhaps studious (Cantor & Mischel, 1977). In sum, when people are rated on personality traits, the ratings reflect the rater's conceptual scheme rather than the subject's actual behavior. Responses to interpersonal checklists, personality inventories, and questionnaire interviews reflect how people (including trait psychologists) view behaviors as related to one another but they do not reflect actual behavior relationships (Shweder, 1975, 1982).

As has been noted, the underlying issue is an old one and much of Mischel's argument had already been made. What was striking about Mischel's book, however, was the clarity with which the problem was articulated, the marshaling of relevant evidence, and the presentation of an alternative personality model based on the role of conditions in the environment, as well as the cognition of these conditions, that regulate the flow of behavior. While the issue was an old one, there was sufficient frustration with traditional "internal" theories and associated assessment devices to ready the field for a shift in emphasis toward more "external" theories and more "behavioral" and environmental measures.

The Response and Debate

Although Mischel emphasized the importance of cognitive mechanisms, and in his 1973 reconceptualization of personality emphasized the importance of such internal personality variables as expectancies and goals, a battle line had been drawn in the sand and the dye had been cast for Mischel to be perceived as the arch enemy of personality psychology. Defenders of traditional personality psychology responded with a barrage of criticism, counterclaims, and evidence in support of the dispositional view.

What was the response of traditional personality psychologists to Mischel's challenge? One of the studies often cited as evidence of situational specificity was Hartshorne and May's (1928) study of honesty in children. As part of the Character Education Inquiry project, children were put in situations where they were tempted to violate standards and where detection appeared to be impossible. Subjects were allowed to play with boxes containing money and were then asked to return the boxes. They did not know that the boxes had been marked, and many of them kept some of the money. Observations were also made of cheating on tests, honesty in work done at home, honesty in reporting scores, and other behavior associated with the traits of truthfulness and honesty. As it turned out, the measures used to assess honesty and truthfulness in children did not correlated highly with one another. This lack of correlation suggested that children are not consistently honest or dishonest but rather that honest behavior is relatively situation specific.

The defenders of the dispositional view argued that the children were too young to have developed "characterological honesty" and therefore to demonstrate consistency in moral behavior. Moral consistency increases with age and therefore such research needs to be conducted with adults. In addition, many children were consistently honest and some consistently dishonest. Perhaps one can expect to find cross-situational consistency only for people high on the trait being measured. Finally, a later reanalysis of the data suggested that the tests were not sufficiently reliable for the demonstration of a more general personality characteristic.

This last point related to a second argument made by "traditionalists": Many studies in the field are poorly done—methodologically inadequate, without conceptual implication, and even foolish. Block (1977) articulated this argument as follows: "It may well be that the current dismal assessment of the personality literature depends too heavily on the poor 'batting average' our sloppy empiricism has attained. Home runs have been averaged with strike-outs, and clearly there have been many of the latter. But some people know how to play ball and others do not. What if the home runs are hit by competent, resourceful athletes while the strike-outs come from the blind and the infirm?" (p. 41).

Are there then any competently performed studies that demonstrate consistency—any home runs? Block points to his own study of *Lives Through Time* (Block, 1971) as illustrative of the kinds of results found when research is done in a careful way. The study involved the independent gathering of a great deal of data about individuals at three points in their lives: when they were in junior high school, when they were in high school, and when they were in their mid-thirties. In other words, the study covered roughly a twenty-year time span. The data at each age were evaluated by psychologists who systematically presented their formulations of the personalities of each subject. Although there was some overlap in the psychologists doing the evaluations at the three time periods, no psychologist evaluated the same subject at more than one age. This means that care was taken to obtain independent personality descriptions of the subjects at each of the three time periods.

What were the findings? Block found that for the time period between junior high school and high school over half of the personality ratings were found to be related at a statistically significant level. For the senior high school to mid-thirties time period, an interval averaging close to twenty years, about 30 percent of the ratings were found to be in agreement to a statistically significant degree. Some of the personality items on which there was considerable evidence of stability were the following: Is a genuinely dependable and responsible person; Tends toward undercontrol of needs and impulses, unable to delay gratification; Basically submissive;

Emphasizes being with others, gregarious; Tends to be rebellious and nonconforming.

Block's study relates to consistency over time. But Mischel suggested that the issue of cross-situational consistency was much more critical to the global trait issue and it is here that he suggested there was minimal support for the trait position. Here the defenders of the trait (and psychoanalytic) position argued that lack of consistency could be evident at the *phenotypic* level, at the level at which behavior appears, but consistent at the *genotypic* level, at the underlying level of the fundamental nature of the behavior. For example, at one level physical aggression and verbal aggression might appear to be different but both are expressive of trait aggression. And, from the psychoanalytic standpoint, one could be dominant in some situations and passive in other situations with both expressing a conflict in the same area. In other words, from the latter point of view even opposite behaviors, perhaps in particular opposite behaviors, can be expressive of the same personality disposition.

Other points made by trait psychologists were that trait consistency was most clearly demonstrated in situations low in constraint where subjects had greatest room to express their personality. Thus, whereas one might not find consistency in laboratory settings, where situational variables dominate, in natural settings, in particular where individuals are free to select the situations they want to be in, consistency will be found. Indeed, perhaps what is most defining of personality is the ways in which individuals select situations to be in and shape the responses of others to them.

Of all the responses to Mischel's critique, however, the one that at the time probably had the greatest influence was Epstein's (1979, 1980, 1982, 1983) emphasis on the concept of *aggregation*, a point made much earlier by Allport. According to Epstein, one can obtain reliable and valid trait measurements only by averaging or aggregating measures of the behavior of interest over a large number of occasions or situations. The problem with much of the past personality research was that only one piece of behavior was sampled, on one occasion, in one situation. Such is typically the case, for example, with laboratory research. However, such limited samples of behavior have a high component of error and a limited range of generality. In contrast, averaging or aggregating responses over many occasions reduces chance error and increases the likelihood of observing stable relationships. Thus, the fact that an extravert does not behave in an extraverted manner on all occasions or in all situations does not make the term invalid or useless. Rather it demonstrates that a person can have a broad dispositional tendency while still responding adaptively to unique situations.

In a number of studies involving both self-report data and observer judgments, both in real-life situations and in the laboratory, Epstein demonstrated that aggregating responses reduces error and provides greater evidence of stability in personality functioning. To illustrate the point further, we can consider a study of naturally occurring prosocial and dominance behavior (Small, Zeldin, & Savin-Williams, 1983). This research involved observations of behavior of four groups of adolescents participating in a wilderness travel program. Prosocial and dominance behaviors were recorded by an observer in three situations: while preparing for or taking down the camp, during meals, and during free time. Illustrative prosocial behaviors were giving physical assistance in setting up a tent and offering to share food or some other possession. Illustrative dominance behaviors were giving verbal directions concerning a task and demonstrating physical aggressiveness. In addition, participants in the program ranked one another on these personality characteristics early in the trip and just before its conclusion.

The results indicated the following: (1) Peer perceptions of prosocial and dominance behavior were significantly in agreement with independent behavioral observation data. (2) There was considerable evidence of temporal stability for both types of behavior; that is, individuals who frequently displayed prosocial or dominance behavior on one occasion also tended to display this behavior on another occasion. (3) There was a high degree of cross-situational consistency for both prosocial and dominance behaviors; that is, regardless of the situation, individuals tended to maintain their rank order relative of other group members on the two behavioral dimensions. The researchers emphasized the importance of obtaining multiple samples of behavior of individuals in the contexts in which they live. Their conclusion, in accord with Epstein's view, was that the data clearly supported "a trait conceptualization of dominance and prosocial behavior. The evidence suggests that trait theories of personality do not have to be discarded—only that we need to revise our methods" (1983, p. 14).

Epstein's view and data were challenged by Mischel (Mischel & Peake, 1982, 1983). First, Mischel argued that all that aggregation does is increase measurement reliability but it does not demonstrate cross-situational consistency. Second, he argued that many of the relationships among behaviors suggested by Epstein were trivial. For example, evidence that people who make many telephone calls also receive many telephone calls hardly constitutes impressive evidence of cross-situational consistency. Third, and probably of the greatest significance, Mischel argued that by canceling out the effects of situations, Epstein had ignored the very data that are of particular interest to the personality psychologist—the individual's unique pattern of stability and change in relation to situations. To support this view, and in contrast with the data from the study just considered, Mischel presented data indicative of cross-situational variability in conscientious behavior in college students. For example, students who attended class regularly were not necessarily on time to class and did not necessarily take thorough notes. This was so even when relationships were based on aggregated measures, and despite the fact that students defined all three behaviors as related to the personality characteristic of conscientiousness. Mischel's conclusion, therefore, was that aggregation does not provide a solution to the consistency paradox. Rather than canceling out the effects of situations, Mischel argued, personality psychologists should recognize that behavior is highly discriminative and reflects the ability of people to respond to changing situational characteristics.

Traits are alive and well.

Epstein, 1977, p. 83

The consistent finding that emotions and behavioral impulses have very high levels of stability when aggregated

over a sample of naturally occurring situations provides
strong evidence for the existence of broad, cross-
situational dispositions, or traits.

Epstein, 1983, p. 112

. . .cross-situational aggregation has the undesirable effect
of canceling out some of the most valuable data about a
person. It misses the point completely for the psychologist
interested in the unique patterning of the individual.

Mischel & Peake, 1982, p. 738

The Interactionist View

It would not be surprising if by now one is left wondering about just what the controversy is, since it seems clear that people are stable in some ways and variable in others and that behavior must inevitably express both person and situation. Perhaps the questions have been poorly posed, needlessly expressing a dichotomy between person and situation. Rather than asking whether behavior is caused by the person or by the situation, perhaps we should be asking the following question: As a function of which person and situation characteristics does the individual remain stable and vary? In other words, people differ in their patterns of stability and change in relation to situations, and it is this pattern of behavior that represents personality. Behavior is always a reflection of the interaction between the person and the situation or between internal and external characteristics.

During the 1970s and 1980s, such an interactional view gained popularity in the personality field, so much so that it prompted one psychologist reviewing the literature to conclude that "if interactionism is not the Zeitgeist (i.e., spirit of the times) of today's personality psychology, it will probably be that of tomorrow's" (Ekehammar, 1974, p. 1045). One of the earliest and best studies of the interaction between persons and situations involved the observation of six preadolescent boys in six different settings (e.g., eating, games, and unstructured group activities). The boys all had problems in being excessively aggressive, and there was particular interest in the extent to which the aggressive behavior was consistent across settings and in how different settings affected different children—the interaction between child and setting. The researchers found that both differences in settings and differences in children generally affected the type of behavior that occurred. With the development of maturity and controls in these hyperaggressive boys their aggressive behavior became more limited to specific situations as opposed to being relatively consistent across all situations. However, at all times it was the interaction between specific settings and individual differences that influenced the aggressive behavior. The effect of the interaction did not involve a mere summation of setting effects and person effects. Rather, the effect of the setting changed according to which child was studied, and the effect of the person changed according to which setting was studied. The kind of behavior the setting evoked was related to the personality of the particular child, and the kind of behavior the child produced was to a considerable extent related to the characteristics of the particular situation that were salient for him.

Do the data argue for a "psychology of traits" or for a "psychology of situations"? The researchers answered this question as follows:

> Our own position is that neither one of these points of view is complete. We would view traits not as a once-and-for-all-time exclusive property of the organism irrespective of the environment but as directional potentialities under certain environmental circumstances; similarly, situations would be viewed as having arousal potential for certain traits. . . . There are some situations where the potential range of individual variation is highly restricted and others where individual variations are maximized. Personality factors may be similarly differentiated—for example, cognitive functions are, it is likely, somewhat less subject to situational variations than are affective aspects of personality.

> *(Raush, Dittmann, & Taylor, 1959, p. 373)*

Trait psychology and psychodynamics, on the one hand, and situationism, on the other, locate the main and causal factors in the person and the situation respectively, each neglecting the importance of factors on the other side of the interaction. The interactional view of behavior seems to be a natural next step in theory and research.

Magnusson & Endler, 1977, p. 31

The study of hyperaggressive boys suggested that the question of whether individual personality or situation was more important was a meaningless one—neither could be separated from the other. Yet, for some time the two tended to be considered independently by psychologists. Then an important series of studies by Endler and Hunt (1966, 1968) again called attention to person-situation interaction effects. In these studies subjects were presented with questionnaires in which a variety of anxiety-arousing or hostility-arousing situations were described. For each situation, subjects rated the likelihood of their responding in one of several different ways. For example, to the description of the situation "You are just starting off on a long automobile trip," subjects would rate the extent to which their hearts beat faster, they had an uneasy feeling, they would perspire, and so on. The responses showed that behavioral variation could not be attributed primarily to individual differences or to situation differences in anxiety and hostility—the interaction between person and situation was of far greater significance than the effects of persons alone or of situations alone. The dispute over whether the main source of variation in behavior is in the situations or in the persons was declared a pseudo-issue. What is important in personality description is the kinds of responses individuals make in various kinds of situations.

A final illustration of the interactional approach to personality research involves my own research with four students (Pervin, 1976). The following question was asked: "In what ways do you remain stable (consistent) and in what ways do you vary according to which situational characteristics?" In other words, the goal was a more differentiated understanding of the transactions between people and situations as opposed to purely an emphasis on persons or on situations. Also, it was felt that in many questionnaire studies subjects are asked to respond to situations that are irrelevant to their daily lives or to rate the applicability of behaviors that are not important parts of their behavioral repertoire. Therefore, in this research the students were allowed to describe situations and responses to situations that were meaningful for them.

In the procedure used, all the subjects listed situations in their current lives that were important to them. Then they listed characteristics to describe each situation, feelings experienced in each situation, and behaviors exhibited in each situation. Thus, for each subject there was a list of situations and a rating of the relevance of situational characteristics, feelings, and behaviors to each of these situations in terms of that particular individual. The data could then be systematically analyzed to determine the ways in which each subject felt and behaved the same or differently according to various situations in his or her daily life. Because the situations and responses were personally relevant, the systematic examination proved to be an interesting, if at times psychologically threatening, one for the subjects.

The results with the four subjects suggested some diversity among them in the kinds of situations they encounter in their daily lives and in the range of feelings and behaviors expressed in these situations. What was particularly instructive about the data concerning personality and person-situation interaction, however, was that each individual had a reported pattern of feelings and behaviors that in some ways was constant across all situations, in some ways was generally present except for some situations, and in some ways was almost never present except for a few specific situations. For example, according to her reports, Jennifer is almost always sensitive, vulnerable, and insightful. She is also friendly, warm, and accepting most of the time except when she is in some volatile home situations, at which times she is uniquely irritable, angry, upset, depressed, uncontrolled, and rebellious. She also tends to be involved and caring, except when she is in uncertain situations, where she is detached, preoccupied, introverted, controlled, and cool.

Each subject had a distinctive pattern of ways in which he or she was stable throughout all situations, varied in some behavior in relation to different groups of situations, and either never or very rarely exhibited other behaviors. The suggestion was made that it makes sense to include both stability and change in our conceptualization of personality as well as the relationship of patterns of stability and change to various kinds of situations:

> In sum, the data suggest that all subjects are stable in some of their behavior across all situations and variable in some of their behavior in relation to different situations. Whether a person exhibits a specific behavior in a situation will depend on whether that behavior is part of

one's repertoire, if so, whether it is stable or varies according to the situation and, if variable, its relationship to the particular situation. One's personality, then, can be defined as one's pattern of stability and change in relation to defined situational characteristics.

(Pervin, 1976, p. 471)

The interactional view suggests that all behavior reflects both person and situation. Within this context some behaviors may be more person determined for some people and other behaviors more situation determined for other people. Instead of deciding whether behavior generally is more person determined or more situation determined, the task of research becomes understanding the person and situation forces that account for the *pattern* of stability and change in behavior. Within such a perspective, several points can be made. First, it is not enough to say that one is an interactionist. One must be clear about what this term means. It means many things to many people (Magnusson & Endler, 1977). For some psychologists it means being able to demonstrate statistical interaction effects. In other words, it has to do with statistical approaches rather than with conceptual issues. For some psychologists interactional psychology means studying people interacting with one another. In other words, it has to do with the description of interpersonal processes rather than with a mode of analysis of such processes. Thus, there was the problem that, because of the popularity and reasonableness of interactional psychology, at times it came to mean all things to all people. The real import of the interactional approach, however, was in the conceptual emphasis it placed on understanding the interdependence between person and situation or between internal and external determinants of behavior. One cannot exist without the other and our research efforts must take cognizance of this fact.

A second implication of the interactionist position was the need for a broader temporal context than the single act. Much of our research to date has involved a freezing of behavior rather than a witnessing of how it unfolds. Observations of the flow or stream of behavior give evidence to both the stability and the plasticity of behavior. In attempting to adapt to the environment, the organism expresses efforts both to preserve its structure and to respond to environmental contingencies. The behaving organism is constantly striving to preserve order in the face of changes in the quality and quantity of internal and external stimuli. Processes such as regulation, adaptation, and exchange seem to be at the core of organismic behavior, and an understanding of such processes of individual-environment interaction require a longer time perspective than is often given in personality research.

Finally, the interactionist position required the study of the behavior of organisms as it occurs in the natural environment. This orientation did not preclude laboratory experimentation. However, it suggested that what is observed in the laboratory must be checked against behavior in the natural environment, where person and situational factors are in constant interplay with one another.

The interactionist position suggested that our task is to define units of the person and of the situation—the critical variables internal to the organism and those external to it—and then study the processes through which the effects of one are tied to the operations of the other. The question is not person versus situation, nor even how much person versus how much situation. Instead the question is *how* person and situation interact with one another. The trait, psychodynamic, and situationist positions all recognized the importance of this question but, unfortunately, never made it the center of investigation.

Given the soundness of the interactionist position, one might have expected the person-situation controversy to have ended with trait and situationist psychologists joining to forge a common ground within that framework. In fact, this did not occur and, with the exception of Magnusson (1999), today one rarely sees direct reference to the interactionist framework. Why was this the case? The reasons for changes in the popularity of concepts in psychology often are difficult to understand; however, my own sense is that the interactionist framework offered a model for how personality psychologists might think about things but did not offer new concepts or research methods. In the absence of these, and because of the remaining strong commitment to the alternative models, for the most part personality psychologists continued to emphasize person dispositions as reflected in behavioral consistency or cognitive processes leading to situational variability. But this is just one point of view. Another assessment of the situation, at least as of 1988, is considered in the following subsection.

Lessons Learned: 1988

This brings us to 1988 and the quote that began this section. In an article titled "Profiting from Controversy: Lessons from the Person-Situation Debate," two personality psychologists, Kenrick and Funder (1988), suggested that although things had not yet quieted down, it was possible to consider the person-situation debate over and to draw some conclusions from it. Considering Mischel's critique, they concluded that the accumulated evidence failed to support the hypothesis that personality traits are simply in the eye of the beholder but that the evidence also failed to support an extreme dispositional view, one that suggested that grand predictions could be made from minute samples of behavior: "As with most controversies, the truth finally appears to lie not in the vivid black or white of either extreme, but somewhere in the less striking gray area" (p. 31).

Although this might seem a balanced, even-handed conclusion, in fact for the most part it represented a defense of traditional trait theory: "When an academic psychologist teaches a course in personality, he or she must either assume consistency in personality or else face a bit of existential absurdity for at least three hours a week" (p. 23). Although it was accepted that one could not expect predictive validity from minute samples of behavior or from assessment devices of questionable reliability and validity, predictive validity was possible when knowledgeable raters and multiple observations were used. In other words, rather than accepting Mischel's fundamental criticism of the traditional dispositional model or rejecting it entirely, the authors attempted to draw a positive conclusion from two decades of debate: "The controversy stimulated by the situationist attack on personality may be seen more as a life-giving transfusion than as a needless bloodletting" (p. 32).

The Simmering Controversy and the Attempt at Rapprochement

Were two decades of controversy, debate, and research sufficient to put the issue to rest? Personality psychologists may differ in their answer to this question but my own answer is a resounding "No!" I remember attending a conference on the debate and one of the suggestions made was, following Chairman Mao of China: "Let a thousand flowers bloom." In other words, let alternative models of personality go their own way and flourish. Rather than destroying the field through controversy, let's pursue each model to its limits and go on from there. But debates in science about fundamental issues rarely follow such a rational course and, I believe, such was not the case in personality psychology.

I want to argue that the person-situation debate is not just about whether persons or situations are more important in determining behavior, or whether behavior is sufficiently consistent to support a trait point of view or sufficiently situation-specific to support a social cognitive point of view. Rather, the person-situation debate is about a fundamental issue concerning how we are to conceptualize personality functioning. Far from being trivial and senseless, the issue is fundamental. We will return to this point but first let us consider where things have gone since Kenrick and Funder attempted to draw a close to the controversy.

On the one hand, as we have seen (Chapter 2), trait psychologists embarked upon an impressive journey of accumulating evidence supportive of the trait point of view. The results of their research emboldened them to equate personality with traits: "Taken together, they (the Big Five) provide a good answer to the question of personality structure" (Digman, 1990, p. 436). In other words, the issue was settled; broad dispositions in the form of traits were to be accepted as the fundamental building blocks of personality. In addressing the question of lessons learned from the person-situation debate, Epstein (1997) suggested that "the existence of traits, conceived of as broad, stable response dispositions, is no longer contested" (p. 18). According to him, recognition of the need for reliable measures and aggregation of behaviors should have put an end to the controversy. And, Funder (2001) in his recent review of the status of the field concludes that "the person-situation debate, concerning whether consistencies in individuals' behavior are pervasive or broad enough to be meaningfully described in terms of personality traits can at last be declared about 98 percent over" (p. 199).

On the other hand, social cognitive psychologists continued with their exploration of *processes* of personality functioning, processes that led individuals to differentiate among situations and to vary their behavior accordingly. For example, Mischel and his colleagues undertook the study of behavior of the same individuals in a variety of settings (Shoda, Mischel, & Wright, 1994). Specifically, systematic behavior observations were made of how the same individuals behaved in a variety of naturally occurring social situations. The general context was a summer residential camp setting for children (mean age of ten years) and observations were made of behavior in such general settings as woodworking and a cabin meeting, and such specific interpersonal situations as the following: *when peer initiated positive con-*

tact; when peer teased, provoked, or threatened; when praised by an adult; when warned by an adult; when punished by an adult. Throughout the 6-week summer, within each hour of camp activity, observers recorded the frequency with which the following five categories of behavior occurred in the five interpersonal situations: *verbal aggression (teased, provoked, threatened); physical aggression (hit, pushed, physically harmed); whined, displayed babyish behavior; complied, gave in; talked prosocially.*

Would individuals display the same behaviors across the interpersonal situations, as suggested by trait theory, or would the behaviors be situation specific and vary accordingly, as suggested by social cognitive theory? More specifically, would there be support for the social cognitive hypothesis that each child would display a distinctive pattern of behavior that varied by context? In other words, rather than there being a stable rank ordering of individuals for each category of behavior across the five interpersonal situations, there would be variability according to context in terms of who was high and low on the categories of behavior. Rather than characterizing each child in terms of traits such as aggressiveness or agreeableness, would it be better and more accurate to characterize each child in terms of his or her profile of situation-behavior relationships: *if* the situation has these characteristics *then* this specific behavior is likely to appear?

Support was found for the latter; that is, the behavior displayed by an individual child was found to vary across situations. For each child a stable *situation-behavior profile* could established. For example, whereas one child was likely to express verbal aggression in response to peer teasing but not in response to adult warnings, another child would display the opposite pattern. The two children might express the same average amount of verbal aggression but the contexts of such aggressive behavior, the situation-behavior relationships, or *if . . . then* probabilities, would differ. For each of the behaviors studied, differences among the children were found in *average levels* but, of greater significance from the standpoint of Mischel, each child had a *stable profile of situation-behavior relationships.* Where consistency of individual differences in behavior were found they reflected a similarity of the nature of the psychological situation. As situations shared more features, consistency of individual differences in behavior across them increased, whereas when situations shared fewer features, the consistency of behavior across them decreased.

According to Mischel's social cognitive conception of personality, each individual has a *behavioral signature,* constituting a pattern of variability in behavior according to contexts or domains of situations, that reflects stable personality processes. It is not that behavior is random or situationally determined, nor that personality does not exist, but rather that individuals have distinctive ways of perceiving situations, specific goals in situations, specific affects associated with categories of situations, and specific outcome expectancies in these situations (Mischel & Shoda, 1995, 1999). It is these personality processes that lead to the interactions between persons and situations emphasized by interaction theorists.

One would have thought that the solution I proposed to resolving the person-situation debate would have been em-

braced by all parties. . . . However a hard core of resistance remained.

Epstein, 1997, p. 15

The person-situation debate, concerning whether consistencies in individuals' behavior are pervasive or broad enough to be meaningfully described in terms of personality traits can at last be declared about 98 percent over.

Funder, 2001, p. 199

One and the same person behaves differently for different purposes, in different activity domains, and in different social contexts.

Bandura, 1999, p. 194

Can the two approaches to personality—dispositional-trait and processing-dynamic—be reconciled and integrated within a unifying framework? . . . at this point in the development of the field they probably can be, and probably should be, if personality psychology is to develop into a cumulative science.

Mischel & Shoda, 1999, p. 213

The above lines of research and quotes suggest that the old issue of the person-situation debate continues to more than simmer. As I suggested above, I believe that it continues to "boil" because it reflects fundamental differences in theoretical orientation, what Mischel contrasts as the dispositional-trait view as contrasted with the process-dynamic view. Is it possible to reconcile, integrate the two? Mischel and Shoda (1998) paint a dire picture of the consequences of our failure to do so: "Absent such a reconciliation, personality psychology is likely to continue to split itself in half. . . at best indifferent to each other, at worst undermining each other, and in either case making it more difficult to become a cumulative coherent science" (p. 232).

What Mischel suggests is that it is time to get past the often bitter competition between the trait and social cognitive approaches to personality, each with its own goals, agendas, and research strategies. Can we be one field rather than two, living together harmoniously? Mischel and Shoda (1998) attempt to make the case that the answer is affirmative, although they recognize that such reconciliation will be difficult to realize. What would such an integration look like? What is proposed is a *cognitive-affective personality system (CAPS)* in which cognitions, affects, and goals within the individual are activated characteristically and stably in relation to features of situations or the self. Without going into the entire details of the theory, what is argued is that stable individual differences in the organization of relationships among the cognitions and affects in the system give rise to processing dynamics and dispositional properties. There is both stable structure and variable processing in the functioning of the personality system, providing for characteristic individual situation-behavior profiles:

> The variability of behaviors within individuals across situations is neither all "error" nor is it "due to the situation rather than to the person." Instead, it is at least partly an essential expression of the enduring but dynamic personality system itself and its stable underlying organization. . . . Just how the individual's behavior and experience change across situations is part of the essential expression of personality.

(Mischel & Shoda, 1998, p. 246)

Is there room for the Big Five in such a model? Obviously there must be for a reconciliation to take place. What is suggested is that perhaps the Big Five can provide a taxonomy linked to the processing dynamics conceptualized within CAPS. But note that this basically remains a social cognitive model, with the trait emphasis on cross-situational consistency continuing to be rejected.

Mischel argues for both structural stability and processing dynamics, which is interesting in that the latest formulation of the five-factor model emphasizes both basic tendencies (the Big Five) and dynamic processes (McCrae & Costa, 1999). But once one goes past what might seem to be similar emphases, the differences in how structures and processes are conceived becomes striking. Whereas Mischel construes structures in terms of the stable organization of the cognitions, goals, and affects that constitute the personality system, McCrae and Costa construe structures in terms of the biologically based five factors. And, whereas Mischel construes processes in terms of how the person operates in response to specific internal and external demands, McCrae and Costa do not define the nature of the dynamic processes emphasized. The latter do suggest that characteristic adaptations (e.g., personal strivings, attitudes) and the self-concept are part of the personality system. However, these are viewed as an outgrowth of the basic tendencies. Finally, whereas McCrae and Costa view personality as for the most part stable over time, Mischel finds considerable opportunity for change. Thus, although remarkably the two points of view choose to use such similar terms as *dispositions*, *dynamic processes*, and *system*, the fundamental premises and models remain far apart.

So, is a reconciliation or integration possible at this time? As noted, Mischel's answer is in the affirmative. But I and others suspect that this is more wish than likely reality. A special issue in the 1999 volume of the *European Journal of Personality* was devoted to the issue of relations between persons and situations, without evidence of much of a consensus. In considering the prospects for an integration of the two approaches, Funder (2001) concludes that "it appears that such integration will not be easily achieved. A major obstacle is the almost dispositional reluctance of some investigators within the social cognitive paradigm to grant the very existence of general patterns to behavior that their theories are well suited to explain" (p. 205). And, addressing the issue from a social cognitive perspective, Cervone (1999) cautions against a simple integration of social cognitive and trait theories, arguing that such an integration is "conceptually problematic and empirically unnecessary. It overlooks the fact that social cognitive and trait approaches differ fundamentally in that they embrace different strategies of scientific explanation" (p. 329).

So What Is Known and Where Do We Go From Here?

Having considered the issue and relevant research, let us take stock of what we do and don't know and then consider where we go from here.

1. *There is considerable evidence for both person and situation determinants of behavior.* Put another way, there is evidence both for person consistency and situational variability in behavior. Interestingly enough, despite the considerable controversy and debate, this is a point on which probably all "dispositionists" and "situationists" agree. For the former there is sufficient cross-situational consistency in behavior to make use of the trait concept. For the latter, there is sufficient behavioral discriminativeness according to the situation to emphasize cognitive mechanisms and a concept such as behavioral signature. The data are such that one can interpret them as evidence for stable individual differences or for the importance of situational variability. Clearly both *person* and *situation* are important and the issue is how to go about conceptualizing the relations between the two.

2. *Some persons are more consistent than others.* This is true in terms of any one specific personality characteristic as well as for more general levels of stability or variability.

3. *Some situations have more powerful influences than others in reducing or maximizing the role of individual differences in personality.* Situations that are high in constraint reduce behavioral differences among people. Individual differences in personality are least likely to show up in highly structured situations and most likely to show up in unstructured life situations where individuals play a role in selecting or creating the situations themselves.

4. *Following from the above, the amount of evidence for consistency or variability will depend on who is being studied, where (e.g., laboratory vs. natural environment), the personality variables considered, and the measures being used.* The importance of who is studied and the situations involved has been considered. In addition, some personality characteristics, such as intelligence and temperament, generally are likely to show greater consistency than others, such as agreeableness. Also, there will be greater evidence of reliable individual differences the more multiple acts rather than single acts are considered, both in terms of forms and occasions. Aggregation improves the reliability and significance of individual differences in personality. However, it cancels out variability and thus cannot account for variability as well as stability.

5.   *People observe their own behavior as well as that of others and develop theo-
     ries to account for the observed events.* The theories developed by individuals,
     in terms of dispositional concepts and causal explanations, generally reflect re-
     ality to some extent but may also err in the importance given to person variables
     or situation variables. Not only are there individual differences in causal expla-
     nations for observed behavior but cultural differences as well.

Having reached these conclusions, we can turn to what we don't know. Here the
challenge is more difficult as well as more interesting. Put quite simply, *we do not
know how to account for patterns of stability and change in personality functioning.* Put another way, we do not know which are the best person and situation variables to emphasize in understanding the process of person-situation interaction. My
own effort in this area (Pervin, 1983) focused on goals as conceptual units and emphasized how the person could have a stable goal structure while also varying the
importance of specific goals according to internal conditions and situational opportunities or affordances. Mischel's CAPS model has many similar properties although
it gives greater attention to cognitive processes and specific behavior-situation relationships. Another possibility, suggested by Funder (2001) and others, is the development of a taxonomy of situations in addition to further development of the current
taxonomy of traits or dispositions. I am not optimistic about such an effort, since the
ways in which individuals categorize situations is highly idiosyncratic and fluid
(Pervin, 1981). In addition, there is large cultural and historical variability in the
nature of situations that influence behavior. However, the pursuit of such a taxonomy, and exploration of its relation to a trait taxonomy, is still worthwhile. If now
ready to "let a thousand flowers bloom," the field still appears to be wide open for
the development of a model that captures both stability and change in personality
functioning.

Summary

We have come a long way from the introductory question: "Am I me or am I the
situation?" We began with our observation that people remain the same yet their
behavior varies considerably over time and across situations. This concern with stability and change in people and their behavior was represented in the dilemma of
Mr. Krim, who could not decide whether to account for his behavior in terms of
himself or the situation and finally concluded that "the situation you're in determines
who you are." His concern with a choice between the two was found to parallel an
issue among personality psychologists—whether to emphasize person variables or
situation variables in explaining behavior.

The person-versus-situation issue was but one aspect of a broader issue within
as well as outside of psychology—the relative significance of internal and external
determinants of behavior. Within psychology there has been a division between
European schools emphasizing the organism and AngloAmerican schools emphasizing the environment. The person-versus-situation issue was also seen to have a historical context. During the 1940s and 1950s, the field of personality was dominated

by internal, centralist theories and related assessment techniques. In the 1960s there developed a serious, "situationist" challenge to these dominant "person" views. The challenge derived in part from studies that questioned the consistency of behavior, such as Hartshorne and May's study of honesty in children, and partly was derived from the growth of a Skinnerian emphasis on the manipulation and control of environmental reinforcers. The issues were articulated and relevant data were presented by Mischel in 1968 in his book *Personality and Assessment.* In this book Mischel questioned the psychodynamic and trait assumptions of hierarchically arranged internal entities and stable patterns of behavior. He suggested the following: (1) There is little evidence of consistency in behavior over time and across situations. (2) Dispositional theories and assessment devices based on such theories are of limited utility in predicting behavior in a situation. (3) Traits and other person disposition terms represent cognitive constructions of people that do not accurately reflect actual behavior. (4) Instead of looking for global traits we should focus attention on evoking and maintaining conditions in the environment.

For the following two decades, 1968–1988, much of the research and debate in the field of personality concerned the person-situation issue. Of particular import on the side of traditional personality psychologists, the trait-dispositionists, was Epstein's emphasis on aggregation. At the same time, Mischel argued that although aggregation increased reliability it also washed out the unique patterning of situational variability that is defining of individual personality functioning. The interactionist model attempted to put the issue to rest by emphasizing the importance of both person and situation variables in the ongoing processes of individual adaptation to internal and external demands. Although widely accepted as a sensible view and research strategy, the interactionist model failed to flourish because it defined neither the units of person and situation to be considered nor the processes governing transactions between individuals and environments.

By 1988, some psychologists were seeking to draw a close to the controversy by proclaiming that the case for traits had been made or by suggesting that the necessary lessons had been learned from the controversy. However, there is considerable evidence that the controversy continues to "simmer" and perhaps "boil." As the century came to a close, trait psychologists continued to push their line of research, suggesting that the Big Five represented the basic structure of personality, and social cognitive psychologists continued to demonstrate evidence of situational variability as reflected in individual behavioral signatures. Concerned that the issue ultimately would split the field in half and preclude the development of a cumulative coherent science, Mischel attempted a rapprochement or unification of the trait and social cognitive points of view. However, to date there has been little response to this attempt and it was suggested that, due to basic incompatibilities in the models, such an integration would be difficult if not impossible. Thus, despite the fact that proponents of the trait and social cognitive models emphasize common concepts such as dispositions, dynamic processes, and systems, large differences remain in the ways in which these concepts are defined and utilized.

The question of consistency is clearly quite complex. One can find evidence both for consistency and for lack of consistency—depending on how one defines consistency, the type of behavior observed, and the conditions of observation. In their extreme forms, the "person" and "situation" positions cannot be reconciled, and neither can do a very good job in accounting for what occurs. Studies of the ways in which people express patterns of stability and change suggest that the question of which is more important, person or situation, is a meaningless one and a pseudo-issue. The real question is *how* do characteristics of the person interact with characteristics of the situation. This is the question asked by the interactionist who sees person and situation, internal determinants and external determinants, as inter-dependent—neither exists in the absence of the other and behavior always expresses both. The question no longer becomes one of understanding which is more important but one of understanding behavior as a constant process of interplay or exchange between the two. Mr. Krim is not the person or the situation, he is the interplay between the two. He is always himself, and his personality is his characteristic pattern of stability and change in relation to the situations he encounters in his daily life. Although a number of models are being developed to capture both stability and change in personality functioning, as well as the relations between person variables and situation variables, what remains unclear is the nature of the model that ultimately will represent the integration called for by Mischel.

CHAPTER 4

Is The Child Father To The Man? The Longitudinal Consistency Of Personality

General Theme

Is personality stable over time? Does what we observe in the child foretell what we will observe in the adult? To answer such questions in a meaningful way, one must distinguish among different possible forms of longitudinal personality consistency. In addition, it is important to consider the possibility of greater or lesser continuity for different personality characteristics, and greater or lesser continuity over different developmental periods. In all, although there is evidence for personality continuity, there is disagreement concerning the amount of such continuity and, perhaps of even greater significance, whether the observed continuity reflects stability in the environment rather than fixed personality structures. That is, to what extent is personality development likely to remain continuous in the face of environmental change?

> *The field of personality development is replete with contested claims, including those about continuity and change.*
>
> *Caspi, 1998, p. 361*

During dinner with my wife one night in New York City, I was struck with how much I had grown to enjoy spending time in the city but still preferred to be in the countryside. In other words, there was both change and stability in my preferences. This got me to thinking about changes in me in general over time, and I was struck with how much I had changed from when I was a beginning college student, to take an arbitrary point in time, and yet how many core aspects of my personality remained the same. I wondered whether others who knew me during this period would agree and whether objective measures of my personality would confirm some of my impressions. At the same time, my thoughts went to some of the biographies I've enjoyed reading and whether anyone could have predicted the unfolding of the lives of these individuals. Could anyone have predicted that Mahatma Gandhi would become the leader he became or that Elvis Presley would so influence the development of rock music? Consider three of the most influential scientists of the century— Darwin, Einstein, and Freud. At what point could one have predicted the magnitude of their future contributions and influence? Freud's admiring biographer Ernest Jones commented that by the time Freud was age 30, he was "a first class neurologist, a hard worker, a close thinker, but—with the exception perhaps of the book on aphasia—there was little to foretell the existence of genius" (E. Jones, 1953, p. 220).

One hears people express two opposite points of view: on the one hand, "I always knew he would be a . . ." or "From the day she was born, you knew she was headed for. . . ." On the other hand, people also say, "Who would have figured that he would end up doing . . ." or "I never would have guessed she would become a . . . ." Some believe you can anticipate the path of the life of at least some people. Others believe you cannot. As the great Yankee catcher Yogi Berra once said: "It ain't over 'til it's over." Or, as the great movie producer Samuel Goldwyn is reported to have said: "Only a fool would make predictions, especially about the future." Considering the question of continuity of personality, the eminent developmental psychologist Jerome Bruner contrasts the discontinuous path of Winston Churchill who started out as an incompetent schoolboy with the continuous path of the philosopher Sartre who "was destined to be a man of letters from the moment he could speak or put pen to paper" (1983, p. 4). He goes on to comment on his own life trajectory as follows: "My childhood, as I look back, seems extraordinarily discontinuous with the rest of my life. I can find little in it that would lead anybody to predict that I would become an intellectual or an academic, even less a psychologist. I 'happened' on what I became and I recreated my childhood as I became what I did" (Bruner, 1983, p. 4).

Which brings us to the issue noted in the previous chapter but which was left without consideration while attention focused on that of cross-situational consistency—the longitudinal consistency of personality. Recall that in Mischel's original critique of traditional personality theory he raised questions concerning both cross-situational consistency and longitudinal consistency. Although subsequently he gave less attention to the latter, differences in the trait and social cognitive positions remain. As noted, whereas trait psychologists view personality as for the most part stable over time, social cognitive psychologists emphasize the opportunity for change over the life course. Beyond them, however, exist fundamental differences in the field concerning how much stability and change occurs over the life course as well as the reasons for stability and change. It is to these issues that we now turn.

The Continuity of Personality: Concepts and Assessment

The issue of stability and change in personality development is not a simple one, and many psychologists have biases toward viewing personality as relatively stable or as relatively flexible. Thus, whereas some believe that "the zebra can as easily change his stripes as the adult his personality" (J. B. Watson, 1928, p. 138), others are much more optimistic in this regard. Sometimes the influence of such biases is subtle: The Personality Science Weekend program at the 1992 convention of the American Psychological Association was titled, "Can Personality Change?" rather than "Can Personality Remain Stable?" or "When Does Personality Change?" Sometimes such biases influence which personality variables are studied, how they are studied, and how the results are interpreted.

The issue is complicated because there are all different kinds of stability and change, and different means of measuring them. In relation to personality development, we can contrast four kinds of change. First, there is *absolute change* and *relative change*. A person may change in absolute height or weight but remain the same relative to others. Or, a person might become more uninhibited over time but still remain average for his or her age and peer group. In each case there has been an absolute change for the individual but not a change relative to others in his or her age and peer group.

Another distinction to be considered is that between *quantitative change* and *qualitative change*. People might gain more knowledge over time but not think about things any differently. On the other hand, there might occur a fundamental change in their way of thinking, in terms of being able to think in more complex ways. The development of self-consciousness can be described as a qualitative change rather than merely a change in scores on some variables. Bodily changes associated with adolescence, such as the development of secondary sex characteristics, represent qualitative changes of considerable psychological importance. Such changes go beyond quantitative changes such as gains in height or weight.

To take another example of the complexity that can be observed in personality development, in recounting her development the social psychologist Sandra Bem describes her transformation from an explosive child to a person in control of her emotions. Following an argument with her mother in which she smashed a mirror, she reports: "I hated myself for that explosion. I should have been able to control myself, I thought. Something changed that day. . . . I learned to control every emotional response that could have been elicited from me, fearful that it might have gotten out of hand the way it did with the mirror" (Bem, 1998, p. 23). Did her personality change or was it just the outer manifestation that had changed while the underlying structure remained the same? What is involved here is a distinction of great import for personality theory, that between *phenotypic change* and *genotypic change*, the former involving change at the observable level whereas the latter involves change at the underlying structural level. It is the same issue, here considered in relation to longitudinal consistency, that was considered in relation to cross-situational consistency in the previous chapter. The change from water to ice or steam represents a phenotypic change. Since the underlying structure remains the same, we do not speak of a genotypic change. In studying personality development we often observe a change without being clear whether it is phenotypic or genotypic. Can we be as sure that different behaviors represent different manifestations of the same personality characteristic as we are that structurally water, steam, and ice are the same?

Finally, we can distinguish between *continuous change* and *discontinuous change*. Continuous change is gradual, lawful, and follows a consistent pattern that can be identified. Although a person changes in bodily characteristics and appearance over the course of a lifetime, one can describe this change as continuous or consistent. In some cases one can see the boy in the man or the girl in the woman. In other cases, comparing photos from widely separated times, it may seem as if they could hardly be of the same person. Yet, following the process more closely allows us to see a gradual, consistent, continuous process of evolution from child to adult. In contrast, discontinuous change is abrupt and fundamental. A person experiencing a serious accident may undergo a significant change in appearance, leaving his or her appearance discontinuous with what it was previously. Or, if people are placed in a "total environment" that is substantially different from their previous environment, such as going into battle conditions, they may undergo a radical personality change that is discontinuous with their past personality. People describe such monumental experiences and their consequent effects as having changed them forever, often making them into virtually new people. I am reminded here of a cartoon that appeared in the *New Yorker* magazine. As described by Bruner (1983), two caterpillars are contemplating a gorgeous butterfly above them. The caption reads that one says to the other, "You'll never catch me up in one of those things." Following the person at close intervals allows us to distinguish between continuous and discontinuous change, between change in which the coherence of the personality is maintained and change in which there is a fundamental shift in system functioning. Seeing the person at two widely separated points in time may permit us to measure the amount of change but remain unclear about the kind of change that has occurred and the intervening processes involved. What at widely separated points in time appears to be discontinuous change may, upon closer inspection, reveal itself to be continuous change.

Caspi (1998; Caspi & Roberts, 1999) describes four types of continuity that capture the distinctions just made. In *absolute continuity* there is constancy in the quantity of a characteristic over time. Such constancy can be observed at the individual or group level. For example, Costa and McCrae (1994) suggest that, both at the individual and group levels, scores on the Big Five are very stable once adulthood has been reached. According to them, personality development ends somewhere between 25 and 30—it is pretty much "set like plaster." In contrast with this, in *differential continuity* there is constancy of individual differences over time although the mean levels change. In other words, the rank ordering of individuals remains constant although absolute score levels change. For example, if individuals are first tested as adolescents and then in adulthood, there is evidence that although rank orders remain fairly constant, with age there is an increase in mean levels for Conscientiousness and Agreeableness but decreases in mean levels for Extraversion, Neuroticism, and Openness to Experience (Caspi, 1998; Costa & McCrae, 1997).

In the third type of continuity, *coherence*, there is change at the phenotypic level but continuity at the genotypic level. For example, Mischel (1999) reports that preschool children found to be able to resist temptation and delay gratification in a laboratory setting in childhood (i.e., choice of a small cookie now or a large cookie later) are later found to be more competent and obtain higher SAT scores than those preschool children found to have difficulties in resisting temptation: "The results give a general picture of the child who delayed in preschool developing into an adolescent who is seen as attentive, able to concentrate, able to express ideas well, responsive to reason, competent, skillful, planful, able to think ahead, and able to cope and deal with stress maturely" (p. 484). Although different in form, the later characteristics are conceptually linked (i.e., cognitive competencies) with the earlier characteristics.

Finally, in *ipsative continuity* there is continuity at the individual level in terms of continuity of structure. Ipsative continuity considers the development of personality organization, the pattern of personality variables, within the individual. According to Block (1971, 1993), studying personality development in the aggregate can mask large individual differences in personality continuity. For example, stability in group means can mask considerable change in the profiles of scores for individuals. Or, continuity at the level of group profiles can mask changes in individual profiles. For example, Asendorpf and van Aken (1999) report that during the period between ages 4 and 12 the same type categories can be defined in children (e.g., undercontrolled and overcontrolled). However, during this period children change in which type they are a member. In other words, there is continuity at the group structural level but moderate to low stability in individual type membership. In another study of ipsative continuity, Robins, et al, (2000) found moderate stability in profile scores on the Big Five during the four years of college. Although students thought they had changed substantially during the four years of college, analysis of both mean scores and trait profiles suggested otherwise. Ipsative studies and analyses are difficult to conduct and have been relatively rare in the literature. However, they are of considerable theoretical significance and are likely to be more prominent in the future.

The preceding discussion indicates the importance of considering the type of continuity being assessed before conclusions are reached concerning personality stability and change over time. Other factors to consider concern matters such as the following: personality characteristics being assessed, ages at which personality is assessed, time interval between assessment, gender differences, and measures used. Concerning personality characteristics, there is both theoretical and empirical reason to believe that temperament traits are likely to evidence greater continuity than are attitudes (Caspi & Roberts, 1999; McAdams, 2001). Concerning ages at which personality is assessed, there is evidence of greater personality stability during adulthood than in childhood (Roberts & DelVecchio, 2000). Although there are good theoretical reasons why this would be the case, a possible confounding factor here is the difficulty of measuring the same personality characteristic at different ages during childhood. That is, it is much easier to use the same, or at least comparable, measures during adulthood than in childhood. For example, it is easier to use comparable measures of cognitive ability in studying adults 20 and 30 years old than in studying children 2 and 12 years old.

In terms of time interval, research suggests less continuity with greater time intervals between assessment (Roberts & DelVecchio, 2000). One cautionary note in relation to this general finding concerns what is known as the "sleeper effect"—a lag between a cause and appearance of an effect (Kagan & Moss, 1962). For example, in 2000 there was considerable interest in the case of a Cuban six-year-old boy who saw his mother drown while sailing to the United States and who then became the center of controversy between efforts on the part of his father in Cuba and relatives in the United States to retain custody of him. Although seemingly a happy child at the time, and dealing with the stress well, many experts in child development suggested that it might take years before the consequences of these events could be observed. In other words, too short an interval in assessment might miss the delayed effects of this trauma that would be observed after a greater interval of time.

Concerning gender, different conclusions can be reached concerning continuity of personality development depending on whether males or females are studied (Block, 1993; Magnusson, 1988, 1999). Where analyses are not conducted separately, conclusions can be reached that apply to neither males nor females. Finally, there is greater evidence of continuity when scores are based on self-reports or peer ratings than when they are based on objective laboratory assessments or observations of actual behavior in the environment (Caspi, 1998). The latter finding is consistent with that found in relation to cross-situational consistency.

Considering distinctions among types of continuity and issues of assessment, it is easy to see why it can be overly simplistic to speak only in terms of stability or change. In studying personality development we want to differentiate among the kinds of continuity and change that are possible and be sensitive to the methodological difficulties involved in longitudinal research. In addition, we want to be aware that ultimately we are interested in the processes involved in personality continuity and change rather than only in quantitative estimates of how much of personality in general or specific personality characteristics have remained stable or changed. With this we are ready to consider two differing points of view that can be drawn concerning stability and change in personality development.

Evidence of Personality Continuity

An extensive database of research attests to personality continuities across the life course.

Caspi & Roberts, 1999, p. 312

---

*In the course of adult life individuals accumulate a lifetime
experience. They age biologically and face acute and
chronic diseases. They pass through a variety of social
roles, from novice parents and workers to grandparents,
widows, and retirees. . . . Yet all these events and experiences have little or no impact on basic personality traits.*

Costa & McCrae, 1997, p. 283

Block's Longitudinal Research

One of the leading figures in longitudinal research on personality has been Jack
Block (1971, 1993). In an important 1971 book, *Lives Through Time*, Block reported the results of research on subjects studied in junior high school, in senior high
school, and in their thirties. Block was picking up on research begun earlier by
members of the University of California (Berkeley) Institute of Human Development. Although there were considerable data on the subjects, there also were many
problems: (1) Much of the data were not in a form that could be quantified. (2)
There were missing data for many subjects. (3) Over time procedures and methods
of testing changed, presenting problems in continuity of evaluation. (4) There was a
lack of agreement on the focus of concern and in conceptual language.

How could such data, albeit on the same individuals, be organized for comparative purposes in terms of longitudinal investigation? What Block did was to have
judges evaluate each of the subjects, at each point in time, in terms of a *Q-sort description*. For example, as adults the subjects were interviewed extensively. On the
basis of these interviews, judges described each subject by sorting 100 statements
from the *California Q Set* into the following distribution, ranging from statements
most characteristic of the individual at one end to statements least characteristic of
the individual at the other end: 5,8,12,16,18,16,12,8,5. This distribution represents a
normal distribution of the statements. Illustrative statements include the following:
"Is critical, skeptical, not easily impressed." "Is a talkative individual." "Seeks reas-
surance from others."

The use of these Q-descriptions meant that although the data on the subjects
varied for the time period involved (junior high school, senior high school, adulthood), a common set of descriptors could be employed. And, since the items were
distributed by the raters in terms of a normal distribution, correlations could be
computed to determine the agreement among ratings for different time periods. Finally, different judges were used to make the ratings at the different time periods.
Thus, the ratings at one period could not have biased those of another period.
Through such procedures Block attempted to overcome the problems noted earlier
and to capture the development of personality over time.

Block found evidence of considerable personality continuity in terms of statistically significant correlations between personality ratings made at the three different time periods. Continuity was greater between junior high school and senior high school than between senior high school and adulthood. Although statistically significant, the correlations generally were low, particularly over more extended periods of time. For example, the across-time average correlations on a measure of psychological adjustment were as follows: .56 for junior high school to senior high school, .28 for senior high school to adulthood, and .22 for junior high school to adulthood.

Block also found important male-female differences in overall change and in the variables indicative of continuity. For example, between the period of senior high school and adulthood, males, relative to females, changed significantly toward a narrowing of interests and less responsiveness to humor. On the other hand, during this period females, relative to males, broadened their interests and became more ambitious and more sympathetic. In terms of overall level of psychological adjustment, females appeared to have a particularly difficult time in high school but were of the same overall level of adjustment in adulthood.

Finally, Block found enormous diversity among subjects in the amount of consistency shown over time. For example, whereas the overall (i.e., all personality measures) across-time correlation for males between junior high school and senior high school was .77, the range of correlations for individuals was from -.01 to 1.00. Similarly, whereas the overall across-time correlation for females between junior high school and senior high school was .75, the range of correlations for individuals was -.02 to 1.00. Thus, what was characteristic of the sample as a whole said relatively little about any particular subject.

In sum, using Q-sort judgments from independent judges at three points in time, Block found evidence of considerable continuity, greater for shorter than for longer periods of time, with evidence of differences in consistency for different personality characteristics, between males and females, and among individuals.

In a subsequent study begun in 1968 and conducted together with Jeanne Block (J. Block, 1993; J. H. Block & Block, 1980), there was particular interest in two personality constructs believed to be of central theoretical importance—*ego-control* and *ego-resiliency*. Ego-control refers to the individual's characteristic expression or containment of impulses, feelings, and desires. It relates to the individual's ability to delay, to inhibit action, and to be insulated from environmental distraction. Individuals fall along a continuum, ranging from overcontrol at one end to undercontrol at the other end. Overcontrolled individuals are overly constrained and inhibited, unduly delay gratification, and tend to show minimal expression of emotion. In contrast, undercontrolled individuals are expressive, spontaneous, and unable to delay gratification and have many but relatively short-lived enthusiasms and interests. Both extremes are viewed as less adaptive than midpoints on the continuum. Ego-resiliency refers to the extent to which the individual can modify his or her level of ego-control to meet the demands of the situation. In other words, the ego-resilient person demonstrates flexibility and adaptiveness in meeting changing life circumstances and is able to plan and to be organized at times as well as to be spontaneous and impulsive at other times. Individuals range on a continuum from unresilient to resilient, expressing increasing degrees of adaptive functioning.

The Blocks began their investigation of these as well as other personality characteristics with the study of 128 children from two nursery schools in the Berkeley, California area. The sample of children was selected to be diverse in terms of parental income, parental education, and ethnicity (65 percent white, 27 percent black, 6 percent Asian, 2 percent Chicano). Extensive individual assessments of the children were conducted at ages 3, 4, 5, 7, 11, 14, 18, and 23. At age 23, 104 of the original sample of 128 subjects were assessed—a remarkably low rate of attrition given the time period involved. During the eight assessment periods a wide variety of data were obtained on each subject: life history data; ratings by teachers, parents, or other knowledgeable observers; data from experimental procedures or standardized tests; and self-report data. An effort was made to assess personality characteristics through multiple measures to achieve dependability and generalizability. When overall evaluations were needed, Q-sorts were obtained from trained observers. For example, at age 3 each child was described using the *California Child Q-Set* by three nursery school teachers trained to use the Q-sort in this context. At age 14, four psychologists described each subject on the *California Adult Q-Set*. At each age the Q-set descriptions of each subject were combined to form a composite, in an attempt to rule out individual idiosyncrasies in observation and judgment. As in the earlier Block study, the assessors at each age were entirely different so as to maintain the independence of each data set. In sum, there were multiple measures of many concepts and data of different kinds. This is a major feature of this study.

Although data collection and analysis continue, what has been reported to date? Let us begin with the concepts of ego-control and ego-resiliency. What is the path of development over time? It is clear that there is change over time—there is a developmental increase in ego-control and ego-resiliency. These changes in absolute scores would be expected. What of changes in relative scores? Do people over time maintain their relative positions on ego-control and ego-resiliency? Regarding ego-control, the evidence suggested that "from an early age individual differences in the level of ego-control are identifiable and continue to distinguish people for at least the next 20 years and, from the evidence of other studies, even beyond" (Block, 1993, p. 34). This was true for both males and females. The average correlation between two time periods was .48, with correlations between pairs of time periods ranging from a low of .22 (age 3 and age 18 for females) and a high of .82 (age 3 and age 4 for males).

Aside from consistency over time, ego-control measured at age 3 was found to be associated with peer behavior at age 7. Children low in ego-control at the earlier age were found to be more aggressive, more assertive, less compliant, and less inhibited at age 7 than children high in ego-control at age 3. While children very high in ego-control at age 3 tended to be shy at age 7, those low in ego-control at age 3 tended to be aggressive, teasing, and manipulative in their peer relations at age 7 (Block & Block, 1980; Buss, Block, & Block, 1980). In a study of adolescents, 14-year-olds rated as high on ego-control were found to demonstrate a high ability to delay gratification in an experimental setting and were described as responsible, productive, and ethically consistent (Funder & Block, 1989).

Concerning ego-resiliency, the findings were different for males and females. For males, there was evidence of continuity in individual differences in ego-resiliency over a period of twenty years. The mean between-age correlation on ego-resiliency for males was .43, ranging from a low of .22 (ages 3 and 23) to a high of .65 (ages 3 and 4, 11 and 14). However, for girls there was virtually no relation between resiliency scores during the childhood years and ego-resiliency in adolescence or adulthood. For females the mean between-age correlation was .21, with a range from a negative correlation of .28 between ages 4 and 14 to a high of .68 between ages 3 and 4. For girls, ego-resiliency scores during the early years and between the ages of 14 and 23 tended to correlate fairly well. However, between the ages of 11 and 14, during the period of puberty, there appeared to be a break in the relationship.

What of the other variables studied? Block (1993) reports the following observations:

1. Males and females were found to differ in the course of their self-esteem scores. For males, self-esteem increased during the course of adolescence whereas for females there was a decrease during this time.

2. Boys who were to experience parental divorce, relative to boys whose parents were to remain married, were characterized by undercontrol of impulse and as being troublesome. Rather than being a consequence of divorce, the behavioral problems of these children appeared to exist prior to the divorce: "Children's behavioral problems may be present years before the formal divorce actually occurs. Indeed, the family discord often characterizing the period before parental separation may well have serious consequences for the children involved" (Block, 1993, p. 29).

3. At age 14, the use of marijuana was associated with ego-undercontrol in both sexes. The use of harder drugs reflected low ego-resiliency in addition to low ego-control.

4. The early antecedents of depression appeared to differ between males and females. Boys who were depressed at age 18 tended to be unsocialized, aggressive, and undercontrolled as children. On the other hand, girls who were depressed at age 18 tended to be intropunitive, oversocialized, and overcontrolled as children (Block, Gjerde, & Block, 1991).

Block summarizes his efforts as follows: "Our research has demonstrated, in many ways, the essential coherence of personality development and the implications of early character structure for later character structure. For a long time, such coherence has been denied by many psychologists" (quoted in Pervin, 1996, p. 182).

Kagan's Temperament Research

One of the areas of greatest interest in terms of continuity of personality development is that of temperament, which some psychologists equate with personality.
Continuity is built into the definition of temperament, such definitions generally
emphasizing individual differences in emotional quality that appear early, remain
fairly stable, are inherited, and are based in biological processes (Kagan, 1994;
Rothbart, Ahadi, & Evans, 2000). Longitudinal studies of temperament have a long
history in the field. In an illustrative early study, Thomas and Chess (1977) followed
over 100 children from birth to adolescence with an interest in relating early differences in temperament to later adjustment. Indeed, such a relationship was found
between early indicators of difficult temperament (e.g., difficult and slow-to-warm-
up babies) and later problems in adjustment. A problem with this and subsequent
studies was that they relied on parent reports. Kagan (1994, 1999) set out to use
objective, laboratory measures of behavior and biological functioning to study the
unfolding of temperament in childhood. In particular, he was interested in *inhibited*
and *uninhibited* types of infants. Relative to the uninhibited child, the inhibited child
reacts to unfamiliar persons or events with restraint, avoidance, and distress, takes a
longer time to relax in new situations, and has more unusual fears and phobias. Such
a child behaves timidly and cautiously, the initial reaction to novelty being to become quiet, seek parental comfort, or run and hide. By contrast, the uninhibited
child seems to enjoy these very same situations that seem so stressful to the inhibited
child. Rather than being timid and fearful, the uninhibited child responds with spon-
taneity in novel situations, laughing and smiling easily.

Would such early differences in temperament, measured as early as four months
of age, be related to later personality development? Kagan suggests that this indeed
was the case. For example, subsequent testing at ages 14 and 21 months of age indicated that high-reactive, inhibited infants showed greater fearful behavior and
physiological response to the unfamiliar than did the low-reactive, uninhibited infants. The former smiled and talked less with an unfamiliar adult, and were more shy
with unfamiliar peers than was the case with the latter. Further testing in the eighth
year of life indicated continuing consistency, with a majority of the children assigned to each group at age 4 months retaining membership in that group. In sum,
there was considerable evidence of temperament stability.

At the same time that we recognize this evidence of continuity of temperament,
a few caveats are worthy of note, particularly in relation to other points of view that
remain to be considered. First, not all infants fit into the extremes of the inhibited
and uninhibited groups. In fact, a majority of the infants were not classified into
either group. Second, there was evidence of potential for change, particularly where
certain environmental conditions prevailed. Thus, for example, most of the high-
reactive infants did not become consistently fearful and changes in these children
seemed particularly tied to having mothers who were not overly protective and
placed reasonable demands on them. And, some of the low-reactive infants lost their
relaxed style. At the same time, early temperament seemed to set a boundary condition on later development since not one of the high-reactive infants became a consistently uninhibited child and it was very rare for a low-reactive infant to become a

consistently uninhibited child. Kagan concludes both that "any predisposition conferred by our genetic endowment is far from being a life sentence; there is no inevitable adult outcome of a particular infant temperament" (1999, p. 32) and that "it is very difficult to change one's inherited predisposition completely" (1999, p. 41).

Caspi's Research on Behavioral Development

Caspi (2000; Caspi & Roberts, 1999, 2001) is one of the major proponents of an emphasis on continuity in personality development and has conducted relevant research. In assessing the findings from a large study of behavioral development during ages 3 through 21, Caspi (2000) emphasizes the pervasive influence of early appearing temperament differences for life-course development. In this research the temperament of children 3 years of age was assessed through observation of their performance on cognitive and motor tasks in a ninety-minute testing session. On the basis of these data, five types of children could be identified, each type being characterized by a configuration or pattern of scores rather than by any single score. In other words, there was an emphasis on the category of *coherence continuity* described above. Three of these types were of major concern and interest since they matched earlier descriptions of temperament types (e.g., the types described in the Thomas and Chess research) and replicated across cultures. These three types and defining pattern of characteristics were the following: *well-adjusted type* (40 percent of the children) including children who were capable of self-control when it was demanded of them, who were adequately self-confident, and who did not become unduly upset when confronting new people and situations; *undercontrolled type* (10 percent of the children) including children who were impulsive, restless, negativistic, distractible, and labile in their emotional responses; *inhibited type* (10 percent of the children) including children who were socially reticent, fearful, and easily upset by strangers. Note that these categories bear some relationship to the concepts of ego-control and ego-resiliency defined by Block and to type categories based on his concepts (Robins, et al, 1996). The two remaining category types noted by Caspi were the *confident type*, characterized by being zealous, eager to explore, somewhat impulsive but neither nonpersistent nor negativistic, and the *reserved type*, characterized by being timid and somewhat uncomfortable in the testing session, but not to the extent that it interfered with performance in the way that was true for the inhibited type children.

Were relationships found between temperament type at age 3 and later personality development? During ages 5 to 11 ratings on the children's behavioral and emotional functioning were obtained from teachers and parents. The undercontrolled children were found to exhibit externalizing problems (e.g., fighting, bullying, lying, disobeying). Major differences in externalizing or internalizing (e.g., worrying, crying easily, fussing) were not found for the other two groups. When assessed again in adolescence (ages 13 and 15), undercontrolled children were again found to exhibit externalizing problems and this time also showed evidence of internalizing problems. At this point the inhibited children were found to exhibit internalizing problems as well.

At age 18 adult personality traits were assessed through the *Multidimensional Personality Questionnaire*, a highly regarded measure of ten traits that define three general personality factors—*positive emotionality*, *negative emotionality*, and *constraint*. The trait profiles for the three groups of children were found to be quite different. At age 18, the undercontrolled children were found to be low on constraint (i.e., reckless, careless, enjoyment of dangerous and exciting activities) and high on negative emotionality. In contrast, the inhibited children were found to be high on constraint (i.e., cautious, prefer safe to dangerous activities) and low on positive emotionality. As young adults the inhibited children were characterized by an overcontrolled personality and nonassertive interpersonal style. The well-adjusted children at age 18 still exhibited a pattern of normal, average functioning, with no extreme scores on any of the ten traits.

Finally, at age 21 the subjects were assessed in terms of their interpersonal relationships, employment history, and psychological functioning. Surprisingly, the three groups did not differ in their likelihood of being in an intimate relationship. However, as young adults the undercontrolled group was involved in more conflicted relationships that also were characterized by less intimacy and trust. Both they and the inhibited group showed less evidence of companionship and emotional support (i.e., number of people who provide lasting affiliation, love, and comfort) than was true for the well-adjusted group. Members of the undercontrolled group were asked to leave school far more often than the members of the other two groups and also spent more time unemployed. In terms of psychological functioning, undercontrolled and inhibited children were more likely than well-adjusted children to be diagnosed with a psychiatric disorder or to be involved in legal difficulties. Undercontrolled children were found to be characterized particularly by alcohol problems, antisocial and criminal activities, and suicide attempts. Inhibited children were found to be characterized particularly by depression.

> *The child is father of the man. . . . Early appearing temperamental differences have a pervasive influence on life-course development and offer clues about personality structure, interpersonal relations, psychopathology, and crime in adulthood.*
>
> *Caspi, 2000, p. 158*

In sum, Caspi suggests considerable continuity in personality development, if not in the stability of specific behaviors then in a continuity of ways of adapting to and influencing life-course tasks. The implications of this degree of continuity are seen as substantial: "Development continuities are pervasive; they have consequences not only for the welfare of the individual but also for the welfare of the wider community" (Caspi, 2000, p. 168). Caspi suggests that the second year of life may be the crucial dividing line for predicting adult personality differences, for that is the time at which important cognitive and emotional developments occur (e.g., object permanence, development of self-conscious emotions). A caveat, again important to remember in terms of the discussion to follow later, is that Caspi considered 60 percent of the population and the temperamental qualities defined at age 3 explained only a "meager" amount of the variance in any single adult outcome. Despite this, the associations found are striking. Caspi notes that the outcomes are probabilistic and do not preclude the possibility of naturally occurring change or planned change. At the same time, he concludes: "The child is father of the man" (2000, p. 158).

Magnusson's IDA Study

Before considering another point of view, let us turn to two further studies of personality development over time for their interesting findings and points that are made. The first study to be considered is a longitudinal study of David Magnusson (1988, 1990, 1992, 1999). This study is presented because it considers both biological and social factors in personality development and is concerned with individuals and development of the organism as a whole. Magnusson began the Individual Development and Adjustment (IDA) study in 1965. The objective of the research was to detail how individual and environmental factors interact to govern development from childhood to adulthood. There was particular interest in the developmental processes underlying social maladaptation as expressed in problems such as alcoholism, crime, and psychological difficulties. The research, now in progress for 30 years, began with the study of all boys and girls attending the third, sixth, and eighth grades in school in a community in central Sweden. Thus, the majority of the students were 10, 13, and 15 years of age when the study began in 1965. This group included a total of about 1,400 individuals.

Most of the data consisted of information obtained from the subjects themselves. In addition, information was obtained from parents, teachers, peers, and public records such as those covering crime, alcohol abuse, and psychiatric admission and diagnosis. Data were obtained on biological factors such as hormonal response to stress and electrophysiological brain activity (EEG) as well as on environmental factors such as characteristics of the home and school. What are some illustrative findings of this research and how are they conceptualized by Magnusson? We can consider here two sets of findings, one concerning biological maturation and social development in girls, the other concerning the development of social problems in boys. In terms of the former, Magnusson and his associates were interested in the role played by biological maturation in social development. Specifically, what was investigated were the effects of early as opposed to late biological maturation in adolescent girls. Would there be any association between such differences in biological development and problem behavior in the home (e.g., running away), school (e.g., truancy), or leisure life (e.g., use of drugs and alcohol)? At the age of 15 there were clear differences in such problem behavior in the direction of more problems for early as opposed to late maturing girls. For example, at age 15, 35 percent of the early maturing girls as opposed to 6 percent of the late maturing girls had been drunk on multiple occasions. Early maturing girls also showed much more conflict with adults and were less interested in school and future careers. To a much greater extent than late maturing girls, the early maturing girls were focused on their social relationships, generally with older males and females.

Although such differences were dramatic at age 15, by the end of adolescence and early adulthood many of them had been reduced considerably. Thus, in adulthood there were few differences between the two groups in terms of problem behavior and social relationships. In other words, the problem behavior of the early maturing girls lasted over a limited period of time. On the other hand, some long-term consequences of early development did appear to hold. For example, such girls tended to marry earlier, have children earlier, enter the labor market earlier, and leave school earlier than did late maturing girls. These differences could not be attributed to differences in intelligence or family background.

To study the development of problem behavior in boys, Magnusson and his associates divided their sample of over 500 boys into groups in terms of their pattern of scores on measures of personality variables such as aggressiveness, motor restlessness, poor concentration, and poor peer relations. Would differences in patterns of scores on such measures taken at age 13 relate to later problematic social behavior such as alcoholism and criminality? Two groups of boys were found to have poor relationships with peers, one group with this problem alone and the other group with the additional problems of excessive aggressiveness and hyperactivity. Whereas the boys in the former group did not show later problematic behavior, the boys in the latter group showed a far greater tendency in this regard. For example, whereas the boys in the first group did not differ from chance in the probability of their later development of alcohol and criminal problems, the probability of such problems was far greater than chance in boys who were also characterized by hyperactivity and aggressiveness. In contrast, boys at 13 years of age who had no problems developed later alcohol and criminal problems at a rate far less than would be expected by chance.

Here too a biological component entered into an understanding of the later developments. Boys with an early pattern of hyperactivity and aggressiveness were also found to have comparatively low levels of adrenaline secretion in their urine. This was important because the secretion of adrenaline is associated with the perception of situations as stressful or threatening. Individuals with low adrenaline output have been viewed by psychologists as low in physiological reactivity and therefore as less likely to perceive situations as stressful or threatening. In Magnusson's longitudinal research it was found that boys with low adrenaline excretions at age 13 were far more likely to show a later pattern of persistent criminal activity than were individuals who had high adrenaline excretions. For the latter group, presumably, the perception of a situation as stressful and threatening acted as a deterrent to engagement in criminal activity, a deterrent that was not present for those with low adrenaline excretion.

Another wrinkle can be added to these findings. Three groups were formed in terms of patterns of later criminal activity: no later crime, teen offenders (recorded crime only before age 18), and persistent offenders (recorded crime during teenage years and in adulthood). Would the three groups show differences in hyperactivity and adrenaline excretion during early adolescence? What was found were clear differences between the three groups. On hyperactivity (i.e., motor restlessness and concentration difficulties), the no crime group showed the lowest scores, the persistent offenders the highest scores, with scores for the teen offenders falling between the two. In terms of adrenaline secretion, only the persistent offender group had a low level of secretion. In other words, the relation between lower physiological reactivity and antisocial behavior held only for the persistent offenders. In sum, males with a persistent criminal career were found to be characterized by adolescent patterns of high hyperactivity and low physiological reactivity (low adrenaline excretion), males with records as juvenile offenders only were found to be characterized by adolescent patterns of somewhat high hyperactivity only, and males without adolescent or adult records of criminal activity were found to be characterized by low hyperactivity and high physiological reactivity (high adrenaline excretion).

These findings illustrate both the continuity and discontinuity that can be found in personality development and the varying relationships that can be found depending on the time at which assessments are made. In addition, they illustrate the value of considering both biological and psychological variables as well as patterns of relationships rather than relationships between single variables and later outcomes. These points relate to Magnusson's emphasis on an interactionist, holistic perspective on individual development. According to this perspective, biological and psychological variables are involved in a constant interplay, as is the individual with the environment. And, development must be understood in terms of the interplay among patterns of variables within the individual rather than in terms of single variables alone. The individual functions as an organismic whole rather than as a bunch of separate parts.

Sroufe's Attachment Research

In the final description of a longitudinal project, we consider the question of continuity in development from infancy through adolescence in attachment and interpersonal relationships—the Minnesota Parent-Child Project (Sroufe, Carlson, & Shulman, 1993). Work in the area of *attachment theory* is largely based on the early theoretical work of the British psychoanalyst John Bowlby and the empirical work of the psychologist Mary Ainsworth (Ainsworth & Bowlby, 1991; Bretherton, 1992). Bowlby was trained as a psychoanalyst and was interested in the effects of early separation from parents on personality development. Such separation was a major problem in England during World War II when many children were sent to the countryside, far from their parents, to be safe from enemy bombing in the cities. Following the war Bowlby began two research projects on the effects of separation, one *retrospective*, involving the recollections of individuals separated from their parents between the ages of 1 and 4 for health reasons, and the other *prospective*, involving the study of children as they underwent separation from their parents to enter institutions for health reasons.

Bowlby's clinical observations led him to formulate a theory of the development of the *attachment behavioral system (ABS)*. According to the theory, the developing infant goes through a series of phases in the development of an attachment to a major caregiver, generally the mother, and the use of this attachment as a "secure base" for exploration and separation. The ABS is viewed as something programmed within infants, a part of our evolutionary heritage that has adaptive value. Thus, attachment behaviors such as crying, cooing, babbling, smiling, and sucking all serve the function of maintaining closeness of contact with the mother. At the same time, as the infant begins to wander and explore the environment, particularly around the end of the first year, the attachment relationship provides a secure base for exploration. Here the infant feels secure to explore but also feels secure that it can return to proximity to the mother if in need of comfort. As a further part of the development of the ABS, the infant develops *internal working models* or mental representations (images), associated with affect, of itself and its primary caregivers. It is these internal working models, based on interactional experience, that provide the basis for the development of expectations of future relationships. In this aspect, that is, in the emphasis on the importance of early emotional relationships for future relationships, attachment theory is similar to psychoanalytic object relations theory, a development out of psychoanalytic theory that emphasizes how early experiences influence the ways in which individuals perceive themselves and relate to others.

A major turning point in the empirical work on this issue occurred with the development by Ainsworth of the *Strange Situation* procedure. In this procedure an infant, generally about 1 year of age, is placed in an unfamiliar setting with a stranger, in both the presence and the absence of the infant's caregiver. The infant is allowed to play with toys that are present and then, at prescribed intervals, the mother leaves the room and then returns to reunite with the infant. At various intervals a stranger is introduced, with the infant sometimes left alone with the stranger before the mother returns to the room. The point here is to observe the behavior of the infant in relation to the mother under conditions of an unfamiliar setting, in the presence and absence of a stranger, and under conditions of separation and reuniting with the mother.

Based on a scoring scheme for observations of infant behavior during the Strange Situation, infants are placed in one of three attachment categories: (1) *anxious-avoidant* infants, (2) *securely attached* infants, (3) *anxious-resistant* infants. Briefly, anxious-avoidant infants (about 20 percent of infants) readily explore the environment, register little protest over separation from the mother, and are relatively accepting of the stranger, even in the absence of the mother. When the mother returns, these children show avoidance behavior in terms of turning, looking, or moving away. In contrast, infants who show secure attachment (about 70 percent of the sample) show ready exploration and acceptance of the stranger in the presence of the mother but are more sensitive to the departure of the mother (e.g., they cry or search for her) and when the mother returns show greeting behavior (e.g., they smile and initiate interaction). These infants also are readily comforted by the mother and readily return to exploration and play once reunited with her. Finally, the anxious-resistant infants (about 10 percent) have difficulty separating to explore, are wary of the stranger, and have difficulty reuniting with the mother upon her return. Upon reunion these infants may mix pleas to be picked up with squirming and insistence that they be let down.

The Minnesota Parent-Child Project focuses on the infant caregiving system as the core out of which personality is formed. Thus, individual differences found during an early developmental period are hypothesized to relate to observed later differences in personality development, in particular in terms of the formation of social relationships. The project began in 1974–1975 with the recruitment of 267 women in the third trimester of pregnancy. Infants and caregivers were seen in a variety of contexts seven times during the first year, twice in each of the next three years, and yearly through age 13. A variety of information was obtained (e.g., temperament, intelligence, parent-child interaction, peer relationships) and observations were conducted in the home, laboratory, and school. After thirteen years, about two-thirds of the original sample remained in the study.

Do individual differences in attachment in infancy, measured via the Strange Situation, relate to later differences in social and emotional behavior? The results of this project as well as others suggest that this indeed is the case. Thus, securely attached infants were rated by preschool teachers and independent observers as less dependent than either anxious or resistant infants. In addition, the securely attached infants were found to show greater ego-resiliency than children in the other groups. This association between infant attachment pattern and ego-resilient behavior continued to be found through middle childhood.

As hypothesized, relationships also were found between infant attachment patterns and peer relationships. In terms of preschool behavior, securely attached infants were found to participate more actively in the peer group, and were more positive in their peer interactions, than were members of the two other groups. This relation held whether quality of peer relationships was rated by independent observers, by teachers, or by children's ratings of one another. These children also were found to demonstrate greater empathy and to deal more easily with rebuff than was true for children from the other two groups. Finally, differences were found in the kind of behavior members of each group elicited from teachers. Securely attached children elicited warm behavior from teachers whereas those showing an earlier pattern of resistant attachment elicited unduly nurturant and caretaking behavior. Children with the earlier pattern of avoidant attachment elicited controlling and occasional angry behavior. Thus, it is suggested that "children actively create their environments based on their history of experiences" (Sroufe et al., 1993, p. 325).

Do such patterns continue through early and middle childhood (ages 10–11)? It would be expected that relationships between infant attachment pattern and later behavior would be increasingly difficult to find because of changes in the way needs and fears are expressed and because of the variety of intervening influences as time goes on. According to the theory, early attachment influences and internal working models are seen as exerting powerful influences on later development but are not seen as immutable. Nevertheless, evidence of such relationships has been found. For example, relative to members of the other two groups, those earlier grouped as securely attached were found to show greater self-confidence and self-esteem, to set higher goals and show greater persistence in these goals, to be less dependent, to spend more time in group activities, and to form close friendships.

Preliminary data also are available concerning adaptation during the adolescent years (ages 14–15). Here too ratings on emotional health, self-esteem, ego-resiliency, and peer competence favor those with histories of secure attachment. In sum, independent ratings at points extending over a period of fourteen years demonstrate a relation between early attachment patterns and later social and emotional development. What is suggested is a coherence to the development of personality wherein change occurs but continuity can be seen between infant patterns and later patterns of behavior. Thus, it is suggested that "prior adaptation and history are not 'erased' by change. Earlier patterns may be reactivated, and early history adds to current circumstances in predicting current adaptation" (Sroufe et al., 1993, p. 317). Such continuity is assumed to occur because of the development of self-maintaining patterns of interaction rather than because of any permanent establishment of a personality structure. Thus, continuity is assumed to exist because of the development of patterns of individual-environment interaction rather than because of the development of fixed structures or the operation of fixed environments. And, room is left for change to occur as a result of powerful relationship experiences that are different from those experienced earlier. In other words, there is a tendency to confirm internal working models but powerful new relationships can lead to the development of new internal working models.

Taken together, the studies described demonstrate an impressive degree of continuity in personality development. The results come from different lines of investigation, by different investigators, covering different personality variables, and in some cases different age groups and time periods. At the same time, it is important to note that all of the investigators recognized the potential for change as well as continuity, and all emphasized the importance of individual-environment transactions that played a role in maintaining stability or producing change.

Some Questions Concerning Continuity and the Reasons For It

> *Based on data alone, there is little support for the argument that continuity best characterizes development.*
>
> *Lewis, 1997, p. 20*

The distinguished developmental psychologist Michael Lewis takes a quite different view than Caspi and others who emphasize continuity of personality over time. In a book chapter in the *Handbook of Personality: Theory and Research* (Lewis, 1999) and in a paper in the journal *Psychological Inquiry* (Lewis, 2001), in which he and Caspi and Roberts (2001) present their differing points of view, Lewis basically reaches two conclusions. First, the evidence in support of developmental continuity is not as impressive as Caspi and others suggest. Therefore, "from a developmental point of view, the idea of predicting individual differences in personality characteristics over time may not be rewarding" (1999, p. 331). Second, continuity in personality development may be due to continuity in the environment rather than to some relatively fixed unfolding of trait characteristics: "In other words, developmental continuity, which we believe is located in the child, may be located in the context to which the child adapts" (Lewis, 1999, p. 339). It should be noted that to a certain extent Lewis' view of the data and the role of the environment are not that different from that of Caspi and Roberts in that the latter conclude that there is "modest continuity from childhood to adulthood" (1999, p. 319) and that the environment is one factor that can lead to greater or lesser continuity throughout the life span. However, the points of emphasis and conclusions reached are vastly different.

Before considering further Lewis's view, let us review some of the findings from his research which lead to his conclusions. Although Lewis has conducted developmental research in a number of areas, his longitudinal work in relation to attachment is particularly relevant to the issues under consideration. For example, in a study of the relation between attachment type at age 1 and emotional difficulties in 6-year-old boys, Lewis found that 80 percent of the boys at age 6 identified as being at risk for emotional problems or actually clinically disturbed were found to have been assigned to an insecure attachment category (i.e., avoidant- or resistant-attachment) in infancy. However, if one took all boys classified as insecurely attached at age 1 and predicted that they would be at risk or clinically disturbed at age 6, one would be correct in only 40 percent of the cases (Lewis et al., 1984). In other words, looking back or retrospectively, the relation between early and later development seems strong. However, looking forward or prospectively, the relation seems far more tenuous. The reason for this is that far more boys were classified as insecurely attached at infancy than were later diagnosed at risk or disturbed. Thus, the clinician or researcher viewing later pathology would have a clear basis for suggesting a strong relationship between early attachment difficulty and later pathology. On the other hand, focusing on the data in terms of developmental outcomes based on early attachment difficulty would suggest a problematic predictive effort. In other words, depending on the number of individuals classified into particular categories at each point in time, the conclusions to be reached from looking back (i.e., retrospectively) may be different from those looking forward (i.e., prospectively).

In a more recent study, Lewis reports on the continuity of attachment from infancy (i.e., one year) to late adolescence (i.e., age 18). Attachment at the later age was measured in terms of scores on an established structured interview measure—the *Adult Attachment Interview*. In addition, at the later age participants gave their recollections of childhood, scores for maladjustment were obtained from mother, teacher, and self-ratings, and data on family divorces were obtained as a measure of environmental stability. The findings were as follows:

1. Attachment in infancy was not related to attachment in late adolescence.

2. Attachment in infancy was not related to maladjustment in adolescence. Although there was disagreement among raters on maladjustment, a not unusual finding in the literature, there was no significant relation between attachment in infancy and whether at least one person rated the adolescent as maladjusted.

3. Adolescent maladjustment was related to current insecure attachment classification.

4. Current maladjustment was associated with negative recollections of childhood.

5. There was a significant relationship between attachment status in adolescence and parental divorce. That is, those adolescents whose parents were divorced were more likely to be classified as insecure, whereas those classified as secure were more likely to come from intact families.

6. Adolescents from divorced families were significantly more likely to rate themselves as maladjusted than were adolescents from intact families.

In sum, the research suggested a lack of continuity between attachment in infancy and adolescence and that the environment, in this case divorce status, had a significant impact on developmental continuity.

The degree to which environmental factors remain consistent represents the degree to which the individual's attachment remains consistent.

Lewis et al., 2000, p. 717

In other words, developmental continuity, which we believe is located in the child, may be located in the context to which the child adapts.

Lewis, 1999, p. 339

Considering the issue of continuity of personality development in a broader perspective, Lewis (1999, 2001) contrasts a trait-like view that emphasizes continuity from childhood to adulthood with a contextual view that suggests that the person's status at any point in time is affected by the environment at that time. For example, in relation to attachment, whereas the trait-like view sees attachment as an attribute of an individual throughout development, the contextual view argues that attachment continuity reflects stability and change in the environment: "The degree to which environment factors remain consistent represents the degree to which the individual's attachment remains consistent" (Lewis, 1999, p. 341). Although discussed within a developmental context, note the similarity here to Mischel's position in relation to cross-situational consistency (Chapter 3).

What Do We Know and Where Do We Go from Here?

Having considered opposing points of view, we again are in a position to take stock of where we are and what remains to be done. The following are suggested as representing a fair evaluation of the evidence at this point in time:

1. *There is evidence for both continuity and discontinuity in personality development over time.* Continuity from childhood to adulthood appears to be weak to moderate while that during the adult years appears to be substantial but not absolute. In terms of the latter, the evidence does not appear to support the extreme "plaster theory" of Costa and McCrae (1997) since there exists evidence in support of a "plasticity theory" in adulthood (Roberts, 1997).

> *One could not ask for a clearer opposition of views on continuity than the essays of Michael Lewis, on the one hand, and Avshalom Caspi and Brent Roberts, on the other. The former scholar questions whether any personality traits are preserved, while the latter pair celebrates preservation. I suspect that most scientists in this field regard a middle position as the one that matches current data best. There is some preservation, but, as Lewis notes, it is modest.*
>
> *Kagan, 2001, p. 84*

2. *Even where there is evidence of continuity in childhood, the nature of the continuity may be sufficiently complex to make prediction problematic.* Although Caspi and Lewis disagree concerning emphasis, they agree that prediction, particularly from childhood into adulthood, is problematic: "The strength of associations between temperament characteristics in early childhood and later behavior problems and personality differences is weak to moderate" (Caspi, 1998, p. 339). At the same time, Caspi (2000) emphasizes that "early appearing temperamental differences have a pervasive influence on life-course development" (p. 158).

3. *Continuity appears to be greater during short periods of time than during long periods of time* (Roberts & DelVecchio, 2000). This is a consistent finding in the literature. However, note should be made of "sleeper effects" wherein relationships between an earlier period and a later effect may take time to appear.

4. *Continuity appears to be greater for temperament and temperament-related traits (e.g., the Big Five) than for other personality characteristics (e.g., attitudes and beliefs).* In the words of McAdams (2001): "Sure people change, but not so much their traits. Significant personality change may occur, but that change may not be captured in a person's trait score" (p. 421).

5. *Conclusions concerning continuity and discontinuity, or concerning relationships between early personality characteristics and later outcome variables, may depend on the measures used and type of continuity considered.* A problem in many developmental studies is that various measures (e.g., self, parent, and teacher ratings) do not agree and show differing relationships with the variables of interest. The efforts to replace or, better yet, to add objective measures of personality characteristics to self-report measures in developmental research are noteworthy. As in all of science, reliable measures are fundamental in developmental personality research. In addition, as considered in the introduction to this chapter, conclusions may vary depending on the kind of continuity being considered—absolute, differential, coherence, ipsative. The research of Robins et al. (2001), in its use of multiple assessments of change and a focus on ipsative change, represents a model for the kind of research that may be conducted in the future. As Magnusson (1999) has emphasized, personality consists not only of the individual parts but the organization of parts into a holistic structural entity.

6. *Relatively little research has been conducted to establish the boundary conditions concerning how much change is possible in various personality characteristics, at specific points in time, and the conditions under which greater or lesser continuity will be observed.* This point is important and contains three elements within it. First, for any personality characteristic of interest presumably there are boundaries concerning how much change is possible and the kinds of changes that are possible. For example, height, weight, and intelligence are all subject to environmental influences but the boundary conditions are probably less great than those for food preferences and political attitudes and beliefs. Second, change may be easier at certain periods in time than at other period in time. Generally, periods of rapid development and periods of transition appear to be special opportunities for change to occur. Third, of perhaps the greatest importance, we need to learn more about the *processes* involved in stability and change as well as the person and environmental conditions that underlie these processes. That is, we need to be concerned with the question of variables in the person and in the environment that foster stability or change in personality functioning. It is one thing to provide evidence of stability or change; it is another to demonstrate understanding of the processes involved.

At this point we have a glimpse of the processes within the individual and the environment that foster stability and consistency in personality. For example, we have evidence that individuals seek self-verification, that they elicit reactions from others that maintain their self-perceptions and ways of behaving, that they select environments consistent with their own personalities, and that others treat them in ways consistent with the images formed of them. As people reach adulthood they tend to narrow and stabilize the range of friendships. All of these forces within the individual, in the environment, and in individual-environment transactions operate to produce relative stability and consistency. At the same time, we know that change, often substantial change, occurs. Here, however, we have a less clear picture of the processes involved. We know that change occurs in psychotherapy, and that the therapeutic relationship appears to be important, but we are very unclear about the change process or processes involved in the various forms of therapy. We also know that powerful environments can produce change, even in adults. Finally, we know that life contains a large element of unpredictability, and that chance encounters and dramatic social or economic events can lead to significant change (Bandura, 1982; Lewis, 1991, 1995). However, we have hardly begun to scratch the surface in our understanding of the boundaries of change in various areas and of the individual and environmental forces conducive to substantial change. Kagan's (1994) research on change as the result of the interplay between infant temperament characteristics and parent treatment represents an illustration of the kind of research that may lead us to a better understanding of processes of continuity and change. Another illustration is research on cross-fostering in animals wherein the offspring of parents with one set of temperament characteristics are raised by parents with another set of temperament characteristics (Suomi, 2000) (Chapter 5). Hopefully the specific processes of continuity and discontinuity considered in the future will be viewed within the framework of a more general theory of personality continuity and change.

Before leaving the issue of personality continuity and change, it is important to recognize that the issue has potential sociopolitical implications. For example, in addressing the question of when personality is fully developed, Caspi and Roberts (1999) suggest that "the answer to this question is critical for both psychologists and society. It pertains directly to whether we choose to rehabilitate individuals or subject people to long-term, palliative care" (p. 302). They give illustrations of possibly different treatments of criminals and employees depending on how much change is considered to be possible. In his "Child is Father of the Man" paper, Caspi (2000) suggests that "developmental continuities are pervasive; they have consequences not only for the welfare of the individual but for the welfare of the wider community" (p. 168). Perhaps mindful of the possible implications that can be drawn from his emphasis on continuity, Caspi (2000) suggests that such continuity "does not preclude the possibility of planned interventions, nor does it negate the possibility of naturally occurring change" (p. 170). For example, he notes that undercontrolled boys are significantly less likely to become involved in crime if they stay in school.

Lewis similarly is aware of the sociopolitical implications of his view: "If continuity is so questionable, then so are the social policy and social intervention strategies founded on it. . . . If discontinuity is to be our model, it will lead to a very different set of social policies aimed at children, families, and societies" (1997, p. 20). What Lewis argues is that the trait-continuity model, whether emphasizing continuity due to genes or the effects of early environments, locates a condition in the person. In contrast, his contextual model locates a condition in the current environmental context or current person-environment transactions. Taking violence as an example, he suggests that the trait model implies that the child will express violence in the future as a consequence of the internal trait—once the trait has been established it resides in the child and will be expressed later. In contrast, the contextual model locates violence in the current context—when children live in a context of violence they are more likely to become violent. According to him, the trait model explains too little of the unfolding of personality to base social policy on it: "From the point of view that I have argued, the altering of behavior will be effective whenever we can alter the context on a long-term basis. If children do not possess an enduring trait, their behavior is contextually determined and maintained...if their environment is altered, so too is their behavior, as well as the structures that underlie their behavior" (1997, p. 189).

Summary

In this chapter we have considered a second aspect of personality continuity and change, in this case the issue of continuity and change in personality development. We began with observations of both continuity and change in people we know and historical figures. We continued with consideration of the different kinds of continuity that can be considered (i.e., absolute, differential, coherence, ipsative) and such issues as the aspect of personality considered and measures used. From there we considered research evidence supporting both continuity and discontinuity in personality development, highlighted by the differing views of Caspi and Lewis. Although the two are perhaps not so far apart in their reading of the data, they draw quite different conclusions from the data. That is, for example, whereas both would probably agree that the evidence of continuity from childhood through adulthood for most personality characteristics is weak, perhaps modest in some cases, Caspi is drawn to an emphasis on continuity and the importance of early characteristics for the later unfolding of personality whereas Lewis is drawn to an emphasis on discontinuity and the importance of the current context in influencing personality functioning. Lewis specifically presents the contrast between a trait view and a contextual view.

Kagan, reviewing the contrasting positions of Caspi and Lewis, takes a middle position and suggests that most scientists in the field would agree that there is evidence of continuity, but the continuity is modest with considerable room for change between infancy and later adulthood. In reviewing the field a number of conclusions were drawn: the evidence for continuity is greater in adulthood than in childhood; the evidence for continuity is greater for short periods than for long periods; continuity for some personality characteristics, such as temperament traits and the Big Five, is likely greater than that for other personality characteristics, such as attitudes and beliefs; that the degree of continuity found may differ depending on the measures used and the kind of continuity considered. Perhaps most important of all, attention was drawn to the need to focus attention on the process of personality development and the factors that govern stability and change in personality development—which person and environmental variables regulate stability and change in which personality characteristics. Finally, attention was drawn to the sociopolitical implications of consideration of the issue of continuity in personality development.

CHAPTER 5

The Nature-Nurture Controversy: Genes, Environments, And Gene-Environment Interactions

General Theme

In this chapter we consider the extent to which views concerning the contributions of genes and environments to personality have been polarized—the nature-nurture controversy. For a variety of areas of personality functioning the evidence is clear in suggesting that genes and environments both are always important, always interacting with one another. Thus, personality development represents the complex unfolding of characteristics at all times influenced by multiple genes interacting with multiple environmental influences.

> *There is no escape from the conclusion that nature prevails enormously over nurture. . .*
>
> *Galton, 1883, p. 241*

> *I should like to go one step further now and say, give me a dozen healthy infants, well-formed, and my own specified world to bring them up in and I'll guarantee to take any*

*one at random and train him to become any type of spe-
cialist I might select—doctor, lawyer, artist, merchant-
chief and yes, even beggar-man and thief, regardless of his
talents, penchants, tendencies, abilities, vocations, and
race of his ancestors.*

Watson, 1930, p. 104

---

*The latest research in genetics, molecular biology, and
neuroscience shows that many core personality traits are
inherited at birth, and that many of the differences between
individual personality styles are the result of of differences
in genes.*

Hamer & Copeland, 1998, p. 6

---

*Now that evidence for the importance of genetic influence
throughout psychology has largely been accepted, it is important to make sure that the pendulum stays in the middle,
between nature and nurture.*

Plomin & Crabbe, 2000, p. 807

I have chosen to present a greater number of introductory quotes than usual so as to
highlight the lengthy history of the nature-nurture controversy and the varying views
that have been taken over time. One would have thought that by now the controversy
would have been settled and, quite frankly, a while ago I would not have included a
chapter on it in this book. However, just as I began work on this book I came across
a paper by McCrae and his colleagues (McCrae, et al., 2000) that stated the following: "The gist of our argument is easily stated: Personality traits, like temperaments,
are endogenous dispositions that follow intrinsic paths of development essentially
independent of environmental influences" (p. 173). The authors, leaders of the Big
Five view and psychologists representing five countries, recognize that what they are
saying may be foreign to the thinking of most psychologists and go on to make their
view explicit, lest there be any misunderstanding: "Five-factor theory deliberately
asserts that personality traits are endogenous dispositions, influenced not at all by
the environment" (p. 175). As they recognize, their statements bring us right back to
"the fundamental issue of nature versus nurture" (p. 173). Shocked that at this point
in time it might still be the case that we are pitting nature and nurture against one
another, I e-mailed one of the authors as follows: "I was surprised to find that you
reraise the 'nature versus nurture' issue and appear to suggest that it is all nature, the
rest just maturation. Do you really mean to say that?" The reply:

> Well, if you want to be technical, we say "nature over nurture" not without it. . . . Parental
> child-rearing practices don't seem to have much impact on adult personality traits; cultural
> variation doesn't have much effect on personality trait structure; life events don't have much

> influence on trait stability, and so forth. Each and every one of those findings was startling to me when we made them, because, like most other personality psychologists, I had anticipated a much larger role for the environment than the data support. . . . At a minimum, I don't think the nature versus nurture issue is dead quite yet.

Perhaps I should not have been so surprised by the suggestion that the nature versus nature issue is not dead yet. After all, in one form or another it is suggested by headlines in the mass media: "Stop Blaming Your Genes: A New Study Shows that Environment Matters More than Genetics in Determining Whether You Get Cancer" (*Newsweek*, July 24, 2000, p. 63); "Is Homosexuality Hard-wired?" (*Nature,* 1991); "In a Nature vs. Nurture Question, a New Book Sides With Nature" (*New York Times,* 1997, p. F4); "Who Is Fat? It Depends on Culture" (*New York Times,* November 7, 2000, p. F1). And, if one only reads some sentences in professional journals one might similarly get the impression that it is genes *or* environment that is important: "The nature-nurture debate is over. The bottom line is that everything is heritable, an outcome that has taken all sides of the nature-nurture debate by surprise" (Turkheimer, 2000, p. 160). Does this mean that everything has an inherited component to it or does it mean that everything is inherited, that is, determined by genes? Reading further in the article makes it clear that although the author emphasizes that all human behavioral traits are heritable (i.e., have an inherited component to them), genes are not more fundamental than environments in shaping these traits. The introductory quote by Hamer and Copeland (1998) similarly appears to have some ambiguity to it: Does the statement that many core personality traits are the result of differences in genes mean that they *only* are the result of differences in genes or that they are the result of genes as well as other factors (e.g., environmental factors)?

As noted in Chapter 1, the contrast between "nature" (heredity) and "nurture" (environment) dates back to the work of Sir Francis Galton. Galton was interested in the inheritance of human attributes, in particular the inheritance of intellectual abilities. His early work was on the question of whether genius and eminence tend to run in families. Through the use of defined criteria for rating such accomplishments, and the careful biographical study of families of men of accomplishment, Galton (1883) found a strong relationship between the biological closeness of two men and the probability of their both being eminent. On the basis of his findings of the tendency for genius and eminence to run in families, he concluded that individual differences in intelligence and talent are largely inherited. This view is captured in the introductory quote suggesting that "there is no escape from the conclusion that nature prevails enormously over nurture. . .," but the rest of the statement has an interesting component to it: ". . .when the differences of nurture do not exceed what is commonly to be found among persons of the same rank of society and in the same country" (Galton, 1883, p. 241). In other words, Galton did recognize that the environment could play a role in the unfolding of talent, as is clear in his discussion of the "relative powers of nature and nurture" (Galton, 1876). Nevertheless, Galton is known for having pitted "nature" against "nurture" and for the unfortunate view that the human species could be improved by controlling heredity—the *eugenics movement.*

Galton's view did not sit well with the American emphasis on the environment and the philosophy of the self-made person. Nor did it fit with the extension of this philosophy into American psychology, as expressed in behaviorism and Watson's introductory quote suggesting that, given control of the environment, anything was possible—doctor, lawyer, beggar-man, or thief. The shaping of behavior through the regulation of environmental reinforcers was expressed most clearly in Skinner's operant conditioning and in his *Walden Two* (1948) novel about the construction of an ideal society based on reinforcement principles. As noted by Lindzey (1967), "the modal emphasis among psychologists in America has been upon learning, acquisition, shaping, or the modification of behavior, and not upon those aspects of the person and behavior that appear relatively fixed and unchanging" (p. 227). Thus, as of the 1970s a leading researcher on the genetic basis of intelligence observed that

"The nature-nurture controversy has not really died or even faded away; with a sprinkling of a few pleasant words about heredity for modern flavor, the nurture side of the argument thrives in quiet complacency" (Erlenmeyer-Kimling, 1972, p. 201).

One might have guessed that Anastasi's (1958) suggestion that the issue was not *which* is responsible for individual differences, genes or environment, or *how much* of the variance was attributable to each, but instead *how* (i.e., the processes involved in genes interacting with the environment) would have settled the controversy and set thinking in the field on the proper course. Unfortunately, this was not to be the case. Thus, over the years we have seen the pendulum swing between an emphasis on nature (genes) and an emphasis on nurture (environment). For the most part the emphasis has been on nurture although during the past few decades there has been a noticeable shift toward a strong emphasis on nature, so much so that even those committed to an emphasis on genetic contributions to personality sound a word of caution: "It is good for the field of personality that it has moved away from simpleminded environmentalism. The danger, now, however, is that the rush from environmentalism will carom too far—to a view that personality is almost completely biologically determined" (Plomin, Chipuer, & Loehlin, 1990, p. 225).

The critical point to remember in all of this is that in the dance of life, genes and environment are absolutely inextricable partners.

Hyman, 1999, p. 27

. . .in the future it would be most important to eschew both genetic determinism and environmental determinism.

Gottlieb, 2000, p. 96

As we undertake consideration of the relevant research methods and findings, let us begin with a clear understanding that genes and environments are always interacting with one another—there is no nature without nurture and no nurture without nature. Further, let us begin with an understanding that complex human behavior reflects the interaction of many genes over the course of time with many environments, with the relative importance of each varying for the behavior and person being considered. Thus, demonstration of the importance of genes or environments for personality characteristics is only a first step toward understanding the processes of gene-environment interaction involved in the unfolding of personality development. To make this point and conclude this introduction, let me note something that came as a surprise to me and perhaps will surprise the reader—even identical twins are not born identical! That is, although identical twins (i.e., monozygotic or MZ twins) are genetically identical, because their intrauterine environments may be different (i.e., unequal nutrition and blood supplies) they may be born with different characteristics (Wright, 1997). I was first alerted to this fact by a friend who described how different his identical twin daughters were at birth, one being born quite healthy and the other having to stay in the hospital a few days because of her illness. Incredulous because I had believed that identical twins are born identical, I asked if he was sure that they were identical rather than fraternal twins. He noted that DNA tests had proven quite positively that they were identical. As I searched the literature it became apparent to me that what my friend reported was quite often the case. But how could it be otherwise and why should I have been so surprised—genes are always interacting with the environment and what is observed always reflects this process of ongoing interaction.

The Goals and Methods of Behavior Genetics

We predict that in the 21st century, as observers look back on personality research during the 20ᵗʰ century, they will see behavioral genetics as a source of some of the field's most novel and important discoveries.

Plomin & Caspi, 1999, p. 269

With the factors considered in the introduction in mind and with the continuing recognition that nature and nurture, heredity and environment, always interact with one another, we can begin to consider the goals and methods of behavior genetics. We can then consider the relevance of the research findings for our understanding of personality development.

The goal in the field of behavior genetics is the discovery of the genes that influence specific kinds of behaviors and an understanding of the process through which such genes affect and are affected by environmental forces. Genes themselves are never directly the causes of behavior of interest to psychologists. Rather, they act as chemical messengers and exert their influence through the development of bodily structures (e.g., the central nervous system) and the biochemical functioning of the body. Such development always occurs within the context of an environment: "It cannot be stressed too often that what is inherited is not this or that 'trait' or 'character' but the way the development of the organism responds to its environment" (Dobzhansky, 1967, p. 8).

A major distinction in behavioral genetics methods lies in methods used in animal research and those used with humans. In animal research, a major method of investigation is that of *selective breeding*. In this type of research, animals with a desired trait for study are selected and mated. This same selection process separates out the animals with the desired trait among the offspring and is continued through a number of successive generations. This produces a strain that is consistent within itself for the desired characteristic. It is basically this process that is used in breeding race horses and it accounts for the high prices bid for winning race horses that will be used for stud purposes.

Although this method is possible with animals, obviously ethical principles of research preclude its utilization with humans. Thus, with humans we must look for "natural experiments" in which there are known variations in degree of genetic similarity and/or environmental similarity. If two organisms are genetically identical, then any later observed differences can be attributed to differences in their environments. If two organisms are genetically different but experience the same environment, then any observed differences can be attributed to genetic factors. While with humans we never have the ideal combination of known variations in genetic and environmental similarity, the existence of identical (monozygotic, MZ) twins and fraternal (dizygotic, DZ) twins offers an approximation to the research ideal. Monozygotic twins develop from the same fertilized egg and thus are genetically identical. Dizygotic twins develop from two separately fertilized eggs and thus are as genetically similar as any pair of siblings, sharing about 50 percent of their genes on the average. The rationale for the study of twins to demonstrate the importance of genetic factors in personality can then be stated as follows: (1) Since MZ twins have identical genes, any difference between them must be due to environmental differences; (2) while DZ twins differ genetically, they have many environmental conditions in common and thereby provide some measure of environmental control; (3) when both MZ and DZ twins are studied, it is possible to evaluate the effect of differing environments on the same genotype and the consequence of different genotypes being acted upon by the same or similar environments. In a simplified form we may say that differences between MZ twins are environmentally determined and differences between DZ twins genetically determined. Therefore, comparison of the extent and nature of both of these effects in relation to the same personality characteristic enables one to estimate the extent to which the characteristic is genetically determined and the extent to which it can be modified by different environmental contingencies.

The necessary conditions for making the above arguments are rarely, if ever, met and the results of such twin studies are not always as conclusive as one might hope. However, at a minimum they are suggestive. The study of twins has been further extended by consideration of similarities and differences between MZ twins who have been raised together and MZ twins who have been raised in different environments. Measured similarities despite rearing in different environments suggest the action of genetic factors whereas measured differences despite identical genes suggest the action of environmental factors. The rearing of MZ twins in different environments generally occurs because they have been given up for adoption and, more broadly, adoption studies offer another method for studying genetic and environmental effects. Where adequate records are kept, it is possible to consider the similarity of adopted children to their natural (biological) parents, who have not influenced them environmentally. One can compare this similarity with the similarity to their adoptive parents, who have not influenced them genetically. The extent of similarity in the former case is indicative of genetic factors while the extent of similarity in the latter case is indicative of environmental factors.

It should now be clear that in twin and adoption studies we have individuals of varying degrees of genetic similarity being exposed to varying degrees of environmental similarity. By measuring these individuals on the characteristics of interest, we can determine the extent to which their genetic similarity accounts for the similarity of scores on each characteristic. For example, we can compare the IQ scores of MZ and DZ twins reared together and apart, biological (nontwin) siblings reared together and apart, adoptive siblings and biological siblings with parents, and adoptive siblings with their biological and adoptive parents. It is here that we come to a statistic of great importance, that of h^2 or heritability. Behavioral geneticists take correlations between groups varying in degree of genetic similarity and groups varying in degree of environmental similarity and use them to estimate the extent to which the variation in scores is due to genetic factors. This estimate is known as a heritability estimate and is represented by the figure h^2. Strictly defined, the heritability estimate is the proportion of observed variance in scores that can be attributed to genetic factors.

Before turning to some of the evidence concerning the heritability of personality, it is important to keep this definition in mind and to understand the origin of the concept. The concept of heritability has its origins in biology where, for example, different seeds of the same plant could be put in the same soil and grown under the same environmental conditions. Differences in plant growth and characteristics could then be attributed to genetic differences in the seeds, with the heritability estimate reflecting the extent to which differences in plant characteristics could be attributed to genetic factors. The rationale for this procedure has been taken over by behavioral geneticists to apply to investigations of heritability of characteristics in humans. An important point to keep in mind in relation to heritability estimates is that they refer to specific populations; that is, they relate to the variance accounted for by genetic factors in the particular population studied. If a different pattern of relationships were observed in two different studies, the result would be two different heritability estimates! The difference between the two different estimates might be great or small, depending on various aspects of the two populations investigated and the measures used. In addition, there are alternative ways of calculating heritability estimates that can result in somewhat differing estimates. For example, Plomin (1990, p. 70) describes six different bases for calculating the heritability of IQ. The resulting heritability estimates vary from .30 to .72, or from 30 percent to 72 percent of the variance being attributed to genetic variance.

It is important to recognize what a heritability estimate is and what it is not—it is an estimate of the variance in a characteristic in a particular population that can be attributed to genetic factors and it is not the discovery of how much of a characteristic is due to heredity! The important point is that it is an estimate associated with a population and not a definitive measure of the action of genes. It also is not an estimate of how much of a characteristic is due to heredity *in an individual* or how much of the difference in a characteristic *between two groups of people* is due to heredity.

Although the major emphasis in behavior genetics has been on the role of heredity, another contribution has been an emphasis on the environment and genetic contributions to environmental effects: "In addition to documenting the influence of genetics, behavioral genetic research provides the best available evidence for the importance of the environment" (Plomin & Caspi, 1999, p. 251). In an important paper, Plomin and Daniels (1987) raised the question: Why are children from the same family so different? Distinguishing between shared environment effects (i.e., effects leading to similarity of siblings due to growing up in the same family environment) and nonshared environment effects (i.e., effects leading to siblings being different due to differences in the ways in which they are treated in the family or different experiences outside of the family environment), they concluded that the reason children in the same family are so different is that, in addition to genetic differences, there are large nonshared environment effects. In other words, contrary to what had been a common belief, the family environment does not appear to produce common effects leading to sibling similarity. This is not to say that the family environment is unimportant in influencing personality development, as some have been led to conclude, but rather that its effects do not lead to similarity among siblings—at least in terms of the personality characteristics measured and the ways in which they have been measured to date. A major exception to this is evidence that a common family environment plays a sizable role in determining attitudes toward involvement in romantic relationships (Waller & Shaver, 1994).

In terms of genetic contributions to environmental effects, behavioral geneticists have emphasized three types of gene-environment interactions. In the first type, the same environmental experiences may have different effects on individuals with different constitutions. For example, an anxious parent can have a different effect on an irritable child than a calm child. In the second type, individuals with different genetic constitutions evoke different responses from the environment. Thus, the irritable and calm children evoke different responses from the same parent. In the third type of gene-environment interaction, individuals with different constitutions select and create different environments. Such effects increase in the course of time as individuals become increasingly able to select their own environments. Thus, behavioral geneticists emphasize that environmental effects are never purely environmental since they always involve constitutional-genetic differences in how individuals respond to the environment, evoke responses from the environment, or select the environment which is to have an effect. As noted earlier, genes and environments are always interacting with one another and by a certain point in time it is impossible to determine the extent to which the individual has been the "recipient" of an environmental effect as opposed to the "creator" of the environmental effect. Nevertheless, as we shall now see, nature and nurture continue to be pitted against one another.

The Nature and Nurture of Personality

For almost every behavioral trait so far investigated, from reaction time to religiosity, an important fraction of the variation among people turns out to be associated with genetic variation. This fact need no longer be subject to debate.

Bouchard, et. al., 1990, p. 227

Whereas researchers using behavior-genetic paradigms imply determinism by heredity and correspondingly little parental influence, contemporary evidence confirms that the expression of heritable traits depends, often strongly, on experience, including specific parental behaviors...

Collins, et. al., 2000, p. 218

In what follows we will consider evidence of the importance of genes for four aspects of personality functioning: intelligence, temperament and the Big Five personality traits, sexual orientation and behavior, and psychopathology and behavior problems. Along the way, and in the concluding discussion, we will consider the views of those who emphasize the role of environmental factors as well.

Genetic and Environmental Factors in Personality: Intelligence

Underlying much of the IQ debate is the nature-nurture question.

Weinberg, 1989, p. 101

Is intelligence inherited? This is one of the questions that has been most investigated and has led to some of the most heated controversies in the field. In part the controversy involves the question of what one means by intelligence and how it is measured. Differences exist between those who emphasize the concept of general intelligence, *g*, as opposed to those who emphasize special abilities or forms of intelligence, *s*. This is a longstanding issue in the field. The evidence suggests that although there are different kinds of abilities or forms of intelligence that are crucial to performance in specific areas, there also is evidence of a general cognitive ability that has broad implications for school and job performance (Carroll, 1997; Gottfredson, 1997, 2000). This individual difference variable in cognitive functioning involves the ability to reason, solve problems, think abstractly, acquire knowledge, and process information in a rapid and effective manner. In terms of measurement, individual differences in intelligence typically are measured with one form or another of an intelligence test, leading to the assignment of an IQ (i.e., intelligence quotient) score. Views differ as to how adequate IQ tests are as measures of intelligence, particularly in terms of possible cultural biases. Although not definitive, there is evidence that current IQ tests have considerable validity as measures of intelligence and that they do not suffer greatly from cultural bias (Carroll, 1997). Related evidence suggests that intelligence is stable over the life span and that it is substantially influenced by genetic factors (Carroll, 1997; Plomin & Petrill, 1997). Although, as noted, each of these statements is controversial, together they form the basis for an emphasis on genes as important determinants of individual differences in intelligence.

The evidence that IQ is largely inherited is overwhelming.

Hamer & Copeland, 1998, p. 10

Our different IQs persist throughout our lives because we each inherit different versions of the genes for intelligence.

Gottfredson, 2000, p. 76

Regardless of the precise estimate of heritability, the point is that genetic influence on IQ test scores is not only statistically significant, it is also substantial. . . . For intelligence, some geneticists need to be reminded that a large part of the variance of IQ scores is not genetic in origin.

Plomin & Petrill, 1997, pp. 59,72

According to Plomin (1989), more behavioral genetic data have been obtained for IQ than for any other trait. There also is a long history to this research. For example, in 1963 there was a review of fifty years of research on the relationship between heredity and intelligence (Erlenmeyer-Kimling & Jarvik, 1963). Although there was some variation in results from study to study, in general there was a clearly marked trend toward an increasing degree of genetic resemblance in direct proportion to an increasing degree of genetic relationship, regardless of environmental communality. For example, the average correlation in intelligence for MZ twins reared together was .87 and that for MZ twins reared apart .75. The average correlation in intelligence for parent-child and sibling combinations was around .50, which closely approximates what would be expected from parents and children or siblings sharing about 50 percent of their genes in common. Virtually no correlation was found between unrelated persons, as would be expected from the absence of a genetic correspondence.

A subsequent review, including additional studies, similarly concluded that as genetic similarity increases, so does the magnitude of the correlations for IQ (Bouchard & McGue, 1981). For example, the correlations in IQ for biological relatives reared together are the following: MZ twins .86, DZ twins .60, siblings .47, cousins .15. If the biological relatives were reared apart, the correlations declined some but still showed evidence of a genetic component: MZ twins .72, siblings .24. The correlation between the biological parent and the child reared in the home is .42, that between the biological parent and the child reared apart is .24, and that between the adoptive parent and the adoptive child is .24. There are two major conclusions one can draw from such data. First, there is clear evidence of a strong genetic component to intelligence with a heritability estimate of approximately .50; that is, approximately 50 percent of the variation in individual differences in IQ can be attributed to heredity. Second, at the same time, the data indicate that the environment contributes to individual differences in IQ. In sum, the behavioral genetic data suggest both that genes play a significant role in individual differences in intelligence (i.e., IQ) and that the environment also plays a significant role in such differences.

There is evidence for both nature and nurture.

There are additional findings that lend depth, complexity, and controversy to the area. First, studies done after the 1970s produced lower heritability estimates for intelligence than did earlier studies. Thus, whereas earlier estimates of the heritability of intelligence were in the 70 to 80 percent range, the current estimate is in the 50 percent range. There is no apparent explanation for these differences (Plomin, 1989). Second, there is evidence of greater heritability as the age of the population studied increases—genetic influences account for 30 percent of the variance in young childhood, 50 percent in middle childhood and adolescence, and more than 70 percent in middle adulthood (Petrill, 1997). In part this may be due to better measures of intelligence with increased age. It also may be due to increased gene influence on cognitive functioning as the person develops. A third alternative is that individual differences in heredity lead to corresponding differences in the selection of environments that are more or less intellectually enriching. There is some suggestion that the shared family environment influence decreases with age as school experiences become more important and as individuals increasingly select their own environments: "The shared effects of a family environment on intelligence disappear with age" (Gottfredson, 2000, p. 89).

Third, there is evidence from many countries of massive IQ gains over time— what has come to be known as the Flynn effect after the discoverer of the phenomenon (Flynn, 1987, 1998). That is, performance on tests of intelligence has been increasing an average of three points a decade over the past fifty years and this increase is more evident on tests presumed to be the best measures of g as opposed to those that would appear to be more influenced by cultural factors.[1] Various environmental explanations have been offered for this phenomenon (e.g., better nutrition, better parental care, better education), but none of these seems satisfactory to account for all of the data (Flynn, 1998). Neisser (1998) considers the question of the heritability of g in the light of the Flynn effect and concludes the following: "The Flynn rise either does or does not reflect real increases in g. If it does reflect real increases, g clearly is affected by environmental factors because no genetic process could produce such large changes so quickly. Whatever those environmental factors may be, we can at least reject the hypothesis that intelligence is genetically fixed. But if it does not reflect real increases. . . then the tests are evidently flawed, and all arguments based on test scores become suspect" (p. 5).[2]

There is a myth that if a behavior or characteristic is genetic, it cannot be changed. Genes do not fix behavior. Rather, they establish a range of possible reactions to the range of possible experiences that environments can provide.

Weinberg, 1989, p. 101

Neisser's comment concerning the Flynn effect was partly an attack upon the themes developed by Herrnstein and Murray in their book *The Bell Curve* (1994). In this book they took a strong genetic view of intelligence and also suggested that an individual's g largely determines what can be accomplished in today's complex society. In other words, not only is intelligence largely inherited and strongly related to achievement, but it is largely fixed and social programs designed to affect intellectual functioning are for the most part useless. I bring this up to once more illustrate how some of the controversies considered in this book can have sociopolitical implications. Probably this is more true for the nature-nurture issue in relation to intelligence than for any other issue in the field. For example, Kamin (1974) has documented how immigration laws in the United States were systematically biased against eastern Europeans partly on the basis of the results of intelligence tests presented before members of Congress by leading psychologists. More recently, in her presidential address to the Society for Research in Child Development, Scarr (1992), who earlier had conducted research demonstrating malleability of IQ and achievement (Scarr & Weinberg, 1976), suggested that within a wide range of environmental opportunities most children "grow up to be individually different based on their indi-

---

[1]There also is evidence of a decreasing gap between black and white scores. In the second edition of this book I gave extended consideration to the issue of racial differences in intelligence. I have decided not to give consideration to the issue in this edition because I do not feel that important theoretical issues are involved and that in many ways it involves an unhealthy preoccupation with race in our society.

[2]Since the writing of this chapter an article has appeared suggesting that the Flynn effect clearly indicates an important role for environment in shaping IQ. The authors suggest that although environments can affect IQ, typically people's IQs are matched to their environments. The model presented allows both for high heritability estimates as well as large environmental effects (Dickens & Flynn, 2001).

vidual genotypes" (p. 1). This view was sharply attacked by others who suggested that other evidence of parental effects contradicted Scarr's view that genotypes drive experience. In addition, they suggested that there was reason to be optimistic concerning the potential effects of intervention programs (Baumrind, 1993; Jackson, 1993). In a similar vein, Weinberg (1989), Scarr's earlier collaborator, noted that "the conclusion that our genetic heritage contributes to the complex accounting of variation in our performance need not be pessimistic nor bode evil for social and educational policy. . . . Although genetic endowment will always influence the acquisition of intellectual skills, the environments and opportunities we create for children do make an important difference" (p. 102). As Gottfredson (2000) notes, research findings neither dictate nor preclude any particular social policy and the nature-nurture controversy in relation to intelligence represents a struggle over how to reconcile our visions of equality with evidence of biological differences.

In 1994, following publication of *The Bell Curve* and the associated intelligence debate, the American Psychological Association set up a task force to prepare a report on what was known and what was unknown concerning intelligence. A few of their conclusions (Neisser, et al., 1996) are presented as a way of summarizing this section and also as a means for setting the tone for further discussion of the nature-nurture issue:

1. "Like every trait, intelligence is the joint product of genetic and environmental variables" (p. 96).

2. "Differences in genetic endowment contribute substantially to individual differences in intelligence, but the pathways by which genes produce their effects is still unknown" (p. 97).

3. "Environmental factors also contribute substantially to the development of intelligence, but we do not clearly understand what those factors are or how how they work" (p. 97).

4. "A common error is to assume that because something is heritable it is necessarily unchangeable. This is wrong" (p. 86).

Genetic and Environmental Factors in Personality: Temperament and the Big Five

For almost every behavioral trait so far investigated, from reaction time to religiosity, an important fraction of the variation among people turns out to be associated with genetic variation. This fact need no longer be subject to debate.

Bouchard, et al, 1990, p. 227

We know that different species have different activity patterns and different patterns of social behavior. Within a species, as with dogs, different breeds appear to be more or less aggressive, more or less friendly, more or less attached to their owner. Early animal research demonstrated that through selective breeding one could develop strains with different temperament characteristics. Additional research indicated an inherited base for traits such as the following: activity level, exploratory behavior, eating behavior, aggressive behavior, dominance, responsiveness to stimuli, and wariness. Today specific genes are being identified that strongly support the view drawn from the earlier literature that emotionality is strongly dependent on genetic factors.

What about humans? Everyday observations of our own behavior and that of others suggests enormous individual differences in activity, temperament, and sociability. Observing newly born babies, we are struck with what once more appear to be striking individual differences in temperament. It is said that parents are believers in "nurture" with the birth of their first child and believers in "nature" with the births of further children—the differences even within families being that striking. Is there some basis for these later views?

You have about as much choice in some aspects of your personality as you do in the shape of your nose or the size of your feet. Psychologists call this biological, inborn dimension of personality "temperament."

Hamer & Copeland, 1998, p. 7

Temperament arises from our genetic endowment. It influences and is influenced by the experience of of each individual, and one of its outcomes is the adult personality. . . we suggest that understanding temperament is central to understanding personality.

Rothbart, Ahadi, & Evans, 2000, p. 122

In the previous chapter on longitudinal continuity in personality we considered the views of Kagan, Caspi, and others that temperament is a stable personality characteristic. Indeed, standard definitions of the concept include not just such stability but an inherited component as well. For example, Kagan (1994) defines temperament as follows: "The concept of temperament refers to any moderately stable, differentiating emotional or behavioral quality whose appearance in childhood is influenced by an inherited biology, including differences in brain neurochemistry" (p. xvii). Note that although Kagan and others suggest an inherited basis for temperament, this does not preclude an environmental influence. Even the statement by Hamer and Copeland (1998) that you have as much choice in temperament as in the size of your feet is followed by the cautionary note that this does not mean that you are "stuck" with your personality from birth: "On the contrary, one of the marvelous features of temperament is a built-in flexibility that allows us to adapt to life's hurdles and challenges. Growing up means not only learning the ways of the world, but also how to deal with yourself. Psychologists cal this more flexible aspect of personality 'character'" (p. 7).

Is there evidence of an inherited basis to temperament? Buss and Plomin (1984) used parental ratings of behavior of their children to define three dimensions of temperament: *emotionality* (ease of arousal in upsetting situations; general distress), *activity* (tempo and vigor of motor movements; on the go all the time; fidgety), and *sociability* (responsiveness to other persons; makes friends easily vs. shy) *(EAS).*[3] Not only was there evidence of continuity of temperament over time but also evidence of heritability in the range of 25 to 40 percent. However, additional research based on elderly twins reared apart suggested that heritability of these traits may be lower later in life (Plomin, 1989). Note again that heritability is not a fixed estimate, but rather depends on the population studied, including the age of that population. Thus, in this case, in contrast with that of intelligence, heritability of temperament may be greater in childhood than in adulthood, although it appears that it is not before the age of 2 or 3 that temperament heritability estimates become substantial (Loehlin, 1992).

Note that the EAS dimensions are similar to some of the Big Five and indeed a connection between childhood temperament and adult personality has been made by many personality psychologists. Plomin (1989) explicitly suggests that the core of extraversion is sociability and the key component of neuroticism is emotionality. In addition, McCrae et al. (2000) suggest that the whole range of personality traits can be subsumed by temperament. Is there, then, evidence of the heritability of the Big Five? In his 1992 review of the relevant behavioral genetic literature, Loehlin concluded that there was evidence in support of the heritability of the Big Five in the range of 28 to 46 percent. Little evidence was found for a shared environment effect. In a later study involving three different measures of the Big Five, Loehlin and his associates again found evidence in support of the heritability of these traits with little or no evidence of a contribution of shared family environment: "In summary, we obtain a simple result—genes accounting for something over one half of individual differences along all five dimensions, with the rest presumably due to the effects of environmental inputs that are distinctive to each individual, temporary situation effects, and gene x environment interactions" (Loehlin, et. al., 1998, p. 449).

These studies involve self-report responses to questionnaires. Would independent observations support similar conclusions? A recent study compared results from self-ratings by MZ and DZ twins on a measure of the Big Five with ratings made by peers of the MZ and DZ twins (Riemann, Angleitner, & Strelau, 1997). These results closely approximated those found in earlier studies, although the percentages for genetic factors tended to be lower for peer ratings than for self-ratings (Plomin & Caspi, 1999). However, data from observation studies are less supportive than those from questionnaire studies and data from adoption studies suggest less genetic influence than do data from twin studies. Of particular importance is a recent finding that

---

[3] A fourth dimension, *impulsivity* (ability to inhibit or control behavior; impulsive; easily bored) also was defined initially but then was dropped because it was not found as a clear dimension in further analyses.

although self-report and peer report data suggest that individual differences on the Big Five are almost exclusively accounted for by genetic and nonshared environmental influences, data from observed behaviors suggest a substantial (25 percent) shared environmental influence (Borkenau, et. al., 2001). Once more we can see the importance of the issue of convergence among findings from different data sources (Chapter 1).

In sum, data from a variety of studies support the view of a major genetic contribution to temperament and major personality dimensions emphasized by trait theorists. This contribution is less than that estimated for intelligence and greater than that estimated for attitudes and beliefs. Overall, estimates of the heritability of personality converge on roughly 40 percent.

My sense is that most personality and developmental psychologists would have little difficulty with the view that genes are important contributors to temperament and more general aspects of personality functioning. The controversy arises when the role of the environment, in particular that of the home-parenting environment, is diminished or negated altogether. For example, as noted earlier, McCrae et al. (2000) suggest that personality traits are endogenous dispositions essentially independent of environmental influences: "Five-factor theory deliberately asserts that personality traits are endogenous dispositions, influenced *not at all* by the environment" (p. 175, italics added for emphasis). And, to take another example, Loehlin et al.'s (1998) statement recognizes the importance of environment and gene x environment interaction effects, but goes on to question the influence of families: "We must emphasize that this does not mean that the environment is unimportant for the development of personality, or as a source of individual differences. It merely means that whatever happens to individuals that makes a lasting difference is *mostly independent of their families*, or depends on their genes, or has effects that are unique to the individual" (Loehlin, et. al., 1998, p. 449, italics added for emphasis).

Is the environment important in personality development? Of course it is. Behavioral genetic data indicate that 50 percent or more of the variance in individual differences in personality is not due to strictly genetic effects. But can much of that remainder be due to the influence of genes on the environment? That is, perhaps the environment is largely shaped by genes as previously considered—genetic differences lead to differences in response to the environment, to what is evoked from the environment, and to the environments that are selected. However, behavior genetic data indicate that as twins grow up they grow apart in personality (McCartney, Harris, & Bernieri, 1990). Although what the important environmental variables are remains unclear, and many of them may be chance events unique to the individual, it is clear that there are environmental effects (Reiss, 1997; Turkheimer, 2000).

. . .*parents in most working to professional-class families may have little influence on what traits their children may eventually develop as adults.*

Rowe, 1994, p. 7

> *There is clear evidence that parents can and do influence*
> *children...as the twig is bent, so grows the tree.*
>
> *Maccoby, 2000, pp. 1,3*

This still leaves us with the issue of parenting effects. Developmental psychologists make a number of points in response to claims of minimal or nonexistent parental influence (Collins, et al., 2000; Hoffman, 1991; Maccoby, 2000). First, research comparing different child-training and parenting practices indicates long-lasting differential effects. Kagan (1994), although emphasizing stability in temperament, also notes that specific parenting practices can produce changes in temperament behavior. As noted, research on attachment suggests a shared environmental effect on the development of views concerning romantic relationships (Waller & Shaver, 1994). Research on socialization in general, and the socialization of aggression in particular, suggests strong parental influence (Dodge, 1993, 2000). In fact, Maccoby (2000) suggests that parenting variables account for 20 to 50 percent of the variance in child outcomes. Behavioral geneticists counter that such parenting effects are specific to each child, thereby representing *nonshared* environment effects. However, developmental psychologists argue that it does not make sense to group such parenting effects with other environmental effects such as peer influences and chance occurrences. To them it seems strange to limit a shared influence to one that makes siblings similar: "But to call an environmental input unshared even though it is experienced by all children in a family (e.g., a father's job-loss, a mother's depression, a move to a better neighborhood) is an unfortunate distortion of the simple meaning of the word 'shared'" (Maccoby, 2000, p. 16). I am reminded here of a patient who struggled with the consequences for his four children of his impending divorce. The children ranged in age from their early twenties to early adolescence and included both males and females. Obviously one could expect different effects of the divorce on the four children, depending on their genetic makeup, age, and peer relationships as well as other factors. But, would one not consider the divorce a shared environmental influence in their development?

Perhaps the best evidence for parenting influences comes from *cross-fostering research*. In such research, done with animals, young animals with certain characteristics are raised by nonbiological mothers with differing characteristics. For example, rodents born to a low-nurturant mother can be cross-fostered to high-nurturant mothers and their development compared with that of siblings raised by the biological mother. Such research suggests reduced reactions to stress in the cross-fostered rodents (Anisman, et. al., 1998). To take another example, young Rhesus monkeys with differing temperament characteristics have been cross-fostered to mothers who are either calm or easily distressed. Genetically excitable, reactive infant monkeys who are reared by calm mothers develop normal peer relationships and competence in dealing with stress. On the other hand, if such infant monkeys are raised by excitable, easily distressed mothers, they develop problematic peer relationships and are quite vulnerable to stress (Suomi, 1999). In other words, through such cross-fostering experiments the effects of genetic differences are controlled for and the effects of differing parenting practices examined. In the words of the researcher: "These and other findings from studies with monkeys demonstrate that differential early social experiences can have major long-term influences on an individual's behavior and physiological propensities, over and above heritable predispositions" (Suomi, 1999, p. 193). This is not to say that genetic effects are nonexistent. Of course there are genetic effects, both direct and indirect through the ways in which the infants alter, to one extent or another, the behavior of the parent. However, what is made clear is that differing parental practices can have an impact that is common across siblings. Given such findings, perhaps it is best to conclude this section with a quote from Maccoby (2000) summarizing her review of parenting effects on children: "I urge that we give up the effort to partition the causal factors influencing children's development into two separate 'nature' and 'nurture' components, and that we abstain from asking ourselves which is more important. The two are inextricably interwoven all along the pathway from birth to maturity" (p. 23).

Genetic and Environmental Factors in Personality: Gender Identity and Sexual Behavior

I want to begin this section with a fascinating and disturbing story. The details come from a book recently published with the title *As Nature Made Him: The Boy Who Was Raised as a Girl* (Colapinto, 2000). The story begins with the birth of identical male twins, Bruce and Brian. Bruce, the older twin having been born twelve minutes before Brian, stays in the hospital a few days because he is underweight but comes home to become the more active child. When the boys are eight months old, a problem urinating is discovered due to a closing of the foreskin and circumcision is recommended. For Bruce the operation ends in a disaster—in a botched circumcision his penis is destroyed. What is to be done? Restoration of the penis as a functioning organ is impossible. Should an artificial penis be constructed, as some doctors recommend? At this point the parents watch a television program featuring John Money, by then a well-known sex researcher interested in issues of gender identity formation. Money is emphasizing how gender identity is socially constructed and learned rather than being biologically determined. That is, according to Money, children establish their gender identity at around the age of 2 1/2, prior to which time which gender identity is assumed is malleable or open to the teachings of the environment. The parents, with their son Bruce now 19 months old, go to see Money at Johns Hopkins University, a well-known and highly regarded institution, and are persuaded that a sex reassignment is best—Bruce is to be given a vagina, to be called Brenda, and raised as a girl. At adolescence "she" will be given female hormones. Since gender identity has not yet been established, if all goes well, and Money is encouraging in this regard, Brenda will develop psychologically as a woman. Although she will not be able to have children, otherwise she should be able to develop a female identity and live a normal life.

This is now the late 1960s, a time when the thinking of professionals in the field is moving toward an emphasis on social learning and the importance of the environment: "Explanations for sex differences had been moving toward a nurturist view for decades. Prior to that, the pendulum had been pointing in the naturist direction—thanks to the discovery at the end of the nineteenth century of the so-called male and female hormones, testosterone and estrogen" (Colapinto, 2000, p. 34). Money himself has been at the forefront of this emphasis on social learning, having studied individuals with genitalia that did not clearly match their biological gender (i.e., hermaphrodites) and individuals who felt they were of the gender other than their genitalia (i.e., transexuals, now called *gender identity disorder*). And, cases of transexuals who had undergone sex change operations and apparently were now leading reasonably normal lives had become public.

So the parents decide to follow Money's advice and Bruce becomes Brenda. Writing in the 1970s, Money presents the case for learning and the environment, rather than biology, being key in defining gender identity. His book *Man &Woman, Boy & Girl* (Money & Ehrhardt, 1972) is published in which he presents the case of Bruce-Brenda under a pseudonym to protect confidentiality. Brenda, now age 6, is described as progressing well. Here and in later publications, Money describes Brenda as developing normally, supporting his emphasis on the environment as key in forming a gender identity. But what is the reality? In fact, Brenda is developing in anything but a normal way. At age 2 a dress is put on her. She tries to rip it off. In play with her brother she clearly is the stronger child. By age 4 problems clearly are emerging. She and her brother observe the father shaving. She and her brother ask for a razor and shaving cream. She cries when the brother is given these to play with and she is told to go to her mother. She rejects the mother's offer to put makeup on her. But beyond this Brenda is not acting like the typical female child. She wants to urinate standing up, moves and speaks like a boy, and wants to play with the boys building forts and having snowball fights. Pictures of Brenda and Brian show attractive opposite-sex children but beyond that both appear to be all-boy. Recalling his childhood, Bruce describes the feeling that he and Brian were brothers.

Once school starts the problems are compounded. Brenda rejects the things that girls do. It is not just that she is a tomboy, but she seems different, not only to the other children but to the teachers as well. She is teased by other children and starts to develop difficulties in school. Money is contacted and reassures the parents that everything will turn out all right. Approaching adolescence, treatment with female hormones is recommended as is surgery for the construction of a more feminine vagina. Brenda, by now developing broad shoulders and a deepening voice, accepts the hormone treatments but rejects surgery. She continues to try and be a girl but it just isn't working. She is confused by all that is going on and considers suicide. Finally, she is told the truth of what occurred—she is a boy, raised as a girl because of the botched circumcision and the suggestion of an expert in the field that she could be raised to become a normal woman. She responds with anger and disbelief but also with relief that she wasn't crazy. After a period of considerable turmoil she decides to return to her biological identity as a male. Testosterone injections are given and an artificial penis is constructed. Eventually he meets a woman with three children, marries her and adopts the children. Now in his thirties, he is described as looking younger than his age, with sparse facial hair, but otherwise looking and sounding like the factory worker and father that he is and enjoying fishing and tinkering with his car engine.

I have presented the details of this story for two reasons. First, it illustrates the limits set by biology for the development of something as fundamental as gender identity. Note that we are not talking here about how masculine or feminine someone is, but rather of their gender identity, whether they believe themselves to be male or female. It also illustrates how professionals in the field and the media are prepared to swing back and forth between nature and nurture. Whereas a review of the book *Man & Woman, Boy & Girl* captured the nurture view by suggesting that "If you tell a boy he is a girl, and raise him as one, he will want to do feminine things," once the full story was presented a newspaper headline read "Sexual identity not pliable after all."

Second, the story is a distressing tale of misrepresentation. It was not until 1997 that a biologist and psychiatrist published the actual story of what had actually unfolded. In other words, for twenty-five years the field believed that Brenda had followed a normal course of development. The case had continued to be presented as illustrative of the plasticity of gender identity, of the importance of nurture over nature. In 1997 Colapinto published an article in *Rolling Stone* giving the details of the story, without identifying the identity of the person involved. Then, with the publication of *As Nature Made Him*, the full details of the story, including with his permission the identity of the individual involved, became known.

It is possible to catalog gender differences in behavior and consider the possible genetic and environmental bases for these differences. To a certain extent this was done in the second edition of this book (Pervin, 1984). At this point, however, perhaps it is best to note that broad theoretical differences exist concerning the causes of gender differences in human behavior. On the one hand, some psychologists emphasize evolutionary and biological factors as the basis for many gender differences. On the other hand, other psychologists emphasize the importance of cultural and social factors as the basis for such differences. We will have a chance to consider these alternative views in greater detail in the next chapter. Here, however, we can consider Baumeister's (2000) interesting discussion of gender differences in erotic plasticity or patterns of sexual desire. According to Baumeister, men and women differ in *erotic plasticity* or the degree to which a person's sex drive can be shaped and altered by cultural and social factors. He suggests that the female sex drive is more malleable than the male sex drive in response to these social and cultural factors: "The balance between nature and culture is different for the two genders, at least in terms of their sexuality. Men's sexuality revolves around physical factors, in which nature is predominant and the social and cultural dimension is secondary. For women, social and cultural factors play a much greater role, and the role of physical processes and biological nature is relatively smaller" (2000, p. 368). In terms of the theme of this chapter, note the contrast between nature-genes and nurture–social and cultural environment. At the same time, it is important to recognize that Baumeister is talking about differences in the relative balance between the two. That is, both nature and nurture contribute to male and female sexuality but it is the relative contributions that differ.

Among the most basic unresolved questions about human sexuality is that of the relative contributions of nature and culture. . . . The general conclusion from the adolescent and adult evidence is that the balance between nature and culture is different for the two genders, at least in terms of their sexuality.

Baumeister, 2000, pp. 347, 368

Baumeister presents data in support of three hypotheses that follow from his theory of gender differences in erotic plasticity. The first hypothesis is that individual women should be more variable than individual men in their sexual desires and behaviors in response to situational factors. That is, intraindividual variability in erotic plasticity should be greater for women than men. Illustrative findings in support of this hypothesis include evidence that women, more than men, show substantial swings in their sexual activity over the course of a lifetime. For example, women more than men become more permissive in their sexual attitudes during dating and marriage and gay females more than gay males are likely to have had heterosexual experiences.

The second hypothesis is that women will vary more than men in their sexual behavior from one culture to another and from one historical period to another. That is, socializing institutions, such as schools and churches, should produce larger changes in sexual behavior in women than in men. Illustrative findings in support of this hypothesis include evidence that rates of premarital sex vary cross-culturally more for women than for men, women change their sexual behavior more than men as they move from one culture to another, women are more influenced by education in their sexual behavior than are men (e.g., higher levels of education are associated in women with delays in starting sexual behavior and greater sexual permissiveness in terms of type of sexual activity), women are more influenced by church attendance and religious beliefs than men (e.g., church attendance and religious belief are associated with not masturbating and premarital virginity more for women than for men), and women are more affected by peer group attitudes toward sex than are men. In addition, and particularly relevant to the nature-nurture issue, heritability estimates for individual differences in sexual activity are greater for men than for women. That is, male sexuality appears to be more determined by genetic factors than is true for women, whereas sociocultural (environmental) factors appear to be more important for women than for men. Similarly, evidence for a genetic contribution to homosexuality is greater for men than for women. In sum, regardless of whether the effect of the sociocultural institution was to constrain or promote sexual activity, the effect was greater for women than for men.

Finally, the third hypothesis is that because plasticity is greater for women than men, the consistency between sexual attitudes and sexual behavior will be greater for women than for men. That is, since the female sexual response is more malleable by situational and social factors, women may be led to behave in ways that contradict their attitudes to a greater extent than is true for men. This hypothesis may seem counterintuitive to many in that it could be argued that men, more than women, will be governed by biological desires regardless of attitudes and therefore will have greater attitude-behavior discrepancies. However, the hypothesis fits with Baumeister's emphasis on the greater plasticity of female sexuality. Thus, one would expect greater inconsistency between attitude and behavior in both directions for women than for men— greater and more diverse sexual activity as well as lesser and more constrained sexual behavior than would be expected from sexual attitudes. Illustrative findings in support of this hypothesis include evidence that girls more than boys engage in sex even when they disapprove of doing so, the same is true for college women relative to college men, women more than men will have sex without the use of protection despite attitudes to the contrary, and the discrepancy between homosexual attitudes and homosexual behavior is greater for women than for men. Baumeister recognizes that these greater attitude-behavior discrepancies for women than for men might be due to greater pressure on women than men to have sex even when it is not desired. However, he suggests that evidence that women are more likely than men to have submissive and masochistic fantasies and yet are less likely than men to engage in such forms of sexual activity runs counter to this interpretation.

Not all of the evidence favors Baumeister's hypotheses. For example, males appear to engage in sexual perversions (i.e., paraphilias) more than women. And, he is prepared to consider a variety of possible explanations for these gender differences. However, he argues against a strictly social structure interpretation (i.e., males control female sexuality as reflected in a double standard and social factors are designed to regulate female sexual activity more than male sexual activity). He rejects such an interpretation in terms of evidence that women report more choice than men regarding sexual orientation and evidence of greater genetic influence on male than female sexual activity.[4] In addition, he cites evidence of greater erotic plasticity for females than males in other species. For example, in one study cited sheep were raised by goats and vice versa. In adulthood they were given the choice of mating with members of their biological species or with members of their adoptive species. Indicative of greater erotic plasticity, females were prepared to mate with members of either species whereas males would mate only with members of their adoptive species (Kendrick, et. al., 1998). Whereas the male sexual mating pattern was fixed by early experience, that for females remained open to change.

Baumeister's conclusion is that "men's sexuality revolves around physical factors, in which nature is predominant and the social and cultural dimension is secondary. For women, social and cultural factors play a much greater role, and the role of physical processes and biological nature is relatively smaller" (2000, p. 368). Not surprisingly, Baumeister's views have not gone unchallenged, both in terms of his interpretation of the data and his conclusion that, because of its greater plasticity, it is easier to regulate female than male sexual activity (Andersen, Cyranowski, & Aarestad, 2000; Hyde & Durik, 2000). Some of this criticism emphasizes differing evolutionary patterns between women and men and some emphasizes a sociocultural or social structural approach. In other words, either nature or culture can explain the

---

[4]An article published in the same year reported no heritability differences between males and females in sociosexuality (casual sex) (Bailey, et. al., 2000).

reported gender differences in plasticity. The point here is not to evaluate the merit of Baumeister's argument but rather to note the way in which it and the ensuing debate are framed—nature versus culture or the relative contributions of nature and culture. In other words, despite recognition that both are important and interact with one another, the nature-nurture issue remains in relation to an understanding of gender differences in sexual activity and other behaviors.

Genetic and Environmental Factors in Personality: Psychopathology and Behavior Problems

> *The major question for genetic research in psychopathology is no longer whether or how much genetic factors play a role in the development of a disorder or disturbance. . . . There are now well-documented genetic influences on a wide range of major mental disorders using a variety of twin, adoption, family history, and, more recently, molecular genetic approaches.*
>
> *O'Connor & Plomin, 2000, p. 219*

As indicated in the introductory quote, genetic contributions to virtually all, if not all, forms of psychopathology and antisocial behavior are widely recognized. Rather than cataloging research studies, we can draw from the data conclusions that fit with points made in earlier sections as well as additional enlightening principles.

Research on schizophrenia illustrates how historically the pendulum has tended to swing between nature and nurture positions, with current thinking emphasizing a gene-environment interaction model—the *diathesis stress model.* In 1946, Kallmann published a twin study of the inheritance of schizophrenia. The study started with individuals diagnosed as schizophrenic, an index case, and then blood relatives were located and their psychological condition evaluated. The rate of agreement in diagnosis between the index case and the blood relative is called the *concordance rate.* The question examined, as in all behavioral genetic research, was whether there was a relation between genetic similarity and concordance rate. That is, did the likelihood of a blood relative being diagnosed as schizophrenic increase as the degree of genetic similarity increased? Kallmann (1946) presented data strongly indicating that this was the case, supporting the view of a genetic basis to schizophrenia.

Kallmann's conclusions concerning the genetic basis of schizophrenia were challenged on methodological grounds. For example, the same investigator often diagnosed the index case and blood relative while knowing the degree of genetic similarity. Thus, there could be a bias in the diagnosis toward greater concordance. However, another factor was the psychoanalytic and more broadly environmental emphasis of practicing clinicians at the time. For example, a popular view was that the "schizophrenogenic mother" was the cause of the development of schizophrenia and the disorder could be cured through psychotherapy. I am quite familiar with this view since I was a graduate student in clinical psychology in 1960 and accepted the prevailing dogma that schizophrenia was environmental in origin and treatable through psychoanalytic methods. It also was a time, however, that Skinnerian behaviorism, with its emphasis on the control of behavior through reinforcers, was becoming quite popular. Thus, I remember observing schizophrenic patients at Metropolitan State Hospital (Massachusetts) pressing levers and being rewarded with candy while experimenters determined whether their behavior followed the reinforcement principles established with pigeons.

A later behavioral genetic study by Gottesman and Shields (1972) corrected the methodological problems of the earlier Kallmann research and found the following:

1. The concordance rate for the diagnosis of schizophrenia was 50 percent for MZ twins as opposed to 9 percent for DZ twins;

2. For MZ twins, the co-twin of the index case was more likely also to be schizophrenic if the illness of the index case was judged to be severe than if it was judged to be mild. In other words, there was an association between severity and the magnitude of the concordance rate for MZ twins;

3. Frequently there was considerable resemblance in the form and age of onset of schizophrenia in the pair of twins;

4. Where the co-twin was not diagnosed as schizophrenic, there often was evidence of a schizoid personality or of other psychiatric difficulties. However, there also were many cases in which the MZ or DZ co-twin of a diagnosed schizophrenic neither was diagnosed to be schizophrenic nor showed other evidence of psychopathology.

Their conclusion was that the magnitude of the concordance rate indicated that genetic factors are largely responsible for schizophrenia but, since many co-twins of schizophrenics never developed the disorder or showed evidence of serious psychopathology, environmental factors also entered in.

Today there is general acceptance of the diathesis stress model of schizophrenia—genetic factors predispose individuals to the disorder but environmental stressors are required to trigger the manifestation of the disorder. At this point neither the specific genes involved nor the specific environmental stressors have been identified. Does the same reasoning hold for other forms of psychopathology? Earlier it was indicated that all of the Big Five personality factors show evidence of an inherited component. One of the five factors is Neuroticism, suggesting an inherited component to neuroticism. Anxiety and depression are major aspects of neurotic functioning. Is there evidence of heritability for these symptoms? Indeed there is but, even more striking is the evidence that genetic factors account for a major part of the overlap of the two symptoms (Eley, 1997). This is important because anxiety and depression often co-occur in the same person (i.e., comorbidity). The fact that the genetic contribution to the comorbidity is considerable suggests the possibility of a common hereditary basis with other factors, such as shared environment and unshared environment factors, determining whether anxiety or depression becomes manifest. In other words, a common genetic base leads to differing phenotypic symptoms (i.e., anxiety or depression) depending on varying environmental factors!

Perhaps genetic factors might be acting as general influences, with environmental factors resulting in the specific manifestation of symptoms. For example, a certain gene could predispose an individual to have an emotional reaction to a stressful life event, but whether this reaction results in symptoms of depression or anxiety might depend on the nature of the environmental stressor involved.

Eley, 1997, p. 91

Psychologists concerned with understanding conduct disorders in children and adults are coming to agree on a gene-environment interaction developmental model, regardless of whether in the main they are coming from an emphasis on one or the other part of the interaction. For example, Lykken (1995) has a strong commitment to behavioral genetics. However, in his book on *The Antisocial Personalities*, he strongly emphasizes *nature via nurture*. According to him, genetically based individual differences in personality traits such as aggressiveness, low fearfulness, low constraint, impulsiveness, and sensation-seeking contribute to criminality. But criminality is not inherited. It is poor parenting in relation to these personality traits that leads to the development of criminal behavior. Using the analogy of training a bull terrier rather than a poodle, he suggests that poor parenting practices in relation to children with predisposing characteristics, as well as other environmental factors, determine whether criminality occurs: "A willful, aggressive, relatively fearless child, like a bull terrier pup, can become an outlaw if he is left to run wild or trained by methods suitable to poodles or Pomeranians. Handled with consistent, patient, loving firmness, however, the bull terrier can grow up to be the neighborhood favorite. . . . Of course parenting makes a difference, but it makes the most useful, helpful difference when it works with nature" (1995, p. 86).

A similar view is expressed by Dodge (2000), whose primary emphasis has been on how cognitive structures (e.g., hostile world schema) and social information processes (e.g., hypervigilance to hostile cues, hostile attributional bias) lead to problematic aggressive behavior. Dodge suggests that antisocial development can occur in numerous ways, all involving interactions among genetic and environmental factors. The common features of antisocial development are being born with a difficult temperament into an environmental context that includes harsh discipline, emotional neglect, and aggressive peers. As a result, "the child never acquires the social skills and regulatory mechanisms necessary to navigate the world of adolescence. The child consistently fails to attend to relevant social cues, readily makes hostile attributions about peers and adults, accesses aggressive responses in social situations, and either impulsively performs these responses, without thinking about their consequences or evaluates their likely outcomes as acceptable and selects them" (2000, p. 458).

Note that Dodge suggests that antisocial development can occur in a number of ways, and here we come to another interesting suggestion on the part of behavioral geneticists. One can contrast two groups that display antisocial behavior in adolescence—a group that displays aggressive antisocial behavior in adolescence that continues throughout the life span and a group that displays antisocial behavior in adolescence that is not aggressive (e.g., truancy, shoplifting) and the behavior does not continue into adulthood. Behavioral genetic data suggest that genetic factors account for more of the variance in individual differences in aggressive behavior than in nonaggressive behavior, suggesting that the behavior of the first group may be more genetically determined than that of the second group. This is similar to the view of Cloninger (1987) that there are two types of alcoholism, one with greater genetic effects and the other with greater environmental effects. In other words, in contrast with the earlier point that the same gene can lead to different phenotypic symptoms, depending on environmental effects, we now have cases where similar, although not identical, phenotypic symptoms (i.e., antisocial behavior, alcoholism) have different genetic and environmental contributions.

In sum, consideration of the area of psychopathology and behavior problems once more reinforces the view that genes and environments are always interacting with one another but now adds two new principles: (1) a common genetic base can lie at the root of different phenotypic symptoms, these differing symptoms representing the outcome of different environmental experiences, and (2) the same phenotypic symptoms can represent the expression of varying degrees of genetic and environmental factors.

Conclusion

The nature-nurture controversy has a long history in the field and, unfortunately, one can still find cases where it rears its ugly head. On the other hand, one increasingly finds adoption of an interactional model that recognizes the ongoing interactions betweens gene and environment—there is no gene without environment and no environment without gene. From a developmental standpoint, genes determine a range of possible outcomes depending on the interaction with the environment. An analogy has been drawn by the biologist Waddington (1957) to the movement of a ball down a landscape. The landscape may have many or few hills and valleys, each varying in height or depth and steepness. The landscape represents what is genetically determined. The ball rolling down the landscape represents development and the influence of environmental forces. It will be difficult for it to move up a hill or out of a valley with steep walls. Thus, such a path of movement or development can occur only through considerable environmental impact. There is a "natural" progression to the ball, or path of least resistance, but it can be deflected in various directions. The number of possible paths depends on the number of different slopes or valleys to the ball at a particular point. Thus, at some stages of development many options or courses of development are left open. Generally, each path taken represents some foreclosure or narrowing of potential for some courses of development. Thus, as the ball moves down the landscape, one would expect its final position to be increasingly defined, just as one would expect that with age various personality characteristics become increasingly defined and less open to change.

Obviously the model of a ball moving down a landscape does not offer any details concerning the ball, the landscape, or the environmental factors influencing its movement. In other words, it does not tell us much about the specific genes that define the landscape, the specific environmental forces that can operate on the ball as it moves along the landscape, or the important processes of gene-environment interaction. This is where progress remains to be made. However, it can serve as a useful model for how we conceptualize phenomena and direct us toward better questions and answers than have polarized views in the past.

Summary

In this chapter on the nature-nurture controversy we have focused on the extent to which views concerning the contributions of genes and environments to personality can become polarized, as well as on views that emphasize the ongoing transactions between nature and nurture, what Lykken calls nature via nurture. Through twin and adoption studies, behavioral geneticists have made important contributions to our appreciation of genetic factors in all aspects of personality functioning. In addition, they have called attention to the ways in which the environment itself expresses a genetic contribution, as when individuals with varying characteristics elicit different responses from the environment and select different environments in which to act. At the same time, the approach has led among many to the neglect of an appreciation of the role of parenting factors in the development of personality. Much of the evidence to date suggests an important role for unshared environmental effects. However, this does not preclude the importance of home-parenting effects that are specific to each child or the importance of common home-parenting influences that lead to different outcomes among siblings depending on genetic differences between them and unshared environmental experiences. Thus, there is evidence in the areas of the development of romantic relationships and behavior problems of shared environment influences.

Personality development represents the complex unfolding of characteristics at all times influenced by multiple genes interacting with multiple environmental influences. In each of the areas considered—intelligence, temperament and traits, gender differences and sexual behavior, and psychopathology and behavior disorders—the importance of this view has been emphasized. The task ahead is one of defining the genes, environments, and gene-environment interaction processes involved in the unfolding of specific personality characteristics. The task ahead is a difficult one because the interactions may vary with different individuals, with chance events sometimes playing a crucial role. In addition, as we have seen, phenotypically similar behaviors may represent the outcome of different gene-environment contributions and interactions. However, the path of progress is not made easier by debate as to which is more important—nature or nurture.

CHAPTER 6

The Nature Of Human Nature: Culture And The Search For Universals

General Theme

This chapter considers the divide between those who emphasize an evolutionary-based view of human universals and those who emphasize a culturally based view of human diversity. The contrasting views can be seen in relation to such important aspects of personality functioning as cognitive processes, emotional experience, and the basis for gender differences. As with nature and nurture, it is suggested that evolutionary and cultural determinants always are part of our functioning, with evolutionary-based adaptations setting the stage for cultural developments and setting constraints on these developments, but also generally leaving considerable room for diversity in custom and experience.

Every person is in some respects

a. like all other people,

b. like some other people,

c. like no other people.

Adapted from Kluckhohn & Murray, 1956, p. 53

The central premise of The Adapted Mind is that there is a universal human nature, but that this universality exists primarily at the level of evolved psychological mechanisms, not of expressed cultural behaviors.

Barkow, Cosmides, & Tooby, 1992, p. 5

Personality is a cultural product.

Cross & Markus, 1999, p. 81

The problem is how to reconcile faith in a single human nature with the reported variations among communities.

Shore, 1996, p. 15

I have always been fascinated with cultural differences. They are part of my intellectual and vacation history. Along with scenic beauty, the opportunity to begin to explore a different culture is one of the guidelines used in choosing vacation spots. Just as I am fascinated with, and challenged by, patients who present a world of experience different from my own, I am fascinated with and challenged by cultures expressing a different way of perceiving, experiencing, and acting upon the world. Just as it often is difficult to fully comprehend the world of experience of a patient, I often find it difficult to fully comprehend the worlds of different cultures. Nevertheless, in both cases the fascination and effort continues.

My first independent paper, as a middle school student, was on the Indian caste system. I remember being fascinated with the ways in which the caste system was organized and the rules regulating behavior, in particular those relating to treatment of the Untouchables. Years later I was able to visit India and found its culture to be one of the most interesting and challenging to understand that I have encountered—a view of the self as spirit more than body, an acceptance of seeming contradictions, a belief in fate and a belief that one's deeds influence the future, a strong belief in astrology, and a commitment to arranged marriages. As one guide said: "In America you say first love, then marriage. In India we say, first marriage and then comes love."

It is a society of contrasts, if not contradictions. There is a very advanced software industry and women carrying stones in a basket on their heads while working on road repairs. There is the discipline of tradition and religion and the chaos of cars, scooters, bicycles, and cows all on the road. As our driver said: "In the United States you drive on the right, in England on the left, and in India we drive on both or in-between." And, there are those who are caught between the old and the new. Our guide had broken with family tradition in many ways. He fell in love with a woman and presented her to his family as the woman he wanted to marry. They did not approve and insisted on an arranged marriage. He could not give up the woman he loved but he also could not violate tradition. He ended up marrying neither.

Most recently, while in Vietnam and reading the Viet Nam News, I was struck with the following headline: "Indian IT Gurus Look to the Stars." The article contained the story of Indian information technology companies turning to astrologers for help with a whole range of issues, from identifying product-launch dates to choosing corporate board members. In the words of one astrologer-adviser: "I read horoscopes of people and make a decision. I have helped revive a number of sick companies." Although I know that many American citizens make use of astrologers, including former First Lady Nancy Reagan, I do not know of any American corporations who use them to make business decisions.[1]

An important part of my graduate training in personality and clinical psychology consisted of courses in anthropology. This was at a time of peak interest in cultural anthropology. I was fascinated with the cultures described in such classics as Ruth Benedict's (1934) *Patterns of Culture* and Margaret Mead's (1935) *Sex and Temperament in Three Societies.* I was equally fascinated with Florence Kluckhohn's (1956) description of cultural differences in answers to such basic questions as the nature of human nature (e.g., good, neutral, or bad and either changeable or fixed), the primary time dimension emphasized (past, present, or future), and man's relation to nature (e.g., man subjugated to nature, man in nature, or man over nature). Influenced by Freudian psychoanalysis, this was a time when there was an interest in defining *basic personality structures* characteristic of different cultures and in relating cultural differences in child-training practices to beliefs concerning causes and cures of illnesses (Pervin, 1999). I also recall being fascinated with the idea that language could structure the very nature of our perception and experience of the world—the Sapir-Whorf hypothesis. As we shall see, many of these concepts and observations have been challenged, perhaps even discredited, but at the time they were a forceful influence on the field and my own thinking.

Finally, a few years ago I had the opportunity to teach at the University of Hawaii-Manoa. Not only is the state of Hawaii a beautiful environment but it is a fascinating mix of cultures—native Hawaiian, Japanese-American, Chinese-American, Samoan, mainlander (i.e., those from the continental United States), as well as others. I remember two events in particular in relation to the issue of cultural differences. First, I was talking in class about the nature of human motives and reflected upon some of my own introspections concerning the matter. A student asked me a question, which at first I had a hard time comprehending. He was puzzled about what I meant by introspection. It wasn't just that he didn't understand the word, but the entire concept made no sense to him. For someone such as myself, for whom introspection is a natural part of daily life, I was thrown into awareness of just how culturally limited my own view of human functioning can be at times. I was so interested in this that I mentioned it to a visiting Japanese psychologist who had invited

---

[1] I am tempted to say that instead American corporations rely upon the advice of economists, who many Indians might view the same way that many Americans probably view astrologers.

me to dinner with his newly arrived wife, children, and mother. He laughed and asked his mother, who only spoke Japanese, what she thought of this. She too was puzzled by the nature of introspection but, as best she could understand it, considered it to be nonsense.

The other event involved a class discussion of the nature of the self. Somehow class discussion led to the distinction between a *real self* and a *phony self*. A student who just recently had arrived from Japan indicated that he could not understand this distinction, in particular what it meant to be phony. One student used the expression of *being two-faced*, which was if anything more puzzling to him. As he struggled with the concept, he described how in Japan there is a public self and a private self. It is understood that both of these are parts of the self and that one is not more basic or real than the other. There are terms for each self, with the understanding among members of the culture that for most people, in particular women, the private self will be smaller than the public self. But nothing in the nature of differences between the public self and private self suggested the concept of being two-faced or phony.

These are just some of my own experiences with cultural differences. Although they involve travel to distant places, I am struck with cultural differences between metropolitan New York and rural Wyoming, or metropolitan New York and rural Georgia, that seem greater than those between metropolitan New York and metropolitan London or Paris. So, the question for us as personality psychologists is to ask whether in the face of such enormous cultural differences, one can speak of a universal human nature. Are these cultural differences relatively superficial or fundamental to personality functioning? Do cultural differences merely represent stylistic differences in the expression of fundamental, universal ways of functioning or does culture shape the very core of personality functioning? Are people all over the world basically the same, so that we can speak of a universal human nature, or are the differences so great that what it means to be human is to function in terms of the expression of a culture? To take the computer as an analogy, to what extent is the basic hardware or architecture of personality functioning the same and to what extent are differences in the software so great that similarities in the hardware become inconsequential? Or, as in the views of some cultural psychologists, is the software of such significance that one can not even speak of an architecture independent of it? That is, according to this view, there is no processing mechanism independent of culture, no personality that can be separated from the culture in which it is embedded (Shweder, 1991).

The field of anthropology is in turmoil in this regard. In its simplest form, the problem is the struggle between those who emphasize psychic unity and those who emphasize psychic diversity, between those who emphasize biology and evolutionary principles of psychic functioning and those who emphasize culture and the role of meaning in psychic functioning. As Shore (1996) describes it: "The problem is how to reconcile faith in a single human nature with the reported variations among communities" (p. 15). Or, as described by another anthropologist, there is a battle between two worlds, the one emphasizing that biology is more important than culture, the other finding such a view shocking, dangerous, and insulting (Cronk, 1999). It is evolutionism versus cultural relativism, biological anthropology versus cultural anthropology, the hardware of psychic unity versus the software of psychic diversity, the view that the fundamentals of human nature set constraints on culture versus the view that culture is as central to being human as genetics, the view that cultural uniformities tell us something about our common evolutionary history versus the view that cultural differences tell us something about what it means to be human.

I do not think that the split in psychology is as great as I sense it is in anthropology. Nevertheless, there are elements of it here as well. For example, recently I was struck with the following lecture title by a distinguished psychologist: "The Origins of Concepts—Evolution vs. Culture." As we have seen in the previous chapter, debate goes on between those who emphasize evolutionary principles in accounting for gender differences and those who emphasize the role of social structures, an issue to which we will return in this chapter. As we will also see in this chapter, there are differences between psychologists who emphasize a psychic unity in cognitive functioning and those who suggest that culture influences the very foundations of cognitive functioning, as well as between those who emphasize basic human emotions, related to our evolutionary history, and those who emphasize the cultural embeddedness of any emotional experience. And, in the next chapter, we will have a chance to consider the following question: Does the concept of the self vary cross-culturally?

In what follows, then, we will consider the views of evolutionary psychologists who emphasize universals in cognitive functioning, emotions, and interpersonal relations, and contrast these views with those of psychologists who emphasize cultural diversity in the same areas of psychological functioning.

Evolutionary Psychology and the Concept of a Universal Human Nature

To understand ourselves and our own world, we need to look not to Sigmund Freud but rather to Charles Darwin.

Burnham & Phelan, 2000, p. 4

The modern evolutionary perspective consists of an array of theories, principles, and assumptions, all of which share a premise: that much of the human mind and human social behavior reflect adaptations to major obstacles to inclusive fitness that humans recurrently faced in evolutionary history.

Simpson, 1999, p. 116

> *Every species has a universal, species-typical evolved architecture.*
>
> Cosmides & Tooby, 2000, p. 94

For some time, evolutionary, Darwinian explanations for human behavior fell into disfavor. In good part this was due to an unfortunate association of them with racist views. Today, they again are being suggested as the basis for understanding basic aspects of human psychological functioning. For some, such as David Buss (1995, 1999), they offer virtually the only hope for bringing the field of psychology into some kind of theoretical order. According to him, human behavior depends on psychological mechanisms and the only known origin of such mechanisms is evolution by natural and sexual selection. According to some, anyone interested in the social behavior of humans must take into account the evolutionary history of the behavior. According to this view, the biological roots of human nature, as expressed in the genes, are the link between evolution and behavior (Goldsmith, 1991; Kenrick, 1994).

> *Evolution by natural selection is the only known causal process capable of producing complex physiological and psychological mechanisms.*
>
> Buss, 1995, p. 2

> *. . .these evolved psychological mechanisms are adaptations, constructed by natural selection over evolutionary time.*
>
> Cosmides, Tooby, & Barkow, 1992, p. 5

What are the basics of the view of evolutionary psychology? First, there is the view that there exists a universal human nature. Second, this universal human nature involves evolved psychological mechanisms. These evolved psychological mechanisms exist and have endured because they have been adaptive to survival and reproductive success. Illustrative evolved psychological mechanisms are a fear of spiders, preferences for certain landscapes, a preparedness to learn language, a cheater detection mechanism in social exchanges, and male-female differences in mate preferences and causes of jealousy. Third, these psychological mechanisms evolved because they were adaptive in solving problems faced by humans in our ancestral history rather than problems faced by humans currently. As noted by Buss (1999), "a mechanism that led to a successful solution in the evolutionary past may not lead to a successful solution now. Our strong taste preferences for fat, for example, were clearly adaptive in our evolutionary past because fat was a valuable source of calories but very scarce. Now, however, with hamburger and pizza joints on every street corner, fat is no longer a scarce resource. Thus, our strong taste for fatty substances now causes us to overconsume fat. This leads to clogged arteries and heart attacks and hinders our survival" (p. 38).

A fourth point is that evolved psychological mechanisms are directed toward the solution of specific adaptive problems. That is, our evolved physiological and psychological mechanisms are task or function specific, rather than being all-purpose mechanisms: "The more important the adaptive problem, the more intensely selection should have specialized and improved the performance of the mechanism for solving it. . .a heart to pump blood, a liver to detoxify poisons, and so on" (Tooby & Cosmides, 1990, p. 27). The analogy is of a Swiss army knife with multiple tools to solve different tasks rather than a single, all-purpose tool. Each mechanism is like a key that fits a particular lock (i.e., adaptive problem) (Buss, 1995). Similarly, it is argued that the human mind consists of many complex, functionally distinct "mental organs" designed to solve specific problems (Chomsky, 1980; Tooby & Cosmides, 1990). In other words, many aspects of our cognitive and emotional functioning are hard-wired into us rather than being products of our unique experiences. Nature could not leave such essential aspects of our functioning to chance.

Finally, a fifth point is that to understand culture, one must first understand our evolved psychological mechanisms. That is, culture depends on and is constrained by evolutionary-based structures (Tooby & Cosmides, 1990). Thus, cultures are not free to develop in unlimited ways. Cultures obviously vary greatly but only in terms of the application of our evolved psychological mechanisms to specific environmental contexts. In other words, evolutionary psychologists suggest that rather than looking at how culture defines human nature, one look at how human nature (i.e., evolved psychological mechanisms) defines culture.

Cognitive Functioning

As indicated, according to evolutionary psychologists we are preprogrammed, or hard-wired to learn a language, although the particular language learned is a result of experience. The diversity of languages spoken and sounds contained within them is enormous. As adults listening to individuals speaking a foreign language, it often is impossible for us to hear differences in sounds considered to be quite fundamental by speakers of that language. In addition, it often is difficult, at times impossible, for us to perform sounds fundamental to that language. Yet, all humans are born not only "wired" to learn a language but able to hear and perform all of the sounds found in any language (Werker, 1989).

To what extent does language structure our cognitive functioning, our perception of the world? In my graduate training I learned of the Sapir-Whorf hypothesis that language structures our experience. Individuals speaking different languages therefore will have different experiences, different ways of processing information. Does this mean that one cannot think of something without a word for it? Does it mean that if the language provides multiple words for something (e.g., ice, sleet, snow) one can be more sensitive to differences than if these words are not available? Does this mean that members of a culture that includes many color terms in its language will be more sensitive to colors, perhaps even categorize them differently, than members of a culture that includes few color terms in its language? Could nature allow for such variability in cognitive functioning?

Early tests of the Sapir-Whorf hypothesis focused on whether members of cultures varying in the availability of color labels would also vary in their ability to recognize color differences (Hardin & Banaji, 1993). If, as suggested by the Sapir-Whorf hypothesis, language structures perception, this should be the case. On the other hand, if color perception is an evolved mechanism, members of all cultures should be adept at identifying parts of the color spectrum. Support for the latter, and evidence against the Sapir-Whorf hypothesis, first came from the research of two anthropologists (Berlin & Kay, 1969). In this research speakers of different languages were asked to give the basic color terms of their language. Then they were asked to pick the best illustration of each color from an array of chips presented to them. First, a limited number of basic terms were found to be present in any of the languages, at most three achromatic (e.g., black, white, gray) and eight chromatic (e.g., red, yellow, blue, green). Second, where more color terms were used in different languages, the selection of terms progressed in the same order—black and white, then red, then yellow, green or blue, and so on. In other words, far from total variability, the physical properties of color seemed to determine the development of linguistic terms. Third, although members of different language groups might use different specific color terms, they would agree on the color that best represented a basic color category (e.g., red, yellow, green, blue) (Berlin & Kay, 1969). Rather than language determining color categories and exemplars of these categories, something more basic about color perception seemed to be present.

In a series of crucial experiments to further test the Sapir-Whorf hypothesis, Heider (1972) found evidence that specific areas of the color space, called "focal colors," are universally the most linguistically "codable" and the most easily remembered. In the first experiment, English-speaking subjects and speakers of ten other languages were asked to provide the basic color names in their language and then to select the best example of that color from an array of fifty-three color chips varying in hue (e.g., red, yellow, green, blue) and saturation (i.e., purity). All subjects selected the most saturated chips, the focal colors, as the best examples of the basic color named. In the second experiment, subjects from different language groups (e.g., Indo-European, Sino-Tibetan) were presented with an array of color chips and asked to write, in their own language, the name of each color. The length of time taken to give each chip a name and the length of the name given was recorded for each of the color chips. The focal color chips were given shorter names and named more rapidly than nonfocal colors. This held true for members of all the language groups.

In a third experiment, an English-speaking group of subjects and a group of subjects from Indonesian New Guinea who spoke a language that lacks basic color terms were compared in terms of their memory for color chips. They first were shown a color chip and then, after a thirty-second delay, were asked to select the chip they had been shown from an array of 160 color chips varying in hue and saturation. Would focal colors be remembered more accurately than nonfocal colors even by speakers of a language that lacks basic hue terms? In other words, would the lack of a color term interfere with the better memory for focal than nonfocal colors or is there something basic about the relative ease with which focal colors are remembered? In both cases, focal colors were remembered better than nonfocal colors, in contrast with what might be expected on the basis of the Sapir-Whorf hypothesis. However, recognition accuracy for both focal and nonfocal colors was greater for the English-speaking subjects than for the subjects whose language lacked basic color terms.

In the fourth experiment, another group of subjects from Indonesian New Guinea were presented with the task of learning a word, taken from their language, in association with each of 16 colors, eight focal and eight nonfocal. Since their language does not contain color terms, the words used were not color words. The question was whether words associated with focal colors would be learned more rapidly than those associated with nonfocal colors. If color is a dominant influence, the words associated with the focal colors should be learned more readily. On the other hand, if language is key (i.e., the Sapir-Whorf hypothesis), there should be no difference in ease with which the two groups were learned. The results indicated that the focal colors became associated with words more rapidly than the nonfocal colors.

In sum, the four experiments indicated that the same colors were most codable and best remembered regardless of the language involved, including a culture where the language involved did not code for color. The conclusion drawn was that the same underlying factors, most likely involving the physiology of color vision, accounted for the results of all four experiments. That is, the data were taken to reflect the effects of basic, universal perceptual-cognitive factors as opposed to the effects of language on thought. And what of the differences in the third experiment where the English-speaking subjects performed better than the group whose language did not contain color terms? Since their performance was better for both focal and nonfocal colors, it was attributed to cultural differences in overall memory performance rather than to the effects of availability of color words in the language.[2]

I have gone into this research in detail because it played a major role in downplaying the influence of language on thought suggested by the Sapir-Whorf hypothesis. Thus, a major figure in the field was led to conclude about research in this area that, although it began in a spirit of strong relativism and linguistic determinism, it "has now come to a position of cultural universalism and linguistic insignificance" (Brown, 1976, p. 152). We will return to this matter when we consider the cultural view, but suffice it here to say that the conclusion drawn fit well with the view of universals in cognitive functioning.

---

[2] I find it rather curious that many reports of this research skip over this detail and that apparently consideration was not given to testing for memory differences on other tasks. It would have been particularly interesting to see whether the same difference in performance occurred on a task more familiar to the other group or on a task equally unfamiliar to both.

Basic Emotions

Are there universal emotions? What would be the adaptive value of such universal emotions? Darwin was impressed with the continuity of facial expressions of emotion among many species, in particular the continuity from nunhuman to human primates. In *The Expression of Emotion in Man and Animals,* Darwin (1872/1965) suggested that emotions have adaptive value and specific expressions and physiological response patterns. The adaptive value of emotions is that of a signal to self and others of a bodily state and preparedness for action. Through facial and bodily expressions of emotion animals, including humans, signal their intention to fight, run, play, or otherwise be engaged in social interplay. A fascinating illustration of the continuity of emotion among the species is evidence that not only do adult humans and children laugh, but laughter also is present in other primates and in rats (Panksepp, 2000). It is suggested that laughter is fundamentally a social phenomenon expressing joyful affect. Consistent with this is evidence that one laughs when tickled by another but it is impossible to tickle oneself.

For many years emotion was a neglected area of psychology, particularly during the early years of the cognitive revolution beginning during the 1960s. A lone voice in the emphasis on emotion, or affect as it was called by him, was Silvan Tomkins (1962, 1963, 1991), who developed what has come to be known as *basic emotions theory.* There are a few basic principles to basic emotions theory. First, it is suggested that there are basic, fundamental, or primary emotions that are universal. The exact number of basic emotions varies somewhat from theorist to theorist, generally ranging from 8 to 14. The 8 basic affects suggested by Tomkins are: interest-excitement, enjoyment-joy, surprise-startle, distress-anguish, disgust-revulsion-contempt, anger-rage, shame-humiliation, fear-terror. In agreement with Darwin, it is suggested that affects are innate, part of our evolutionary heritage, and have evolved because of their adaptive value. We do not learn to be afraid, startled, disgusted, or angry, although we do learn when, where, and in response to which stimuli to respond with these affects. For example, although there appear to be universal stimuli for disgust, namely those having contamination properties, what is considered to be disgusting by some individuals or cultures can be considered a source of joy by others (e.g., eating ants can be considered disgusting or a delicacy) (Rozin & Fallon, 1987).

Second, according to basic emotions theory the basic, universal emotions have unique features. Most significantly, each affect is associated with a pattern of facial movement involving specific facial muscles. This pattern of facial movement or facial expression, unique to each affect, is innate and universal. It can be seen in young infants as well as adults, and in members of differing cultural groups. In addition to the universality of these facial expressions, it is suggested that the basic emotions have distinctive physiological patterns of response associated with them.

Third, the affect system is the primary motivational system. It is suggested that emotions, rather than drives, have an energizing or motivational effect. Emotions have the capacity to organize and maintain sets of thoughts and actions. Fourth, as a result of constitutional factors as well as experience, individuals differ in the frequency and intensity with which particular emotions are experienced. Since affects are motivational and organize cognition and action, it is not surprising that they would be central to an individual's personality. And, as each emotion influences thought and action in relatively distinctive ways, specific emotions help to shape specific traits in each individual. For example, the emotions of interest, enjoyment, and shyness have been found to be related to the trait of Extraversion, while the emotions of sadness, contempt, fear, shame, and guilt have been found to be related to the trait of Neuroticism (Izard, 1993).

In sum, basic emotion theorists suggest that there are innate, universal emotions that are part of our evolutionary heritage, have adaptive value, and have universal expressions and distinctive physiological properties. These emotions have importance for motivation, cognition, and action and play a central role in the organization of personality functioning. Although the basic nature of each affective response is innate and universal, it is recognized that there are learned associations between each emotion and specific stimuli as well as cultural rules concerning when and how each affect is to be expressed. Culture is important but it acts more as an overlay rather than as a determinant of the nature of the basic emotional response itself.

Is there support for the view of universal emotions? According to Ekman, "the strongest evidence for distinguishing one emotion from another comes from research on facial expressions" (1992, p. 175). In cross-cultural research conducted independently by Ekman (1993) and by Izard (1994), it has been demonstrated that members of vastly different cultures select comparable emotion terms to fit facial expressions. In other words, members of different cultures share the same basic facial expressions associated with the basic emotions and can recognize these facial expression–emotion relationships in one another. In an interesting recent extension of this research, American and Indian college students were presented with videotaped expressions of 10 classic Hindu emotions (anger, disgust, fear, heroism, humor-amusement, love, peace, sadness, shame-embarrassment, and wonder) and 15 neutral expressions. In this case the portrayals included the body as well as the face. Could both American and Indian subjects correctly identify the emotions? Consistent with the findings of Ekman and Izard, the subjects correctly identified the emotion being portrayed in more than 60 percent of the cases (Hejmadi, Davidson, & Rozin, 2000).

Additional support for the universality of emotions comes from studies indicating that included in the languages of different cultures are groups of emotions similar to those suggested by basic emotions theory (Church, et al., 1999; Church & Lonner, 1998) and evidence that members of different cultures associate similar patterns of subjective feelings, physiological symptoms, and expressive behavior for the major emotions (Scherer & Wallbott, 1994). Although the latter findings were based on responses of subjects to a questionnaire, laboratory research suggests that it may be possible to identify specific patterns of physiological response that are associated with each of the basic emotions (Levenson, 1992). There also is some preliminary evidence that these patterns of physiological response show consistency across cultures (Levenson, et al., 1992).

In sum, the evidence in support of the view of basic emotions, or the universality of emotions, comes from four sources: evidence of the ability of individuals from different cultures to recognize one another's facial expressions, evidence of cross-cultural similarity of grouping of emotion terms, evidence of differentiation of physiological response for various emotions, and evidence of continuity of facial expressions of emotion between human adults and children, and perhaps between humans and other primates as well.

Before leaving this section, it may be worth considering a caveat to the research on cross-cultural similarity of facial expressions. A difference in facial expression of emotion has been found between occasions where the person is being observed and when he or she is not being observed. In other words, when an observer is present culturally prescribed display rules enter in. These display rules, of course, vary from culture to culture. However, the results of these display rules do not wipe out the basic facial expressions. Rather, they operate as an overlay on top of them.

Interpersonal Relations

Evolutionary theory leads to a variety of hypotheses concerning human social behavior. Here we consider two aspects of such behavior addressed by evolutionary theory—the development of bonds between parent and offspring, and differences between males and females in mate preferences and determinants of jealousy.

Bowlby's Attachment Theory. At birth, the human infant is in a very vulnerable position, and continues to be so for longer than is true for members of other species. For the infant to survive, for parental genes to be passed on, a mechanism had to be established to insure a bond between infant and caregiver, a protective bond. This bond provides the basis for the human as a social animal and experiences established during the early years of life set the framework for later social relationships.

These principles form the basis for the attachment theory of the British psychoanalyst John Bowlby (Simpson, 1999). In his conceptual work, Bowlby was influenced by Darwin's ideas and by developments in two fields of biology: ethology, which focuses on the study of animals in their natural environment, and general systems theory, which focuses on general principles of operation of all biological systems. In terms of ethology, Bowlby was particularly struck with the ethologist Lorenz's description of the separation distress and proximity seeking of birds who had become attached to the mother, and of the strong bond that was not based on oral gratification. These observations appeared to match Bowlby's observations of infants and young children.

Attachment theory is an evolutionary theory.

Simpson, 1999, p. 115

If the attachment system described by Bowlby is part of our evolutionary heritage, one would expect to find evidence of it in other species and evidence of it cross-culturally. As has been indicated, Bowlby's formulation of attachment theory was influenced by observations ethologists made of other species. According to Suomi (1999), who has done considerable research with other primates, "attachment is not an exclusively human phenomenon. . . . Virtually all of the basic features of human infant behavior that Bowlby's attachment theory specifically ascribed to our evolutionary history could be observed in the normative mother-directed behaviors of rhesus monkey infants and other primates" (p. 181). In addition, as noted in Chapter 5, according to Suomi (1999) there is evidence from studies with these other primates that early social experiences can have long-term consequences on an individual's development. In addition to this cross-species evidence, a recent review of the cross-cultural research suggests considerable evidence for the cross-cultural validity of attachment theory: "The cross-cultural studies support Bowlby's idea that attachment is indeed a universal phenomenon, and an evolutionary explanation seems to be warranted" (Van Ijzendoorn & Sagi, 1999, p. 728). These studies not only suggest the universality of views of early attachment behavior but also views of the successful outcome of transition through this period.

At the same time that there is evidence of universality of the attachment system, it should be noted that attachment does not take the same form in all cultures. For example, the model of attachment to a single caregiver characteristic of much of modern Western culture is not the norm in most societies. In most societies attachment takes the form of a network of multiple caregivers (Van Ijzendoorn & Sagi, 1999). In addition, the specific form of the caregiver's mothering or attachment that most leads to optimum development varies from culture to culture, depending on the relevant environmental requirements: "There is no best mothering (or attachment) style, for different styles are better in different circumstances, and natural selection would act to favor individuals with a range of potential styles from which they select appropriately. . .a mother-child relationship which produces successful adults in one situation may not do so in another" (Hinde, 1982, pp. 71–72). Once more we see an evolved mechanism that provides both for specificity and flexibility.

Male-Female Differences in Mate Preferences and Causes of Jealousy. According to evolutionary theory, dating back to Darwin, males and females have evolved different mate preferences as a result of prior selection pressures. Basically the theory revolves around two fundamental differences between men and women. First, there is the *parental investment theory*—the view that women have a greater parental investment in offspring than do men because women pass their genes on to fewer offspring. This is because of both the limited time periods during which they are fertile and, relative to men, the more limited age range during which they can produce offspring. Thus follows the suggestion that females will have stronger preferences about mating partners than will males (Trivers, 1972). Also, there is the suggestion that males and females will have different criteria for the selection of mates, the former focusing more on the reproductive potential of a partner (i.e., youth) and the latter on the mate's potential for providing resources and protection.

Second, there is the matter of *parenthood probability*. Since women carry their fertilized eggs, they can always be sure that they are the mothers of the offspring. On the other hand, males cannot be so sure that the offspring is their own and therefore must takes steps to ensure that their investment is directed toward their own off-spring and not those of another male (D. M. Buss, 1989). Thus follows the sugges-tion that males have greater concerns about sexual rivals and place greater value on chastity in a potential mate than do females.

The following are some of the specific hypotheses that have been derived from parental investment and parenthood probability theories (Buss, 1989; Buss, et al., 1992):

1. A woman's "mate value" for a man should be determined by her reproductive capacity as suggested by youth and physical attractiveness. Chastity should also be valued in terms of increased probability of paternity.

2. A man's "mate value" for a woman should be determined less by reproductive value and more by evidence of the resources he can supply, as evidenced by characteristics such as earning capacity, ambition, and industriousness.

3. Males and females should differ in the events that activate jealousy, males be-ing more jealous about sexual infidelity and the threat to paternal probability, and females more concerned about emotional attachments and the threat of loss of resources.

Buss (1989) obtained questionnaire responses from 37 samples, representing over 10,000 individuals, from 33 countries located on 6 continents and 5 islands. There was tremendous diversity in geographic locale, culture, ethnicity, and religion. What was found? First, in each of the 37 samples males valued physical attractive-ness and relative youth in potential mates more than did females, consistent with the hypothesis that males value mates with high reproductive capacity. The prediction that males would value chastity in potential mates more than females was supported in 23 out of the 37 samples, providing moderate support for the hypothesis. Second, females were found to value the financial capacity of potential mates more than did males (36 of 37 samples) and valued the characteristics of ambition and industrious-ness in a potential mate to a greater extent than did males (29 of 37 samples), consistent with the hypothesis that females value mates with high resource-providing capacity.

Contrary to the view that humans have no nature, except for the capacity to learn and the capacity for culture, it turns out that humans universally have clearly defined de-sires that are part of our human nature.

Buss, as quoted in Pervin, 1996, p. 141

In subsequent research, three studies were done to test the hypothesis of sex dif-ferences in jealousy (Buss et al., 1992). In the first study, undergraduate students were asked whether they would experience greater distress in response to sexual infidelity or emotional infidelity. Whereas 60 percent of the male sample reported greater distress over a partner's sexual infidelity, 83 percent of the female sample reported greater distress over a partner's emotional attachment to a rival.

In the second study, physiological measures of distress were taken on undergraduates who imagined two scenarios, one in which their partner became sexually involved with someone else and one in which their partner became emotionally involved with someone else. Once more males and females were found to have contrasting results, with males showing greater physiological distress in relation to imagery of their partner's sexual involvement and females showing greater physiological distress in relation to imagery of their partner's emotional involvement.

In the third study, the hypothesis that males and females who had experienced committed sexual relationships would show the same results as in the previous study but to a greater extent than would males and females who had not been involved in such a relationship was explored. In other words, actual experience in a committed relationship was important in bringing out the differential effect. This was found to be the case for males for whom sexual jealousy was found to be increasingly activated by experience with a committed sexual relationship. However, there was no significant difference in response to emotional infidelity between females who had and had not experienced a committed sexual relationship.

A follow-up of this study was conducted in the Netherlands and Germany, as well as in the United States (Buunk, et al., 1996). Comparable results concerning male-female differences in the causes of jealousy were found, although the magnitude of these differences were found to vary from country to country (largest for the United States, least for the Netherlands). These results were interpreted as particularly significant since, according to the authors, the German and Dutch cultures have a more relaxed attitude toward extramarital sex than does the American culture. In addition, they are described as having a greater emphasis on sexual equality: "The fact that the sex differences still emerged in these cultures provides support for the evolutionary psychological hypothesis" (Buunk, et al., 1996, p. 362).

In sum, the results from these studies are interpreted as supportive of the hypothesis of sex differences in activators of jealousy. Although alternative explanations for the results are recognized, it is suggested that only the evolutionary psychological framework led to the specific predictions.

Culture and the Emphasis on Diversity

To presume Western concepts of the mind, along with its methods of study, not only lends itself to research of little relevance to other cultures, but disregards and undermines alternate cultural traditions.

Gergen, et al., 1996, p. 496

The introduction to this chapter focused on diversity. The emphasis was on differences in the ways in which people from different cultures perceive and experience the world. In the next section the focus was on the evolutionary-based view of human nature. The emphasis there was on universal human nature, what Cosmides and Tooby (2000) refer to as the species-typical evolved architecture. In this section we return to consideration of the cultural point of view. At its extreme, this view suggests that culture and personality are so intertwined that one cannot speak of a person without culture, and there is no culture without persons. In contrast with the evolutionary view of a basic, species-typical architecture, the cultural view argues against any concept of a central processing mechanism (Shweder, 1991). Rather than a focus on universal ways of thinking, feeling, and relating, the cultural view focuses on the unique meanings given to events by members of various cultures. According to the latter, to focus on the universal is to miss much of the richness of experience and that which makes us truly human.

As suggested in the introductory quote to this section, the clash between the evolutionary and cultural views also can be a clash between methods. Too often Western psychologists have assumed that what they learn from their subjects is universal. Indeed, in some cases it is suggested that cross-cultural testing of theories and research findings is unnecessary (Messick, 1988). Where research on other cultures is conducted, often it involves the presentation of questions and materials translated from English into a foreign language rather than first examining whether the questions asked are meaningful in other cultures and beginning with materials relevant to that culture. In other words, rather than looking at another culture from a Western framework, perhaps it is useful to consider another culture within its own framework. In other words, the very questions we are asking from a Western standpoint, as well as the way we are asking them, may not be meaningful within another cultural context. To return to an issue considered in Chapter 2, compare the following two approaches. In one case trait terms from English are translated into another language and subjects are asked to rate themselves on these traits. Is the Big Five structure duplicated in these ratings? In another case, subjects are asked to generate terms they would use to describe themselves and others. These might be trait terms; they might not. Where they are trait terms, they might duplicate those found in English but they might not. And, at an even more fundamental level, suppose the entire enterprise of describing oneself or another does not make sense within some cultural contexts. That is, suppose one asks the following question: "Does the concept of the person vary cross-culturally?" (Shweder & Bourne, 1984).

In this section we will consider cultural differences in cognition, emotion, and interpersonal relationships, following the sequence considered in relation to evolutionary interpretations of a universal human nature. In doing so, however, we should be aware that some cultural psychologists would suggest that even using these categories of knowledge does an injustice to cultures that may differ in how they carve up the world of experience and behavior.

Cognitive Functioning

We have considered Heider's (1972) work on color categories and the switch from the view of linguistic determinism to cultural universalism and linguistic insignificance (Brown, 1976). According to Hardin and Banaji (1993), this research led to the view that the Sapir-Whorf hypothesis of linguistic influences on thought had been disconfirmed. However, according to these authors, this rejection of the hypothesis may have been premature. First, not all cross-cultural studies of color categorizations were inconsistent with the hypothesis. Second, because of constraints set by the physiology of the color system, color perception and color memory might not be the best place to look for linguistic influences on thought.

> *It appears that the continued rejection of the hypothesis that language influences thought is unwarranted. . .*
>
> *Hardin & Banaji, 1993, p. 284*

According to Hardin and Banaji (1993), there exists considerable experimental evidence consistent with the view of linguistic influence, perhaps even linguistic determinism. That is, there is evidence that language *causes* cognitive processes to function the way they do. First, in terms of perception, there is evidence that language can influence perception. For example, already noted was the finding that infants are able to recognize all speech sounds but by adulthood there is a reduced ability to perceive differences among speech sounds that are not differentiated in one's own language (Werker, 1989). Second, there is evidence that verbal labels can facilitate or inhibit memory for visual forms and person characteristics. Having labels for behaviors and person characteristics facilitates memory for these behaviors and characteristics. According to the authors, language functions to package and organize information in ways that makes such information more or less accessible. Third, there is evidence that language can structure the way we perceive people in terms of categories of traits and personality types. In addition, language can structure the ways in which we perceive similarities and differences between men and women.

In what follows we will have the chance to consider other evidence of cultural differences in cognitive functioning that may be expressive of linguistic influences. At this point suffice it to say that Hardin and Banaji (1993) suggest that the evidence supports the view that language influences cognitive functioning in fundamental ways.

Culture and the Fundamental Attribution Error. A major area of research in social cognition in personality and social psychology has been that concerning causal explanations people offer for events. To what do people attribute events? A person succeeds or fails. Was it luck or did it have to do with them? Was it under their control, internal to them, or under external control? A person behaves in a particular way. Is their behavior expressive of some personality characteristic or is it due to the situation they are in? Within the context of research on causal explanations, there has been enormous interest in what came to be known as the *fundamental attribution error*. Largely studied by social psychologists, the fundamental attribution error calls attention to the tendency, among subjects from Western cultures, to attribute the behavior of others to personality characteristics (i.e., traits) to a greater extent than they do their own behavior. Conversely, these subjects tend to attribute their own behavior to situation influences to a greater extent than they do the behavior of others. Where is the error? To social psychologists, the error is in attributing the behavior of others to internal dispositions, such as traits, rather than to the influence of situations. Presumably people are aware of the variability of their own behavior from situation to situation but tend to see others in a more limited range of situations. As a result, they incorrectly see others as much more trait-like in their behavior than they really are.

For the longest time the concept of the fundamental attribution error was used as part of the critique of trait theory and was assumed to be universal. Then, in 1984, a study by Miller (1984) reported on the differences between American and Indian Hindu explanations for everyday social events. Evidence was presented indicating that Americans give greater weight to dispositions in accounting for social behavior than do Hindus. Conversely, Hindus give greater weight to the context in accounting for social behavior than do Americans. Even more striking was the reversal of the fundamental attribution "error." Whereas American subjects tended to weight dispositions more heavily than context, the reverse was true for Hindus. This held for both deviant and prosocial behaviors. The point made by Miller was that cultural factors that influence meaning and everyday social explanation had been neglected by psychologists. According to her, the emphasis on the individual person in Western culture lends itself to a dispositional view of events whereas the greater Hindu emphasis on social roles lends itself to a contextual view. In both cases it is culture that is influencing the perceptions of, and explanations for, events.

In a further study of possible cultural differences in the relative emphasis on dispositional and situational causal explanations, Morris and Peng (1994) compared American and Chinese attributions for events. In the first study, American and Chinese subjects watched cartoon displays of physical and social events and reported their causal perceptions. They found that the two groups did not differ in their causal perceptions of physical events but did in their causal perceptions of social events. Americans perceived more influence of internal factors and Chinese more influence of external factors. In the second study, they compared English-language and Chinese-language newspapers in terms of their explanations for crimes. The former were found to be more dispositional and the latter more situational in their explanations for the same crimes. Finally, in the third study, American and Chinese subjects were compared in terms of their attributions for murders. Consistent with the earlier findings, American subjects gave greater weight to dispositional factors than did Chinese subjects, whereas situational factors were given greater weight by the Chinese subjects than by the American subjects. American subjects emphasized such dispositional factors as chronic psychological problems and Chinese subjects emphasized situational factors such as corruption by bad example and disruption by social change. The authors concluded by indicating that although their studies indicated that the two cultures were biased toward differing explanations for events, neither could be viewed as more accurate or objective than the other.

An interesting aspect of the Morris and Peng research was that parts of it were based on doctoral dissertation research conducted under the guidance of Richard Nisbett, one of the individuals most responsible for development of the concept of the fundamental attribution error. Research such as that just considered led Nisbett to a variety of studies comparing members of different cultural groups in their cognitive functioning and to the conclusion that members of such groups can differ substantially in this regard. Noting that psychologists have long believed that fundamental reasoning processes are the same in all cultures, Nisbett moved toward an emphasis on cultural differences in cognition. Specifically in regard to the fundamental attribution error, whereas until recently it was held to be invariable across cultures, "it turns out, however, that the fundamental attribution error is much harder to demonstrate with Asian populations than with European-American populations. . . . The cultural difference seems to originate primarily from a stronger East Asian tendency to recognize the causal power of situations" (Norenzayan & Nisbett, 2000, p. 132).

East Asian and American causal reasoning differs significantly. . . . These culturally differing causal theories seem to be rooted in more pervasive, culture-specific mentalities in East Asia and the West.

Norenzayan & Nisbett, 2000, p. 132

These are just a few of the differences in cognitive functioning that have been found among members of differing cultural groups (Markus, Kitayama, & Heiman, 1996). The findings include differences in moral reasoning, differences in optimism, differences in theories of psychological functioning (i.e., theories of mind), and, as will be considered in Chapter 7, differences in views of the self. Collectively, what is significant is that they lead some psychologists to the view of basic differences in cognitive functioning among members of different cultural groups. In other words, it is not just differences in content or what one attends to that is being considered, but more fundamental differences in the way information is processed (Nisbett, Peng, Choi, & Norenzayan, 2001).

I can remember hearing Nisbett present some of these ideas to my colleagues at Rutgers University. His paper focused on how members of different cultures use different mental processes to solve similar problems. Coming from the view that our cognitive processes are universal and part of our evolutionary heritage, my colleagues were startled and for the most part rejecting of what Nisbett had to say.

Emotion

> *One of the most interesting and provocative ideas that have been put forward in the relevant literature is the possibility of identifying a set of fundamental human emotions, universal, discrete, and presumably innate. . . . I experience a certain unease when reading claims of this kind.*
>
> *Wierzbicka, 1986, p. 584.*

As noted, basic emotions theorists suggest that there are universal basic emotions, with corresponding physiological concomitants, although the stimuli that trigger these responses and external displays of them may vary from culture to culture. Cultural anthropologists recognize that there may be some "basic emotions" but question how many there are, the role they play in daily life, and, most importantly, how free of cultural context and meaning they are in terms of the actual experiences of individuals.

> *The truth may well be that when it comes to basic emotions we are not only basically alike in some ways, but are basically different from each other as well.*
>
> *Shweder & Haidt, 2000, p. 410*

Part of the difference between those who emphasize basic emotions and an evolutionary point of view as opposed to those who emphasize cultural diversity has to do with the nature of the emotions being considered as well as the nature of the emotional experience itself. At its broadest level, all humans, and probably most animals, are capable of experiencing pleasant as opposed to unpleasant emotions. Also, most, if not all, languages distinguish between pleasant and unpleasant emotions (Church & Lonner, 1998). However, beyond this, languages vary considerably in the size of the vocabulary of emotion terms and in the ways in which these terms are linked with one another. According to cultural anthropologists, even where the same or comparable emotion terms appear in different languages, the actual nature of the emotional experience is so embedded in culture that one cannot assume identical emotional experiences in individuals from different cultures (Shweder & Haidt, 2000; White, 1993; Wierzbicka, 1986). According to this view, emotional experience is dependent on the meaning of the entire social context within which that experience occurs. Thus, for example, in some cultures one's experience of self-worth largely depends on accomplishing one's own goals and focusing on one's own internal experience, whereas in other cultures the focus is much more on the group, social sharing, and the shared evaluation of the situation (Mesquita, 2001). Such differences are suggested as altering the entire nature of the emotional experience, to the extent that the emotional experiences of members of one culture would be hard to comprehend by members of the other culture.

To a certain extent the point made by cultural anthropologists can be made as well by considering the experiences of individuals within the same culture. For example, consider the emotions of guilt, shame, embarrassment, and humiliation. Suppose you were asked to define each and give illustrative situations in which each would be experienced. To what extent would these definitions and illustrative situations match those given by other students? In my experience, although students are familiar with these emotion terms and can relate to them, they have a hard time defining them, often disagree about aspects of their definition, and often disagree about which experience would be expected in a particular situation. In part these constitute personality differences and in part differences in the ways in which the terms are used. And, in part the differences express different linkages with other emotions such as anger, anxiety, and sadness. But, according to those who emphasize cultural diversity, these are some of the very components that go to make up the nature of our emotional experience. In other words, although one can seek to objectify universal emotions, to do so is to lose the diversity of meanings that people associate with experience and that go toward defining the nature of the emotional experience itself. In a sense, without meaning there is no experience of emotion and there is no meaning without culture.

Interpersonal Functioning

In the section on universals in human nature, we considered views emphasizing evolutionary explanations for universals in attachment and gender differences. As was true for the areas of cognition and emotion, interpretations of the data and conclusions reached by those who emphasize social factors have been quite different.

Attachment Theory. Whereas attachment theorists maintain that cultural differences are minor and focus on universals, others emphasize cultural variation and suggest that attachment theory is value laden and culturally biased (Rothbaum, et al., 2000). According to this view, the conceptions of desirable caregiving and measures of such caregiving, as well as of desirable outcomes, are biased toward Western ways of thinking.

> *We attempt to show that core tenets of attachment theory are deeply rooted in mainstream Western thought and require fundamental change when applied to other cultures or minority groups.*
>
> *Rothbaum et al., 2000, p. 1094*

Rather than downplaying the role of culture as is done in the evolutionary emphasis, Rothbaum et al. (2000) suggest that culture is a fundamental part of attachment. Contrasting practices in the United States and Japan, they suggest that when parents in the United States care for babies in ways valued by Japanese parents, "they are considered insensitive, and their babies are found to be insecurely attached" (p. 1097). Parental behaviors considered to be encouraging of secure attachment in one culture (Japanese) would be considered to be encouraging of an unhealthy dependence in the other culture (U.S.). Indications of competence in U.S. children, such as independence and the ability to venture forth on one's own, are contrasted with indications of competence in Japanese children, such as an orientation toward the group and dependence on others to meet one's needs. Whereas emotional openness is valued in the former, it is less likely to be seen as desirable in the latter. Similarly, indications of competence in adulthood can be contrasted in the two cultures. Whereas in the U.S. autonomy is valued, in Japan it is interdependence that is valued.

In sum, Rothbaum et al. (2000) question the universality of attachment theory and suggest that the core elements of the theory do not apply in all cultures. The importance of early attachments and the evolutionary dispositions that underlie attachment are not questioned. However, what is proposed is greater attention to the specific cultural contexts in which early attachments are formed and the cultural contexts in which later consequences are expressed.

Gender Differences. Earlier we considered the view of Buss and others concerning male-female differences in mate preferences and the causes of jealousy. The emphasis there was on different evolved psychological dispositions, reflecting different adaptive problems, that are part of our evolutionary heritage. According to this view, the different behavioral patterns and social positions of men and women can be viewed as derived from biologically based differences in evolved psychological dispositions. In contrast with this evolutionary emphasis, Eagly and Wood (1999) locate the basis for differences between men and women in the contrasting social positions. That is, according to their *social structural theory,* women have less power and status than men and control fewer resources, and these are the major factors in accounting for gender differences in behavior. Although biological differences (e.g., differences in size and strength and women's role in childbearing) contribute to determining the different social roles filled by men and women, it is the differing social roles that lead to gender differences in behavior that are of critical significance. As a result of these differing social roles, for example, men are more competitive and women more nurturant, men become breadwinners and women become homemakers, men value women for their "good housekeeper and cook" qualities and women value men for their "good earning capacity." However, where these differences in the social structure are removed and gender equality is approximated, the associated gender differences erode. In sum, the gender differences attributed by evolutionary psychologists to genetically based differences in evolved dispositions are better understood as the result of differences in social structure and social roles. In the future, to the extent that men and women fill comparable positions in the labor market, differences in psychological attributes will disappear.

> *In the origin theory proposed by evolutionary psychologists, the critical causal arrow points from evolutionary adaptations to psychological sex differences. . . . In contrast, in the social structural origin theory, the critical causal arrow points from social structure to psychological sex differences.*
>
> *Eagly & Wood, 1999, p. 408*

And what of the findings concerning gender differences in causes of jealousy? An alternative, social cognitive view of jealousy suggests that this emotion is triggered by threats to self-esteem (Harris, 2000). Thus, men and women might be expected to differ in the realms in which there is threat to their self-esteem. In our culture, within the context of romantic relationships, males might be expected to feel more threatened by sexual infidelity and females more threatened by romantic infidelity. In addition, Harris (2000) questions the basis for some of the conclusions reached by Buss and his associates. First, she notes that the difference between imagining sexual infidelity and imagining romantic infidelity was much weaker for women than for men. Second, she questions whether the physiological data necessarily were indicative of the emotion of jealousy as opposed to other emotions such as anxiety, anger, or sadness. Third, there may be gender differences, based on cultural roles, in reactivity to sexual and romantic stimuli independent of whether they involve one's partner. For example, it might be that in Western cultures men have had greater exposure to, and greater acceptance of arousal by, sexual stimuli (e.g., pornography) than have women, whereas women are relatively more comfortable with exposure to, and arousal by, romantic situations. In other words, in the earlier research perhaps gender differences had more to do with the nature of the stimuli that are arousing, rather than with infidelity and differences in the causes of jealousy.

In some relevant research, Harris (2000) conducted three studies in which physiological responses were recorded to fantasies of a mate's infidelity. In the first study, as in the earlier Buss research, male and female subjects imagined sexual and romantic-emotional infidelity scenarios. Although for men the physiological responses were greater for the sexual scenarios than for the romantic-emotional scenarios, for women there was no evidence of a difference in reactivity between the two. The data supported the earlier report of male differential responsivity to imagining the two forms of infidelity but did not support the report of differential female responsivity. In the second study, there was investigation of whether the differences for males had to do with infidelity or whether sexual as opposed to romantic-emotional stimuli were involved, regardless of whether infidelity was involved. Half of the male subjects imagined scenarios in which their partner was engaged in sexual or romantic infidelity and half imagined scenarios in which they were interacting with their partner in a sexual or romantic-emotional activity. No differences between the two forms of imagery were found on the physiological measures of reactivity: "Imagining sexual activity appears to be more arousing than imagining emotional activity, regardless of whether these male participants were imagining their mates with someone else or with themselves" (p. 1086). These data challenged the earlier interpretation of sexual jealousy as the basis for the differential male response.[3]

In the third study, female subjects were studied under the same conditions as in the first study but with the addition of another measure of physiological response. In addition, the female subjects were asked whether they would find sexual infidelity or emotional infidelity a more serious form of betrayal and whether they had previous experience with committed sexual relationships. Once more there was a lack of evidence of differential physiological response to the emotional infidelity and sexual infidelity scenarios. When answers to the question of prior experience with committed sexual relationships were considered, it was found that women with such experience showed a greater reactivity to sexual infidelity imagery than to romantic-emotional infidelity imagery. Women without such experience showed the opposite pattern: "Women who have sexual relationship experience tend to show reactivity patterns more like men, not less" (p. 1089). In terms of self-report, in agreement with the Buss results, the vast majority (80 percent) of the subjects indicated that emotional infidelity was the more serious form of betrayal. However, there was no relation between these self-report responses and the measures of physiological response. This discrepancy between the two forms of data were seen as questioning the view of an innate basis for the jealousy response.

Harris suggested that the data did not support the view that men are "innately" more upset by sexual infidelity than by emotional infidelity whereas the reverse is true for women: "Both genders could be equally distressed by sexual infidelity, but men may be more successful at imagining sexual infidelity than romantic infidelity. For men, sexual imagery may lend itself more readily to a concrete image, whereas emotional imagery may seem more nebulous" (p. 1088). Certainly the data suggest that the greater male response to sexual than romantic imagery may be due to a general difference in arousal rather than specifically to jealousy. In sum, the data were viewed as more supportive of a social cognitive view of gender differences as opposed to a biologically based evolutionary view.

Evolutionary and Cultural Views: Is an Integrated View Possible?

In this chapter the evolutionary and cultural views have been contrasted, the former emphasizing biologically based universals and the latter learning-based diversity. Proponents of the evolutionary view of human universals emphasize that any theory of human functioning must be tied to our evolutionary heritage and to our ties to members of other species, in particular the great apes. On the other hand, while not denying that we have an evolutionary history, proponents of the cultural view suggest that humans have progressed to the point where they are much freer of genetically programmed responses. In addition, rather than focusing on problems of sur-

---

[3]It is not clear why a group of female subjects was not similarly studied in this condition.

vival and reproduction, it is suggested that we focus on efforts to adapt to current social problems (Cantor, 1990).

Are the two views necessarily in fundamental opposition to one another? Note that some of the authors cited have suggested that the evolutionary and the cultural can coexist with one another. Rather than it being universal versus cultural, perhaps we can consider the issue in terms of the following: To what extent, and in which ways, has our evolutionary heritage defined our psychological functioning? We can all agree, I think, that we do not come into the world a tabula rasa or blank slate on which anything can be written, or at least written with equal ease. As evolutionary psychologists suggest, apparently we come into the world prepared to learn language structures, prepared to become more afraid of some objects than others, and prepared to form attachments. At the same time, as cultural psychologists emphasize, there is enormous diversity to the content and structure of languages people speak, to the emotional responses of people from different cultures, and to the nature of the relationship bonds formed by members of different cultures.

Recognition of the importance of both evolutionary and cultural determinants suggests that the appropriate questions may be the following: How broad or *pervasive* are the effects of our evolutionary heritage? What are the *constraints* set by our evolutionary heritage on culture and individual development? How do cultures build on what is universally human in a way that is adaptive to changing environmental and social circumstances? And, in what ways does the diversity of psychological functioning found in humans suggest important differences between humans and members of other species, including those closest to us in our ancestral history? Much like the discussion of nature and nurture in the previous chapter, we can take the view that evolutionary and cultural determinants always are parts of our functioning. Neither can exist independent of the other. To return to the initial quote in this chapter, our evolutionary heritage is what makes everyone alike to some extent. A shared culture is part of what makes members of a group similar to one another and different from members of another culture. And, our unique genetic structure and history of experience is what makes each of us unique individuals like no other person.

Summary

This chapter began with consideration of the split between those who emphasize an evolutionary-based view of human universals and those who emphasize a culturally based view of human diversity. Evolutionary psychologists emphasize the adaptive problems faced by our ancestors and the evolved psychological mechanisms developed in response to these adaptive tasks and challenges. If these mechanisms were not adaptive in terms of survival and reproductive success, they would not exist. Conversely, what is common to us as humans must exist because it served some adaptive function in our evolutionary history.[4] Evidence presented by evolutionary

---

[4]The possibility that some common characteristics developed as byproducts of adaptations is not considered within the context of this chapter (Buss, et al., 1998).

psychologists of universal aspects of cognitive functioning, basic emotions, attachment, and gender differences in mate preferences and causes of jealousy was considered.

At the same time, many psychologists emphasize evidence suggesting diversity in cognitive functioning, emotion experience, attachment, and gender functioning. In addition, in a number of cases research data are presented challenging the findings of those supportive of a universalist view of human nature. For example, research suggests that language can impact on how perceptions are organized and remembered and that social structure explanations for gender differences are possible.

Finally, it was suggested that evolutionary and cultural explanations need not be considered in opposition to one another. That is, it was suggested that our evolutionary heritage may set constraints on which culture may operate, the constraints being greater in some areas of psychological functioning and lesser in other areas, greater during some historical periods and lesser during other historical periods. Cultures must help us to answer basic questions and to solve basic human problems. Many of these questions and problems are basic to our functioning as humans with an evolutionary heritage. Other questions and problems reflect specific environmental and historical challenges such that cultures will differ in accord with the specific nature of the challenges presented. And, similarly, cultures will change as the nature of these challenges change for the members of that culture. In this sense there is cultural evolution just as there is biological evolution. Finally, evolution and culture, genes and experience, contribute to making all humans alike in some ways, groups of humans alike in some ways, and each individual unique in some ways.[5]

---

[5] After completing this chapter I came across a book by the primatologist de Waal (2001), *The Ape and the Sushi Master*, that has implications for the issues considered in this chapter as well as previous chapters. de Waal's main point is that culture, defined as knowledge socially transmitted from generation to generation, is not unique to humans—it is found in other primates (e.g., apes) as well. From there he goes on to argue against a dualism of culture and nature, suggesting that culture is shaped by our evolutionary history and that "culture takes human nature and bends it this way or that way, careful not to break it" (p. 9). For de Waal there are fascinating cultural differences but also a shared humanity that makes interactions across cultures possible. Influenced by Eastern as well as Western culture and primate research, he would appear to suggest that it is not a question of nature over culture or culture over nature, but of culture and nature in relation to one another.

CHAPTER 7

Is The Concept Of The Self Useful And Necessary?

General Theme

Interest in the concept of the self has waxed and waned throughout the history of the field. Phenomena associated with the self seem of critical importance to understanding personality. Yet, conceptual and measurement problems have been recurrent. In this chapter the following questions are considered: Does the person have a single self or many selves? Can the psychoanalytic and social cognitive concepts of the self be integrated? What is the evolutionary basis for the development of self-consciousness? Is the concept of the self universal? Are related motivations universal?

> *"The self" has a long and controversial history in psychology. Some eras, such as our own, exalt it to a central position in personality and social psychology, whereas others relegate it to the realm of the unobservable, unknowable, and scientifically unthinkable.*
>
> *Westen, 1992, p. 1*

> *It was the Self, the character and nature of which I wished to learn. I wanted to rid myself of the Self, to conquer it, but I could not conquer it, I could only deceive it, could only fly from it, could only hide from it. Truly nothing in the world has occupied my thoughts as much as the Self, this riddle, that I live, that I am one and am separate and different from everybody else, that I am Siddartha; and about nothing in the world do I know less than about myself, about Siddartha.*
>
> Hesse, Siddartha, 1951, p. 40

> *Many aspects of human behavior seem inexplicable without the notion that people have a self.*
>
> Robins, Norem, & Cheek, 1999, p. 443

At various times throughout this book we have found ourselves confronted with some perplexing aspects of personality theory and research. In this chapter we again consider a paradox brought home by the following question: Is the concept of the self useful and necessary? The phenomena associated with the concept of the self seem so obvious; yet, when we try to study them empirically, it is often as if we are grasping at straws in the wind. As a result, as we shall see, periods of great interest in the self have alternated with periods of virtually complete rejection of it as a topic of useful inquiry.

Some answers to the question of why the need for a concept of the self seem apparent. The concept of the self makes sense in our daily lives and phenomenological experience. Terms such as *self-conscious*, *self-esteem*, *selfish*, *self-hatred*, *self-love*, *self-actualization*, and *phony* give testimony to the importance of the self from an existential point of view. These terms and associated feelings form a major part of what patients talk about in virtually all forms of psychotherapy. However the therapist construes what the patient is saying, in most cases the patient is concerned because there is dissatisfaction with some aspect of the self or with the total self.

Second, the self would appear to represent an important part of the way a person construes the world. The self emerges fairly early in infancy and begins to form an important part of the child's construction of the world. With our ability to differentiate ourselves from others and to reflect back upon ourselves, we use our self-concept as a way of evaluating and organizing information. As in any cognitive operation, new information concerning the self has to be evaluated against old concepts and then either be integrated into them or effect changes in them. In other words, not only is the self experiential, but it is a concept with potentially important implications for the functioning of our cognitive system,

Finally, one could suggest a need for the concept of the self-based on its potential for integrating what otherwise appear to be discrepant or unrelated findings. People perform differently when they are motivated, ego-involved, or self-involved as opposed to when they are not so involved. Wouldn't we appear to need a concept of the self to understand such differences? In fact, would it not make sense to suggest that the concept of the self is a necessary expression of the organized, integrated aspects of human psychological functioning?

Given these existential, cognitive, and organismic justifications for the concept of the self, why should there be a chapter concerned with the question of its utility? The answer to this question is partly a result of the historical waxing and waning of interest in the self in the field of psychology, and partly in the conceptual and methodological problems that remain. Historically the concept was introduced into American psychology by William James in 1890. During the 1920s there was a decline in interest in the self in conjunction with the Watsonian opposition to the study of internal processes and the use of phenomenological self-report. During the 1940s there was a surge in interest in the concept, particularly as seen in the works of Carl Rogers and Gordon Allport. There was interest in the goal of self-consistency (Lecky, 1945), or the individual's efforts to maintain a consistent picture of the self, and a portion of a presidential address to the American Psychological Association was directed to the importance of the concept of the self (Hilgard, 1949). Yet, in the 1950s Allport found it necessary to address the question: "Is the concept of the self necessary?" (Allport, 1955), and a review at the end of the decade suggested that there were many problems with the research that had been done to that time (Wylie, 1961). During the 1960s and early 1970s there was some continued research but no major breakthroughs. Social learning theory was developing a full head of steam and at the time gave little attention to the concept of the self. Thus, in 1973 it was again asked whether the concept of the self was necessary (Epstein, 1973), and another review of the research indicated that thinking and research in the field had not advanced terribly far in the course of the decade since the previous review (Wylie, 1974).

Yet, despite the paucity of consistent research findings, psychologists continue to be impressed with the topic. The self will not go away. Indeed, since 1973 the topic has returned with a vengeance. Whereas in 1975, when I began working on the first edition of *Current Controversies and Issues in Personality,* I debated whether to include a chapter on the self, today one could hardly imagine not including such a chapter. A recent review of the literature lists thirty-seven self-concept theories (Robins, Norem, & Cheek, 1999) and another review refers to thousands of articles that have been published on the self (Baumeister, 1998). Both reviews point to the importance of the concept and gains made in research. However, both also point to the questions, confusion, and controversies that remain.

What is the self? In some ways, the thousands of journal articles dealing with the self have seemed to make the answer to that fundamental question more elusive rather than clearer. . . . Trying to keep abreast of the research on self is like trying to get a drink from a fire hose.

Baumeister, 1998, pp. 680, 681

How are we to proceed given the thousands of articles on the self and the "blooming, buzzing confusion" (Robins, Norem, & Cheek, 1999, p. 444) that many psychologists see as surrounding the concept? In this chapter we will limit ourselves to three main areas of inquiry. First, we will consider cognitive, affective-motivational, and behavioral aspects of the self. In this section we will address the question of whether the self is best conceptualized as a single entity or the self is best considered in terms of many parts or selves: Does the person have a self-concept or many selves? If the latter, what is it that gives a sense of coherence to the self and allows us to avoid suffering from a multiple personality disorder? Second, we will consider psychoanalytic and social cognitive views of the self: Can we get these two theoretical views of the self together? Third, we will consider evolutionary and cultural views of the self: Do other species have a sense of self? Is the concept of the self cross-cultural?

Cognitive, Affective-Motivational, and Behavioral Aspects of the Self

In this section we will consider the self from three major perspectives: *cognitive*, how people represent themselves in their thinking, *affective-motivational*, how people feel about themselves and what they are motivated to do in relation to their self-concept, and *behavioral,* how people present themselves behaviorally in everyday life. Although these are considered separately, it should be clear that the self always has cognitive, affective, motivational, and behavioral components associated with it.

The Cognitive Self: The Representation of Self in Everyday Life

Today in psychology there is considerable interest in what has been called *implicit personality theory.* Implicit personality theory is concerned with the theories that people develop as they go through their lives and with the theories they use in their daily activities. As George Kelly suggested, every person is a scientist and therefore each person has a unique theory concerning human behavior. The theory is implicit in the sense of not being spelled out, as a scientist does, but this does not make the theory any less present. Furthermore, we can use techniques to discover each individual's implicit personality theory concerning, for example, which traits or personality characteristics are linked with which other personality characteristics. These personal theories allow us as lay people to assume that if a person has one personality characteristic the chances are good that the person also possesses other specific personality characteristics. The hypotheses emanating from the theory are used to make predictions in our social encounters so that we do not need to consider every social encounter an entirely new experience.

One critical part of our implicit personality theory, or cognitive representation of what people are about, is the way in which we come to think about, represent ourselves—the self-concept. Combining early experiences we have of our bodies with reflected appraisals, or ways in which we see others perceiving us, and utilizing observations of our own behavior, we develop a cognitive representation of the self. According to one psychologist, the self concept is a self-theory: "It is a theory that the individual has unwittingly constructed about himself as an experiencing, functioning individual and is part of a broader theory which he holds with respect to his entire range of significant experience" (Epstein, 1973, p. 407). The theory one has about the self is used to organize experience so that one can cope effectively with the internal and external world. Like any theory, the theory about the self can be very differentiated or very simple, it can cover a great deal of experience in a parsimonious way or cover minutiae in an overcomplicated fashion, it can be a useful representation of reality and lead to predictions that are verified by events or it can be a distortion of reality leading to repeated disconfirmation and surprise.

Implicit personality theory and the self as part of a theory of the world clearly emphasize cognitive processes. It is here that some of the most interesting recent research is being conducted. This research emphasizes the self as a cognitive structure that can be considered in the same way as other cognitive structures, that is, in terms of its influence on such cognitive processes as attention, information search, information storage or memory, and information retrieval or recall (Markus & Sentis, 1982). An impetus for work in this area was the research by Markus (1977) on the self as cognitive structures or schemata: "Self-schemata are cognitive generalizations about the self, derived from past experience, that organize and guide the processing of the self-related information contained in an individual's social experience" (p. 63).

In her early research Markus compared subjects who rated themselves as independent with those who rated themselves as dependent, and with individuals who did not show any clear tendency to rate themselves as independent or dependent, on four tasks: (1) speed of judgment of words as self-descriptive that were independent adjectives (e.g., adventurous, self-confident), dependent adjectives (e.g., conforming, submissive), or unrelated to either; (2) ability to provide behavioral illustrations from their own past experience of each trait or adjective; (3) ratings of the likelihood of their behaving in ways considered to be characteristic of independent and dependent people; (4) acceptance of feedback information describing the self in ways that were congruent with or contrary to the ways in which they described themselves. The first two groups of subjects were considered to have relevant self-schemata, while the third group of subjects was considered to be aschematic for this personality trait.

Would the availability of relevant self-schemata influence performance on the four tasks? Indeed, Markus found the following: (1) Subjects with independent self-schemata were found to judge more of the independent adjectives as self-descriptive and to be faster in their judgments of the words than were subjects with dependent self-schemata. The reverse was true for dependent adjectives. Aschematic subjects were midway between and did not differ in their response speeds to the two sets of words. (2) In terms of behavioral illustrations, independent self-schematic subjects gave the most for independent adjectives and dependent self-schematic subjects the most for dependent adjectives. (3) In terms of probability of behavior ratings, independent self-schematic subjects rated themselves as more likely to behave in independent ways than dependent ways. The reverse was true for dependent self-schematic subjects, while there was no difference for aschematic subjects. (4) Finally, both groups of schematic subjects were found to resist information that was incongruent with their self-schemata or contrary to the ways they thought about themselves. In sum, the self-schemata were found to be associated with performance on a number of tasks involving the recognition, recall, and receptivity toward potentially self-relevant information.

Since this research, additional evidence has been gathered suggesting that once self-schemata are established they influence a wide variety of cognitive processes. Thus, for example, there is evidence that we attend to and learn self-relevant information more than information that is not relevant to the self, that we can recall self-relevant information better than nonrelevant information, and that we not only resist information discrepant with our self-schemata but we actively elicit from others self-relevant or self-confirming information (Baumeister, 1998; Fong & Markus, 1982; Markus & Sentis, 1982; Swann & Read, 1981). Finally, there is evidence that we tend to perceive others in terms of schemata that are relevant to the self, though we sometimes also are able to use different categories in these judgments. In sum, it appears that "all incoming stimuli are evaluated according to the relevance to the self" (Markus & Smith, 1981, p. 245) and that "the self can be reasonably viewed as a system of cognitive structures" (Markus & Sentis, 1982, p. 63).

Individuals differ in their self-schemata. They also differ in the extent to which they focus attention on and are influenced by what is going on inside them as opposed to what is going on in the surrounding environment (Duval & Wicklund, 1972). An important concept in this regard has been that of self-monitoring or the extent to which people monitor or regulate their behavior according to situational cues. Snyder (1979; Snyder & Campbell, 1982), who developed the concept of self-monitoring as well as a test to measure relevant individual differences, suggests that high self-monitoring individuals are sensitive to cues of situational appropriateness and regulate their behavior accordingly, whereas low self-monitoring individuals behave more in accord with internal feelings and attitudes. These differences are seen as reflecting differences in global self-conceptions that have important implications for the way people think, feel, and act. High self-monitoring individuals are seen as having a *pragmatic self.* They see themselves as being flexible and adaptive, they are sensitive to information concerning situations and other people, they tend to attribute their behavior to situational causes, and they see themselves as varying in behavior from situation to situation. The latter does not appear to be merely a case of self-perception since there is evidence that high self-monitoring, pragmatic individuals do tend to behave in ways that are situation specific and not always in accord with their personal beliefs and attitudes.

In contrast with such individuals, low self-monitoring individuals are seen as having a *principled self.* They see themselves as being principled in their actions, defining themselves in terms of their personal characteristics. They are sensitive to internal cues, tend to attribute their behavior to internal causes, and see themselves as being relatively stable in their behavior across situations. Also, there is independent evidence suggesting that principled individuals do tend to behave in ways that are stable and congruent with their beliefs and attitudes. Finally, it is suggested that both pragmatic and principled individuals choose to be with those people and in those situations that conform to their self-conceptions and general patterns of behavior. In sum, these differing self-conceptions are of enormous significance for what people think, feel, and do.

It is worth considering implications of this distinction between pragmatic and principled individuals for the person-situation controversy considered in Chapter 3. In this regard, Snyder notes that at the level of specific traits and attitudes one would find considerable behavioral consistency for low selfmonitoring, principled individuals but perhaps little for high self-monitoring, pragmatic individuals. On the other hand, at the level of more general patterns of behavior, we may see that "both high self-monitoring individuals and low self-monitoring individuals may demonstrate meaningful congruence between global conceptions of self and the events of their lives" (Snyder & Campbell, 1982, p. 205). In sum, the degree of consistency found may have to do with the kind and level of data considered.

One or Many Selves? Is there one concept of the self or many self-concepts? Are people's conceptions of themselves stable and enduring or do they shift from situation to situation and from time to time in life? These continue to be questions of concern. In the past, psychologists tended to talk about the self-concept as if the individual had one self-concept that covered a broad range of experience over time and across many situations. In other words, the assumption was that people functioned as trait psychologists concerning themselves as well as others. With the rise in criticism of the trait approach and the social cognitive emphasis on the situational specificity of behavior, some psychologists were led to suggest that we do not have one concept of the self but many self-concepts (Gergen, 1982). We may have concepts of the self that vary according to the situation we are in and conceptions of the self that change from time to time. In other words, the selfconcept is neither global nor fixed. Our many concepts of the self at times may be inconsistent with one another. For those who hold such a view, neither our construction of our self, nor how we experience our self, nor what others tell us about our self provides a satisfactory definition of the concept of self: "There appears to be precious little of sufficient clarity or palpability concerning the experience of mental or emotional life to furnish a reliable self-definition" (Gergen, 1982, p. 66). According to this view, the self is constantly being presented, formed, and changed in the course of social interaction.

> *Properly speaking, a man has as many social selves as there are individuals who recognize him and carry an image of him in their head.*
>
> *James, 1890, p. 294*

> *A vital point to stress is that in spite of certain pressures*
> *toward self-stability and consistency over time, the phe-*
> *nomenal self shifts from moment to moment and is con-*
> *stantly evolving and changing.*
>
> Jones & Pittman, 1982, p. 233

> *. . .the one most basic need of the individual is to maintain*
> *unity or coherence in the individual's conceptual system.*
>
> Epstein, 1981, p. 27

> *But the concept of the self loses its meaning if a person has*
> *multiple selves. . . . The essence of self involves integration*
> *of diverse experiences into a unity. . . . In short, unity is*
> *one of the defining features of selfhood and identity.*
>
> Baumeister, 1998, p. 682

In tune with this view, two social cognitive psychologists, Cantor and Kihlstrom (1987, 1989), have suggested that each person has a multiplicity of selves, called a *family of selves*. These selves may be tied to situational contexts such that one has a work self, a family self, a social self, and an alone self. Each of these selves might be divided into further selves. For example, within the family, there might be a child self, a sibling self, and a partner self. The important point is that the self-concept is like any other concept that has multiple elements that can be arranged in a hierarchy. For example, one might have a broad concept category of vehicle, under which are subcategories such as car, truck, and bus. Under each might be further subcategories, such as sports car and sedan under *car*, pickup truck and tractor-trailer under *truck*, and city bus and cross-country bus under *bus*. Similarly, then, an overall sense of self might be at the top of a hierarchy, representing the general self-concept, with subcategories representing units of the family of selves that are tied to specific situations or periods of time in one's life.

Two questions of particular interest may be asked in relation to such an analysis of the self. First, what are the implications of greater or lesser consistency among these self-representations? Second, what is it that gives a sense of coherence among the self-representations so that we do not end up suffering from a multiple personality disorder? In terms of the former, there is evidence that greater consistency among self-representations across situations (e.g., with friends, at work, at school) is associated with better psychological adjustment (Donahue, et. al., 1993). In terms of the latter, Cantor and Kihlstrom (1989) suggest three bases for the sense of integration within the family of selves. First, overlapping resemblances give us a sense of unity. Parts of the self remain consistent from situation to situation, or at least consistent over many situations. Second, unity to the self is given by our autobiographical record, our sense of continuity over time. In this sense, our sense of self may be more or less tied to the past ways in which we viewed ourselves. Third, we may always be able to focus on features of a basic, core self regardless of whether these features are present in all, or even most, situations. For example, we may see ourselves as kind and considerate even if we don't always act that way. Thus, an answer is provided to the question of why we are not all multiple personalities—because of overlapping resemblances, an autobiographical record, and a basic or core self-conception.

In sum, apparently the concept of self is neither whole nor part, neither stable and enduring nor chaotic and conforming to changes in circumstances. People vary in how responsive they and their self-concepts are to situational variations as well as in how integrated these self-conceptions are into a total self-concept. For most people it would probably make most sense to be, in Snyder's terms, neither completely pragmatic nor completely principled, neither a chameleon nor a caricature of stability. That is, it would appear to be most adaptive to maintain some sense of stability in the self, some sense of continuing identity, while leaving room for variations in situations and periods of time. From the research and conceptual standpoint, the answer to the question of one or many selves would appear to depend on the questions of interest to the psychologist. That is, for some purposes, such as assessment of subjective well-being, it might be best to inquire about the overall self-concept, whereas for other purposes, such as prediction of performance and feelings in specific situations, it might be best to inquire into one or more of the many selves that make up each of our family of selves.

Affect and Motivation as Aspects of the Self-Concept

The phenomenal self concerns all aspects of how we sense or experience ourselves. The earliest roots of a sense of self probably lie in experiences associated with the body. Throughout life we rely on kinesthetic cues from the body to guide us in our movements. Reliance upon bodily cues and images becomes so integral a part of our daily existence that we often cease to take notice of it. Yet, their significance becomes apparent when there is a change in bodily image or a disturbance in our ability to make use of these cues. The processes involved here start at a very early point in life, and it is sometimes said that the early definition of the self by the infant is based on the experiences it has of feeling and being felt at the same time. Whereas with other objects the infant only experiences the sense of touching or feeling, with its own body the infant experiences the sense of touching and being touched, of feeling and being felt. The experience obviously is different if the infant bites its cradle than if it bites its own foot or hand—and the infant certainly does such biting.

The psychologist Carl Rogers (1947, 1951, 1961), popular and influential during the 1940s and 1950s, made the phenomenal self central to his theory of personality and form of psychotherapy. For him the self, the *I* or *me* as experienced by the person, was the key structural concept. A related concept was that of the ideal self, the self-concept that the individual would most like to possess. Psychopathology was defined, in part, in terms of discrepancies between the self and ideal self, with therapy operating to reduce such a discrepancy. Following Lecky (1945), Rogers emphasized efforts to maintain consistency among self-perceptions. That is, according to this view, individuals strive to behave and view their behavior in ways that are consistent with their self-image. Eventually this led Rogers to an emphasis on the importance of consistency, or congruence, between the self and experience. In this case psychopathology was viewed as based on the individual's efforts to deny experiences that were not consistent or congruent with the self.

Speaking personally, I began my work with the settled notion that the "self" was a vague, ambiguous, scientifically meaningless term. . . . Consequently I was slow in recognizing that when clients were given the opportunity to express their problems and their attitudes in their own terms, without any guidance or interpretation, they tended to talk in terms of the self.

Rogers, 1959, p. 473

Disturbances in the way the self is experienced are well-known to clinicians working with patients. For example, the noted psychiatrist R. D. Laing in his early work *The Divided Self* (1960) described how schizophrenics and schizoid personalities experience themselves as automatons, machinery, robots, and animals. In many cases of severe psychopathology there is a disturbance in the body image, confusion concerning the boundary of the body, and in some cases a complete loss of a sense of self as an entity. I can recall a patient who during periods of stress would feel herself becoming removed from her body. Thus, for example, during sexual intercourse she would feel herself becoming isolated from her body as if she were observing her "self" have intercourse rather than herself having intercourse. Other individuals experience themselves as unreal, dead, blobs that can be swallowed up by other people, and so on among the variety of possible perceptions of self and body. Whereas some obese patients may experience themselves as mouths that can engulf everything, other patients (e.g., those with anorexia nervosa) may avoid eating to the point of becoming emaciated, always insisting that they are too fat and weigh too much. At various times, and with various patients, I have heard people refer to themselves as bad, weak, fragmented, and empty. One patient, upon feeling abandoned by her partner, reported: "I feel as if I am nothing, as if I don't exist."

Given the clinical significance of the phenomenal self, it is perhaps surprising that for a considerable period of time little empirical attention was given to affective and motivational aspects of the self relative to cognitive variables. In part this was because of earlier difficulties in the assessment of concepts such as self-esteem and in part this was due to the general neglect of affect and motivation during the early part of the cognitive revolution. Over the past two decades, however, there has been increased attention to affective and motivational variables in terms of self-enhancing biases and efforts to maintain self-esteem (Baumeister, 1998, 1999; Greenwald, 1980; Kunda, 1990; Tesser, 1988). Thus, there is evidence that people will use a wide variety of defensive maneuvers to protect their self-esteem and enhance their self-image. In addition, there is evidence that people are motivated to move toward some *possible selves* (Markus & Nurius, 1986), such as the ideal self, and away from other possible selves, such as the *undesired self* (Ogilvie, 1987). According to Higgins (1987, 1997, 2000), people are motivated to bring the self into line with *self-guides* such as the *ideal self* (i.e., one's hopes, wishes, desires) and the *ought self* (i.e., one's duties, responsibilities, obligations). Failure to do so has important affective consequences, depression in the case of self-ideal self discrepancies and anxiety in the case of self-ought self discrepancies.

A great deal of the research in social psychology relies on the assumption that people are motivated to protect and enhance their self-esteem.

Baumeister, 1998, p. 695

The good, the correct, the responsible, the consistent and the successful aspects of one's activities are much more likely to be recalled than the bad, the incorrect, the irresponsible, the inconsistent, or the unsuccessful.

Markus, & Sentis, 1982, p. 49

The Cognitive-Affective Crossfire. There is evidence for people being motivated to maintain a consistent self-concept, what Swann (1997) calls a motive for self-verification. That is, people will actively solicit self-confirming evidence from others and present themselves in ways that will elicit such evidence, even if the self is viewed negatively and such self-confirming evidence also is negative. In the words of the comedian Groucho Marx: "I'd never join a club that would have me as a member." According to Swann, self-confirmation affords a degree of predictability and control that is not possible when events, such as feedback from others, violate our self-schemas. But, as previously noted, there also is evidence that people seek self-enhancement. That is, people seek to view themselves positively and to receive information that will bolster their self-esteem. The former motive, self-verification, can be viewed as a cognitive motive, whereas the latter motive, self-enhancement, can be viewed as an affective motive.

What happens, then, when the two motives conflict? When push comes to shove, do we prefer accurate feedback or positive feedback, the disagreeable truth or what fits our fancy, to be known for who we are or to be adored for who we would like to be? In other words, what happens when our cognitive need for consistency or self-verification conflicts with our affective need for self-enhancement—the cognitive-affective crossfire? The answer to this question is not yet at hand and there may be individual differences or circumstances that determine preferences. For example, in relation to the latter, there is evidence that self-enhancement is more important during the early stages of a relationship but self-verification becomes increasingly important as the relationship becomes more intimate (Swann, De la Ronde, &

Hixon, 1994). Although not researched, one might speculate that narcissistic individuals might prefer self-enhancement to self-verification whereas intimacy-seeking individuals might show the reverse preference. In any case, to return to the theme of this section, it is clear that the self is not just a cognitive construction but has important affective and motivational consequences as well.

The Relationship of the Self to Behavior: The Presentation of Self in Everyday Life

We do not merely represent ourselves cognitively and experience ourselves affectively, but we also present ourselves behaviorally to others. The relationship between the representation of self and the presentation of self, between cognitive constructions and behavioral performances, is complex. Each has some influence on the other, though the two are by no means identical. A self-concept tends to lead one to behave in ways that are in accord with the concept. To behave consistently otherwise is to create dissonance or conflict. In other words, having a picture of ourselves as honest, we can occasionally cheat or lie, either by accepting that a trait need not apply to every instance to be true or by attributing the behavior to some unusual situational circumstances. However, if we routinely cheat or lie, there is pressure either to change our self-concept or to change our behavior. We all recognize that we may behave in certain ways to create an impression in others as to what we are like. Such impression-managing behaviors, however, would appear to have some influence on our own self-concept. It would be hard to behave in a particular way much of the time without seeing oneself in that way, unless one is prepared to take the cynical attitude that all the world is a stage and how we act need not relate to who we are.

In considering overt behavioral aspects of the self we are immediately drawn to the sociologist Goffman's (1959, 1971) discussion of the presentation of self in everyday life. Goffman uses the metaphor of the theatrical performance to consider our behavior in social interaction with others. According to this metaphor, we present ourselves behaviorally to others in an attempt to guide and control the impressions they form of us. We are, in other words, like actors presenting a character to an audience. Goffman suggests that while all the world is not a stage, "the crucial ways in which it isn't are not easy to specify" (1959, p. 72). When we believe in the performance of actors, we say they are sincere and expressing their real selves. When we don't believe in the performance of actors, we say they are phony. People who never believe in the acts of others or in their own acts are cynics. Cynics toy with the world of presentations of self, a world that the rest of us take seriously.

All the world is not, of course, a stage, but the crucial ways in which it isn't are not easy to specify.

Goffman, 1959, P. 72

> *It is proposed that a wide range of social behavior is de-*
> *termined or influenced by self-presentational concerns.*
>
> *Baumeister, 1982, p. 3*

Goffman is very insightful in calling attention to the world of presentation of self and in detailing how we manage the impressions others will have of us. The clothes we wear, our speech, and our body gestures all contribute to impression management. Except for psychoanalysis, where the rule is to say whatever comes to mind, we select what we tell others about ourselves to present a certain image. Not only do we behave selectively, but we try to elicit behaviors in others that will support and confirm the image we are attempting to create. Berne's popular book *Games People Play* (1964) can be understood in part as an elaboration of the ways in which we get others to collude with us to sustain certain impressions. Typically we emphasize our positive characteristics and withhold negative feelings from public view so as to acquire the liking and acceptance of others (Jones, Gergen, & Davis, 1962). However, at times we may also present ourselves less favorably or be ingratiating to gain such acceptance by others (Jones, Gergen, & Jones, 1963).

Efforts toward strategic self-presentation need not be false and can be viewed as matters of tone rather than deceit. They are not always present, being less so when one is very involved in a task, when one is expressing pure emotion, or when one is concerned with the authenticity of one's actions. However, generally they are present and are motivated by a desire to maximize the ability to affect favorable outcomes in social exchange (Jones & Pittman, 1982). The desired outcome may be to be liked, to be seen as dangerous and feared, to be seen as competent and respected, or to be seen as helpless and to be nurtured. In any case, the goal of strategic self-presentation is to have the power to influence and control the social environment.

Goffman's conclusion from his analysis of the art of impression management is that the self is a performed character: "The general notion that we make a presentation of ourselves to others is hardly novel; what ought to be stressed in conclusion is that the very structure of the self can be seen in terms of how we arrange for such performances in our Anglo-American society" (Goffman, 1959, p. 252). Undoubtedly there is much to what Goffman says, but are we ready to conclude that the self consists of the impressions we create in others and the means we use to create such impressions? Is the world but a stage or are there crucial ways in which it is different?

There are at least three critical ways in which the world is not a stage. First, whereas actors control their behavior, this is not always possible when we are not actors. Sometimes we are able to perform in accordance with some image we are attempting to present to others, but often some slight deviation in performance gives the act away. Second, whereas on the stage there are not real consequences for the actor's behavior, in life there are such consequences. In particular, there are negative consequences or sanctions for being found out to be only an actor or an impostor. Finally, whereas the actor on the stage can explain the discrepancy between his construction of his self and his behavior on the stage, this is generally hard to do in real life. It is true that some people try to treat life as a stage. Thus, such people may, in Laing's words, exhibit themselves but never expose themselves. One can hide behind acting and always fall back on statements such as, "I was only pretending," or "Don't take things too seriously." However, in real life such performances generally put a strain on the integrity of one's internal functioning and create a distance from others that often leads to a serious sense of loneliness. Indeed, some psychologists consider self-disclosure to be indicative of healthy personality functioning and a discrepancy between the public and private selves to be indicative of pathology (Derlega & Chaikin, 1975; Jourard, 1971). People not only try to manage impressions but they try to be self-disclosing, and they alter their views of themselves according to observations of their own behavior (Locksley & Lenauer, 1981). We can present an act to others for just so long before we begin to believe the act ourselves.

Does this mean that Goffman is wrong in his emphasis on the self as overt behavior and impression management? It is not so much that Goffman is wrong but rather that his presentation is limited. Goffman is concerned with normative, role-related behavior. He is concerned with the rituals we perform to maintain some order in our social interaction. In a way, this is analogous to the function of rituals in the behavior of members of other species. However, there are important differences between self and role or between ritual and personality (Thomas, 1968). Whereas roles depend on cues in the environment concerning appropriate behavior, self and personality are also influenced by internal controlling variables. Whereas role consists of what is common or shared, self and personality also include what is particular and perhaps unique. Whereas roles relate to overt behavior, the self and personality include covert functioning such as feelings, fantasies, and wishes. Whereas role behavior is situationally determined and often transitory, self and personality tend to persist and to show some coherence over a range of situations.

Thus, while the self would appear to have behavioral significance, it seems questionable to equate the self with overt behavior. As with so many phenomena expressive of personality, cognitive, affective, and behavioral aspects of the self appear to have a reciprocal relationship with one another. The cognitive view we hold of ourselves leads us to accept information that is consistent with this view and to reject inconsistent information. The cognitive representation of the self influences how we behave. Similarly, the affective aspect of the self or the way we feel about ourselves influences our behavior. At the same time, how we behave influences the cognitive representation and appraisal of the self. Getting people to change their behaviors can lead to a change in their self-concepts. Experiences of success and accomplishment do affect the way we view and feel about ourselves (Wylie, 1968). Experiences of success and competence do increase our sense of self-efficacy (Bandura, 1997, 1999). Although at times such changes are dependent on rewards and social confirmation from others, often they are a direct result of observed changes in our own behavior. We can consider cognitive, affective, and behavioral aspects of the self independently, but they appear to be parts of an interlocking system.

The Psychoanalytic Self and the Social Cognitive Self: Can We Put Our Selves Together?

As noted, during the 1970s there was a surge of interest in the concept of the self. What is interesting in this regard is that it occurred in diverse literatures—psychological, psychoanalytic, and the popular media. It was a period described as the age of narcissism or preoccupation with the self. Particularly noteworthy was the independent development of the psychoanalytic and social cognitive literatures. In 1992 Westen, a scholar of both the psychoanalytic and social cognitive literatures, examined the two views and asked: Can we put our selves together? Westen was aware of the fact that the two literatures had arisen out of different observations, the one clinical and the other experimental. In terms of the former, psychoanalytic object relations theory developed out of clinical work with patients with severe personality disorders. Such patients had severe disturbances of self and many conflicting representations of other people and their relationships with them. In contrast, the social cognitive literature, as discussed above, grew out of experimental work with normal college students. Could the insights gained from the two differing approaches be joined to make something greater than either? Was it possible to integrate the psychoanalytic self and the social cognitive self in a way that did justice to both and furthered advances in the field?

Westen began by describing key elements of the psychoanalytic object relations view of the self. First, the person is seen as having many self-representations, some of which can be contradictory. Thus, for example, the person can have a self-representation as good and one as bad, one as moral and one as immoral, one as successful and one as a failure. Such contradictory self-representations can explain conflict within the self and sudden mood swings within the same individual. Second, self-representations are seen as affectively laden. That is, self-representations are not just cognitive constructions but are associated with affects such as joy, anger, love, hate, shame, guilt, and pride. Further, self-representations may be linked by their connecting affects rather than by rational categorizations. In other words, a family of selves may be defined by similarity of affects rather than by similarity of situations or similarity of meanings. Third, self-representations are assumed to have both conscious and unconscious components. Particularly important from the psychoanalytic standpoint are the unconscious self-representations, especially those that are maintained for defensive purposes such as to protect self-esteem. For example, the person may have an unconscious self-representation as invulnerable so as to protect the self from threats of injury. Fourth, self-representations are assumed to be associated with wishes and fears, and thereby to have motivational properties. That is, we strive to be like self-representations that are associated with positive affect (i.e., wishes) and to avoid being like those associated with negative affect (i.e., fears). Finally, such self-representations are assumed to have developed during interactions with important people, particularly during the earlier stages of development.

And what of the social cognitive view of the self? We have already considered some of the relevant literature and from this we know that the social cognitive view of the self includes cognitive, affective, and motivational properties. Beyond this, social cognitive psychologists increasingly have emphasized the importance of unconscious cognitive structures and processes, as will be considered in the next chapter. Thus, seemingly this is not a point of controversy between the two. Finally, social cognitive psychologists certainly have an interest in developmental aspects of the self, including the role of interactions with important figures in the social world of the developing child.

Given these points of agreement, it would seem that an integration of the two would be feasible and desirable. Such an integration of the two would capitalize on the clinical insights of the psychoanalysts and the experimental insights of the social cognitivists. Hopefully such an integration would provide for avoiding the pitfalls of the object relations theorists who do not put their ideas to the experimental test and the pitfalls of the social cognitive theorists who do not study the complexity of self-representations observed in in-depth studies of the individual. Since the weaknesses of one appear to be the strengths of the other, why not an integration?

Westen's effort at integration was considered by representatives of each point of view. What was their conclusion as to whether the two selves could be put together to form a unified self? The answer was not very encouraging. Although members of each group recognized the contributions of the other, they were at least equally impressed with the other's limitations and their own unique contributions. Thus, the drama and power of the self observed in the clinical context was sufficiently impressive to the psychoanalysts to make them reluctant to move toward the approach emphasized by the social cognitivists. And, members of the latter group were sufficiently impressed with the conceptual and methodological advances being made that they were reluctant to give up their methodological rigor for the drama of the self observed by clinicians.

Are we, then, one happy family, with cognitive and psychoanalytic psychologists marching proudly together under the banner of the self?. . . As the situation currently stands, psychoanalytic theories have as little explanatory power in interpreting experimental findings as most cognitive theories do in interpreting complex clinical events. . .psychoanalysis and social cognition may well be star-crossed lovers.

Westen, 1992, pp. 4, 74

What are other stumbling blocks to integration, an idea that would appear to have so much merit? At one time a major stumbling block was the lack of contact between members of the two groups. But, there now exist individuals in each "camp" who are familiar with and respectful of the work of members of the other camp. Rather, the problem would appear to be one of fundamental conceptualization and approach to research. Three central issues relate to conceptualization: (1) the importance of unconscious self-representations; (2) the importance of early experiences in the formation of self-representations; and (3) the affective and motivational power of these self-representations, particularly in terms of their dynamic interplay. Psychoanalysts emphasize the importance of unconscious self-representations, the importance of early experiences in their formation and ongoing functioning, and the dynamic interplay among self-representations. Conflict among self-representations, for example, is a matter of major importance and interest. Social cognitivists are more interested in conscious self-schema, or nonconscious self-schema controlled by automatic cognitive processes, in current self-representations or current selves associated with memories of the past, and with the ability of individuals to differentiate among members of the family of selves. Interfacing with these differences are the differences in approaches to research, the one emphasizing clinical work and the other experimental work. Thus, although the idea of putting the various selves together would appear to have merit, and although we may be coming closer to the point at which a true integration is possible, at this time the two approaches remain separate and distinct, at best second cousins in the family of selves.

Evolutionary and Cultural Aspects of the Self

In the previous chapter we considered evolutionary and cultural explanations relevant to personality. For the most part these explanations were pitted against one another. That is, in the previous chapter evolutionary and cultural explanations were viewed as conflicting with one another. However, this need not always be the case. It is possible for evolutionary and cultural views to be in harmony with one another. Such a possibility is illustrated in relation to the self.

The Symbolic Self in Evolutionary Context

According to standard evolutionary theory, characteristics that emerged over time did so because of their adaptive value in response to specific environmental challenges. Is there evidence that the self is part of our human evolutionary history and, if so, what was the adaptive value of such a development?

> *Our central thesis is that the symbolic self is an adaptation. That is, we argue that the symbolic self is a broad-based capacity that was selected and distributed in the human population because of its high adaptive significance.*
>
> *Sedikides and Skowronski, 1997, p. 81*

An answer to these questions was the challenge undertaken by Sedikides and Skowronski (1997) in their paper on the evolution of what they call the symbolic self, basically what has been considered in this chapter as the self-concept. Sedikides and Skowronski suggest that there are various levels of development of the self and these fit evolutionary history. First, it is suggested that all species have the capacity to distinguish "crudely" between the organism (the self) and the environment. That is, all species have the ability to distinguish between the organism itself and the external environment. However, this does not involve the ability to reflect back upon the self, to have self-consciousness. This kind of self-awareness or self-consciousness presumably is limited to the great apes (e.g., chimpanzees, orangutans, humans).

One of the tests that has been used for such self-awareness is the mirror self-recognition test. Members of species lower than the great apes do not recognize themselves in a mirror. For example, when a mirror is placed in front of male Siamese fighting fish, in the presence of a female, they respond as if the image in the mirror is a competitor. I can remember doing this with the fish in my fish tank and enjoying how the male fish enlarged its body and became extremely colorful. Dogs and cats typically ignore their images in a mirror. Thus, ignoring the image in the mirror or treating it as another member of the species is typical of lower species. In contrast, with experience chimps will use the mirror to groom themselves (self-directed behavior) and, of course, we are well familiar with the extent to which such behavior is characteristic of humans. Developmental research with humans suggests that such mirror self-recognition behavior occurs at about the age of one year to age one-and-a-half (Lewis & Brooks-Gunn, 1979). This also is the age at which various self-conscious emotions as shame and pride appear to develop (Lewis, 1990).

Other behaviors associated with self-awareness appear to be characteristic of chimpanzees, orangutans, and humans (e.g., attribution of knowledge states to others, concealment, deception). On the other hand, symbolic self-awareness, the ability to form abstract representations of the self (i.e., the self-concept), to communicate these representations to others, and to deceive oneself appear to be uniquely human.

What were the challenges faced by humans during our ancestral heritage and how did the development of self-awareness provide adaptive value? According to Sedikides and Skowronski, first there was the movement from the forest to the savanna and the transformation to hunters. As part of this shift in ecological environment, there was the shift to the formation of groups for hunting and for protection from predators. The development of the brain provided for greater skill in food procurement and for greater social complexity. For example, in terms of the former, greater development of cognitive skills provided for greater acquisition of food supplies over time and space. Also, limitations in size and speed, affecting hunting ability, could be compensated for by the development of weapons. The development of self-awareness, then, was part of the development of these cognitive capacities that provided adaptive value in terms of food acquisition. Beyond this, as noted, the formation of stable social groups provided for hunting efficiency and protection from predators. In terms of the latter, for example, groups could divide up tasks such as warnings of predators and fighting defense against predators. The development of the symbolic self, including the development of language as a means of communication and abstract thinking, provided for sensitivity to the appraisals of others in the group (i.e., groups norms and regulations) and for sensitivity to the needs of others in a way that enabled cooperative behavior. The development of symbolic activities, such as in the formation of the self-concept, was part of this cognitive development that was adaptive in terms of the problems of group living.

In sum, the development of cognitive capacities was adaptive in terms of the tasks of food acquisition and protection from predators. The development of self-awareness was part of this cognitive development, particularly in terms of the development of language capacities. In addition, the development of self-awareness provided adaptive value in group living in terms of sensitivity to group norms and the needs of others.

This evolutionary account of self-awareness provides for an interpretation of the relation of the self to culture. According to Sedikides and Skowronski, self-awareness and the concept of self should be universal, part of our evolutionary heritage. On the other hand, specific aspects of the self could be expected to vary among members of different cultures and to reflect the experiences unique to each individual. Which leads us to the question considered by cultural psychologists: Is the concept of the self cross-cultural?

Cultural Aspects of the Self

People in different cultures have strikingly different construals of the self. . . . These construals can influence, and in many cases determine, the very nature of individual experience, including cognition, emotion, and motivation.

Markus & Kitayama, 1991, p. 224

Is the concept of the self universal? Recall discussion in the previous chapter of the fundamental attribution error. After years of research it was discovered that people in some cultures do not make what was called the fundamental attribution error and, in fact, it is questionable whether people in some cultures make these causal attributions at all. Could the same be true of research on the self? That is, is it possible that members of different cultures have different conceptions of the self and different self-related processes? Is it possible that some of the cognitive, affective, and motivational processes associated with the self that were described earlier in this chapter are culture-bound? Beyond this, is it even possible that members of some cultures have no concept of the self at all? According to the view of Sedikides and Skorownski just considered, all living organisms distinguish between the self and the environment, all members of the great apes show self-consciousness, and all humans show self-awareness in terms of a symbolic self or self-concept. If the concept of the self is not universal, does this have implications for their view of the evolution of the concept of the self? Of greater significance, what would be the implications for a theory of personality if the concept of the self were not found to be universal?

Cultural anthropologists have long been interested in how members of different cultures construe the self and the concept of the person. One of the leading figures in this regard, Clifford Geertz (1974), takes the view that concepts of the self and person cannot be understood outside of their cultural context. Thus, he suggests that the Western conception of the person as a bounded, unique, distinctive unit separate from others is, "however incorrigible it may seem to us, a rather peculiar idea within the context of the world's cultures" (1974, p. 29). Consider, for example, his observation that in Java the inner world of emotion and outer world of behavior are considered to be separate realms of the self. Or, consider his observation that in Bali there is a dramaturgical self, expressed in the effort to always behave in a stylized ways that fit a prescribed role or type rather than behaving in ways that express individuality: "It is dramatis personae, not actors, that endure; indeed, it is dramatis personae, not actors, that in the proper sense really exist. Physically men come and go, mere incidents in a happenstance history, of no genuine importance even to themselves. But the masks they wear, the stage they occupy, the parts they play, and most important, the spectacle they mount remain and comprise not the façade but the substance of things, not least the self" (p. 32). In line with this, Balinese are given birth-order names but there are only four of these—firstborn, secondborn, thirdborn, and fourthborn. And what of the fifth child? The birth order here is recycled so that the fifth child becomes the firstborn, the sixth the secondborn, and so on. In other words, birth-order naming may tell you nothing about the order of birth as we understand it and does not identify individuals as individuals—nor, Geertz suggests, is it intended to.

In 1991 Markus and Kitayama published an important paper on culture and the self, exploring the implications of differing cultural views of the self for cognition, emotion, and motivation. They began by noting that despite anthropological evidence that people of different cultures hold divergent views of the self, most of what psychologists believe to be true is based on the Western view of the individual as independent and self-contained. In this paper they contrasted such an *independent* view of the self with an *interdependent* view of the self. Found in Japan and other Asian cultures, the interdependent view of the self emphasizes belongingness to a group and social relationships. It is the contrast between what Triandis (1989, 1995) calls the *individualist self* as autonomous and independent with personal goals and personal attributes, as opposed to the *collectivist self* as connected to groups and influenced by group goals, roles, and group norms. It is, in simplified terms, the difference between individuality and conformity, between the American view that "the squeaky wheel gets the grease" and the Japanese view that "the nail that stands out gets pounded down" (Markus & Kitayama, 1991, p. 224).

What are the cognitive, emotional, and motivational implications of such differences in the self? According to Markus & Kitayama, those with an independent self would be expected to attend to and emphasize information that makes them distinctive, whereas those with an interdependent self would be expected to attend to and emphasize information that represents them as part of a group. Indeed, there is evidence that whereas American subjects typically emphasize dissimilarities between themselves and others, Asian subjects typically emphasize their similarities to others. In addition, whereas those with an independent self tend to view themselves in terms of traits that are context-independent, those with an interdependent self tend to view themselves in terms of roles played and behavior in specific contexts in relation to others (Cousins, 1989; Kanagawa, Cross, & Markus, 2001; Shweder & Bourne, 1984). Whereas Western subjects describe themselves in terms of the extremes of ratings, Asian subjects describe themselves in terms of mid-points (Chen, Lee, & Stevenson, 1995).

Although a rapidly expanding volume of studies suggest that some aspects of cognitive functioning are relatively hard-wired, many features of the way people perceive, categorize, or assign causality are probably not basic processes. . . . Rather, these processes are to a large extent personal, reflecting the nature of the self that anchors them.

Markus & Kitayama, 1991, p. 246

Turning to the consequences for emotion, Markus and Kitayama suggest that individuals with an independent self tend to experience what they call *ego-focused emotions* (e.g., anger, frustration, pride) whereas those with an interdependent self tend to experience what they call *other-focused emotions* (e.g., sympathy, feelings of interpersonal communion, shame). They cite evidence that American subjects tend to experience ego-focused emotions longer and with greater intensity than do Japanese subjects. Whereas the former focus on the expression of their inner feelings, seeking to express themselves, the latter focus on the public aspect of their emotional expression, which may or may not be related directly to their inner feelings. Emotions such as pride, which are associated with individualism, are much more associated with Western subjects than Asian subjects. Whereas self-esteem in the Western culture is associated with individual abilities and accomplishments, in the Asian culture self-esteem is associated with the ability to maintain harmony in the social context and with group accomplishments. Indeed, in a footnote to their summary of differences between independent and interdependent construals of the self, Markus and Kitayama suggest that "esteeming the self may be primarily a Western phenomenon, and the concept of self-esteem should perhaps be replaced by self-satisfaction, or by a term that reflects the realization that one is fulfilling the culturally mandated task" (1991, p. 230). In addition to differences in the expression of common emotions, there are emotions specific to cultures that are not readily translated into other cultures, either because there are no comparable words or because the emotion is so embedded in the particular cultural context that its meaning is lost in the translation.

Theories of self-esteem and other self-related processes that are based on the assumption of a relatively fixed and stable self-concept may not properly capture the malleable and evolving nature of the Japanese self.

Kanagawa, Cross, & Markus, 2001, p. 102

Turning to consequences for motivation, two differences are particularly note-worthy. First, as noted earlier in this chapter, there is strong evidence of a self-enhancement motive. However, Asian (interdependent) subjects appear to be much more oriented toward self-effacement, self-criticism, and self-improvement than they are toward self-enhancement. For example, Chinese subjects tend to rate themselves lower relative to peers than do American subjects (Yik, Bond, & Paulhus, 1998). Japanese students tend to evaluate their family members and their university less positively than do Canadian subjects: "Cultural differences in enhancement biases are robust, generalizing to individuals' evaluations of their groups" (Heine & Leh-man, 1997, p. 1268). The motive for positive self-regard is a major part of the per-sonality theory of Carl Rogers and also is intrinsic to the emphasis on self-enhancement biases and positive illusions about the self. Yet, these and other data suggest that such a motive may not be universal (Heine, et. al., 1999). In addition to this difference in self-enhancement motivation, there is some question about whether the conditions that foster intrinsic motivation are the same across cultures. Accord-ing to some personality psychologists (Ryan & Deci, 2000), people have a need to act in autonomous, self-determined ways. Situations that provide for such freedom of choice are assumed to foster intrinsic motivation, whereas situations that empha-size external control are assumed to foster extrinsic motivation. Yet, a study compar-ing Anglo-American children and Asian-American children casts some doubt on the universality of this proposition (Iyengar & Lepper, 1999). In this research the two groups of children were compared in terms of their relative intrinsic motivation when choices were made for them as opposed to when they made their own choices. Intrinsic motivation was determined by the children's reports of interest in the task and the amount of time they spent on the task during a free-play period. Whereas the Anglo-American children showed less intrinsic motivation when the choices were made for them, the Asian-American children showed the greatest intrinsic motiva-tion when the choices were made for them by trusted authority figures or peers. In sum, once more there is evidence of important cultural differences in relation to self-related processes.

The suggestion, then, is that tendencies to possess, en-hance, and maintain positive self-views may not be basic to humankind, but may depend, in large part, on significant aspects of contemporary North American culture.

Heine, et. al., 1999, p. 766

Perhaps the greatest contribution of the present findings is the challenge they provide to some of our most fundamen-tal assumptions regarding human motivation, and perhaps the most general lesson they teach is the recognition of the

> *many ways in which our theories and paradigms are a re-*
> *flection of the culture in which they were developed.*
>
> *Iyengar & Lepper, 1999, p. 364*

Before concluding discussion of cross-cultural aspects of the self, it is worth-while to consider one point and one question. First, although we have considered individuals as independent and interdependent, individualist and collectivist, it is important to recognize that both self-construals exist in most individuals. In the words of Singelis (1994), most individuals contain two selves, an independent self and an interdependent self. Thus, many of these contrasts may be of degree rather than of a more fundamental qualitative nature. This point relates to the question that may be asked: How deep and fundamental are the differences observed? Do they get to differences in degree of emphasis in relation to different self-concepts and to dif-ferent expressions of the same cognitions, emotions, and motives, or are the differ-ences more fundamental?

For example, do Asians lack a self-enhancement motive or is it expressed dif-ferently than by Western subjects? A study by Kitayama and Karasawa (1997) sug-gests that the latter might be the case. Thus, in this research Japanese subjects were found to prefer letters and numbers associated with their names and birthdays. The authors suggested that the Japanese may have a deep-seated need for positive self-regard but mask this need when responding to self-referential questions and public displays. Views on the matter differ, with some suggesting that the evidence for fun-damental differences is equivocal (Church, 2000; Kashima & Yamaguchi, 1999) and others suggesting that the evidence is more substantial (Kitayama & Markus, 1999; Markus, Kitayama, & Heiman, 1996). It is a question raised by Markus and Kita-yama in their groundbreaking 1991 paper: "A persistent issue is how deep or perva-sive are these cultural differences? Are the observed differences primarily a reflec-tion of differences in styles of behavioral expression, or do they also reflect differ-ences in the phenomenology accompanying the behavior?" (p. 247). Are the differ-ences primarily of content, situational context, and behavioral expression, or do they relate to more fundamental differences in structure and process? In its most basic form, is the concept of the self universal or does it vary cross-culturally? Ten years later, we have learned a great deal but are still without a definitive answer to this important question.

Conclusion

In this chapter we have been concerned with the question: Is the concept of the self useful and necessary? To consider this question, we have examined the ways in which the concept of the self has been used in personality theory and research—the self-concept as a cognitive representation of the person, affective and motivational implications of the self, and the presentation of self in everyday life as a behavioral phenomenon. In addition, we have been concerned with two issues in the literature:

Can we put the psychoanalytic and social cognitive selves together? Can we understand the self in both evolutionary and cross-cultural contexts? The material presented, which only begins to touch on the actual amount of work done in relation to the self-concept, suggests that we have here an important, perhaps critical, psychological concept.

However, many conceptual and methodological problems remain in relation to the concept of the self. There is no one theory of the self but many self theories, no one measure of the concept but many measures, and relationships among cognitive, affective, and behavioral aspects of the self remain to be determined. There is the question of whether the concept of a single self is too broad and general. Are there many self-concepts, many sources of self-esteem, a variety of presentations of self? If we have many selves, how are these organized in relation to one another? Are some aspects of the self more stable than others and what are the implications of change in one aspect of the self for other aspects of the self?

In addition, there is the question of how to conceptualize the varying aspects of the self that are more or less available to conscious awareness. At one level we have a representation or representations of the self that are in full awareness and can be articulated without great difficulty. At another level we have aspects of the self that we are not always in touch with or that we do not reveal publicly except in very special circumstances. To one extent or another we all have our own *Secret Life of Walter Mitty,* a world of fantasies and feelings that rarely is made known to others. At another level, we have aspects of the self of which we are completely unaware. Crippling images of the self often emerge in the process of psychotherapy, as do painful feelings about the self. Ways of behaving or presenting ourselves may come to our attention as a complete surprise. How are we to conceptualize these varyng self-representations?

Finally, there is the question of the universality of the concept of the self and self-relevant processes. We know that the concept of the self varies enormously cross-culturally. Are the differences so great as to question the universality of the concept? We know that there is cultural variation in cognitive, affective, and motivational aspects of the self. Are the differences only of degree or expression or are they of a more fundamental nature? We know that the content of the self shows enormous diversity. Is content of such importance that universal laws of functioning are of limited explanatory value? Could it be, as many anthropologists and psychologists suggest, that culture and personality are so intertwined that it is impossible to speak of the person independent of culture or of culture independent of the person?

In sum, we are left with a dilemma that all too frequently is present in the study of personality. The concept of the self appears to be useful and necessary. It relates to major aspects of human experience and appears to hold promise for explaining phenomena that otherwise make no sense at all. Yet, an affirmative answer to the question concerning its utility is largely based on subjective considerations rather than on established theory or cumulative research findings. Thus, the utility and necessity of the concept of the self remains an issue in the field today.

Summary

We began this chapter by asking whether the concept of the self is useful and necessary. We also noted that intuitively, in terms of our daily existence, phenomena associated with the self seem of critical importance. Yet, it has been hard to solve the conceptual and methodological problems associated with serious scientific inquiry into this important realm of experience. Thus it is that interest in the concept of the self historically rises and declines.

Along with the general increase in interest in cognition has been an interest in how individuals come to construe or represent themselves, and in the self as a component of the individual's implicit theory of personality. The individual gathers information from internal and external sources, which leads to a concept of the self or, as some psychologists have suggested, many concepts of the self depending on the situation one is in. Research has focused on the self as a cognitive structure or schema that organizes and guides self-related information. There is considerable evidence that such cognitive structures influence all aspects of information processing—attention, organization, memory, and recall. There also is evidence that individuals resist information that is discrepant with existing schema, that they elicit schema-relevant information from others and use self-relevant schema in the perception of others. In terms of individuals, a critical difference appears to be in the extent to which situational or internal cues are used to monitor behavior. High self-monitoring individuals, described as having a pragmatic self, are attuned to situational cues whereas low self-monitoring individuals, described as having a principled self, are attuned to internal cues. A variety of cognitive and behavioral differences are associated with this general difference in view concerning the self. Since all individuals vary somewhat in their self from situation to situation, we can ask whether the self is best considered as a unitary concept or it is best to consider many selves organized in terms of a family of selves.

The earliest sense of self probably comes from the body as something that uniquely feels and is felt and something that uniquely is under the control of the person. The body is experienced as a source of pleasure or pain, as something diffuse or something with definite boundaries, as something vulnerable or as something relatively invulnerable. In severe conditions of psychopathology there is a disturbed sense of self and often a disturbed sense of body boundaries. In some of these cases people experience a terrifying sense of depersonalization and dissolution of the body, feeling as if they are being merged into others around them. Another aspect of psychopathology, including mild forms of disturbance, is negative feelings about the self or low self-esteem. Almost all patients in psychotherapy talk about negative feelings about themselves and the problem of low self-esteem.

The self has motivational properties, undoubtedly associated with its cognitive and affective properties. Thus, there is evidence of a need for consistency or self-verification so as to make the world, and our functioning in it, predictable. In addition, there is evidence of a need for self-enhancement so as to protect our self-esteem and make ourselves feel good. The question of the cognitive-affective crossfire asks about what happens when these two motives conflict, when the cognitive need for consistency conflicts with the affective need for self-enhancement. The answer to this question remains open, with differences likely among individuals and relationships. What is clear, however, is that both motives may have significant implications for behavior.

The self as presented in everyday life has a complex relationship with the self as experience and the self as representation. Some theorists, such as Goffman, consider the self to be a performed character. The world is a stage, and in everyday life we act out roles and manage the impressions of others while presenting ourselves. While the self as presented to others appears to be an important area of inquiry, it can be seriously questioned whether the concept of the self is limited to such behavior. Rather it appears that the self also involves affective and cognitive components, each of which may be associated with but not coincident with overt behavior. In other words, one can consider affective, cognitive, and behavioral aspects of the self. Each can be studied independently with an understanding that there is some relationship to the other aspects of personality functioning. It would also appear possible to focus on relationships among these aspects of self-functioning, though this is rarely done in personality research.

We have considered two questions among the many that can be raised in relation to the concept of the self. First, there is the question of whether the psychoanalytic and social cognitive selves can be put together. Although there is evidence of mutual interest, significant differences remain. In the main, these revolve around differences in emphasis on unconscious, affective, and motivational aspects of the self. In addition, there is a fundamental difference in the nature of the data obtained in the clinical setting and that obtained in the laboratory. Second, there is the question of whether the concept of the self is universal. Recent research, particularly over the past decade, points to significant differences in how the self is construed among members of various cultures. In particular there has been an emphasis on differences associated with an independent self as opposed to an interdependent self, the former associated with Western society and the latter with many Asian societies. Contrasts between these two selves involve matters of cognition, affect, and motivation. That is, there are differences in how the self is defined, how self-esteem is gained and maintained, and in the motives for self-consistency and self-enhancement. These differences may be so great as to question the universality of the concept of the self. On the other hand, there is evidence that members of both societies have independent and interdependent selves. In addition, differences in affect and motivation may be more of degree and expression than of a more substantial, qualitative nature. These are issues that remain to be further defined and resolved.

The rise and decline in interest in the concept of the self can be understood through the apparent meaningfulness of the concept and the serious conceptual and methodological problems that interfere with successful inquiry. Conceptually, there are problems of different meanings associated with the same terms, and of deciding whether the concept of self relates to conscious experiences alone or also relates to unconscious elements (e.g., elements that cannot be tapped by verbal self-report). Intuitively, the concept seems both useful and necessary. However, in the absence of further conceptual and methodological progress, such utility is a promise of the future.

CHAPTER 8

The Unconscious: What Is It? How Important?

General Theme

In this chapter we consider a topic of enormous importance to the field of personality psychology—the unconscious. Emphasis is placed on the contrast between the psychoanalytic and cognitive views of the unconscious. Four issues are considered: Is there evidence for the Freudian mechanisms of defense? Is the use of defensive processes reflective of healthy or maladaptive functioning? Is there evidence supportive of the recovery of repressed memories? Can the psychoanalytic and cognitive views of the unconscious be brought together?

> *The unconscious is the sovereign means of believing whatever one likes in psychology and of turning what might become a science into a tumbling ground for whimsies.*
>
> *James, 1890, p. 163*

> *We become obliged then to take up the position that it is both untenable and presumptuous to claim that whatever goes on in the mind must be known to consciousness.*
>
> *Freud, 1915, p. 99*

While people are not fully conscious of every aspect of their thinking, neither is their thinking largely unconscious. People generally know what they are thinking.

Bandura, 1986, p. 125

Our minds contain knowledge of which we are unaware. Our feelings can be impervious to the assertion of conscious will. Our behaviors subsume acts that are unintended, even opposed to those that are intended or consciously desired.

Banaji, 2001, p. 8

In this chapter we consider a topic that is central to personality theory and research—the unconscious. In the previous chapter we considered the concept of the self, which involved consciousness and the ability to reflect back upon the self. There it was suggested that individuals may have unconscious self-representations and that such self-representations may have important implications for psychological functioning. In this chapter we consider the broader implications of the concept of unconscious functioning. Are we, as Freud suggested, "lived" by unknown forces? How important is unconscious functioning and what are the implications of such functioning for the use of self-report measures? Is the unconscious, as asked by psychologists in 1992, smart or dumb (Loftus & Klinger, 1992)? Do people defend against unconscious thoughts, feelings, and motives? And, if so, is that good or bad for their health? Finally, what are we to make of recovered memories? Is it possible that memories can lie buried in the unconscious for years, as suggested by psychoanalysts, and then be recovered in their original form? These are among the issues we will address as we trace some of the history of the relevant theory and research.

Freud's Concept of the Unconscious

Not surprisingly, we begin with consideration of Freud's concept of the unconscious. Interest in the unconscious predates Freud (Ellenberger, 1970). However, it is Freud who made the concept central to a theory of personality and psychopathology: "Psychoanalysis aims at and achieves nothing more than the discovery of the unconscious of mental life" (1924, p. 397). Freud's concept of the unconscious influenced psychology, art, and literature for decades and it is likely that his scientific legacy will stand or fall on an evaluation of his work in this area.

Why the concept of the unconscious? According to Freud (1915), the concept of the unconscious was necessary to account for such diverse phenomena as dreams, symptoms, slips of the tongue, and irrational feelings which otherwise remained inexplicable: "It is necessary because the data of consciousness are exceedingly defective; both in healthy and in sick persons mental acts are often in process which can be explained only by presupposing other acts, of which consciousness yields no evidence" (p. 99). Freud struggled long and hard about how to conceptualize the unconscious. He ended with a tripartite formulation of the *unconscious* (i.e., that which is unavailable to consciousness), the *preconscious* (i.e., that which is not currently in consciousness but is available to consciousness), and the *conscious* (i.e., that which is currently in awareness).

The key elements of the Freudian unconscious were those that had been put there by the mechanisms of defense, in particular the central defense mechanism of repression. Could emotions and motives (instincts, drives) be part of the unconscious as well? That is, could one have unconscious emotions and motives as well as unconscious thoughts? This was an issue with which Freud struggled. Although his focus was on ideas, and he suggested that it was only ideas that could be represented in the unconscious, he suggested that it was possible to speak of unconscious emotions and motives: "Though we do speak of an unconscious or a repressed instinctual impulse, this is a looseness of phraseology which is quite harmless" (1915, p. 109). Certainly over time it has been common for psychoanalysts to speak of unconscious emotions, motives, drives, and instincts.

A few questions are central to Freud's concept of the unconscious and to a comparison of it with other views of the unconscious: What are the characteristics of unconscious functioning? How important is unconscious functioning in our daily life? How are we to determine the meaning of conscious acts that are influenced, or determined, by unconscious processes? In his essay on the unconscious, Freud (1915) devoted an entire section to consideration of "special characteristics" of the unconscious. Within the context of his energy system, he viewed the contents of the unconscious as having an energy that was pressing for discharge via entry into consciousness. A counterforce therefore was necessary to keep the contents outside of awareness, that is, in the unconscious. While in the unconscious, these contents were characterized by different qualities than contents that were part of the conscious. For example, they tended to have a wish-fulfillment quality to them, there were no logical contradictions between them (e.g., one could be in two places at the same time), they were timeless (e.g., one could be old and young at the same time, move rapidly back and forth in time), and, as in symbolism, one object could stand for another (e.g., tree for a penis): "The processes of the Unconscious are just as little related to reality. They are subject to the pleasure-principle; their fate depends only upon the degree of their strength and upon their conformity to regulation by pleasure and pain" (1915, p. 119). He described these attributes of the unconscious as characteristic of *primary process* thinking, in contrast with *secondary process* thinking characteristic of conscious functioning. The former is illogical, irrational, and governed by the pleasure principle while the latter is logical, rational, and governed by the reality principle.

How important is the unconscious in our daily functioning? In a sense, this question is answered easily—very important, fundamental. However, in another sense the answer is not readily apparent. Recall the phenomena with which Freud was concerned—dreams, symptoms, slips of the tongue, symbols, inexplicable acts. To this day, these are the phenomena with which psychoanalysts are concerned and to which the concept of the unconscious seems so relevant. It is not our answer to a simple math problem or a history question that is at issue. Although unconscious "forces" can come into play here as well, ordinarily such acts are free of unconscious influence. Such unconscious "forces" are more important in relation to pathological functioning than in relation to healthy functioning, more important in relation to our psychological functioning when we are at our worst than when we are at our best. According to Freud, they are seen in the patient who picks at his blackheads and hides from contact because he fears others will notice the deep holes in his face:

> Analysis shows that he is working out his castration complex upon his skin. . .it gave him great pleasure to squeeze them (the blackheads) out, because, as he said, something squirted out when he did so. Then he began to think that there was a deep cavity wherever he had got rid of a blackhead and he reproached himself most vehemently with having ruined his skin for ever by "constantly fiddling with his hand." Pressing out the content of the blackheads is clearly to him a substitute for onanism (masturbation). The cavity which then appears in consequence of his guilty act is the female genital, i.e., stands for the fulfillment of the threat of castration (or the phantasy representing it) called forth by the onanism. (1915, p. 132)

According to Groddeck (1923), in *The Book of the It*, in the unconscious writing can symbolize a sexual act—the pen is the male organ and the paper is the woman who receives the ink (the semen) in the quick up-and-down movements of the pen. And, according to him, the number three has the following significance for him:

> I cannot recall her (my nurse's) appearance. I know nothing more than her name, Bertha, the shining one. But I have a clear recollection of the day she went away. As a parting present she gave me a copper three-pfennig piece. A Dreier. . . . Since that day I have been pursued by the number three. Words like trinity, triangle, triple alliance, convey something disreputable to me, and not merely the words but the ideas attached to them, yes, and the whole complex of ideas built up around *them by the capricious brain of a child. For this reason, the Holy Ghost, as the Third Person of the Trinity, was already suspect to me in early childhood; trigonometry was a plague in my school days. . . . Yes, three is a sort of fatal number for me. (1923, p. 9)*

In sum, the unconscious is more important for some things than other things, for some people more than for other people, at some times more than at other times. However, according to psychoanalysts the concept of the unconscious is always of fundamental importance to understanding some phenomena (e.g., dreams, symptoms, slips of the tongue, irrational acts) and always must be understood in terms of its own qualities of psychic functioning.

Finally, there is the question of how we are to determine the meaning of these otherwise inexplicable phenomena. According to Freud, it is clinical evidence that lies at the heart of understanding unconscious processes: "In many quarters our justification is disputed for assuming the existence of an unconscious system in the mind and for employing such an assumption for purposes of scientific work. To this we can reply that our assumption of the existence of the unconscious is *necessary* and *legitimate*, and that we possess manifold *proofs* of the existence of the unconscious (1915, p. 99, italics in the original). It is through the process of psychoanalysis, in particular through the methods of dream analysis, free association, and transference analysis, that one gains insight into the workings of the unconscious. In particular, it is dreams that provide the "royal road to the unconscious" and, for many, Freud's book *The Interpretation of Dreams* (1900) represents his crowning achievement.

Freud's ideas concerning the unconscious remain controversial. For analysts, so many of the phenomena they observe remain inexplicable without an appreciation and application of these principles of unconscious functioning. For others, the unconscious is where analysts put their conscious ideas for what otherwise would remain inexplicable.

In part, as I have emphasized, such differences are due to differences in the phenomena observed and the criteria used to evaluate explanations. For Freud, and for many psychoanalysts, clinical evidence is the ultimate and sufficient basis for belief in certain views. For others, experimental tests provide the necessary and sufficient basis for establishing the scientific utility of concepts. We will have the opportunity to consider the issue further later in the chapter when we compare the psychoanalytic and cognitive views of the unconscious. Here I will state my own view, based on my own clinical experience and a reading of the empirical literature: The principles of unconscious functioning *can* and *do* at times operate in the ways suggested by Freud and later analysts. However, the importance attributed to the concept, as well as the accompanying principles of operation, far exceed what is justified by the evidence.

The New Look in Perception and a Return to Interest in Unconscious Processes

Freud's ideas concerning the unconscious never were far from the interest of some psychologists. Interpretations of Rorschach inkblot tests were strongly influenced by psychoanalytic thinking (Schafer, 1954). The development of the *Thematic Apperception Test* (TAT) by Henry Murray and Christina Morgan (Murray, 1938), also was expressive of the influence of Freud's ideas. At the same time, much of psychology was influenced by the radical behaviorist rejection of such mentalistic concepts. Then, at the end of the 1940s and during the following decade, there developed what came to be known as "The New Look in Perception." What was new about this "New Look" was the idea that values, motives, and needs could influence perception, an idea that certainly was not too far from the heart of psychoanalytic thinking. And, what could be better from the standpoint of such thinking than the suggestion that such influences could occur outside the awareness of the person? In other words, there could be unconscious, motivated influences on perception.

A few studies highlight this early period of renewed interest in unconscious processes. The first begins with a study of the role of value and need on perception by Bruner and Goodman (1947). In this research, children from poor and wealthy families were asked to adjust the size of a circle of light to match the size of various coins. The coins ranged in value from a penny to a quarter. The questions asked were whether value would influence the size estimation of the coins and whether need (i.e., poor vs. wealthy) would also have an effect on size estimation. The answer was yes for both questions. That is, it was found that the size of the more valuable coins was overestimated relative to the size of the less valuable coins, and the effect was greater for the children from poor families than those from wealthy families. It should be noted that although this research fit with the psychoanalytic emphasis on motivation (drive), it was not conducted within the context of psychoanalytic thinking. Rather, it was directed more generally toward demonstrating that perception reflected other ongoing processes in the person. The emphasis here was on the person as an active organism in the construction of what was perceived (Bruner, 1992). In itself, the research had nothing to say about the psychodynamics of the unconscious.

> *The New Look was not initially about the unconscious. . . . It had little, if anything, to do with the unconscious or with Freud. . . . Very soon, however, the corner was turned into psychodynamics.*
>
> *Bruner, 1992, pp. 780, 781*

How did this turn toward psychodynamics occur? In 1949 McGinnies conducted research involving the concept of *perceptual defense*. In this research McGinnies (1949) presented emotion-laden, "taboo" words (e.g., *whore, bitch, penis*) and neutral words (e.g., *house, apple, flower*) through a tachistoscope, an instrument for presenting material to subjects at varying speeds. The words were first presented at very fast speeds and then gradually at increasingly slower speeds until the subjects were able to identify the words correctly. Would there be a difference in the recognition thresholds for the two types of words? In addition, a physiological indicator of emotional response (i.e., GSR or galvanic skin response) was recorded during the session. Would the subjects show a differential emotional response to the two types of words and, if so, would this differential response coincide with differences in the recognition thresholds for the two types of words? Would the subjects perceive the emotion-laden or neutral words faster? Would they respond emotionally in a comparable way? Would the "mind" and the "body" operate in the same way or would there be a disconnect between the two?

McGinnies reported two interesting findings. First, it took the subjects longer to recognize the taboo words than it did to recognize the neutral words. Second, the physiological measures indicated an emotional response to the taboo words prior to their being perceived by the subject. In other words, the subjects were responding to the taboo words prior to conscious recognition of them. This suggested that there was *perception without awareness* and that a process of perceptual defense intervened between the unconscious perception of the taboo words and the conscious recognition of them. Was this the basis for Freud's mechanisms of defense? The research results were startling and criticized by others. In particular, it was suggested that the subjects were less familiar with perceiving the taboo words than the neutral words and were more reluctant to report perception of them (Howes & Solomon, 1950). However, subsequent evaluations suggested that the results were not due to such factors and that a process such as that of perceptual defense was possible (Erdelyi, 1974).

A third study of the time also demonstrated perception without awareness and laid the groundwork for what came to be known as *subliminal perception*. In this research, Lazarus and McCleary (1951) presented nonsense syllables to subjects, some of which were paired with electric shock and others were not. The nonsense syllables were then presented tachistoscopically to subjects at decreasing speeds until they were correctly identified. As in the McGinnies research, a physiological measure (GSR) of emotional response was recorded during the process. The question asked was whether an emotional response to the nonsense syllable associated with shock would appear prior to the perceptual recognition. Note that here there is no issue of taboo words and reluctance to report them. Would there be evidence of perception without awareness in terms of an emotional response to the shock-associated nonsense syllables prior to the conscious perception of them? Indeed this was the case. That is, the emotional response (GSR) to nonsense sylla-bles associated with shock but not correctly identified was greater than that to nonsense syllables that were not associated with shock. In other words, once more there was evi-dence of unconscious perception or the ability to respond to stimuli at levels below con-scious recognition.

Actually, these results should not have been that surprising, for in the 1930s a study of unconscious perception had already been reported. In this study of classical condition-ing (Diven, 1937), subjects were presented with a list of words and received a shock whenever the word *barn* appeared. This word was always preceded by the word *red* but followed by a variety of words. Physiological responses (GSR) to the words on the list were measured during the process. In addition to showing signs of anxiety in response to the word *barn*, the subjects showed such signs in relation to the word *red* which, as noted, always preceded the word *barn*, as well as to all words having a rural association (e.g., hay, plow, pasture, sheep). The latter was in contrast to the lack of an anxiety reac-tion in response to words with an urban association (e.g., *pavement, subway, streetcar*). In other words, the anxiety reaction generalized to other stimuli associated by contiguity in time and in meaning with the stimulus that was followed by shock. But what was par-ticularly striking about this result, and why it is presented here, was that it occurred even when the subject failed to recognize that the word *barn* was the signal for the shock. In other words, there was generalized anxiety to meaning-related stimuli even though the person was unaware of the original stimulus signal for the shock. This suggests that through unconscious perception one can develop fears for which there is no conscious explanation.

In his retrospective look at the New Look in perception, Bruner (1992) viewed these studies as a turning point in the field, dividing the more psychoanalytically inclined from the more cognitively inclined: "The fat was in the fire. . . . What resulted, I realize in retrospect, was a split between those who were principally interested in psychodynamics and those who were committed to the study of cognition" (p. 781). We will turn shortly to the latter, but for now let us pick up the story of those interested in psychodynamics.

The Psychoanalytic Unconscious

Later psychoanalytic experimental research on the unconscious focused on what is known as *subliminal psychodynamic activation* (Silverman, 1976, 1982; J. Weinberger, 1992; J. Weinberger & Silverman, 1987). In this research, there is an effort to stimulate unconscious motives without making them conscious. In general, the experimental pro-cedure involves using a tachistoscope to show subjects material related to wishes or fears that is expected to be either threatening or anxiety-alleviating. Observations then are made as to whether the expected effects occur. In the case of threatening wishes, the ma-terial being presented subliminally (below the threshold for conscious recognition) is expected to stir up unconscious conflicts and thus increase psychological disturbance. In the case of an anxiety-alleviating wish, the material being presented subliminally is ex-pected to diminish unconscious conflict and thus decrease psychological disturbance. In either case, what is key is that the content that is upsetting or relieving to various groups of subjects is predicted beforehand on the basis of psychoanalytic theory and the effects occur only when the stimuli are perceived subliminally or unconsciously.

We can consider here three relevant pieces of research. The first concentrates on arousing positive, anxiety-alleviating wishes (Silverman & Weinberger, 1985). These studies are based on the psychoanalytic view that many people, and particularly some patient populations, have wishes to merge or unite with the good mother of early childhood (i.e., the comforting, protective, nurturing mother). In illustrative research, the stimulus *Mommy and I Are One* is presented subliminally to schizophrenic patients. The assumption is that these individuals have strong wishes to merge with the good mother representation and therefore will find such messages pleasurable or anxiety-alleviating. The effects of such messages are contrasted to those of a neutral message such as *People Are Walking*. In some cases a threatening message such as *Mommy Is Gone* also is presented subliminally. The research to date suggests that presenting the message *Mommy and I Are One* subliminally to these patients indeed lessens their pathology and enhances their progress in therapeutic and educational settings (Weinberger, 1992).

The second illustration involves a test of the concept of the Oedipus complex, involving the young boy's fear of castration by his father as a result of his competitive wishes for his mother. In this research, stimuli were presented subliminally to subjects. The stimuli were designed to activate unconscious conflicts and either intensify or alleviate these conflicts. The stimulus chosen to intensify the oedipal conflict was *Beating Daddy Is Wrong*, whereas that selected to alleviate such conflict was *Beating Daddy Is OK*. In addition, a number of other stimuli were presented, such as the neutral stimulus *People Are Walking.*

Before the subliminal presentation of one of these stimuli, subjects were tested for performance in a dart-throwing competition. Performance in such competition was measured again following the subliminal presentation of one of the three messages. The prediction, based on psychoanalytic theory, was that the *Beating Dad Is Wrong* message would intensify oedipal conflicts and lead to poorer performance whereas the message *Beating Dad Is OK* would alleviate such conflicts and lead to improved performance. The neutral message was expected to have no specific effects on performance. This is exactly what was found to be the case (Silverman, et. al., 1978).

A few additional points about this research are noteworthy. First, the results were not obtained when the stimuli were presented above threshold. The psychodynamic activation effects appear to operate at the unconscious rather than at the conscious level. Second, the experimental stimuli had to relate to the motivational state of the subjects and the response measured had to be sensitive to changes in this motivational state. In this case, subjects were first "primed" with picture and story material containing oedipal content and then the task was presented as one involving competition. In sum, the subjects were primed to an increased competitive motivation level, the stimuli presented subliminally related to such motivation, and the performance measure reflected changes in such motivational levels.

The third piece of research again involves the activation of conflicts and the observation of effects on dynamically related behaviors. In contrast to the previously presented research, here groups differing in theoretically significant ways were compared. Normal college women and women with eating disorders were compared in terms of how many crackers they would eat following subliminal presentation of three messages: *Mama Is Leaving Me, Mama Is Loaning It, Mona Is Loaning It*. Although subjects were told they were participating in tests of visual and taste discrimination, in fact the study was designed to test the hypothesis that subjects with eating disorders would increase their eating in response to the *Mama Is Leaving Me* message relative to the other subjects and the other messages. The crucial message affected the cracker eating of only the eating disorder group. In addition, this effect was not found when the stimuli were presented above threshold (Patton, 1992).

These three studies are illustrative of the subliminal psychodynamic activation effects derived from psychoanalytic theory. By now about 100 such studies have been reported that on the whole support the theory and the existence of the effect. At the same time, the results remain controversial both within and outside psychoanalytic circles (Balay & Shevrin, 1988). Part of the problem here lies in the fact that the results have not always been replicable, although one review suggests that the overwhelming body of evidence supports the existence of these effects. According to this reviewer, "the reason the work has been and may remain controversial is that it does not seem to fit into what is accepted in present-day academic psychology and even has the flavor of magic" (J. Weinberger, 1992, p. 176).

The Cognitive Unconscious

> After 100 years of neglect, suspicion, and frustration, unconscious processes have now taken a firm hold on the collective mind of psychologists.
>
> *Kihlstrom, Barnhardt, & Tataryn, 1992, p. 788*

Psychoanalytic psychology is credited with taking unconscious processes seriously at a time when this was unfashionable among academic psychologists. However, as noted in one of the introductory quotes to this chapter, this does not mean that cognitive psychology owes a debt to psychoanalytic theory in terms of subsequent research (Kihlstrom, 1990, 1999). As noted, following the New Look a split developed in the paths taken by psychoanalytic and cognitive psychologists. At the beginning of the cognitive revolution, cognitive psychologists were relatively uninterested in the unconscious. However, influenced by a variety of observations and the development of techniques for measuring cognitive processes, a strong interest in unconscious, or nonconscious, processes emerged. Today, cognitive neuroscientists make use of sophisticated techniques for measuring brain activity to study unconscious processes and to locate the parts of the brain involved in specific unconscious processes (Morris, Ohman, & Dolan, 1998; Schacter & Badgaiyan, 2001)—a far cry from Freud's clinical observations and theoretical work on repression.

An early spur for the development of an interest in unconscious processes was the work of the neurophysiologist Libet (1965, 1966). Libet was able to measure brain activity in terms of when a stimulus was registered. This point in time was assessed in relation to a conscious intention to make a movement in relation to the stimulus and the actual beginning of the voluntary movement itself. What Libet found was that there was the beginning of the voluntary movement prior to the conscious intention to make the movement. In other words, brain activity was associated with the intention to act *prior to* awareness of the intention to act. According to Libet, there is an unconscious readiness to act *prior to* a consciously experienced decision to act. Thus, the will to act begins to form unconsciously prior to the conscious decision of intentional action.

A second spur for the development of this interest was observation of patients with cognitive dysfunctions due to brain damage. Consider, for example, the phenomenon of *blindsight* (Weiskrantz, 1986). In this case, patients with a lesion in a part of their brain report that they are unable to see. Yet, they are able to respond correctly to stimuli when required to do so. For example, the patient might report being unable to see a pencil on the table but be able to pick it up. There is a disconnect between the conscious perception of the object and ability to act on the perception of the object. Unconsciously, or nonconsciously, the person perceives without being aware of his or her ability to perceive.

A third spur for the development of interest was the work of Marcel (1983). Marcel demonstrated, through the use of a priming technique, that individuals could be influenced by a stimulus that was not consciously perceived. Marcel presented subjects with a stimulus (prime) tachistoscopically, followed immediately by a stimulus (mask) that prevented conscious recognition of the original stimulus or prime. Subjects then were asked to identify words flashed on a screen. What was found was that the prime (i.e., the word presented tachistoscopically and prevented from reaching consciousness due to the mask) could facilitate recognition of related words flashed on the screen. Perhaps most striking of all was the finding that this facilitation of recognition extended to words that were related in meaning to the unconsciously perceived prime (e.g., *boat* as the prime and *ship* as the recognized word). Note the similarity to the research on classical conditioning of anxiety to barn-related words in the absence of conscious recognition of the word associated with shock (Diven, 1937). The importance of this work was twofold. First, there was a demonstration of the effects of unconscious perception of a stimulus on further cognitive activity. Second, there was the demonstration of the utility of the priming technique for investigation of these phenomena.

So, we have developments in the areas of neuroscience, cognitive pathology, and cognitive science converging on an interest in unconscious as well as conscious processes. Kihlstrom (1999) has reviewed developments in research on the cognitive unconscious in terms of the following categories:

- *Implicit Memory.* Individuals can report not being able to recall stimuli presented to them yet have better recall for them when presented with a subsequent task than for stimuli not previously presented. The contrast is drawn between facilitated recall associated with the conscious, explicit memory of previously presented stimuli and facilitated recall associated with the unconscious, implicit memory of the previously presented stimuli (Schacter, 1987).

- *Implicit Perception.* In contrast with explicit perception, which involves the conscious perception of a stimulus, in implicit perception there is perception without awareness. Whereas in implicit memory the stimulus once was perceived but then forgotten, in implicit perception the stimulus never achieves conscious recognition.

- *Implicit Thought.* Implicit thought involves problem solving in the absence of conscious thought. For example, research suggests that people can have unconscious insights (Siegler, 2000). That is, people can begin to solve problems using newly discovered rules or principles before they are able to articulate the relevant principles.

- *Implicit Emotion.* It is clear that individuals can respond emotionally without being aware of the basis for their emotional reaction (e.g., finding a face attractive without being aware of the determining features). Beyond this, in implicit emotion the person experiences an emotion without being aware of that emotional experience. Sometimes the word *feeling* is used to distinguish between the conscious recognition of an emotion and the unconscious experience that is reflected in physiological recordings or in changes in response to various external stimuli.

- *Implicit Motivation.* Related to implicit emotion is the phenomenon of implicit motivation. Here the person is motivated by some goal without being consciously aware of the goal. Problems of volition, where the person feels compelled to do things they do not want to do or are blocked from doing things they intend to do, typically involve implicit (unconscious) motives (Pervin, 1991). Measures of conscious motivation typically do not correlate with measures of implicit motivation (McClelland, 1980; McClelland, Koestner, & Weinberger, 1989).

In sum, Kihlstrom sees unconscious processes as operating in virtually every arena of psychological functioning. However, once more it is important to note that he sees these processes as very different from those described by psychoanalysts. We will return to this issue later in the chapter.

The Unconscious in Social Psychology

The application of principles of cognition to social psychological phenomena is known as *social cognition*. The involvement of unconscious processes in social cognitive phenomena is known as *implicit social cognition* (Greenwald & Banaji, 1995). Implicit social cognition involves unconscious attitudes, beliefs, feelings, and behaviors toward the self and others. Research in this area makes use of the same techniques that have been described earlier for demonstrating the effects of unconscious processes (e.g., priming, subliminal presentation of stimuli). The difference is that the phenomena investigated with these techniques are social in nature. The broad principle is that many of our responses to others, the ways in which we perceive, experience, and behave in relation to others, is governed by unconscious memories, feelings, and motivations. Although considered as part of the field of social psychology, research in this area has obvious implications for personality psychologists as well. As hopefully has been evident throughout, the border between personality and social psychology is a fuzzy one, with research in one area often having important implications for the other.

Research has found much of an individual's complex psychological and behavioral functioning to occur without conscious choice or guidance—that is, automatically.

Bargh & Ferguson, 2000, p. 941

Social behavior is like any other psychological reaction to a social situation, capable of occurring in the absence of any conscious involvement or intervention.

Bargh, Chen, & Burrows, 1996, p. 242

An early study in this area involved the use of priming to see whether trait characteristics presented outside of awareness would influence the impressions of a person described to the subjects (Bargh & Pietromonaco, 1982). In this research subjects were primed with lists of words with differing proportions of hostility words, ranging from 0 percent to 80 percent, all at a level below recognition. As in earlier research (Marcel, 1983), the prime also was subsequently masked by another stimulus (a string of Xs). In what was presented as an unrelated second task, subjects were given a description of a person that was ambiguous with regard to hostility and asked to rate the person on several trait dimensions. Despite not perceiving the hostile words, subjects rated the person increasingly more negatively as the proportion of hostile words to which they were exposed increased. The conclusion drawn was that social stimuli of which people are not consciously aware can influence conscious judgments.

A second illustration of unconscious influences on attitudes and social behavior comes from a study of subliminal conditioning of attitudes (Krosnick, et. al., 1992). In this study, two groups of subjects were shown a series of pictures of the same person. For one group of subjects, the pictures were preceded by subliminal exposure to positive affect-arousing pictures while subjects in the other group were subliminally exposed to negative affect-arousing pictures. Illustrative positive affect-arousing pictures were of a bridal couple, a group of people playing cards and laughing, and a couple in a romantic setting. Illustrative negative affect-arousing pictures were of a skull, a werewolf, a face on fire, and a bucket of snakes. After being shown the common group of slides of the target person, at a level above threshold, subjects in both groups filled out a questionnaire in which they reported their attitudes toward the target person, their beliefs about her personality, and their beliefs about her physical attractiveness.

Would the prior subliminal exposure to positive or negative affect-arousing stimuli influence the ratings and would it do so to different degrees for the three types of ratings—attitudes, beliefs about her personality, and beliefs about her physical attractiveness? What was found was that subjects in the positive affect-arousing group had more positive attitudes toward the target person and gave her more positive personality ratings but did not give her more positive physical attractiveness ratings. Presumably the latter occurred because more objective data concerning the target's physical attributes were available from the photographs than was true for her personality characteristics. In sum, attitudes toward the target were conditioned by prior subliminal exposure to stimuli, again demonstrating the unconscious elements of such attitude formation.

The unconscious activation of trait characteristics has implications for stereotypes. Considerable research indicates the automatic, unconscious operation of race and gender stereotypes (Greenwald & Banaji, 1995). One of the important issues in this areas is the extent to which people are in touch with their racial and gender stereotypes and biases. This is particularly important in relation to individuals who pride themselves on being liberal or politically correct, and who therefore may not consciously recognize the operation of their stereotypes. In many ways the issue is parallel to that between explicit, conscious motives and implicit, unconscious motives. As noted earlier, often there is considerable discrepancy between the two sets of measures. The same is true for measures of explicit and implicit attitudes (Greenwald & Farnham, 2000; Greenwald, McGhee, & Schwartz, 1998). For example, in one research study subjects were found to have much more negative prejudice against female authorities on the measure of unconscious attitudes than on the conscious measure. The difference was particularly great for the female subjects. That is, while female explicit attitudes were more favorable to female authority figures than male explicit attitudes, their implicit attitudes were similarly negative (Rudman & Kilianski, 2000).

These trait constructs and stereotypes not only operate at the cognitive level but spill over into action as well. Three priming experiments by Bargh and his colleagues (Bargh, Chen, & Burrows, 1996) illustrate this. In the first experiment, subjects primed with the rude concept (e.g., words *rude*, *disturb*, *obnoxious*, *disturb*) interrupted the experimenter on a subsequent task more quickly and frequently than did subjects primed with the polite concept (e.g., words *respect*, *honor*, *polite*, *yield*). In a second experiment, participants primed with an elderly stereotype (e.g., words *old*, *helpless*, *cautious*, *Florida*) walked more slowly leaving the experiment that did subjects primed with unrelated words (e.g., *thirsty*, *clean*, *private*). In the third experiment, subjects primed with the subliminal presentation of the face of a young African-American male reacted with more hostility to an annoying request by the experimenter than did subjects primed with the subliminal presentation of the face of a young Caucasian male. Thus, in all three cases the activation of a trait construct or stereotype below the level of consciousness resulted in behavior consistent with the construct or stereotype.

Can such automatic behavior be controlled? The authors suggest that control is possible if these stereotypes and their potential influence are recognized, and if there is motivation to control such behavior. However, they also suggest that given these requirements, it is easy to see why such control often is not implemented: "Even with the best of underlying intentions, one cannot control an influence if one is not aware of its operation, or at least its potential for operating" (p. 241).

Bargh, who has done so much work on demonstrating the effects of priming on attitudes and action, also suggests that the unconscious is a repository of goals and motives (Bargh & Barndollar, 1996). He argues that many of our goals operate without conscious guidance. However, this does not mean that our goal-directed behavior is irrational or foolhardy, as might be suggested by a Freudian view of unconsciously motivated behavior. Rather, goals are viewed as operating automatically, in the way that typing or driving a car is done automatically. In addition, goals are viewed as being activated or triggered automatically (unconsciously) by environmental stimuli. Thus, the entire motivational process, from activation through completion, can have an unconscious quality to it. However, this is not to deny the intentional, goal-directed, adaptive quality of the associated behavior.

In our view the unconscious has received a "bad rap.".... The unconscious is actually quite adaptive and usually does not produce errors, but instead produces appropriate and rational decisions, choices, and behaviors.

Bargh & Barndollar, 1996, p. 460

In agreement with Kihlstrom, it is clear that social psychologists view the importance of unconscious processes as demonstrated and accepted. However, also in agreement with Kihlstrom, it is a view of an unconscious that is different from that suggested by Freud and psychoanalysts generally. It is, in the words of Greenwald, "intellectually much simpler than the sophisticated agency portrayed in psychoanalytic theory" (1992, p. 766). He suggests that the psychoanalytic view of defenses that manage repressed drives and memories is a much "smarter" unconscious than that suggested by cognitive and social psychologists.

I'm not sure that smart–dumb is the best dimension along which to contrast the two views, but certainly there are major differences between them. In fact, the differences are so great that I have suggested that the cognitive and social psychological unconscious be called the *nonconscious* rather than the *unconscious*. This is an issue to which we will turn shortly, for it is time to consider a variety of related issues: Is there evidence for mechanisms of defense? If so, are they adaptive or maladaptive, associated with health or illness? Is there evidence of repression, and what are we to make of stories of recovered memories, particularly of recovered memories of childhood sexual abuse?

Is There Evidence for the Mechanisms of Defense?

The concept of defense mechanisms is central to psychoanalytic theory. The suggestion is that people unconsciously use various protective measures to defend against the painful emotion of anxiety. Although the central emphasis has been on the defense against painful memories, emphasis also has been placed on the defense against recognition of painful feelings (e.g., anger, depression) and wishes or motives (drives, instincts) associated with threat (e.g., hostility, sex). If defense mechanisms do not exist, there is little of significance left to psychoanalytic theory.

As is true for the unconscious generally, interest in the mechanisms of defense among academic psychologists has waxed and waned (Cramer, 2000; Caprara & Cervone, 2000). For an extended period of time there was an absence of interest. This was due to ambiguities in definitions of the concept, difficulties in measurement, and reviews suggesting the absence of evidence to support the existence of mechanisms of defense such as repression and projection (Holmes, 1974, 1990). Unfortunately, as frequently has been the case, there was a gap between clinical observations and experimental studies. In particular, often the experimental studies were not testing psychoanalytic concepts in ways that were relevant to their clinical significance. For example, one would not expect projection and repression to be used by all individuals in relation to all content, but only by individuals who use that mechanism of defense in relation to memories, emotions, or wishes that are associated with anxiety for them. The individualistic or idiographic nature of the specific defense mechanism utilized, and content in relation to which it is employed, place enormous burdens on researchers interested in the investigation of defensive processes. In any case, an interest in the mechanisms of defense has returned and evidence exists that, as a minimum, is consistent with the view that people unconsciously exclude from awareness contents that may be threatening to them.

Interestingly enough, some of the best evidence for defensive processes comes from research by social psychologists. Greenwald (1980), in a classic paper, described how the self distorts the past and manipulates the present, and exaggerates successes and minimizes failures, in the service of protection of the self. Often the relevant studies are grouped under the heading of *self-deception processes*. For example, Baumeister (1998) describes the following self-deceptive "tricks" by which people sustain favorable views of the self:

1. People show a self-serving bias, taking credit for success and blaming external circumstances for failure.

2. People accept that which puts them in a positive light but are critical of the evidence that depicts them in an unflattering light (e.g., think a test is fair when they do well but unfair when they do poorly).

3. People tend to minimize or ignore bad feedback but linger over praise.

4. People selectively forget failure feedback and undesirable traits while recalling positive information and their desirable traits.

5. People compare themselves against others who will make them look good.

6. People tend to think that their good traits are unusual and faults are common.

More directly relevant to the psychoanalytic concept of mechanisms of defense is research on projection, denial, and repression. In a study of how people deal with undesirable personality traits, Newman, Duff, and Baumeister (1997) found evidence of projection, defined as the act of perceiving in other people those characteristics that one wishes to deny in oneself. Although their model of projection differed some from the Freudian model, they were in basic agreement with "the Freudian view that people are prone to overperceive in others the traits that they seek to deny in themselves" (p. 980).

Denial is one of the defense mechanisms for which there is the greatest and most varied evidence. Consider, for example, the following description by the mother of former President Clinton as to how she deals with adversity: "When bad things do happen, I brainwash myself to put them out of my mind. Inside my head, I construct an airtight box. I keep inside it what I want to think about and everything else stays behind the walls. Inside is white, outside is black. The only gray I trust is the streak in my hair" (*New York Times*, August 18, 1998, p. A12). Although she may be aware that this is what she does, she probably is unaware of when she is doing it. Or, consider former President Reagan's account of his involvement in the Iran-contra affair: "A few months ago, I told the American people I did not trade arms for hostages. My heart and my best intentions tell me that's true, but the facts and the evidence tell me it's not." This event is recounted by former Senator Warren Rudman who describes the former president's incredible ability to deny elements of reality, in this case economic reality, as follows: "The man inhabited his own reality. That was both his greatness and his failure as a political leader. His greatness was his ability to make American share his vision of reality. . . . His failure was that, at least in economic affairs, his reality was a delusion" (Rudman, 1996, p. 73).

Beyond such anecdotal evidence of denial, is empirical evidence. For example, consider the results of a study of how students at the University of California at Los Angeles dealt with the threat of damage to buildings should an earthquake occur. For some time a major earthquake had been predicted and the report of a panel studying the vulnerability of campus buildings was distributed to students. Who would read the report? Incredibly enough, although not from a defense mechanism standpoint, the students in the most vulnerable structures were the ones who were most likely to deny the seriousness of the situation and doubt the experts' predictions:

> The results of this study suggest that individuals at risk for a catastrophic event whose occurrence is highly likely, but whose timing is unknown, may cope with that threat by ignoring or denying the seriousness of the situation. . . . That respondents were typically aware of the threat and that residents of very poor seismic structures showed more questioning and denial than individuals in good seismic structures suggest that these perceptions are efforts to cope with the event, rather than a result of simple ignorance or misinformation.

> *(Lehman & Taylor, 1987, pp. 551, 553)*

The study of UCLA students relates to denial of an external threat. There also is evidence of denial of internal threats. For example, a study of homophobic men found that they responded with erections to erotic stimuli of a heterosexual nature, as did nonhomophobic heterosexual men. However, in contrast with the nonhomophobic heterosexual men, the homophobic men also responded with erections to erotic stimuli of a homosexual nature, despite self-reports to the contrary. The conclusion drawn was that "homophobia is apparently associated with homosexual arousal that the homophobic individual is either unaware of or denies" (Adams, Wright, & Lohr, 1996, p. 440).

Of broader relevance is evidence of denial as a mechanism of defense against death anxiety. Pyzczynski, Greenberg, and Solomon (2000) begin with the view that "one of the least controversial propositions in all psychology is that people are not always aware why they do the things they do" (p. 156). They go on to suggest that wide varieties of behaviors represent unconscious defenses against anxiety associated with the awareness of the inevitability of one's own death—what they call *terror management theory*. The fear of death is seen as inherent in the human condition. People are viewed as avoiding this fear by, among other means, maintaining faith in a worldview that provides an explanation for existence and that provides the promise of either literal or symbolic immortality to those who live up to the standards of the cultural worldview. Many experimental studies in diverse cultures has demonstrated that increased self-esteem and faith in a cultural worldview serve to protect against death anxiety, and that the arousal of such anxiety unconsciously leads to greater striving to maintain self-esteem and faith in the cultural worldview. Terror management theory is based on the psychoanalytic view that behavior is driven by powerful unconscious forces. However, it assumes that basic anxiety lies in the threat of death, rather than in the threat of the instincts. It also dismisses the psychoanalytic emphasis on primary process thinking as part of the unconscious. Instead, terror management theory emphasizes the processes by which unconscious concerns are translated into conscious goals and relevant behavior.

Finally, we come to repression, the linchpin of psychoanalytic theory. There is considerable empirical evidence for the fundamentals of repression. That is, there is evidence that many processes occur outside of awareness, that people can exclude from awareness threatening information, and that previously conscious material that is forgotten can subsequently be recalled. However, to date it has been impossible to experimentally demonstrate the process of repression (Caprara & Cervone, 2000; Erdelyi, 1985). The most supportive evidence comes from the study of individual differences in repression as a mechanism of defense. Typically "repressors" are defined as individuals who score high on measures of social desirability and low on anxiety. In some early research in this area, relative to nonrepressors, repressors were found to recall fewer negative emotions and to be significantly older at the time of the earliest recalled negative memory: "The pattern of findings is consistent with the hypothesis that repression involves an inaccessibility to negative emotional memories and indicates further that repression is associated in some way with the suppression or inhibition of emotional experiences in general. The concept of repression as a process involving limited access to negative affective memories appears to be valid" (Davis & Schwartz, 1987, p. 155).

A 1994 review of the literature comparing repressors with nonrepressors suggests that repressors show the following: dismissal of negative feedback given privately, avoidance of material that is threatening, investment in maintaining self-control, deficits in emotional self-disclosure, difficulty in insight-oriented therapy, high stress reactivity despite reports of low subjective distress, and evidence of negative health consequences probably associated with the dissociation between verbal reports of stress and physiological measures (Weinberger & Davidson, 1994). Since that review, other studies indicate that repressors underestimate how anxious they are (Derakshan & Eysenck, 1997), have a particularly difficult time in being aware of negative emotions (Schimmack & Hartmann, 1997), and tend to use happy thoughts automatically as a defense against negative emotional material (Boden & Baumeister, 1997). Although repressors here are characterized in terms of a general style, it also appears to be the case that the style is specifically employed under conditions of threat to the self rather than under all conditions (Mendolia, Moore, & Tesser, 1996).

There is no research evidence to support the theory of repression.

Holmes, 1974, p. 649

> *For much of this century, laboratory evidence for the existence
> of repression was weak. . . . During the past quarter of a cen-
> tury things have changed. Repression has returned. Well-
> controlled laboratory research reveals that people's psycho-
> logical experiences indeed are affected by material that they
> banish from awareness to protect their self-image.*
>
> Caprara & Cervone, 2000, p. 320

What are we to conclude, then, in relation to the question of whether the evidence supports the view of unconscious defensive processes? Caprara and Cervone (2000), in a comprehensive review of the recent literature, suggest three relevant questions: (1.) Is there unequivocal evidence of the existence of unconscious defensive processes? (2.) Are the mechanisms of them understood? (3). Does the evidence support the psychoanalytic model of defensive processing that launched this field of study? Their answers are yes, somewhat, and no—*yes* that well-controlled research studies demonstrate that people are unconsciously motivated to defend against threatening material, we *somewhat* understand the relevant motivational and cognitive processes involved in defensive processes, and *no* in terms of whether special psychoanalytic principles, as opposed to more general psychological principles, are necessary to understand the relevant phenomena.

In general, I find myself in agreement with their conclusions, although I think that more credit and attention might be given to psychoanalytic thinking in this area. What I have in mind here, first, is the psychoanalytic contribution in bringing these phenomena to the attention of psychologists, a contribution that is recognized by Caprara and Cervone. Second, I think that more credit should be given to the psychoanalytic emphasis on individual differences in the use of various mechanisms of defense and, more generally, to the involvement of these defensive processes specifically in relation to threatening material and under conditions of threat to the self.

Defense Processes: Healthy or Sick? Good or Bad?

The standard psychoanalytic view of the defense mechanisms is that they serve a function, the defense against anxiety, but basically distort reality in an unhealthy way. The more primitive the mechanism of defense (e.g., denial and projection), the more serious the psychological disturbance. In addition, there is the view that the mechanisms of defense are debilitating in terms of energy and can also be bad for one's physical health.

In the late 1980s this view was challenged by a distinguished social psychologist, Shelley Taylor. In an article in a major professional journal (Taylor & Brown, 1988), and in the book *Positive Illusions* (1989), Taylor expressed the view that self-deceptions can be healthy and adaptive, particularly when one is threatened with adversity. Taylor was well aware that she was challenging the traditional view that mental health corresponds with the accurate perception of reality. However, she was impressed with the successful coping efforts of individuals who survived one or another kind of trauma: "Many of the psychological recoveries recounted by these victims seemed to depend on certain distortions of their situations, especially overly optimistic perceptions concerning the chance of recovery from a disease, or the belief that they could actively control the likelihood of a repeat victimization in the future" (1989, p. ix). What was particularly striking was that the individuals characterized by these overly optimistic perceptions and beliefs in control often were actually better adjusted to their circumstances than those not characterized by such perceptions and beliefs. According to Taylor, it was adaptive for people to have "benign fictions" about the self, the world, and the future—what could be called *positive illusions*. These illusions fell into three general categories: *self-enhancement*, or the perception of oneself in a more positive way than is actually the case; an exaggerated belief in one's *personal control* or ability to make positive things happen and avoid negative outcomes; and, *unrealistic optimism*, the belief that the future will bring positive outcomes and a relative absence of adverse events.

Not surprisingly, this view was challenged by supporters of the view that a reality orientation is central to mental health. Reviewing the literature emphasized by Taylor, Colvin and Block (1994) questioned the conclusion that positive illusions are associated with mental health. Instead, they suggested that well-adjusted individuals have higher self-esteem than poorly adjusted individuals but the basis for this higher self-esteem is not an illusion. In relation to beliefs about control, they argued that "perceptions of control are beneficial when they are indeed reality based. When the threat is severe but not controllable, an individual who manifests an illusion of control may well be exhibiting maladaptive behavior" (p. 11). Similarly, they questioned the connection between unrealistic optimism and mental health. Colvin and Block accepted that normal, healthy individuals often distort reality, but they also suggested that such individuals self-corrected such distortions. Support for their view could be found in a study demonstrating that defensive subjects with an illusion of mental health showed signs of greater stress than either healthy subjects or nondefensive psychologically unhealthy subjects (Shedler, Mayman, & Manis, 1993). Additional support comes from a study suggesting that positive illusions about the self can have short-term benefits but long-term costs (Robins & Beer, 2001).

In many ways, the healthy mind is a self-deceptive one. . . . Normal human thought is distinguished by a robust positive bias.

Taylor, 1989, pp. xi, 7

We do not believe that cognitive distortions about oneself and one's social surroundings can result in adaptive behavior over long periods of time. . .

Colvin & Block, 1994, p. 17

A further exchange between the representatives of these two differing views failed to result in a reconciliation (Block & Colvin, 1994; Taylor & Brown, 1994). What are we to make of the situation? First, it may be that it is a question of degree. Thus, one view is that a moderate level of defense is healthy but a lack of defenses or an excessive reliance on defenses is unhealthy (Baumeister, Dale, & Sommer, 1998). In other words, according to this view optimal mental health is defined by the avoidance of both excessive realism and excessive distortion. Another view would be that two different processes are involved, one that might be called *adaptive coping efforts* and the other *mechanisms of defense*. Some suggested differences between the two would be that adaptive coping efforts are more conscious, more under voluntary control, more specific to a situation, more temporary, and less distorting of reality (Cramer, 2000). Both of these views would appear to have merit, although my own view tends toward an emphasis on the latter. It is a question I am frequently asked by students: "Is it ever healthy to use mechanisms of defense?" The question has not yet been answered, although my sense is that most psychologists would agree that there is a difference between adaptive coping efforts ("benign illusions") and pathological mechanisms of defense. However, the means for differentiating between the two and establishing the consequences of the use of each remain for the future.

Recovered vs. False Memories

One of the most controversial issues in the clinical literature over the past period has been the recovered memories versus the false memories debate. One the one hand, there are those who emphasize the Freudian concept of repression and the potential for individuals to bury memories of traumatic experiences in the unconscious and then recover them later in life. On the other hand, there are those who question the concept of repression and the accuracy of adult recall of childhood experiences. Perhaps not surprisingly, the former view tends to be held by clinicians, the latter by experimental psychologists. The former cite their clinical experience, the latter evidence that false memories can be planted in individuals who believe their memories to be real (Loftus, 1997).

The issue is not just of academic and theoretical importance, but of judicial and psychological importance for many individuals. This includes both individuals who are struggling to understand the significance of their recovered memories and individuals who believe themselves to have been falsely accused of committing sexual abuse. I can recall meeting with a group of clinicians, of diverse orientations, where the issue came up for discussion. On group felt that we had to be prepared to believe reports of recovered memories of sexual abuse in childhood lest we prevent patients from gaining freedom from repressed experiences and emotions. The other group felt that there was little evidence to support the validity of these memories and we had to be on guard against the power of suggestion associated with the therapeutic context and the mass media that was playing up the reports of recovered memories.

Where do things stand? We know that people can forget events that they subsequently recall and that unconscious contents can influence current thinking (e.g., implicit memory, implicit emotion). We also know that people can be motivated to forget unpleasant events and there is evidence that some women who are known to have been sexually abused in childhood could not recall this abuse as adults (Williams, 1994). But, we also know that people generally recall powerful emotional experiences better than neutral experiences and that memories tend to be constructed over time rather than being buried and then recovered in their original form. And, we know that people can believe they are remembering something that evidence shows never occurred.

Both the American Psychiatric Association and the American Psychological Association set up task forces to come to grips with the issue. The leader of the latter task force began by suggesting that everyone could agree on two ideas: First, there is evidence that people can forget and then remember things that actually occurred. Second, there is evidence that people can falsely recall something that did not occur. There was consensus on these two statements. Could this lead to consensus concerning the recovered memory–false memory debate? Evidently not, with the clinicians on the task force emphasizing the former, the experimentalists on the task force emphasizing the latter. Both the association task forces ended up with reports that concluded that although both actual and false recovered memories are possible, we have no way of differentiating between the two. At this point the situation remains that there are those who believe that the evidence for repression is substantial and those who believe that it is without scientific basis (Schacter, 1996), and there are those who suggest that reports of recovered memories are largely to be believed as well as those who suggest that such reports are largely to be viewed with skepticism.

The Psychoanalytic Unconscious and the Cognitive Unconscious: Can We Get Them Together?

In the chapter on the self we considered whether it was possible to get the psychoanalytic and social cognitive selves together. In this chapter, we have a parallel question: Is it possible to get the psychoanalytic and cognitive views of the unconscious together? There are those who view Freud's contributions to our understanding of the unconscious as basic, and much of subsequent research as supportive of Freud's view of the unconscious (Westen, 1998). There are those who see Freud as having made fundamental contributions, with evidence for unconscious processes such as the mechanisms of defense, but with different interpretations of the basis for these processes: "We have suggested that defense mechanism theory may need to downplay its original focus on impulse transformations and instead focus more directly on how possible images of self are protected and rejected" (Baumeister, Dale, & Sommer, 1998, p. 1116). And, there are those who view the cognitive unconscious as fundamentally different from the psychoanalytic unconscious and with little owed to Freud's legacy (Kihlstrom, 1999).

> *It is impressive to consider how well modern findings in social psychology, mostly obtained in systematic laboratory experiments with well-adjusted American university students, have confirmed the wisdom of Freud's theories, which were mostly based on informal observations of mentally afflicted Europeans nearly a century ago.*
>
> *Baumeister, Dale, & Sommer, 1998, p. 1115*

Modern research on cognition and the cognitive unconscious
owes nothing whatsoever to Freud and that is also the case with
modern research on emotion and the emotional unconscious.

Kihlstrom, 1999, p. 430

Psychoanalysts and cognitive psychologists agree that individuals can be influenced, in important ways, by information below the level of conscious awareness. Beyond this, the two views have a number of major differences between them. First, the contents of the two views tend to differ. The psychoanalytic unconscious contains sexual and aggressive wishes, fantasies, thoughts, and feelings. The contents of the cognitive unconscious are primarily thoughts that may have no special motivational significance for the individual. Second, the functions are different. In the psychoanalytic view, unconscious processes serve a defensive function; that is, they protect the individual from conscious awareness of painful thoughts and feelings. No such defensive function is associated with the cognitive unconscious. The contents of the cognitive unconscious are there primarily because they never reached consciousness or have become overly routinized and automatic.

A third difference between the two views is the qualitative nature of unconscious processes. The psychoanalytic view emphasizes primary processes as the language of the unconscious—the unconscious is illogical and irrational. Symbols, metaphors, and dreams are all expressions of the language of the unconscious. The cognitive view suggests no fundamental differences between conscious and unconscious processes. Fourth, there is a difference in views concerning availability to consciousness. The psychoanalytic view suggests that there are defensive barriers against the contents of the unconscious reaching consciousness. Special circumstances, such as those that occur in psychoanalysis, are necessary for this to occur. In contrast, the cognitive view suggests that no such barriers exist and that the transformation of unconscious contents into consciousness follows regular laws of memory.

In sum, we have major differences between the psychoanalytic and cognitive views of the unconscious. In addition, we have differences in the kind of evidence that is considered acceptable by representatives of the two points of view, clinical evidence in the case of psychoanalysts and empirical evidence in the case of cognitive psychologists. These differences in the two views of the unconscious and how unconscious processes are to be investigated are summed up by Kihlstrom as follows:

> Our modern view of unconscious mental life is quite different from Freud's. Freud's unconscious was irrational, hallucinatory, full of primitive affects and impulses. By contrast, the psychological unconscious of modern psychology is cognitive, rational, and propositional. Most important, we have agreed-upon rules by which we can infer the existence of unconscious percepts and memories from the results of formal experiments, whereas Freud was limited to speculations, which could never be tested, about the cases that he studied.

(Quoted in Pervin, 1996, p. 223)

Thus, the situation in regard to the unconscious would appear to be not terribly different from that in regard to the self. At this point in time it seems that we stand as little chance of reconciling the two views of the unconscious as we stand of getting our selves together. And, the reasons in the two cases appear to be the same—differences in relative emphasis on affect, conflict, and motivation, as well as differences in the kind of evidence that is considered acceptable.

Summary

In this chapter we have considered a topic of enormous theoretical and methodological importance to the field of personality psychology—the unconscious. Are there memories, emotions, and motives that exist outside of consciousness and, if so, what are the implications for how we understand and study people? Although the concept of the unconscious was not original to Freud, it was he who gave enormous importance to the unconscious for all aspects of human functioning and who set forth methods for investigation of the unconscious.

Prior to the 1950s, radical behaviorists excluded issues of consciousness from the realm of systematic psychological investigation. However, during the 1950s, with the New Look in Perception, and then with progress in the cognitive revolution and related developments in measurement techniques, investigation of unconscious phenomena became a serious area of inquiry. On the one hand, psychologists influenced by the ideas of Freud were particularly interested in investigating the influences of unconscious emotions and motives on behavior. On the other hand, cognitive psychologists were interested in unconscious processes that were more directly tied to conscious processing of information—implicit memory and implicit perception. Social psychologists adapted many of the concepts and techniques emphasized by cognitive psychologists to the investigation of social phenomena such as stereotypes and views of the self. In general, their view of unconscious processes coincided with that of cognitive psychologists.

Four issues were considered in relation to the unconscious. First, evidence concerning the existence of the Freudian mechanisms of defense was considered. In general there is evidence that people engage in a variety of self-deceptive processes and for mechanisms of defense such as projection and denial. There are differing views concerning the evidence for the concept of repression, a concept fundamental to psychoanalytic theory. Psychologists tend to agree that memories can be forgotten and recovered, and that some of this can be for motivated reasons. What is at greatest disagreement is whether there is a defensive barrier against the recall of some memories, a barrier that serves as a protection against anxiety and can be lifted under defined conditions. There is evidence that individuals differing on measures of repression (i.e., repressors vs. nonrepressors) show a variety of differences in recall and behavioral functioning. However, to date there has been no experimental demonstration of the phenomenon of repression.

Second, the issue of the relation between the use of defensive mechanisms and mental health was considered. On the one hand, there is the view that self-deception and positive illusions serve adaptive functions and are associated with healthy psychological functioning. On the other hand, there is the view that distortions of reality are associated with unhealthy psychological functioning. It is possible that what is important is the extent to which defensive processes are used. It also is possible that what is fundamental is the distinction between coping methods that involve conscious control that is, for the most part, realistic and situational, as opposed to defense mechanisms that are unconscious, characterological, and generally not open to correction by information. There may also be differences between short-term and long-term benefits and costs.

The third issue brought us back to the issue of repression and the question of recovered memories versus false memories. This is an important theoretical, legal, and personal issue for those associated with recovered memories. We know that people can recall experiences previously forgotten and that people can falsely recall events that never occurred. However, the extent to which we can trust recovered memories, particularly those recovered in situations where suggestion is a possible element, remains in debate. Two professional organizations considering the issue of recovered as opposed to false memories both concluded that it was impossible at this time to distinguish between the two. Generally there is more support among clinicians, particularly psychoanalytically oriented clinicians, for recovered memories and more support among experimental psychologists for false memories. These views tend to coincide with differing views on the evidence concerning repression.

The final issue considered was that of the relation between the psychoanalytic unconscious and the cognitive unconscious—could the two views be brought together? There are major differences between the two views in terms of contents, functions, processes, availability to consciousness, and evidence required to substantiate views. These differences suggest that at this time a reconciling of the two views is as likely as bringing the psychoanalytic and cognitive views of the self together.

In limiting discussion to these four issues, it should not be forgotten that the issue of the unconscious has tremendous implications for the assessment of personality, considered in Chapter 1 and touched upon in this chapter in relation to the distinction between explicit and implicit measures.

CHAPTER 9

Why Do And Don't People Change?

General Theme

Why do and don't people change? This is an issue of fundamental importance to personality psychology. Although addressed most specifically in the area of psychotherapy, it is of broader relevance. Are cognitions, emotions, or behaviors most central to the change process? Do all forms of therapy contain the same therapeutic ingredients or are there specific ingredients unique to each? These are some of the issues addressed in this chapter.

> *Life, at its best, is a flowing, changing process in which nothing is fixed.*
>
> *Rogers, 1961, p. 17*

> *I used to feel quite hopeful of reconditioning even adult personalities. . . . But with humans as lazy as they are*

about themselves. . .the zebra can as easily change his stripes as the adult his personality.

Watson, 1928, p. 138

Over the years, as a clinician, friend, and more general observer of human functioning, including my own, I am struck with the remarkable capacity for people to change, as well as their difficulty in changing. At times change, for better and for worse, seems so apparent and so much an intrinsic part of human functioning. Individuals who seem unable to get their lives together, all of a sudden do so. For example, at one point the life of football quarterback Kerry Collins seemed in a shambles. He had a drinking problem, was accused of making a racial slur and alienating his teammates, and was dropped by two professional football teams. A few years later, he appeared to have his life together, having become a recovering alcoholic and finding a home as quarterback of the New York Giants.

Often change seems inexplicably rapid and unanticipated. A patient of mine told me about sexual difficulties he and his wife had been having for some time. At some later point she shared with him a trauma that had occurred to her in childhood. There was a great outpouring of feeling and he in turn shared with her some childhood events that had led him to associated sex with considerable feelings of guilt. Following these disclosures, their sexual relationship improved dramatically. Why the sudden change for the better?

In contrast with such positive changes, there are individuals who appear to have their life in order, only to act out in some way that destroys the lives of others or their own life. Following a tragic suicide of cult members, newspaper reporters interviewed people who knew the cult members in the past. Inevitably one reads that "That wasn't the same person I knew," or "How could a person have changed so much?" Some time ago the *New York Times* carried a story about Gilles Gilbert, a professional hockey player (December 4, 1982). Gilbert, a goalie, was experiencing a skin condition that threatened his career. For a while he thought he was allergic to pucks. As the condition continued to worsen, he was forced to stay at home and consider his future. At that point his "entire personality" changed: "I was reacting like it was not me." Rather than being patient, he was always angry. He feared he was going crazy. Finally, the condition improved and he was able to return to playing hockey, with a return to his earlier personality functioning. How are we to understand such dramatic changes in personality functioning?

It was so bad. I think I'm a great father, but all of a sudden I changed, day and night. My wife said, "If you keep going that way, what will they think? You've changed so much."

Gilles Gilbert, Professional Hockey Player

And, of course, there are many for whom life, and their personality, goes on and remains pretty much the same.

How are we to understand such differences? We can ask the classic question in the field: Is it the person or the situation? That is, are some people more open to change and others less so, or does change revolve more around the circumstances in a person's life? Does change during the college years say something about the student or something about the environment and the pressures for change? Or, perhaps once more we have to consider interactions between persons and situations, with change in this case reflecting student characteristics, college characteristics, and the interaction between the two. Although such questions certainly are of interest to us as personality psychologists, most of all we want to know about the processes of change. That is, we want to understand what goes on when people change, including the factors that facilitate change and those that inhibit change.

What better place to study such questions than the process of psychotherapy? When people come to a therapist for help, they are seeking some change in their condition. They may not see a change in personality functioning as required, but in all forms of psychotherapy at some point it becomes clear that a change in them is required—a change in their behavior, a change in their emotions, a change in the way they think about things, a change in their situation, or some combination of these. Why has change been so difficult for them in the past? Why are some addicts (e.g., smoking, drinking, gambling, shopping) able to change on their own, while some require the assistance of a support group, and some find it impossible to change under any circumstances? Does psychotherapy help and, if so, are some forms of therapy better with some patients or problems and other therapies helpful for other patients and problems? Why do all forms of therapy fail with some patients? Is it something about the therapist? The patient? The match between the two?

These are enormously difficult questions and we will not be able to answer them in this chapter. What we will be able to do is consider some of the major views concerning the nature of psychotherapy and behavior change. From there we will consider the evidence concerning the effectiveness of psychotherapy and the ingredients of change that are common to all methods or specific to each. In focusing on psychotherapy, it should be clear that our effort is to understand why people do and do not change, rather than on whether one form of therapy is better than another or on issues concerning the evaluation of research in the field. A therapeutic procedure can be effective but for reasons very different from those suggested by the practitioners. In such instances, we want to know that this is the case and ask what the true effective ingredients are. In other words, although patients primarily are interested in results, our interest is in an understanding of the processes involved.

The Power of Suggestion

During the latter part of the eighteenth century, the Austrian physician Franz Mesmer successfully treated many patients. Mesmer was interested in the effects of the stars and gravity on humans. He believed that heavenly bodies, such as the stars, sun, and moon influence all bodies through the medium of a fluid that pervades the universe. His effort was to make use of the universal fluid of gravity and magnetism to cure illness. Thus, he first used magnets to treat patients, believing that a universal fluid with healing properties could enter the body by way of the magnets, restoring the proper balance of *animal magnetism.* Following this he was led to believe that magnets were not necessary and that other objects, including himself, could serve as conductors of the vital universal fluid. Typically patients would fall into a trance, experience a convulsion of sorts, and then find themselves able to function better. Even group treatment was possible. Presumably the healing could be attributed to the working of the animal magnetism, the universal fluid with its healing powers.

It should be clear that Mesmer was not a charlatan. Although we now believe that his curative powers resided in his powers of suggestion, what we now refer to as a *mesmerizing* effect, he viewed his efforts within a scientific framework. But, even by calling it suggestion, does this mean that we understand the processes involved? It is interesting that for a new drug to be approved by the government, it must be demonstrated to be better than a *placebo*, a pill that looks similar to the drug of interest but has no effect at all. In virtually all studies, the placebo is found to have some positive effect.[1] If the experimental drug is demonstrated to be superior to the placebo (i.e., it produces more positive effects and fewer negative effects), the pharmaceutical company and government agency (i.e., the Food and Drug Administration) are satisfied. They may not fully understand why the drug works and, perhaps of even greater relevance to our interests in this chapter, they do not care about why the placebo worked.

The point here is that therapeutic results can occur for unknown reasons or for reasons different from those suggested by honest, ethical practitioners. In the case of Mesmer, an explanation was offered that we now know was not accurate. In the case of the placebo, no explanation is offered or we attribute the effect to the placebo, the *placebo effect*, which is another way of saying that we do not understand why it occurred. In this chapter we are interested in results, but only insofar as they lead us toward an understanding of the processes involved. In the case of psychotherapy, we are interested in whether it is effective only insofar as this leads us toward an understanding of why people do and do not change.

Theoretical Approaches to Change in Psychotherapy

A great variety of approaches to psychotherapy exist, most offering some theoretical rationale for why they are effective. There are Freudians, Adlerians, Jungians, be-

---

[1] Since completion of this chapter a report has appeared that questions the existence of a placebo effect other than in the area of pain (Hrobjartsson & Gotzsche, 2001). According to this report, in nontreatment groups some proportion of patients improve in their condition, whether given a placebo or not. Thus, if treated patients are only compared with a placebo group, and some of the latter show improvement, one is incorrectly led to conclude that the placebo produced the improvement. It still is too early to tell whether this finding will stand up under further scrutiny. However, if it does, two points are noteworthy. First, it demonstrates how scientists can believe something incorrectly for an extended period of time. At the same time, it demonstrates the ultimate self-correcting nature of the scientific process. Second, such a finding in no way invalidates the basic point that psychological factors influence physical functioning.

havior modificationists, behavior therapists, cognitive behavior therapists, and so on. Is there some way in which we can find some uniformities among what otherwise may seem to be a bewildering array of possibilities? What I want to suggest is that although most forms of psychotherapy focus to some extent on emotional, behavioral, and cognitive processes as ingredients of change, they differ on which is viewed as the primary ingredient of change. Therefore, let us proceed in terms of whether psychotherapy is viewed primarily as a process of emotional change, behavioral change, or cognitive change.

Psychotherapy and Affective Modes of Change

In this section we consider treatment methods that suggest that affective or emotional change is the key element of constructive, therapeutic personality change. Such an emphasis on emotions goes back to the early work in psychoanalysis and includes Rogerian client-centered therapy and related experiential therapies. During the 1970s there was a great deal of interest in therapies that emphasized the expression of feelings as fundamental to change. For example, in *Gestalt therapy*, developed by Fritz Perls, who was trained as an analyst, the emphasis was on the immediacy of feelings in the here and now. Patients were encouraged to attend to their feelings so as to get in touch with their "true selves" and free themselves from the bondages of current and past others. Structured, emotion-producing situations and group encouragement often were used to facilitate the process. In one Gestalt workshop I attended, one member of the group worked on feelings in relation to his father by wrestling with another member of the group. While doing so he got in touch with and expressed the feelings of rage, fear, and helplessness he had felt toward his father and others. In another case, a member of the group worked on feelings in relation to his mother. The therapist had the group member lie down on the floor and then pressed her hands over his nose and mouth, producing a suffocating experience. The person experienced a flash of panic and terror as he got in touch with fears of being suffocated by his dominating mother and fears of dying without her assistance.

Another illustration of a therapeutic approach during this time that emphasized feelings was *scream therapy*. The underlying rationale for this approach was that psychologically disturbed individuals are bothered by frozen feelings of anger, fear, and pain. According to this view, patients have long-buried emotions, buried because of the fear induced by parents and because of societal punishments for the expression of emotions and rewards for affectless role playing. Therefore, the goal of scream therapy was to provide a means for the emergence of fear-frozen feelings. This was done in group sessions where members began a meeting by forming a circle, holding hands, and then screaming. The view was that screams release emotions repressed since childhood and thereby promote significant positive personality change. In one session I observed, group screams were followed by a member pounding a pillow, expressing rage at his father that he got in touch with during the beginning screams. Another member got in touch with the feeling of needing people as he screamed. He was encouraged to tell a member of the group that he needed her. He said "I need you" with increasing intensity, until finally he broke down sobbing while experiencing the full weight and pain of these previously buried feelings.

Approaches such as Gestalt therapy and scream therapy have faded from the field. They are presented here as illustrative of extreme approaches to emotional expression and change as the basis of the therapeutic enterprise. They also are presented here as illustrative of how approaches to therapy can be popular during a time and then fade, perhaps because they are expressive of psychological issues current in society at the time. Two more traditional approaches that emphasize emotions as fundamental in personality change are psychoanalysis and Rogerian client-centered therapy, the latter represented today in what are known as *experiential therapies*.

Psychoanalysis. Psychoanalysis as a method of therapy emphasizes both affective and cognitive change, and there has been some debate concerning the relative importance of the two. The cognitive emphasis is seen in the psychoanalytic emphasis on the recall of early memories or making conscious what was previously unconscious, and in the emphasis on the patient's gaining insight into the nature of his or her psychological functioning. Even the announced goal of "where Id was Ego shall be" suggests an increase in cognitive control over instincts. At the same time, emotional change has always played a critical role in psychoanalysis and remains central to the change process. Freud's earlier work emphasized not only the recall of memories but also cathartic abreaction—the discharge of blocked emotions. While a somewhat mechanistic notion, the view was that improvement occurred when the person was able to express, discharge, or release painful feelings associated with past traumatic events. Indeed, patients often feel better after they express or release anger or sadness. Often we experience such relief when we express feelings we are uncomfortable about to a trusted friend.

During World War II the drug sodium pentothal ("truth serum") was used to help combat personnel who had developed hysterical symptoms recall with full feeling the emotional event that led to the development of the symptom. While under the influence of the drug, they would recall events they had previously forgotten and release the painful feelings of fear, grief, and guilt associated with these events. The release of such feelings was often followed by a dramatic change and improvement in their symptom. A soldier with a paralysis of the trigger finger might recall the fear of shooting at an enemy soldier and the guilt about killing another human being, thereby recovering the use of his finger. Such instances of change associated with *catharsis*, the release of blocked emotions, fit well within the psychoanalytic framework.

Freud's thinking concerning the role of emotions, of course, proceeded beyond the emphasis on catharsis. The cornerstone of his entire theory of psychopathology is the emotion of anxiety. While psychoanalytic writings emphasize almost every emotion, it is anxiety that by far receives the greatest attention. It is anxiety that leads to the development of defenses that are the basis for symptom development and psychopathology. Therefore, in psychoanalysis it is the uncovering of anxiety and the diminution of anxiety that is the basis for positive change. The defenses must first be given up, often leading to a temporary increase in anxiety. Thus, a patient of mine described the feeling of tension and near panic as the wall of distance, aloofness, and emotional uninvolvement started to come down. Feelings previously warded off (e.g., anger), because of their association with anxiety, now start to be expressed and for a time may still be accompanied by anxiety. However, as the person examines his or her feelings in the relative safety of the therapist's office, gradually there is a recognition of the basis for the anxiety in the past that is no longer relevant in the present.

The emphasis on feelings is clearly seen in all analytic work. It is clearly seen in the emphasis on the transference or the response of the patient to the therapist in terms of earlier parental figures. Transference involves feelings. It is not the thoughts about the analyst that are of critical significance, but rather the feelings—the rage at frustration, the fears of abandonment, the anxiety about attack, and so forth. The reenactment of these feelings in relation to the analyst lies at the heart of psychoanalysis and provides the basis for insight and emotional growth. The patient gains insight into the earlier roots of his or her functioning and appreciates the basis for much of the defensive efforts. While insight thus includes a cognitive component, it should be clear that it contains an emotional component as well. It is not just the recall of memories and the intellectual understanding of one's functioning that is important. It also is the emotional reexperiencing of these events and the emotional turmoil and release associated with insight that are significant.

Analysis of the transference is one of the corner-stones of psychoanalytic technique. . . . Analysis of transference helps the patient understand how one misperceives, misinterprets, and relates to the present in terms of the past.

Arlow, 1995, p. 32

This recognition is not merely intellectual insight but is at the same time an emotional experience. . .what I call the corrective emotional experience. This is not the discovery of a new therapeutic factor; it is only an explicit recognition of the essential therapeutic agent in the psychoanalytic process, as formulated by Freud himself.

Alexander, 1956, pp. 41–42

The psychoanalytic emphasis on insight as an emotional experience that is basic to therapeutic change is most clearly seen in Alexander's concept of the *corrective emotional experience* (Alexander & French, 1946). According to this view, it is the emotional experience that is part of the transference process that is the key ingredient of psychoanalytic therapy. The corrective emotional experience is the central therapeutic agent in the change process. In the corrective emotional experience the patient feels the irrationality and inappropriateness of the reactions to the therapist. There is a feeling of recognition of the difference between the old situation and the new, between the parents or other significant earlier figures and the therapist and other significant persons in the present. The corrective emotional experience is possible in therapy because the therapist acts differently than did the parents, because the patient is older now and can use resources previously unavailable, and because the conflict and anxiety can be handled gradually rather than all at once.

Rogerian and Experiential Psychotherapies. The client-centered therapy of Carl Rogers departs from psychoanalytic therapy in many ways, but it too places a major emphasis on getting in touch with and changing feelings in therapy. In fact, as Rogers developed his therapeutic approach, there was an increased emphasis on the clarification of feelings in the patient and on the emotional aspects of the relationship between client and therapist. According to Rogers, people deny feelings access to consciousness because of the threat of loss of positive regard from others. In therapy, then, the proper climate must be created to allow clients to experience these feelings and integrate them into their self-concept. The process of personality change involves experiencing feelings freely in the immediate moment and risking being oneself in relating to others (Rogers, 1961).

How is such change to come about? One of the remarkable contributions of Rogers was his suggestion that the therapeutic climate is the most important ingredient of positive change. According to him, there are three necessary and sufficient conditions for therapeutic change—unconditional positive regard or warmth on the part of the therapist, empathic understanding by the therapist of the client's experiences, and congruence or genuiness of expression of the self in relation to the client. Note the emphasis here on *necessary* and *sufficient.* In other words, no therapeutic procedure could succeed if it did not provide these conditions, and any therapy that provided these conditions would be successful. All three involve affect and establishment of these conditions is viewed as leading to affective change in the client in terms of greater positive regard for self and others, greater empathic understanding of others, and greater congruence or genuiness of expression of the self in relation to others.

Experiential therapies cover a broad category of approaches that are similar in their emphasis on the client's ongoing experience, on the therapeutic relationship as central to therapy, and on new awareness as the basis of change (Greenberg, Elliot, & Lietaer, 1994). In contrast with psychoanalysis, they view the client-therapist relationship as real rather than an unconscious recreation of relationships from the past (i.e., transference): "Experiential therapies all define the facilitation of experiencing as the key therapeutic task, and almost all also view the therapeutic relationship as potentially curative...they generally share the view that a real relationship with the therapist provides the client with a new, emotionally validating experience and an opportunity to discriminate between past and present and to discover and own experience" (Greenberg, Elliott, & Lietaer, 1994, p. 509).

As indicated, psychotherapies that focus on emotions as fundamental to personality change can vary greatly in the specifics of how change comes about. However, their common emphasis distinguishes them from approaches that emphasize overt behavior or cognitions, to which we now turn.

Behavior Change—Behavior Modification

The clearest and most consistent emphasis on overt behavior is the Skinnerian-based program of *behavior modification*. Underlying this approach is the view that pathology consists of either learned maladaptive responses or the absence of adaptive responses. Therapy, or behavior modification, consists of the shaping of new behaviors. These behaviors will either conflict with and replace maladaptive responses or represent new adaptive responses. Concern is not with feelings inside the body or thoughts inside the head. Instead it is with the shaping of behavioral responses through the manipulation of environmental reinforcers. Behavior is assessed through the events that lead to problem behaviors and the reinforcing consequences that maintain them. These same reinforcers often are then used to shape and control the desired behavior. Necessary new behaviors are shaped by successive approximations. For example, in teaching language to autistic children, one may give reinforcements first for attending to the instructor-therapist, then for uttering sounds or vocalizations, and then for making sounds that progressively approximate letters and words. To teach the same child to get dressed involves breaking the behavior down into its component parts (e.g., putting on underwear, putting on pants, and putting on shirt) and then reinforcing the child for each part and for the linkages or chains between the parts.

Skinner's radical behaviorism was seen most clearly in his establishing schedules of reinforcements for pigeons pecking at a key. I can recall being amazed in 1958 at the adaptation of this learning model to research on schizophrenia. There were schizophrenic patients at a hospital tapping keys and being reinforced with candy or other reinforcers at various intervals and ratios. Could schizophrenic behavior be regulated by reinforcers in the same way as pigeon behavior or, according to Skinner, behavior in general? Following this there were efforts to set up *token economies*—psychiatric wards run completely on the basis of Skinnerian reinforcement principles. On such wards patients were given token reinforcers for producing behaviors considered desirable for their treatment. The tokens then could be cashed in for desired privileges or food. For example, in a treatment setting where individuals had problems in controlling their behavior, contracts would be established where privileges (e.g., greater ward freedom, a pass for the weekend) were made contingent on demonstrating the proper control of behavior and following established regulations. In some cases these token economies followed established principles of Skinner's operant conditioning program. In other cases, however, the rationale behind the token economy was corrupted by individuals purely interested in manipulating patients to do what they wanted them to do. That is, in some cases reinforcers were given in an arbitrary way for behaviors that were not necessarily part of the treatment plan or established contract. In addition, in some cases patients started their own "black market" economy, trading tokens for cigarettes and other such desired objects.

Behavior modification efforts were important in bringing attention to what the person *does*, not just what they are *feeling* or *thinking*. In addition, they were important in calling attention to the importance of external reinforcers in the regulation of behavior, a point that often was missed in other approaches. For example, often it could be pointed out to parents that they were unwittingly rewarding the very behaviors that they were trying to eliminate in their children. Beyond this, individuals could be taught to regulate their own behavior by establishing contracts with themselves and rewarding themselves for behaving in particular ways (e.g., buying an article of clothing for not smoking for a week or staying on a diet for a week). Nevertheless, limitations of behavior modification programs began to be recognized. With the cognitive revolution, there began a decline in the exclusive use of Skinnerian reinforcement principles as the basis for therapeutic change. Nevertheless, as we will see, behavior, what the person does, continues to be an important part of many current cognitively based therapeutic efforts.

Cognitive Modes of Change

Cognitive modes of psychotherapy emphasize changes in attitudes-beliefs as the essential ingredient of therapy. Two illustrations of the emphasis on the role of cognitions in the process of therapeutic change will be considered: the views of Albert Ellis and Aaron T. Beck. Ellis and Beck were trained as analysts prior to coming to their current views and modes of approach. Their approaches to therapeutic change differ radically from the psychoanalytic approach in their emphasis on change in cognitions, such as irrational or maladaptive beliefs, as the major element of the therapeutic endeavor. Changes in emotions are seen as following from changes in cognitions. In addition, the therapist is seen as playing an active role in directing patient efforts at change in contrast with the psychoanalytic emphasis on the blank screen analyst who allows for the development of transference.

Rational-Emotive Therapy (RET) deals with all kinds of irrationalities, illogicalities, superstitions, and unrealistic statements that people devoutly believe and use in a self-defeating way.

Ellis & Harper, 1975, pp. 202–203

The goals of cognitive therapy are to correct faulty information processing and to help patients modify assumptions that maintain maladaptive behaviors and emotions.

Beck & Weishaar, 1995, p. 242

Ellis's Rational-Emotive Therapy (RET). Albert Ellis calls his system of change *Rational-Emotive Therapy (RET)* (Ellis, 1995; Ellis & Harper, 1975). It is perhaps the most extreme system of cognitive emphasis because of its efforts to persuade, convince, and cajole the patient into a change in attitudes and beliefs. In fact, it was originally called *rational psychotherapy* and only later was extended to *rational-emotive psychotherapy*. While emotions are, as indicated in the title RET, recognized as important, they are seen as following from beliefs. The ABCs of RET suggest that antecedent (A) events or activators lead to beliefs (B) that then lead to emotional consequences (C) and behavior. Whereas we often skip the mediating link of cognitive beliefs and think that our feelings and behaviors follow from events, in fact they follow from our interpretations of these events. Neurotic feelings and neurotic behavior do not follow from events in the world or from dangerous instincts or wishes from within the body. Rather such feelings and behavior follow from irrational or illogical thinking. The causes of psychological disturbance are the irrational statements we make to ourselves—that we *must* do something, that we *have* to feel some way, that we *should* be some kind of person. Since the causes of disturbance do not lie in actual events or feelings but rather in our cognitive constructions, there is great potential for freedom and change—we can become liberated and change through changing our beliefs, attitudes, and statements we make to ourselves.

What are some of the major irrational beliefs people hold that run them into difficulty? The following are ten such beliefs that Ellis has found to be especially common in his patients.

1. *Need for Approval.* I must have love or approval from all of the people I find significant.

2. *Perfectionism and Fear of Failure.* I must prove that I am thoroughly competent, adequate, and achieving. I must have great competence or talent in some important area.

3. *Blame.* When people act obnoxiously and unfairly, I should blame and damn them, and see them as bad, wicked, or rotten individuals.

4. *Frustration = Catastrophe.* I have to view things as awful, terrible, horrible, and catastrophic when I get seriously frustrated, treated unfairly, or rejected.

5. *Helplessness.* Emotional misery comes from external pressures, and I have little ability to control or change my feelings.

6. *Preoccupation.* If something seems dangerous or fearsome, I must preoccupy myself with it and make myself anxious about it.

7. *Avoidance.* I can more easily avoid facing many life difficulties and self- responsibilities than undertake more rewarding forms of self-discipline.

8. *Victim of the Past.* My past remains all-important and because something once strongly influenced my life it must keep determining my feelings and behavior today.

9. *Chasing Nirvana.* People and things should turn out better than they do and I must view it as awful and horrible if I don't find good solutions to life's grim realities.

10. *Passivity and Boredom*—Avoiding Risks. I can achieve maximum human happiness by inertia and inaction or by passively and uncommittedly enjoying myself.

Many, perhaps most, of these beliefs will ring true to many readers. What characterizes them is their extreme nature, as if everything depended on the way the person behaves or the way others treat the person. What they suggest is a rather simplified, black–white, childlike view of the world. The self is seen as virtually helpless and totally dependent on others. If frustration occurs, the person blames the self or others rather than accepting that life has inevitable frustrations and acting to minimize future frustrations.

Probably therapists of all theoretical orientations would recognize these beliefs in their patients, thought they might understand them differently and treat them differently. How does Ellis treat them? First, he seeks to make the individual aware of his or her irrational beliefs. Most individuals are not aware of the irrational beliefs they hold. Even if they are aware of them in a general way, often they are unaware of how these beliefs enter into so many aspects of their thinking, feeling, and behaving. Thus the task for Ellis, or any RET therapist, is to make the individual aware of his or her irrational beliefs, both generally and in terms of each and every place that they may arise. The patients may try to deny their irrational nature, seek to hold onto them by minimizing their importance, or suggest that they are bound by them since they can't imagine thinking any other way. In each case Ellis confronts the person with the illogical nature of the belief, including the belief that the individual must believe as he or she does or is helpless to look at things any other way. To get people to recognize their irrational beliefs, Ellis may draw them to ridiculous extremes. To get people to change their beliefs, he may argue with them, ridicule their beliefs, use wit and humor to remove the power and mystique of the beliefs, and urge them to test out reality concerning what they and others can do. Often his style is aggressive and challenging, but generally people recognize that it is their belief system that is being attacked rather than themselves as people or their worth as individuals.

In an Ellis workshop I attended I observed him interview a woman who was obsessed with jealousy and envy concerning her successful former husband. In a short period of time Ellis elicited many of the beliefs that she held and that generally are involved with jealousy and possessiveness. Among the beliefs she held were the following: Her former husband was the only real mate for her; she must be perfect to be loved by any man; she must be loved totally; if she is not loved totally then she is unloved totally and totally unlovable; she must be absolutely sure that no man will ever leave her again before she can get involved again; because her husband is successful and "seemingly happy," she must blame herself for the divorce and remain a prisoner of the past; she must prove herself superior to her former husband by competing with him but since success here is not possible she might as well give up. The woman was surprised that so many of the people in the audience questioned whether that was the only way she could view things. Whatever happened to her afterwards, she left the interview with at least something of a new perspective on what previously had been a totally baffling situation.

Ellis's therapy is active, direct, and present-oriented. While he does not exclude emotion and overt behavior from discussion, the emphasis steadfastedly remains on the belief system of the individual. Irrational beliefs are the basis for neurotic difficulties; the changes in these beliefs provide the foundation for therapeutic change and growth.

Beck's Cognitive Therapy. As was noted earlier, Beck was trained as an analyst. However, he felt that psychoanalytic techniques were not working with many of the depressed patients that came to him for help, and gradually he developed his current cognitive emphasis (Beck, 1972, 1993). The rationale for Beck's treatment of depression is that the depressed patient systematically misevaluates ongoing and past experiences, leading to a view of the self as a "loser" and a view of the future as bleak. It is this unrealistic belief system and associated negative thinking that lead to unpleasant affects and the self-defeative behavior associated with depression—passivity, self-blame, sadness, loss of the pleasure response, and suicidal feelings. The depressed patient has a cognitive problem in that thinking focuses on the theme of loss, either exaggerating a loss or overgeneralizing from it. Note that the problem in thinking does not follow from difficulties in other areas, as would be true according to other views. For example, the psychoanalytic view of depression would emphasize how the depressed individual has turned his or her rage inward against the self and attempts to ward off feelings of anxiety associated with a sense of helplessness. According to Beck, on the other hand, the problem of depression is a cognitive one. It is thinking that affects feeling. The depressed person feels sad and lonely because he or she erroneously thinks of the self as inadequate and deserted.

What are the thinking problems of depressives? The problem with depressives is their negative thoughts concerning the self, the future, and the environment. The negative view of the self leads to unfavorable comparisons with others, self-criticism, and self-reproach. The negative view of the future is associated with pessimism and the expectation of failure. The negative view of the environment leads to frustration, gloom, and a sense that life is overwhelming. People with the problem of depression exaggerate events so that everyday difficulties are magnified into disasters. Such people also over-generalize so that a single instance of rejection is assumed to mean "nobody likes me" or a single instance of failure is taken to mean "I can't do anything. I'm a complete failure." As with Ellis, Beck notes some common misconceptions of depressed people: I have to be successful in everything to be happy; if I'm not on top, I'm a flop; if I make a mistake, it means I'm inept; if somebody disagrees with me, it means they don't like me.

What is to be done about such negative thoughts and thinking errors? Beck suggests the use of cognitive and behavioral approaches to alter the patient's conception of the self and the world. The patient is asked to keep busy and is given exercises or tasks that have maximum likelihood of success and pleasure. The patient is given training in the correction of faulty thinking so that negative statements are replaced with positive, balanced statements. Unrealistic pessimism is questioned. The patients are asked to consider whether they are too hard on themselves. The role of the therapist is to help to clarify, test out, and objectify faulty interpretations of experience by the patient. Invalid statements are pointed out and questionable statements are challenged. On the basis of his extensive experience and the treatment of depression, Beck suggests that such an approach leads to change in the evaluation of ongoing and past experiences and thereby to a lifting of the depression.

Although this discussion has focused on depression, the same elements are present in the cognitive therapy approach to other psychological disorders. Each disorder is assumed to have associated with it a specific constellation of beliefs that are problematic and require change for psychological improvement to occur. In all cases the therapist and patient engage in what Beck calls the enterprise of collaborative empiricism where, with the model of the scientist in mind, beliefs are checked out against data. Where irrational beliefs are held, the person is challenged to revise them in the light of data. Where experience confirms beliefs, the person is challenged to consider alternative ways of behaving that can lead to different experiences that will provide supportive data for new beliefs. In sum, in common with Ellis and with other cognitive approaches, Beck's focus is on the correction of faulty cognitions as the main therapeutic task. The correction of such faulty cognitions is seen as occurring both through the development of better cognitive skills for evaluating data and by behaving in ways that will lead to new kinds of data. In both cases therapeutic change is seen as involving the development of more realistic and adaptive ways of viewing the self and the world.

Does Psychotherapy Work? Are Some Approaches More Effective than Others?

Our interest in this chapter is in understanding why people do and do not change. We have taken the area of psychotherapy as the focus for consideration of this issue since the task of psychotherapy is personality change and alternative procedures exist for producing change. As we have seen in the previous section, these alternative forms of therapy differ in their focus on what needs to be changed as well as in their views concerning how change comes about. We now are ready to ask the question of whether there is evidence for the effectiveness of psychotherapy, whether some forms of therapy are more successful than others, either generally or in the treatment of specific problems, and whether the data concerning effectiveness shed any light on the processes involved in personality change. This is a complicated area of research with differing views concerning what should be measured (e.g., specific problems as opposed to general personality functioning), how it should be measured (e.g., patient reports, therapist reports, actual behavioral observations), whether studies conducted in the laboratory have relevance for daily clinical practice, as well as a host of other issues. Our effort here will not be to consider these issues but rather to focus on what the literature can tell us about why people do and do not change.

Does psychotherapy work? I remember sitting with a patient. She had read an article by Hans Eysenck which questioned whether psychotherapy did any good since there was evidence that, with or without psychotherapy, about one-third of the people with difficulties showed major improvement, about one-third showed some improvement, and about one-third showed no improvement at all. Her reading of the article was quite accurate and raised a very fundamental and difficult question, one that has occupied psychologists for many years and continues to do so today. Does psychotherapy work? For whom? With which therapists? Why?

Copious evidence already exists for the proposition that psychotherapy in general is effective for clients in general.

Chambless & Ollendick, 2001, p. 699

The evidence from these analyses supports the conjecture that the efficacy of bona fide treatments are roughly equivalent. . .the equivalence of outcome in psychotherapy has been called the Dodo bird effect.

Wampold, et al., 1997, p. 203

Although there are a large number of therapies, each with its own rationale and specific techniques, there is only modest evidence to suggest the superiority of one school or technique over another.

Lambert & Bergin, 1994, p. 161

Fortunately, we are in a better position to answer questions concerning the effectiveness of psychotherapy than we were at the time of my patient's reading of the article by Eysenck. A number of studies comparing various forms of psychotherapy with one another or with a no-treatment control group have concluded that diverse therapies appear to be equally effective (Wampold et al., 1997). These studies support the 1979 headline in the *New York Times* that read "Consensus Is Reached: Psychotherapy Works." The conclusion that all therapies are of roughly equivalent outcome has come to be known as the *Dodo bird effect,* after the Dodo bird in *Alice in Wonderland* who said: "Everybody has won, and all must have prizes."

The conclusion that "all must have prizes" is based primarily on empirical comparisons of treatments. Another approach to the evaluation of the effectiveness of psychotherapy was taken by *Consumer Reports* (November, 1995). In 1994, 180,000 subscribers to the magazine were asked to respond to a survey about mental health and psychotherapy, along with its customary inquiries about appliances, services, and so on. About 4 percent of the subscribers responded to the mental health questions, of whom about 60 percent (nearly 4 percent of the original sample of subscribers) reported having gone to some combination of mental health professionals, family doctors, and support groups. What were the experiences reported by the respondents? Among the major findings reported by Seligman (1995), a consultant to the study, are the following:

1. Treatment by a mental health professional worked—most respondents reported getting a lot better.

2. Long-term therapy produced more improvement than short-term therapy.

3. There was no difference between psychotherapy alone and psychotherapy plus medication for any disorder.

4. While all mental health professionals appeared to help their patients, psychologists, psychiatrists, and social workers did equally well and better than marriage counselors.

5. Respondents who tried self-help groups, especially Alcoholics Anonymous, did especially well.

6. Active shoppers and active clients did better in treatment than passive recipients.

7. "No specific modality of psychotherapy did any better than any other for any problem. These results confirm the 'dodo bird' hypothesis, that all forms of psychotherapies do about equally well" (p. 969).

These conclusions have been criticized on a variety of grounds (e.g., percentage of respondents, self-report only, lack of distinction among success of specific forms of treatment with specific disorders, etc.), and it has been called a survey of consumer satisfaction rather than one of therapeutic effectiveness (Nathan, Stuart, & Dolan, 2000). However, the final point noted above, confirmation of the Dodo bird effect, is striking in that it agrees with reviews of empirical studies.

Clearly support for the Dodo bird hypothesis poses a challenge for those who support the effectiveness of specific forms of therapy. If all forms of therapy are overall of about equal effectiveness, what does this say about the theory behind each technique? Do they all work for the same reasons or is it possible that different techniques are of equal effectiveness but work for different reasons? Or, is it possible that different techniques work with different disorders or different people? The Dodo bird hypothesis is rejected by some as absurd: Would one ever recommend the same form of psychotherapy regardless of the nature of the problem (Rachman & Wilson, 1980)? For others it is left as a hypothesis neither confirmed nor denied; that is, the question of differential effectiveness among psychotherapies generally, and in relation to specific disorders, is left open (Nathan, Stuart, & Dolan, 2000; Wampold et al., 1997). Regardless, we are left with the question of *why*: Why do and don't people change? What are the processes involved? Are there common ingredients to all forms of therapy or ingredients specific to each?

The Effectiveness of Psychotherapy: Common or Specific Ingredients?

> *We know that psychotherapy is generally effective but we are uncertain as to why. . . . The traditional view that the different psychotherapies—similar to medication treatments—contain unique active ingredients resulting in specific effects has not been validated.*
>
> *Kopta, Lueger, Saunders, & Howard, 1999, p. 461–62*

> *Future research needs to ascertain the variables that actually produce positive patient change.*
>
> *Garfield, 1998, p. 124*

Let us assume, for the time being, that the Dodo bird effect in general is valid. How are we to account for such an effect? One possibility is that there are common, nonspecific ingredients to all methods of effective therapeutic change. What might be such nonspecific ingredients? Note that we are not talking here about some placebo effect, which typically is considered to be some "inert substance." The inert substance of a placebo may be related to the power of suggestion, though just how the healing power of suggestion works is not clear. But when we speak of nonspecific effects, we are talking about actual therapeutic ingredients that are common to all effective forms of psychotherapy.

Ingredients Common to All Forms of Psychotherapy

An early suggestion concerning a nonspecific ingredient of all psychotherapies was that of *hope.* In his 1973 book on *Persuasion and Healing*, Jerome Frank suggested that the therapeutic ingredient of all forms of therapy is that they help to combat demoralization. Here, and in his later book (Frank & Frank, 1991), he suggested that despite the diversity of complaints, patients are suffering from a demoralization that results from the inability to cope with the stressful aspects of life. There is a lack of faith, a loss of morale, and a loss of hope. The effectiveness of all forms of psychotherapy, then, lies in their ability to combat the state of demoralization that exists in the patient. In sum, according to Frank all successful forms of psychotherapy restore in the patient morale, hope, faith, and a sense of control over life events.

A second suggestion concerning nonspecific effects was made by Carl Rogers. As noted earlier in this chapter, Rogers suggested that the necessary and sufficient conditions for therapeutic change were that the proper therapeutic climate be established. This climate was seen as depending upon the therapist being genuine and communicating both unconditional positive regard and empathic understanding. One of the most consistent findings in the psychotherapy literature is that the therapeutic alliance is a critical factor in successful therapeutic change (Beutler, 2000). Central to the development of such an alliance are therapist characteristics such as warmth, respect, and expertness (Lambert & Bergin, 1994). Although specific terms may differ, the importance of the therapeutic alliance, and of these therapist characteristics in helping to establish this alliance, fit well with Rogers' views concerning the necessary and sufficient conditions of therapeutic change.

In 1961 Bandura published a paper which unfortunately has been lost from the literature. In this paper Bandura (1961) interpreted psychotherapy as a learning process and suggested that learning processes mediate behavior change. The relevant learning processes included *counterconditioning* (i.e., the conditioning of responses, such as relaxation, that are incompatible with anxiety), *extinction* (i.e., the unlearning of a response when it is not followed by reinforcement), *discrimination learning* (i.e., the ability to discriminate among situations that are and are not problematic and to respond differentially accordingly), *positive reinforcement* (i.e., the development of new responses and patterns of behaving as a result of therapist reinforcement in the form of interest and approval), and *social imitation* (i.e., modeling of healthy therapist behavior).

This emphasis on psychotherapy as a learning process that can be tied to basic principles of learning has always made sense to me. However, with the cognitive revolution, and the decrease in interest in the older theories of learning (e.g., S-R theory and operant conditioning theory), this emphasis was lost from the field. Bandura himself went on to emphasize cognitive variables and to suggest that the common ingredient of all successful therapy is the development of *self-efficacy beliefs* (i.e., the perceived ability to cope with specific situations). According to Bandura (1982), all forms of psychotherapy work through an increase in the level and strength of the patient's self-efficacy beliefs. Bandura emphasized that actual experience was critical for the development of these beliefs and recommended procedures to help patients to overcome anxieties associated with perceptions of self-inefficacy. Regardless of the procedures used, however, according to him it was changes in self-efficacy beliefs that is the common ingredient to all forms of therapeutic change.

Finally, we come to Pennebaker's (1997) suggestion that "the mere act of disclosure is a powerful therapeutic agent that may account for a substantial percentage of the variance in the healing process" (p. 162). I must say that I find Pennebaker's work among the most intriguing and amazing in the field. In one of his earliest studies, Pennebaker examined whether writing about traumatic experiences for 15 to 30 minutes a day for four days would have therapeutic effects on physical health. His view was that inhibition, or holding back thoughts and feelings, is associated with stress and the potential for disease, so perhaps writing about traumatic experiences would reduce such inhibition and have therapeutic value. In this research he compared the effects of writing about traumatic experiences with writing about superficial topics on number of visits to the health center, measures of immune system functioning, blood pressure levels, and subjective distress. Lo and behold, just writing about traumatic experiences during a four-day period was associated with a decline in health center visits, better physiological functioning (immune system, blood pressure), and lower levels of subjective distress relative to writing about superficial topics (Pennebaker, Kiecolt-Glaser, & Glaser, 1988). His conclusion was that "opening up" or confiding in others had healing power (Pennebaker, 1990).

Frankly, I was skeptical that these results would be replicated by others. However, the finding of value in writing about emotional experiences has been replicated in many studies, with varied populations, in diverse cultures. Writing or talking about emotional experiences, relative to writing or talking about superficial topics, has consistently been found to be associated with the following: decreases in physician visits, improved immune system functioning, fewer absences from work, higher grade-point averages, and improvement in mood and other indicators of psychological well-being (Pennebaker, 1997). In sum, what Pennebaker calls the "disclosure phenomenon" appears to generalize across settings, individuals, and cultures.

Why does writing work? What is the nature of the "disclosure phenomenon?" As noted, Pennebaker originally thought that disclosure worked through reduction of the negative effects of inhibition. However, he has not been able to find evidence in support for the view that disclosure improves health through the reduction of inhibition. For example, individuals appear to benefit as much from writing about traumas already discussed with others as from writing about traumas they have kept secret. And, self-reports of changes in inhibition have not been found to be associated with health changes. Catharsis does not appear to be the theapeutic ingredient (Kelly, Klusas, von Weiss, & Kenny, 2001).

At this point Pennebaker believes that putting traumatic or emotional experiences into words—as seen in writing, praying, undergoing psychotherapy, talking with friends, or confessing to the police—helps to organize our thoughts and feelings, and thereby reduces the biological upheavals of stress. Apparently, communicating about one's deepest thoughts and feelings facilitiates cognitive understanding of traumatic events and helps to maintain social ties (Pennebaker & Graybeal, 2001). Continuing research investigates questions concerning the specific processes through which "opening up" helps physical and emotional well-being. However, at this point the effect appears to be well documented and important.

. . .the mere act of disclosure is a powerful therapeutic agent that may account for a substantial percentage of the variance in the healing process.

Pennebaker, 1997, p. 162

So, we have a number of candidates for common, nonspecific agents of therapeutic change—hope, therapeutic alliance, principles of learning, changes in self-efficacy beliefs, and disclosure. They vary in degree of empirical support, in clarity of exposition of the processes involved in therapeutic change, and in the extent to which they are related to broader psychological theory. Interestingly enough, none has formed the basis for a widely practiced form of therapy. This is because practitioners continue to believe in the efficacy of ingredients specific to their approach.

Ingredients Specific to Each Form of Psychotherapy

Is there evidence in support of the view of specific ingredients? In medicine we would not expect to treat all illnesses with the same medication. We would want to know which medications were effective for which illnesses, and hopefully to understand the basis for their effectiveness as well. Is there evidence, then, that different forms of therapy work for different reasons, or that they are differentially effective with different patients because of the specific therapeutic ingredients associated with each procedure? The view of differential effectiveness with specific psychological disorders, as a result of the application of specific therapeutic procedures, continues to be held by many. This is particularly the case among proponents of cognitive therapy and cognitive behavior therapy. The suggestion is that studies supportive of the Dodo bird effect fail to examine differential effectiveness for different disorders. This has led to clinical trials comparing the effectiveness of alternative procedures for specific problems, as is done in the medical field, and the development of lists of empirically supported treatments (ESTs) (Chambless & Ollendick, 2001).

What is the evidence in support of differential effectiveness and specific ingredients? First, concerning differential effectiveness, there is some evidence that some forms of therapy are more effective with specific disorders but it remains too early to form firm conclusions. And what of the matter of specific ingredients? That is, is there evidence of different therapeutic procedures working because of the specific processes emphasized? Little if any evidence can be found to support the psychoanalytic emphasis on the importance of transference and the corrective emotional experience. It has proven to be difficult to distinguish between psychoanalysis and psychodynamic therapy, and training programs to improve the use of transference phenomena in therapy have not been proven to be successful (Henry, Strupp, Schacht, & Gaston, 1994; Wallerstein, 1989).

Most of the research on specific therapeutic ingredients has been done in relation to cognitive behavior therapy (CBT). As indicated, there is considerable evidence of the effectiveness of various forms of cognitive therapy. However, a variety of experts in the field, including many who are committed to these forms of therapy, suggest that the mechanisms through which change occurs are poorly understood (Brewin, 1996; Wilson & Fairburn, 1993). For example, in the treatment of depression, it is not clear whether cognitive processes *cause* changes in depression, are *associated with* other processes that lead to changes in depression, or *follow from* changes in depression (Hollon, DeRubeis, & Evans, 1987). In addition, it is suggested that there is not a close tie between the therapy and experimental work in cognitive psychology (Brewin, 1989).

Quite recently I came across some research which, it seemed to me, suggested support for the relation of specific cognitive processes to therapeutic change. In this research, sudden gains in therapy were found to be preceded by sessions in which there was evidence of substantial cognitive change, suggesting that the cognitive changes *caused* the sudden gains in well-being (Tang & DeRubeis, 1999a,b). Illustrative cognitive changes were bringing a belief into awareness, identifying an error in a belief or way of thinking, arriving at a new belief, and accepting a new cognitive technique. What was particularly striking was that the cognitive changes could be identified, that they occurred early in treatment, and that the effects seemed to hold over the course of an 18-month follow-up. What was left unclear was what led up to the cognitive changes, but the finding nevertheless seemed significant.

What surprised me was the response of other researchers in the field, all of whom were proponents of cognitive behavior therapy (CBT). For example, the suggestion was made that sudden gains occur in other treatments as well as in CBT and, in any case, that these gains occurred too early in treatment to alone account for the therapeutic results (Ilardi & Craighead, 1999; Rachman, 1999; Wilson, 1999). Indeed, in their commentaries these experts suggested that the results once more focused attention on nonspecific ingredients in therapy and brought into question the cognitive theory underlying the therapy. In other words, rather than moving us toward clarification of specific effects, the research was viewed as returning us to the issue of nonspecific effects and causal mechanisms.

These results suggest that cognitive change is an important therapeutic factor in CBT.

Tang & DeRubeis, 1999a, p. 900

Rapid response to CBT. . .focuses renewed attention on specifying the so-called 'nonspecifics' of therapy.

Wilson, 1999, p. 289

The rapid early responses raise the uncomfortable possibility that a large part of the response to treatment is nonspecific, and the responses bear some resemblance to the rapid early response that is characteristically found in placebo reactions.

Rachman, 1999, p. 293

It is to the credit of the cognitive behavioral researchers that they are seeking to understand the causal mechanisms involved and are not ready to leap to conclusions based on limited evidence. At the same time, we are left with the following conclusions: We have not found clear evidence in support of the hypothesis of active ingredients specific to different forms of therapy and we are without a close tie between therapeutic practice and basic theory in the field.

Why Don't People Change?

I used to feel quite hopeful of reconditioning even adult personalities. . . . But with humans as lazy as they are about themselves. . .the zebra can as easily change his stripes as the adult his personality.

Watson, 1928, p. 138

Unfortunately, all forms of therapy, with all disorders, report failures. At least as important as the question of why therapy works, then, is the question of why it doesn't work. Why people *don't* change is part and parcel of an understanding of change processes. Yet, many approaches to therapy fail to address the issue.

Early in my own clinical work I became impressed with what patients appeared to be saying: that they wanted relief from pain and suffering but did not want to change. It was as if there was some fantasy that relief could occur without change. More recently, I was struck by the comment of a patient concerning his goals for therapy. He sated that he did not want a change in feeling or a change in belief, but a change in his actual situation. The problem was that he had an obsessive fear of death. He hoped for immortality rather than for a decrease in anxiety concerning death. He was not psychotic, understood that what he hoped for was impossible, but still clung to this wish with great tenacity. How often is it the case that people do not change in therapy because it means giving up some wish or fantasy that they consider central or necessary to their emotional well-being and cognitive belief system?

One explanation for why change doesn't occur in therapy is that the proper techniques were not used. For example, Rogerians would suggest that the necessary and sufficient conditions of unconditional positive regard, empathic understanding, and congruence were not established. Another suggestion is that reinforcers outside of therapy maintain pathological patterns of thinking, feeling, and behaving. For example, it is not unusual for a person in treatment to find resistance to his or her changing on the part of a partner. The two may have worked out an arrangement where one is dependent on the other. If one seeks to be less dependent, or seeks to be less of a caretaker, the other may do everything possible to maintain the established relationship pattern. This can occur on a conscious or unconscious basis.

In terms of cognitive therapy, change may not occur because not all of the irrational thoughts have been uncovered. One such thought might be "I can't change." Another might be "Life without neurotic conflict is dull." Thoughts such as these can be a fundamental part of the cognitive belief system of an individual without his or her being aware of them. Another, to me rather unusual explanation, is that people have an "innate" tendency to hold onto irrational ideas (Ellis, 1987). Much more based on experimental work is Swann's (1997) emphasis on the need for self-verification so as to maintain cognitive system functioning. To the extent that therapy involves changes in the way one views the self, the self-verification motive may interfere with change, even where such change is associated with self-enhancement.

The psychoanalytic group probably has given the greatest attention to the question of why patients do not change. Their concept of *resistance*, suggesting that patients are motivated to resist change, has been adopted by other schools although the suggested basis for resistance may differ. According to the psychoanalytic view of resistance, patients may actively resist change in ways that are expressive of their broader difficulties. For example, I remember a patient telling me that he would like to feel better about himself and life at the end of therapy. I indicated that I would like this for him as well, following which he responded: "Then I don't want it." He would do anything to avoid gratifying my needs or the needs of others or, in his mind, having to feel grateful. What came up here, in the form of resistance, was fundamental to the difficulties with which he struggled more generally.

Psychoanalysts suggest that resistance occurs when patients experience anxiety associated with facing old conflicts. Another source of resistance is the wish not to give up old pleasures. For example, one patient asked if they would have to give up masturbation if they got married: "I've always been a loner and intercourse could never be as good as masturbation when I only focus on my own pleasures." Another source of resistance emphasized is the blow to one's narcissism when one has to say "I'm not all right the way I am." Or, there may be the threat that no new parts will be found to replace discarded parts of the self.

In sum, anxiety and the loss of rewards associated with change may be associated with active resistance to change. Change means uncertainty about what comes next and the potential that things will get worse rather than better. For these and perhaps other reasons as well, change is not easy. In all therapies, obstacles must be overcome to produce change. Yet, our understanding of the basis for these obstacles is no further along than our understanding of the processes that lead to change.

Conclusion

In many ways it is easy to summarize what is known concerning psychotherapeutic change: (1.) There is evidence that psychotherapy does work. (2.) Although there may be some variation in the effectiveness of different approaches, generally and in relation to the treatment of specific disorders, the Dodo bird effect of "equal prizes for all" remains the most consistent finding. (3.) Despite diverse theoretical accounts, we still do not understand why people do and do not change. (4.) No current form of therapy that is broadly practiced is closely tied to theoretical developments in other parts of psychology.

From my own standpoint, one of the problems in this area has been the narrow focus of practitioners and researchers in the field on the practice of psychotherapy rather than more broadly on the issue of processes of personality change. Aside from maturation, for many people change is a natural part of life. Anthropologists are interested in change in terms of how people adapt to cultural change. Sociologists are interested in how people adapt to social change. Social psychologists are interested in attitude change. Developmental psychologists and personality psychologists are interested in how people change during periods of transition, such as from high school to college, from single living to partner living, from marriage to parenthood, from marriage to divorce, from early adulthood to middle age and old age. All of these involve processes going on in the individual, and between the individual and the surrounding environment, that reflect forces promoting and inhibiting change.

Given the ubiquity of change, in some ways it is surprising that so little broader theoretical attention has been given to the forces promoting and inhibiting change. For example, we might speculate that change is more likely when there is internal motivation for change (e.g., pain under the current circumstances or anticipated gain from change) and external pressure for change. Internal motivation for change is what draws patients into psychotherapy and external pressure for change occurs when a society is undergoing change, for example, when communist countries changed to capitalist economies. Conversely, we might speculate that change is less likely where there is little internal motivation for change and little external pressure to change. Facility for change may be both a general personality characteristic and a response to specific situational ingredients. For example, some people are comfortable with change, even seek it, while others rigidly maintain the status quo. Some new environments represent dramatic shifts in ways of living while others are less challenging in this regard, and some provide considerable support during the change process while others are less supportive. I think here of the challenges faced by immigrants to this country as well as to other countries. For some the change involved is enormous, for others less so. And, for some there is considerable social group support for change while for others this is completely absent. In these cases some immigrants show tremendous adaptive resources in coping with change, while others are overcome with feelings of helplessness.

In sum, the challenges of, and opportunities for, change occur in many walks of life. Presumably the processes involved do not differ greatly from one to the other. Each would appear to offer to personality psychologists the potential for greater understanding of why people do and do not change.

Summary

In this chapter we have been concerned with understanding the processes involved in personality change and in answering the question of why people do and do not change. The area of psychotherapy was selected as a focus of inquiry since it is specifically concerned with this question. Although all forms of psychotherapy recognize the importance of cognitions, feelings, and behaviors in pathology and change, they differ in their focus on one or the other. Some forms of therapy emphasize affect as central to the change process, as in the psychoanalytic emphasis on the corrective emotional experience. The transference relationship is viewed as one place in which both cognitive and emotional insight can be gained into how current difficulties are related to patterns of relationships established earlier in life. Other forms of therapy emphasize behavior as central to the change process, as in the behavior modification procedures based on Skinnerian operant conditioning. And, some forms of therapy emphasize cognitive change as central, as illustrated in Ellis' RET and Beck's cognitive therapy.

Many years of research on the effectiveness of various forms of therapy have led to support for the Dodo bird hypothesis—all forms of therapy deserve prizes since they are equally effective. At the same time, many suggest that with further research we will find that various therapies are differentially effective in general and in relation to specific problems. In either case we are left with the task of considering whether the various forms of therapy contain common ingredients or ingredients of change that are specific to each. Suggested common ingredients include Frank's emphasis on hope and the combatting of demoralization, Rogers' emphasis on the necessary and sufficient conditions of therapeutic change, Bandura's emphasis on changes in self-efficacy beliefs, and Pennebaker's emphasis on the value of self-disclosure. Suggested specific ingredients are part of each theoretical approach. However, to date there is little evidence supportive of the view that a form of therapy makes use of ingredients unique to it. Thus, while evidence has been accumulated that therapy is effective, we are without an understanding of the ingredients of this effectiveness. In addition, we are without the close ties between clinical practice and broader psychological theory that are considered desirable. Attempts to explain psychotherapy in terms of established learning principles were made in the past but these did not lead to new therapeutic practices and fell into disfavor with the advent of the cognitive revolution.

All forms of therapy experience failures. Thus, it is essential to understand the processes that interfere with positive change as well as those that promote it. Various explanations have been offered for why people do not change in therapy: the proper therapeutic procedures have not been employed, external reinforcers operate against the changes being promoted in therapy, the self-verification motive that leads people to maintain a self-view even when it is negative or painful, and the psychoanalytic emphasis on anxieties and rewards that underlie resistance as an active force against change. These possible factors inhibiting change have received less empirical investigation than those promoting change and we similarly are without a clear understanding of them.

Personality change occurs in varied walks of life and is not limited to the process of psychotherapy. Adaptation to change is an important task faced by most organisms. For humans it is seen clearly in transitions between stages of life and during periods of rapid social and cultural change. Thus, we have to understand personality in this broader context and seek principles of change that apply over diverse settings. As well as broad individual differences in potential for change as opposed to rigidity, the potential for change likely involves a dynamic interplay between costs and benefits associated with change as opposed to those associated with fixity.

CHAPTER 10

Mind, Brain, And Behavior: Psychology, Biology, And The Question Of Reductionism

General Theme

In this chapter we consider the question of the relation of mind to body, and the associated question of the relationship between psychology and biology. These are historical questions that have become of increasing importance as developments in biology have quickened, as the field of psychology has expanded (e.g., biopsychology, behavioral neuroscience), and as some departments have found it necessary or useful to split into separate departments of Psychology and Neuroscience. How one understands the relation of mind to body also has sociopolitical implications, as in the treatment of mental illness. Research on stress and illness, and on social support and health, suggests the utility of a mulilevel approach in which connections are established among different levels of organism functioning.

> *In the middle of the Decade of the Brain...we need to tackle some of the difficult, confusing issues about the logical relationship between biology and psychology.*
>
> *Miller, 1996, p. 619*

Much controversy remains about where biological phe-
nomena fit into psychological science and vice versa.

Miller & Keller, 2000, p. 212

We are confronted in this chapter with perhaps the most challenging issue of all those considered in this book. It is an issue that has challenged philosophers for centuries: What is the relation of what we call the *mind*, including our most personal thoughts and subjective experiences, to the *brain* and other parts of the *body*? Can the smell of a rose, the joy of a symphony or rock concert, the love of a partner or child be "reduced" to brain structures, cells, or neurons? Can one say that the mind "directs" the brain and body to do things? Or, can one say that the brain "causes" the mind to think the way it does and the body to behave the way it does? Is there such a thing as free will? Is mental illness a "disease of the brain" or a disturbed way of thinking and experiencing the world? The questions before us are of fundamental importance and are likely to become increasingly so as biological advances increase in the future.

The Mind-Body Question: The Case of Mental Illness

So we are still haunted by such questions as: Is there more
to personal behavior than molecular biology can tell us?
Or, is there more to personal behavior than neurology can
tell us?

Ramsey, 1965, p. 175

Do we treat people's brains or mind? As the argument
evolved in the seventies and eighties, if psychiatric illness
is biological, it should be treated with drugs; if it is psy-
chological, it should be treated with therapy.

Luhrman, 2000, p. 262

The question of mind-body relationships is not just of scientific, theoretical, or philosophical interest. It has important social and political implications as well. In the course of looking for a book relevant to this chapter, I came across a 1965 edited book titled *Biology and Personality*. Not familiar with the book, and intrigued both by the date of publication and the subtitle *Frontier Problems in Science, Philosophy, and Religion*, I began to read through it. Here were some of the questions considered by the distinguished group of biochemists, zoologists, neurophysiologists, philosophers, and psychologists: How far do developments in molecular biology drain human personality of any distinctiveness? Can an adequate account, in principle, be given of personality in terms of such disciplines as molecular biology, evolutionary theory, and neurology? What is the relationship of subjective feelings to physical events in the brain? Is there a contradiction between the subjective sense of free will and material causations? Do genes determine our destiny? What are the implications of developments in neuroscience for religion, free will, and morality?

Today the issue before us comes up most dramatically in terms of the understanding and treatment of mental illness. Is alcoholism a biological disease or a psychological difficulty? Is weight gain a biological problem or a question of will power?[1] Is mental illness a disease of the brain or a social and psychological problem? Luhrman (2000), in her book *Of Two Minds: The Growing Disorder in American Psychiatry,* suggests that psychiatrists have inherited a Cartesian dualism. This dualism is expressed in the division between psychodynamic psychiatrists who emphasize the treatment of the mind through psychotherapy and the biological psychiatrists who emphasize treatment of the brain through drugs. According to her, these represent "two profoundly different notions of what it is to be a person: to feel, to choose, to do good, to have meaning" (p. 5).

The worst consequence of the biology versus psychology war is the assumption that dysfunctions conceived biologically warrant interventions conceived biologically and similarly for dysfunctions and interventions conceived psychologically. This assumption is rampant in the popular press and common in prominent scholarly works, but it is groundless.

Miller, 1996, p. 625

The issue is well represented in an article in the *New York Times* (June 24, 2000, p. B9) with the headline "Seeing Drugs as a Choice or as a Brain Anomaly." On the one hand, Alan Leshner, director of the National Institute on Drug Abuse, is quoted as declaring that science shows that the brain of an addict is fundamentally different from that of a nonaddict—it is a brain disease. The article asks whether addicts should be treated as sick people in need of help or as bad people in need of punishment. Leshner is viewed as coming down squarely on the side of illness-help, although he also recognizes an element of individual responsibility. On the other hand, the article quotes others who reject this view of addiction as a disease of the brain and suggest a much greater role for volition or free will. Thus, although not

---

[1] Consider the following quote from the former director of the Food and Drug Administration: "I recognized that understanding the nature of addiction was fundamental to our investigation. Over the years, the word has acquired multiple meanings, signifying one thing to a scientist studying brain chemistry and another to a layman simply judging behavior. The definition had also evolved over time. In the early 1960s, addiction was viewed as a personality disorder, and the assumption was that the addict was somehow to blame for a lack of willpower. The biological basis of addiction, and particularly how substances act on the brain, was not well understood until several decades later" (Kessler, 2001, p. 120).

necessary connections, a contrast is drawn between brain-illness-nonvolition-treatment and mind–bad behavior–volition-punishment. In other words, there can be a tendency to go from attributions for the cause of an illness, to views concerning appropriate treatment of the illness, to views concerning moral responsibility (Weiner, 1993). The issue is well stated by an undergraduate of mine who had spent the semester working with an individual previously hospitalized for schizophrenia and who was unaware of the chapter I was writing:

> I would like to start this discussion about the nature-nurture debate concerning schizophrenia by first describing to you what I think each side is saying. To me, the essential difference between the two poles of the nature-nurture controversy is the way in which each side views a person. "Nature" advocates a view of schizophrenia as a biological phenomenon. That is, schizophrenia is an organic disturbance of some sort, and the symptoms of schizophrenia are nothing more than the manifestations of the organic aberrance. Since schizophrenia is an organic disease, the most effective way to treat it is with chemotherapy, shock treatment, surgery, or some other technique that will correct the biological disruption. Thus, in this view, a person with schizophrenia is a biological organism with a biological disruption, and schizophrenia is no different from a condition of Down syndrome or Albinism.

> On the other side of the coin, the "nurture" advocates hold a different view of schizophrenia and of the person with schizophrenia. They view schizophrenia not as an organic disruption, but as an experiential disruption. Instead of looking at a person as a biological organism, they look at a person as a conscious, thinking, feeling, experiencing being. They view schizophrenia as a problem that is caused on a conscious level, and should thus be confronted on a conscious level. "Nurture" advocates would use a treatment such as psychotherapy to address the person's problems, which confronts the disorder on an experiential level.

> I'm sure you've noticed that I have taken both the nature and the nurture positions to extremes, and have kept them rigidly distinct from one another with no room for overlap, like oil and vinegar. I am well aware that I have trimmed away a multitude of variations and intermediate stances of such a view. But as a starting point, I want to clear away all of that intermediate fuzziness, so that I have something clear to look at. So now that I have done this, which one is it? Is a human a biological or a conscious being? Drawing from my own contemplation, and my personal experiences with "Albert," I can conclude that the answer is indeed both. Humans are biological organisms. However, humans are not just biological organisms. Because of the complex and altogether unique way in which we are constructed, we possess an awareness of our agency in the world. This extra is what separates us from other things that are just biological organisms, such as the bacteria and the wheat and the elephant. We biologically function in the world, and we also consciously experience the world. As far as schizophrenia goes, I have read too many case studies and biographies that point to a personal, conscious explanation to think that schizophrenia is solely an organic phenomenon. On the other hand, I have read too many adoption studies and twin studies that point to a significant hereditary influence to think that it is solely an experiential phenomenon.[2]

The issue also is well represented in a paper by DeGrandpre (1999), in which he argues that psychological, behavioral phenomena, such as attention deficit hyperactivity disorder (ADHD), are found to be *correlated* with biological measures and then incorrectly interpreted as being *caused* by biological factors. According to him these biological attributions reflect a biological, neurological reductionism and have moral and treatment implications. Treatment with drugs is prescribed and research money is directed toward an understanding of the biological basis for the disease.

---

[2] My appreciation to the student, Nathaniel Okpych, for permission to quote this part of his paper.

However, he suggests that many disorders treated as brain diseases are developmental and psychosocial problems, requiring attention to the socioenvironmental context and possible social and psychological change procedures. Rather than prescribing drugs, we can prevent or treat psychological problems by altering the conditions under which people live. Not surprisingly, as in the above quote from my student, debate concerning illnesses such as ADHD is drawn back to the nature-nurture question. That is, on the one hand some argue that ADHD is a biological disorder caused by genes, while on the other hand some argue that it is a psychosocial disorder caused by environments (*Cerebrum,* 2000, Vol. 2, No. 3).

In her 1984 book, *The Broken Brain: The Biological Revolution in Psychiatry,* Andreasen helped to destigmatize mental illness by developing the view that psychiatry deals with brain disorders. In her later book, *Brave New Brain: Conquering Mental Illness in the Era of the Genome* (2001), she notes that an unintended effect of viewing mental illness within a medical framework, as a disease of the brain, was the dehumanization of psychiatry. Due to economic factors, managed-care companies began to insist that psychiatrists write prescriptions and stop doing psychotherapy—the latter is just too costly. Again, there is the division between mind and body, treatment with psychotherapy or treatment with medication.

We now need to ask, How do the biological processes of the brain give rise to mental events, and how in turn do social factors modulate the biological structure of the brain?

Kandel, 1998, p. 464

Despite this tendency toward bifurcation in terms of biological-drugs and psychological-psychotherapy, there remain those who call for a multilevel, integrative framework. Thus, for example, as far back as 1977 Engel, a professor of medicine and psychiatry, called for a *biopsychosocial model* that would go beyond mind-body dualism and avoid the split between psychotherapy and pharmacotherapy. Such a model rejects reductionism (i.e., the reduction of complex biological, psychological, and social illnesses to strictly biological elements) and mind-body dualism in favor of a multilevel, systems view. The person is treated as a whole, with problems at each level of organization (e.g., cell, tissue, organ, person, family, community) being recognized in terms of their distinctive contributions to the illness and their potential contributions to recovery from illness. Similarly, the psychiatrist and neuroscientist Kandel (1998) argues for an approach in which each level of analysis is recognized for its own contributions, and that psychotherapy and pharmacotherapy may induce similar alterations in personality and brain functioning. Thus, from this perspective, the psychological and biological approaches are joined.

The Mind-Body Question: Psychology and Biology as Disciplines

---

My feeling is that molecular biologists are going to move into psychology and take over the field. I think that's the way psychology is going to be rejuvenated.

Silver, quoted in Weiner, 1999, p. 243

There is a growing unease about the progressive divestiture of different aspects of psychology to biology. . . . It is feared that as we give away more and more psychology to disciplines lower down on the food chain, there will be no core psychological discipline left.

Bandura, 2001, p. 18

Biologists know what a brain is, but they are as confused as ever about the mind. . .

Lewonfin, 2001, p. 105

I am a member of a department of psychology. A few years ago consideration was given to a proposal to split the department in two. One part would consist of the biopsychology-behavioral neuroscience and cognitive science groups, the other part to consist of social, personality, and developmental psychology. The status of clinical psychology was left undefined. There were various reasons for consideration of such a split, but one component was the feeling among some members of the biopsychology-neuroscience group that they represented the "true" science of psychology, the future of the field. Although for some such a split seemed strange, the point was made that many other universities had a department of psychology and one of neuroscience, or some similar division. At other universities there were life sciences programs, with the behavioral neuroscience psychologists being closely allied with other members of the program, in particular biologists.

For various reasons, the split in my department did not occur and harmony among us as a family of psychologists was established. However, a short time thereafter a candidate was interviewed for a position in the department. The candidate gave a lecture in their area of expertise and a possible appointment was considered at a subsequent faculty meeting. The candidate was recommended by members of the neuroscience group but the following sentiment was expressed by a number of members of the department: "We went to the lecture but could not understand what was being said. Is this psychology? Perhaps this person is a more likely candidate for an appointment in the Biology department."

The issue being faced in my department, as in other psychology departments throughout the country, concerns the boundaries of the field and its future as a science. This is true for psychology in general, and personality in particular. Is there a basis for an independent science of psychology, or should it be folded into biology? Are psychological and biological explanations, what some refer to as mind and brain, incompatible or can they be brought together? Whereas some in the neurosciences claim that biological approaches have eclipsed traditional psychological approaches, some in the latter suggest that these biological approaches are irrelevant to understanding the phenomena of interest to them (Cacioppo, et.al., 2000).

In his book *Consilience,* the biologist Wilson (1998) argues for a reductionism in which biology becomes a unifying science. According to him, reductionism, followed by synthesis, is the primary and essential activity of science: "The love of complexity without reductionism makes art; the love of complexity with reductionism makes science" (p. 54). On the other hand, the psychologist Jerome Bruner, in his book *Acts of Meaning* (1990), argues for a psychology of culture and meaning, and warns against a form of reductionism in which biology is seen as directing human behavior. Can memory, motivation, the self, and culture be understood in terms of genetics and molecular biology, or are more traditional psychological concepts necessary? Bandura's answer is clear: "Mapping the activation of the neuronal circuitry subserving Martin Luther King's 'I Have a Dream' speech would tell us little about its powerful socially inspirational nature" (2001, p. 19).

Thus, in this chapter we are confronted with questions concerning how phenomena of fundamental interest to personality psychologists will be defined, explored, and analyzed in the future. It probably is not too much of an extreme to say that the future of the field will be defined in the next decade, the decade following the Decade of the Brain (1990–2000). The issue addressed in this chapter cross-cuts many of the issues already considered in the text. It is not just the questions of nature-nurture and evolution-culture that are involved, but those concerning the units of personality, research methods, the nature of the self, the unconscious, and personality change. In other words, almost every phenomenon of importance to personality psychologists involves the question of the relation of findings in biology to these phenomena.

Let us consider a few illustrations. Genetics and Darwinian evolutionary theory clearly are relevant to the nature-nurture and evolution-culture issues. The nature of the self is of great interest to neuroscientists as well as psychologists and philosophers. The list of those concerned with understanding the self includes the "who's who" in these fields, with the Nobel Prize likely going to the scientist who solves the riddle of the biological basis for the self. We know, for example, that what the neuroscientist Damasio (1994) calls brain diseases can lead to the sense of more than one self (i.e., multiple personality disorder or dissociative identity disorder) or the sense of lacking a self. In his book *Altered Egos: How the Brain Creates the Self,* the neurologist and psychiatrist Feinberg (2001) asks questions such as the following: What is the self? Where is the self? How does the brain produce a unified self? He describes various neurological disorders such that the person cannot recognize parts of the body as his or her own and is unable to identify the self in a mirror. In a fascinating and disturbing illustration of the latter, a patient is described who each time she sees herself in the mirror thinks it is another person. No amount of persuasion can convince her otherwise, that the image in the mirror is her reflection. She wonders who this woman is that follows her everywhere as she sees the image not only in mirrors but in all reflective surfaces (e.g., store and car windows).

Since the sense of self is so linked to consciousness, and thereby to unconscious phenomena, it is no wonder that some cognitive social psychologists call for the development of a field of social neuropsychology as a way of bridging the gap between social-personality psychology and neuropsychology (Klein & Kihlstrom, 1998). Finally, in terms of the issue of personality change, there are investigations underway of brain changes that occur during the process of psychotherapy (Schwartz et al., 1996).

We need to know how the brain, which is composed of billions of neurons, creates the single and unified entity we call the self.

Feinberg, 2001, p. 148

At present, "What is the self?" can be answered only tentatively by neuroscience. . . . "Where is the self located in the brain?" is both too ambitious and a question neurology's methods are poorly equipped to address.

Derrington & Parker, 2001, p. 97

We have no idea how our brain makes us who we are. There is as yet no neuroscience of personality.

LeDoux, quoted in Horgan, 1999, p. 31

In sum, we have before us the challenge of understanding phenomena of mutual interest to psychologists and biologists, and of determining whether advances by each can be of benefit to the other. In other words, are psychology and biology competing disciplines or can they exist as distinct but related? If the latter, what kind of relationship might exist between the two? These are some of the questions we will seek to address in the course of the chapter.

Some Historical Notes

Attempts to establish linkages between biology (brain, body) and psychology (mind) have a long history. Greek physicians in the fifth century B.C. related four temperament types (i.e., melancholic, choleric, phlegmatic, sanguine), to a predominance of one or another type of humor. Much later, Eysenck (1967, 1990) attempted to relate his major trait dimensions of personality (i.e., *Introversion-Extraversion, Neuroticism, Psychoticism)* to differences in biological functioning. More recently, Zuckerman (1995), in an article entitled "Good and Bad Humors: Biochemical Bases of Personality and Its Disorders," suggests that "the Greek physicians had the right idea, but the wrong humors" (p. 325). Personality traits, such as the Big Five (Chapter 2), have been related to such biological variables, as genes, hormones, and neurotransmitters, as well as more general differences in brain functioning.

In the early nineteenth century, the anatomist Franz Joseph Gall, often viewed as the founder of phrenology, attempted to locate areas of the brain responsible for various aspects of emotional and behavioral functioning. Although the view was later discredited as quackery and superstition, Gall was a fine anatomist and serious scientist. He did postmortem inspections of brains and attempted to relate observed differences in brain structure to reports of patient traits prior to death. Although remembered largely for what seemed like a foolhardy effort, Gall's work is seen by some as an early and serious effort to locate aspects of personality functioning in specific parts of the brain, what is now a part of the field of neuroscience. In his fascinating exploration of the relation between biology and personality, the eminent neurologist Antonio Damasio (1994) gives many illustrations of the effects of damage in specific brain areas on personality functioning. He begins this endeavor with the famous case of Phineas Gage, the railroad construction foreman who suffered major personality changes as a result of an iron rod being blown through a part of his brain: "Gage's disposition, his likes and dislikes, his dreams and aspirations are all to change. Gage's body may be alive, but there is a new spirit animating it. Gage was no longer Gage" (Damasio, 1994, p. 7). Currently there are studies of Einstein's brain in an effort to find the neural basis of genius (Lepore, 2001).

Although Freud is known as a psychologist of the mind, he was very much a biologist, so much so that Sulloway's (1979) biography of him is titled *Freud, Biologist of the Mind.* Freud's thinking was greatly influenced by his early training in medicine and by the views of Darwin. In the early part of his career he did research and practiced in the field of neurology. Throughout his career, but particularly during the early years, he attempted to establish a biological basis for psychological phenomena. This is expressed most clearly in his *Project for a Scientific Psychology* (1895), described by Sulloway as an expression of Freud's quest for a neurophysiological, psychobiological theory of mind: "He never abandoned the assumption that psychoanalysis would someday come to terms with the neurophysiological side of mental activity. . . . Perhaps no one synthesized the biological assumptions of his scientific generation more boldly than did Freud" (1979, pp. 135, 496).

Sulloway viewed Freud as a dualist, separating the physical (brain) from the psychological (mind), which brings us to the seventeenth-century philosopher Descartes, also described as the father of physiological psychology (Boring, 1950). Descartes viewed the body as a machine, separate from the soul or mind, thus the basis for what came to be known as *Cartesian dualism.* This split of the mind from the body, of the operations of the mind from the operations of the body, is what Damasio (1994) refers to as *Descartes' Error.* Damasio is critical of such dualism but also is critical of neuroscientists who insist that mind is only brain events. But how, then, are we to understand the relation between mind and brain, between psychology and biology? This is an issue that has bedeviled philosophers for centuries and continues to do so to this day (Searle, 2000). If the brain is a computer, then what is the mind and what is consciousness? If the mind is not just neurons firing, then what else is it? As our understanding of the brain, and biological functioning in general, increases, we seem nearer to an answer to the question. Yet, the answer remains so distant and hard to grasp, as does an answer to the question of the of the relation between psychology and biology.

> *How could neuron firings at synapses cause the experience of hearing a Beethoven symphony, or seeing a red rose, or worrying about how we are going to pay our income taxes? . . . But one thing we are certain of: brains do it. Brains cause all of our conscious states.*
>
> *Searle, 2000, p. 45*

Mind and Body: Illustrative Research

In 1999 I received a report from the Dana Foundation Brain-Body Institute. It began with the following question: "Why does the state of our mind seem to have such a powerful effect on the state of our health?" The foreword to the report went on as follows:

> For centuries, keen observers of human nature have noted an obvious link between our emotions and our health. Happy people tend to get sick less often and recover quicker. Angry people often have more health problems than their even-tempered peers. . . . But why does our state of mind have such an impact on our health? How can happiness or anger or the warm connection we feel with a loved one travel from our minds to our bodies? After all, emotions are just in our heads, aren't they?
>
> *(Foreword, Brain-Body Science, The Charles A. Dana Foundation Brain-Body Institute)*

The report went on to indicate that these questions have puzzled scientists for centuries but that a new field of study, brain-body science, was beginning to provide some answers.

One of the outgrowths of Freud's work was an interest in how emotional conflicts could lead to bodily disorders, the field of *psychosomatic medicine.* Freud had studied the relation between unconscious conflicts and conversion reactions—disturbances in bodily functioning that had no known biological basis and that, in some cases, did not fit what was anatomically possible. For example, the hand might lose sensation at a point on the body that did not fit nerve endings, what was called *glove anesthesia.* In the case of psychosomatic disorders, such as those studied by the psychoanalyst Franz Alexander (1950), there was an interest in the relation between unconscious conflicts and disorders such as ulcers. For example, successful executives with repressed dependency needs might develop ulcers and require a diet that included milk—symbolically a form of oral gratification. Or, to take another example, asthma was thought to result from a suppressed need to cry.

Taylor (1999) suggests that this approach became discredited because of a simplistic linkage between personality and illness but that it "laid the groundwork for a profound change in beliefs about the relation of the mind and the body" (p. 6). Another important development in this regard was the work of Hans Selye (1956) on stress. Selye suggested a common physiological response to stress, called the *general adaptation syndrome.* This syndrome consists of a sequence of *alarm* and the mobilization of resources, *resistance* and efforts to cope with the stressor, and *exhaustion* if coping efforts are not successful. It was viewed by Selye as the basis for many forms of illness. In other words, the field of stress disorders was born. Although Selye gave inadequate attention to stress as a psychological variable (i.e., what is stressful for one person is not for another), and advances have since been made in our understanding of the physiology of the stress response, he laid the groundwork for the study of stress-illness, mind-body relationships. Thus, for example, the biologist Robert Sapolsky (1994) can ask the question of why zebras don't get ulcers and answer it as follows: Whereas short-term stress, such as that experienced by zebras, is adaptive, chronic stress, such as that experienced by many humans, is not. Chronic stress increases the risk of getting diseases and of overwhelming disease-fighting biological processes.

In Chapter 9 mention was made of the placebo effect, the ability of an inert substance, such as a sugar pill, to have beneficial effects. As noted, the placebo effect is incorporated into research on the effectiveness of drugs and also is seen as a nonspecific psychotherapy effect, although the mechanism by which it works remains unclear. Beliefs about a threat can cause illness, perhaps even death (e.g., what is called *voodoo death*), and beliefs, as in placebos, can promote health—the mind-body connection. Two major areas of research are illustrative of this connection: the relationship between stress and illness and the relationship between social support and health. Both draw attention to the mind-body issue and thereby to the issue of the relation between psychology and biology.

Stress and Illness

> *Thoughts, feelings, and behaviors affect our health and well-being. Recognition of the importance of these influences on health and disease is consistent with evolving conceptions of mind and body.*
>
> *Baum & Posluszny, 1999, p. 138*

> *The link between psychosocial factors and the development or progression of several chronic diseases seems to be established.*
>
> *Schneiderman, et. Al.*, 2001, p. 573

The field of *psychoneuroimmunology*, the study of relations among psychological variables (e.g., stress), neural and endocrine functions (e.g., stress hormones), and immune functions, is alive and well (Ader, 2001; Cohen, 1996; Maier, Watkins, & Fleshner, 1994). By now there is clear evidence that stress impacts on the immune system in a way that lowers resistance to disease and makes the fight against established disease more problematic. Stress has been linked with susceptibility to the common cold. For example, chronic stress lasting a month or more has been found to double the incidence and severity of the common cold (Cohen, et al., 1998). In addition, stress has been linked to increased risk of heart disease, poor wound healing, and delays in postoperative recovery (Kiecolt-Glaser, et. al., 1998). The functioning of the immune system is seen as the clear mediator of this relationship. Thus, for example, suppression of immune functioning has been linked with stressors such as taking important examinations, caring for relatives with chronic diseases, bereavement, marital conflict, divorce, battle task vigilance, high levels of unpleasant daily events, and negative moods (Cohen, 1996; Kiecolt-Glaser & Glaser, 2001). Comparable effects of stress on the immune system have been shown in animals after exposure to electric shocks, maternal separation, loud noise, and social defeat (Maier, Watkins, & Fleshner, 1994).

Recently a study gave clear indications that traumatic experiences in childhood can have lasting effects in terms of responses to stress and thereby to illness. In this study women with no history of childhood abuse were compared with women who were sexually or physically abused as children in terms of response to a laboratory psychosocial stressor (i.e., public speaking and mental arithmetic task in front of an audience). Physiological indicators of the stress response indicated clear differences between the two groups, with women who were physically or sexually abused in childhood showing exaggerated physiological responses to the psychosocial stressor. These exaggerated stress responses were particularly characteristic of women with symptoms of depression and anxiety. The conclusion reached was that exposure to early traumatic stress created a vulnerability to later responses to stress and thereby to the development of psychopathological conditions (Heim, et al., 2000).

Further contributing to the stress-disease linkage is evidence that positive emotional states are associated with positive health outcomes. For example, optimism has been associated with a faster rate of recovery from coronary artery bypass surgery (Scheier, et. al., 1989) and positive emotional states have been associated with improved immunological system functioning and healthy outcomes (Salovey, et. al., 2000). There also is evidence that stress management techniques can improve immune system functioning (Schneiderman, et. al., 2001). In sum, there is evidence that stress and negative emotion can make you sick, as well as evidence that reduced stress and positive emotion can be beneficial to your health.

Social Support and Health

Social relationships are a ubiquitous part of life, serving important social, psychological, and behavioral functions across the life-span. More important, both the quantity and quality of social relationships have been reliably related to morbidity and mortality.

Uchino, Cacioppo, & Kiecolt-Glaser, 1996, p. 488

Your closest relationships seem to matter most for your health.

Kiecolt-Glaser, quoted in the New York Times, December 15, 1992, p. C1

There is evidence that humans, as well as other primates, have a need to have a relationship with other individuals or to feel membership in a group. Therefore, it is not surprising that social support has been linked with health, both in terms of the absence of social support being associated with poorer health functioning and the presence of social support being associated with improved health functioning (Uchino, Uno, & Holt-Lunstad, 1999). Social support involves the feeling that one is connected to and cared about by others. It has been associated with such diverse health outcomes as coronary heart disease, cancer, and infectious illnesses. The mediating process appears to be the effects of social support on the functioning of the endocrine glands and immune system, in particular through the buffering of the effects of stress on that system's functioning.

In terms of the effects of the experienced absence of social support, lonely individuals and those who have experienced losses in interpersonal relationships have been found to be vulnerable to both mental and physical illnesses. This relationship holds for recovery from illness as well as for the initial development of illness. For example, socially isolated survivors of heart attacks are much more likely to die sooner than those who are less socially isolated (Berkman, Leo-Summers, & Horwitz, 1992). These relationships have been found to be particularly striking in older adults (Kiecolt-Glaser & Glaser, 2001). Apparently it is the subjective feeling of loneliness or social isolation that is key rather than objective indices of such states. In addition to these findings with humans, relationships between social disruption and poorer health functioning have been found in health studies of animals. Here too the evidence suggests that the key ingredient may be the effects of stress, created by the social disruption, on physiological processes (Manuck, et. al., 1995).

Viewing matters from the other side, there is clear evidence that providing social support increases resistance to, and facilitates recovery from, illness. Ordinarily we are told to stay away from contact with others to avoid getting a cold. However, whatever the truth to this recommendation, it also is the case that people with the most ties to others are the least likely to catch a cold (Cohen, et. al., 1997). One of the most dramatic reports of the effects of social support was the demonstration that participation in support groups could both lower the pain associated with breast cancer as well as prolong life (Spiegel, et. al., 1989). Participation in support groups also has been found to increase the immune functioning and survival rates of individuals with malignant skin cancer (Fawzy, et. al., 1993). Finally, to return to Pennebaker's work on writing about traumatic experiences (Chapter 9), there is evidence that such writing is associated with improved immunological functioning in part via the sense of increased social connectedness (Pennebaker & Graybeal, 2001).

Perhaps not unrelated to the link between social support and health is evidence that faith or spirituality is good for one's health (Plante & Sherman, 2001; Seybold & Hill, 2001). According to a report of the Weill Medical College of Cornell University (2001), belief is strong medicine. Summarizing evidence presented at a conference on "Spirituality and Healing in Medicine" sponsored by the Harvard Medical School and the Mind/Body Medical Institute, the report indicated that faith (i.e., strong belief systems) can play a role in affecting the course of a wide variety of illnesses—further evidence that "the mind plays a strong role in healing the body."

Views of the Mind-Body, Psychology-Biology Relationship

It is clear from the research on stress, social support, and health-illness that not only can illness affect one's psychological state but one's psychological state can affect the development and progression of illness. In other words, there is a clear, reciprocal relationship between mind and body. The question is the following: How are we to conceptualize this relationship? At least three views of the mind-body, psychology-biology relationship have been suggested and can be considered: (1.)The mind and body are separate and distinct entities. One cannot move from analysis, understanding, and explanation in terms of one to analysis, understanding, and explanation in terms of the other. (2.) Psychological explanations can be reduced to biological explanations. (3.) There are different levels of explanation, each with its own strengths and limitations. Psychological and biological explanations, analyses in terms of mind and body concepts, can be usefully related to one another.

Psychology and Biology as Separate, Alternative Constructions

At its extreme, the view of psychology and biology as completely separate endeavors reminds one of Descartes' mind-body dualism. Few, if any, psychologists or biologists would take such a Cartesian view. However, some border on it in terms of their emphasis either that the phenomena of mind cannot be reduced to the processes of the body or, on the other hand, that the phenomena of mind are of little scientific interest in and of themselves, mere epiphenomena that are secondary to the underlying processes. As we shall see in the next section, some biologists come close to stating the latter position. And, perhaps as a response to such biological imperialism, some psychologists come close to stating the former position.

As indicated in an earlier quote in this chapter, Bandura (2001) expresses concern with the threat of reducing the psychological to the biological. He states, for example, that processes of the mind (e.g., cognitive processes) are emergent phenomena that differ qualitatively from the neural events that are part of them and cannot be reduced to these neural events. He draws the analogy of the properties of water such as fluidity, viscosity, and transparency not being reducible to the components of hydrogen and oxygen. It is not that Bandura discounts the importance of understanding brain and other biological processes, or the legitimacy of their investigation, but rather that such understanding cannot be accepted as a substitute for analysis and understanding of these phenomena on their own terms: "Psychological principles cannot violate the neurophysiological capabilities of the systems that subserve them. However, the psychological principles need to be pursued in their own right" (2001, p. 19).

---

*The field of psychology should be articulating a broad vision of human beings, not a reductive fragmentary one. . . .
Mental events are brain activities, but the physicality does not imply reduction of psychology to biology.*

Bandura, 2001, pp.

Another expression of this point of view is represented in Miller's (1996) presidential address to the Society for Psychophysiological Research. In that address Miller expresses concern that a "naively reductionistic" view of psychological concepts is prevalent. He suggests that "we need to tackle some difficult, confusing issues about the logical relationship between biology and psychology" (p. 619). He notes that there often seems to be an ideological war between the psychologically and biologically inclined researchers and rejects the view that biology is more fundamental than psychology. Along these lines, he rejects such phrases as "biological underpinnings," "biological substrates," "neural substrates," and "physiological foundations." Remember that this is in a presidential address to a psychophysiological group. He argues that we should stop thinking in terms of what underlies what, since that is the wrong way of characterizing the relationship between psychological and biological concepts.

I was particularly drawn to Miller's rejection of these phrases, with their potential for expression of the view that biological phenomena are more fundamental than psychological phenomena, since I had struggled with how to title a relevant chapter in my personality text (Pervin & John, 2001). What I ended up with was a title related to the phrases rejected by Miller: "Biological Foundations of Personality."

I am not sure that it is useful to assert that biology underlies psychology, or vice versa. We would not say that the gears in a clock underlie the concept of time keeping or that gears are more fundamental than the concept of time keeping. . . . Time keeping and gears simply belong to different conceptual domains.

Miller, 1996, p. 620

Fundamentally psychological concepts require fundamentally psychological explanations.

Miller & Keller, 2000, p. 212

It is clear that both Bandura and Miller accept the importance of biological concepts and findings. It also is clear that both are against disciplinary elitism and a reductionism where the concepts of one discipline are viewed as unnecessary and eliminated in favor of the concepts of the other discipline. However, in their efforts to maintain the distinction between psychology and biology, and the legitimacy of both psychological and biological descriptions and explanations of phenomena, they remain somewhat vague about what should be the relationship between the two. If the psychological and biological are separate and distinct, representing different languages and different ways of approaching related phenomena, then how are we to interpret the mind-body connections established in studies of stress-illness and social support-illness relationships?[3]

Psychology as Reducible to Biology

The term *reductionism* tends to have a negative implication, suggesting that something of value is lost or eliminated in the process of going from one group of units to another. Thus, for example, the arguments of Bandura and Miller against the reductionistic explanation of psychological phenomena in biological terms. In contrast with such a view, the biologist Wilson (1998) argues that the reduction of wholes and large units into smaller units makes for good science. According to him, we must first reduce the level at which we analyze phenomena and then work back toward synthesis. Although he accepts the view that there are different levels of explanation, each with its own laws and principles, he argues for biology as the most relevant discipline for unifying the life sciences.

I suspect that Wilson represents the kind of explanatory and disciplinary elitism that so troubles Bandura and Miller. It is not just that he sees biology as unifying knowledge, it is that he also argues against holistic explanations and against cultural relativism. Thus, Bandura (2001) specifically links Wilson with a view of biological

---

[3]In fairness to their positions, it is important to note that both have studied mind-body connections. For example, Bandura (1992) has been active in studying the relationship between self-efficacy beliefs and biological functioning.

determinism that rejects the importance of culture. In his emphasis on the ability of humans to exercise control over the nature and quality of their lives, Bandura rejects what he views as Wilson's biological determinism and the rule of nature.

So here we come to a difference not only in preferred level of explanation or kind of phenomena to be investigated, but a difference in the view of human nature. Are such linkages inevitable and can either psychology or biology answer all questions concerning human nature? I am reminded here of a lecture I just went to by Craig Venter, one of the molecular biologists responsible for the sequencing of the human genome. Someone in the audience asked whether we were beholden to our genes or had free will. His answer was: "I don't think we (biologists) are capable of answering that question. If one identical twin is schizophrenic, the chances of the other being schizophrenic are approximately 50–50. So clearly experience makes a difference and there is plasticity to the biological system" (April, 17, 2001, lecture given at Princeton University). Perhaps different questions are better addressed by different concepts and no one discipline has hegemony over all others.

Psychological and Biological Levels of Explanation

My sense is that the concept of levels is gaining increased usage in the personality literature. However, somewhat troublesome is the fact that generally there is not discussion of what is meant by levels of description, analysis, or explanation, or what kinds of relationships are possible among the different levels. We can consider three senses in which the term *levels* has been used. First, there is reference to levels in a hierarchical organization, where the higher levels represent more comprehensive categories of the lower-level units. For example, the category *car* is a higher level category than the level of specific types of cars (e.g., sports car, sedan, sport utility vehicle, etc.). In the personality realm, Eysenck (1970) diagrammed a hierarchical organization of personality, going from the specific response level, to the habitual response level, to the trait level, and then to the supertrait level. For example, various behaviors would be expressive of anxiety and other behaviors expressive of depression, with both anxiety and depression being parts of neuroticism. Note that in this case the *levels* designation refers to larger or smaller categories or units of analysis. These units are not independent of one another and one would not say that the units at one level cause or interact with those at another level.

A second reference to levels in a hierarchical organization involves units that have an independent status from one another. For example, one can speak of levels of government—township, county, state, and federal. The actions at one level may have implications for those at another level, but each exists independent of the others. Another illustration would be a business organization with various levels of administrative responsibility, ranging from a unit manager, to a division head, to a vice-president, to a chief executive officer or chairman. Each level of the business organization includes different individuals with different responsibilities. Decisions at one level can impact upon actions at another level, typically with actions at higher levels having a broader impact than actions at a lower level. As in the first illustration, there are more units at the lower levels than at the higher levels. However, in this case the units at each level are distinct from one another and actions at one level can be said to cause or have an impact upon actions at another level.

A third reference to levels involves units at lower levels that are embedded in units at higher levels, but each level has distinct properties and one can speak of interactions among, or causal connections between, the different levels. For example, we can consider the individual, group, and society levels of organization. Although a society is made up of many groups, and each group is made up of many individuals, each level has properties of its own. For example, conflict and coalitions among members within a group has no equivalent within the individual. Similarly, the concept of group cohesion has no direct equivalent at the individual level. At the same time, one can speak of processes at one level having an impact upon processes at another level. For example, an individual can be disruptive to a group process and a group process can affect the psychological functioning of each individual in the group. The suggestion that the whole is different from, and perhaps greater than, the sum of the parts (e.g., a team is more than a collection of individuals) reflects the view that there are phenomena that may be unique to each level of analysis.

As further illustrations of this third model, let us consider illustrations from economics and biology. In economics we have macroeconomics and microeconomics, the former referring to the analysis of the economy as a whole, the latter to specific actions made by such groups as businesses, consumers, and governments. Decisions made at one level have implications for those at another level, and findings at one level have implications for analyses at the other level, but the two levels of analysis are distinct from one another and economists identify themselves as macro- or microeconomists.

In biology there are analyses at the molecule, cell, tissue, organ, system, and organism level. Again, events at one level can have implications for those at another level (e.g., tissue damage has implications for organ functioning). Each level is accepted as an appropriate choice for description, analysis, and explanation. Biologists may make distinctions among one another (e.g., molecular biologists and cellular biologists), and in some cases separate departments have been formed, but it is accepted (hopefully) that different levels of investigation are more suitable for answering different questions. And, one would not say (hopefully) that one or another level of analysis is more fundamental, basic, or scientific than another. Each level of description, analysis, and explanation is better suited for different purposes, with the findings at one level having implications for understanding phenomena being considered at another level.

In sum, there are different ways of defining levels, with some definitions suggesting independence of units from one another and others not, and some definitions suggesting interactions among the different levels, and others not. Now, the question is the following: When the view is expressed that psychological and biological explanations (i.e., those in terms of mind and those in terms of brain or body) represent different levels of analysis and explanation, which levels model is being suggested? As mind-body connections and explanations have gained in popularity, it is important to be clear about what we mean by levels. If we take a *multilevel, integrative approach* (Cacioppo, 1999; Cacioppo & Berntson, 1992), does this mean that the units at each level exist independent of one another? Have cause-effect relationships with one another? Have implications for one another but are not reducible to one another? Are mind and body in relation to one another like trait and response, like chairman and division head, like organ and cell, or what?

> *At each level of complexity entirely new properties appear, and the understanding of the new behaviors requires research which I think is as fundamental in its nature as any other. . . . Psychology is not applied biology, nor is biology applied chemistry.*
>
> *Anderson, 1972, p. 393*

> *Social and biological explanations traditionally have been cast as incompatible, but advances in recent years have revealed a new view synthesized from these two very different levels of analysis.*
>
> *Cacioppo, et. al., 2000, p. 829*

> *A psychobiological approach to personality is often accused of reductionism. This charge is usually baseless. All types of phenomena may be studied at different levels, from the most molecular to the most molar. Each level has its own methods, constructs, and limitations. . . . The cognitive, behavioral, and biological are complementary and not conflicting modes of explanation. Great discoveries will occur at the borders of the different levels.*
>
> *Zuckerman, 1998, p. 150*

So, let us accept that it is useful to study mind-body relationships, that the units of analysis differ from level to level, that processes at one level have implications for processes at another level, and that different levels of analysis and explanation are complementary rather than alternative to one another. Let us accept that all psychological functioning is biological but that biological reductionism is not the answer to understanding psychological phenomena (Cacioppo & Berntson, 1992). Have we solved the mind-body problem? I think not. Accepting all of these valuable components of a multilevel approach, we still are left with some puzzling questions about the relationship between mind and body, between the psychological and the biological. For example, the philosopher Searle (2000) rejects mind-body dualism but then struggles with what is called the "puzzle of consciousness." His solution to the puzzle is that lower-level brain processes cause conscious states, that consciousness is a biological phenomenon, but that consciousness is a higher-level feature of the brain system. However, arguing against reductionism, he suggests that consciousness cannot be reduced to the lower-level brain processes. In principle this makes sense, and it certainly is supportive of the legitimacy of a multilevel, integrative approach to the study of mind-body relationships, but I am not sure that it has answered the question of the basis of consciousness.

In other words, there may remain a gap in our understanding of the connection between mind and body. On the other hand, as some suggest, consciousness and mind may be nothing other than the coordinated activity of brain processes, just as walking is nothing other than the coordinated activity of a number of muscles and nerves. Is there something truly unique about the phenomena of consciousness and self-consciousness, and, if so, how are the disciplines of psychology and biology to be defined in relation to them?

Conclusion

We come to the conclusion of consideration of the mind-body, psychology-biology issue, the one that almost caused a split in my department and has resulted in splits in other psychology departments. We can see that the issues are diverse and challenging, engaging the interests of psychologists, biologists, neuroscientists, and philosophers. They also involve preferences for research at one or another level of investigation and, unfortunately, competition for research funds and dominance of the scientific enterprise. It seems clear that progress has been made in establishing mind-body and psychology-biology connections. Such connections are likely to continue to be made in the future. Answers to some of the questions raised in this chapter may be found. In other cases we may find that we were not even raising the correct question. In the meantime it is important that we be aware of how the issue pervades so many other areas of psychological inquiry, as well as how positions on the issue have potential implications for social and political views.

Summary

In this chapter we have considered an issue that has run through many of the previous chapters—the relation between psychology and biology. We have seen how the mind-body question has been of historical interest to philosophers, psychologists, biologists, and others. It becomes of increased relevance for psychologists as we witness the enormous gains in scientific understanding made by biologists and neuroscientists.

The connection between mind and body is illustrated in the findings of research on determinants of health and illness. It is clear that stress has implications for immune system functioning, and thereby for the development and course of a wide variety of illnesses. It also is clear that social support has similar implications for the development and course of a wide variety of illnesses. Just as physical illness can influence one's psychological state, the mind can be powerful medicine. Such mind-body connections can be linked back to earlier interests in psychosomatic disorders. However, in contrast with earlier psychoanalytic views suggesting links between specific psychological conflicts and specific illnesses, current thinking suggests a much broader link between stress and illness. In addition, current thinking is based on a greater foundation of research and increased understanding of the processes involved in health and illness.

How best to conceptualize the relation between mind and body remains a challenge and an issue that often divides psychologists and biologists. One view suggests that psychological and biological phenomena are best treated as separate, distinct, and independent. In other words, just as chemistry and biology, and physics and biology, are separate disciplines, each with its own methods of investigation and scientific concepts, psychology and biology are best viewed as separate disciplines. The phenomena of interest to one are not those of interest to the other, and the methods of investigation and concepts used are different. At the same time, most individuals who take this view would probably accept that there are areas of overlap between psychology and biology. And, just as there are biochemists and biophysicists, there are biopsychologists (or psychobiologists). A second view suggests that biological processes underlie phenomena of interest to psychologists. In the form expressed by Wilson, biology is the unifying discipline of the life sciences and reducing complex wholes to their less complex units is part of the scientific enterprise. A third view suggests that mind and body, psychological and biological processes, be understood in terms of levels. According to this view, each level of analysis has its own strengths and limitations, with distinctive contributions to make to understanding and explanation. No single level of explanation is best for understanding all of the phenomena of interest to psychologists and biologists, and appreciation of the contributions from research at all levels is desirable. It is useful to draw connections among levels but dangerous to try and reduce the units and concepts of one level to those of a lower level.

The question of mind-body relationships may seem abstract and of little practical importance. However, aside from the question of how scientists view their work and relationships with other scientists, positions on the issue can be of social and political significance. This can be seen in the linkages sometimes made in the popular media, as well as scholarly journals, between mind-illness-volition (will)–psychotherapy on the one hand and brain-disease-nonvolition-pharmacotherapy on the other hand. Such connections are not necessary ones. That is, it is possible to believe that an illness with a strong psychological component can be usefully treated with drugs (e.g., depression) and that an illness with a strong biological component can benefit from psychosocial interventions. And, as suggested by the biopsychosocial model, one can appreciate the connections among processes going on at the same level as well as connections between levels. One can consider the parts of the organism as well as the organism as a whole. At the same time, there is a tendency to move from an attribution of the cause of an illness to a view of treatment and to a view of moral responsibility. Thus, in staking out our individual views on the mind-body issue, it is important to be aware of their potential sociopolitical implications as well as their potential scientific implications.

CHAPTER 11

The Nature Of The Scientific Enterprise: Personal, Sociopolitical, And Ethical Features

General Theme

The public image of the scientific enterprise tends to be one of objectivity, detachment, and rationality. However, in fact it is very much a human endeavor, with personal and social forces influencing theory and research, and with scientists being very invested in their ideas. What distinguishes science from other activities is not its neutrality but rather its self-correcting features, as evidenced in evaluating data according to accepted standards. The scientific enterprise is influenced by social and political forces in terms of the questions asked, the methods used to address these questions, and the response to findings. Scientists have a responsibility to follow ethical principles in their research, including the protection of the interests of subjects and the presentation of results in a responsible manner.

> . . . *science seldom proceeds in the straightforward logical manner imagined by outsiders. Instead, its steps forward (and sometimes backward) are often very human events in which personalities and cultural traditions play major roles.*
>
> Watson, *The Double Helix, 1968, p. ix*

> *Science and society are complexly related. Scientists are cultural members, their research often motivated by social needs, funded by public agencies, and interpreted in the light of prevailing beliefs and values.*
>
> *Thompson, 1996, p. 168*

> *Psychologists are committed to increasing knowledge of behavior and people's understanding of themselves and others and to the use of such knowledge to improve the condition of individuals, organizations, and society. . . . This Ethics Code provides a common set of values upon which psychologists build their professional and scientific work.*
>
> *American Psychological Association Ethics Code Draft, 2001, p. 79*

In this chapter we will be concerned with personality theory and research as a human, personal enterprise. In addition, we will be concerned with the social, political, and ethical aspects of the pursuit of the science of personality. The study of people by people lends itself to deeply personal influences and potential sources of bias. In addition, the study of people occurs within the context of a particular time period, reflecting and at times challenging the values and beliefs prevalent in society. In sum, the scientific enterprise is a human one in which personal, social, and political forces come into play. This is true of the scientific enterprise in general, certainly no less so for the science of personality.

The quote that introduced this chapter comes from the book *The Double Helix* by the Nobel Prize-winning biochemist James Watson. The book recounts the story of an incredible scientific breakthrough—the discovery of the structure of the heredity molecule DNA. As advertised, it is an intensely human story and serves to correct the view that scientific progress proceeds in orderly steps taken by impersonal observers. The story of the discovery of the structure of DNA involves tales of rivalry between American and British scientists, and personal rivalries between scientists that make them rigidly maintain one view and totally disregard other lines of development, and it involves rules of fair play that prevent one scientist from jumping in on the work of other scientists. It is a story of contrasts between personalities who proceed with excessive caution and those who rush into the adventure of discovery, of contrasts between scientists who are afraid to compete for the prize and those who are driven forward by such competition. There is a description of how scientific research can be experienced as play and how it also can become ensnared in departmental and university politics. Some experimental results are presented publicly, but others are kept secret lest they be used by some researchers to move ahead in the race for the prize. Blind alleys are followed at length and at other times there are significant chance discoveries. In all, the story of *The Double Helix* presents us with a picture of a remarkable combination of careful analytical thought and intense personal involvement in a competitive enterprise.

This is not to say that all research proceeds in the way described in *The Double Helix* or that all researchers experience their work as described by James Watson. In fact, as Watson notes, styles of scientific research vary almost as much as human personalities. Thus, the point is not only that there was intense personal involvement in this particular research, but also that the nature of the personal involvement reflected the personalities of the researchers. Psychology, because of its subject matter, may particularly lend itself to coloration by subjective factors, but it is not distinctive or unique as a scientific endeavor in this regard.

Turning from the private and personal, we may consider the social and political factors that enter into scientific inquiry. Margaret Mead was an eminent anthropologist whose writings were read by millions. In 1928 she announced her finding of a culture that, because of the nature of adolescent development, proved the dominance of culture over biology. Her book *Coming of Age in Samoa* became the best-selling anthropology book of all time and a focal point for the nature-nurture debate. In 1983 Freeman published a book, *Margaret Mead and Samoa*, that created considerable storm and controversy. In this book Freeman traced the history of the nature-nurture debate and suggested that Mead's observations were in error and derived from an ideology of cultural determinism over biological determinism. Going back to Samoa and reexamining Mead's observations, Freeman concluded that her concepts and data were twisted by ideology: "It is thus evident that her writings during this period had the explicit aim of disproving biological explanations of human behavior" (1983, p. 282). Thus, the book raises significant questions both about the nature-nurture controversy and about the relation of political ideology to scientific inquiry.

We are taught to believe that science is objective and value-free, that scientists tend to be cool and dispassionate observers of phenomena. Rationality is seen as a check on emotions that can deceive the observer and bias the interpretation of data. Yet, studies in the sociology of science suggest that scientists become affectively involved with their ideas and discoveries, and Michael Polanyi (1958), an eminent philosopher of science, argues that the personal character of science is part of its entire structure and enters into all aspects of knowing. In this chapter, then, we will have the opportunity to explore the ways in which personal and social factors influence the course of personality theory and research. In doing so, we will consider the extent to which personality theory and research serve as a magnifying glass, detailing the essence of human nature, as opposed to their serving as a mirror reflecting the images and life experiences of particular theorists.

Personal Factors in the Science of Personality

Critics of Freud and psychoanalytic theory suggest that many of the phenomena held to reflect the functioning of all people in fact reflect the issues that concerned Freud and middle- to upper-class patients of the Victorian era. In particular, critics of his Oedipus complex point out that Freud was a very special son of a relatively young woman married to an older man. It is probably true that Freud's early experiences played a role in the formulation of the content of his theories. It also seems fairly clear that Freud's energy model of psychological functioning was significantly influenced by the hydraulic model current at the time in the area of physiology. Given this background, two questions remain. Is the influence of Freud's life experiences on the development of his theory of personality unique to Freud or can such influences be found in all theories of personality? Second, does the existence of such influences discount the potential utility and validity of the theoretical formulation?

Some psychologists suggest that to one degree or another each theory of personality reflects the life and times of the theorist involved. The issue has drawn increasing attention and was clearly presented in a paper by Atwood and Tomkins (1976). They suggest that all personality psychologists rely on their own lives as a potential source for material for the development of their theory. The theory presented by the theorist is a system for comprehending his or her own experience as well as a system for explaining the behavior of other people.

Every theorist of personality views the human condition from the unique perspective of his own individuality. As a consequence, personality theories are strongly influenced by personal and subjective factors.

Atwood & Tomkins, 1976, p. 166

One example given by Atwood and Tomkins concerns the life and theory of the psychoanalyst Carl Jung. According to their account, during his childhood years Jung acquired a conviction that he was two persons or two personalities. In the outward personality he was oriented to the world about him, often feeling humiliated by other children. The other personality was a hidden inner self that was unknown to others and entertained secret fantasies of omnipotence and communication with God. In many ways his life represented a counterplay of these two personalities. During some periods the former personality would become ascendant, and he would become actively involved with others. During other periods the latter personality would become ascendant, and he would be preoccupied with his grandiose inner world. The first personality was expressed in a concern with science and medicine. The second personality was expressed in an interest in religion and mythology and in a world of feelings and intuition.

Observing the conflict between Freud and Alfred Adler, Jung was led to the belief that both viewpoints contained truth and that the differences between them reflected different temperaments. The differing temperaments assumed by Jung to underlie the Freud–Adler conflict and then to be basic to all human functioning were those of introversion and extraversion. Thus, the differences between Freud and Adler could be resolved in their representing different attitudes derived from differing temperaments. Here, the severe conflict between introversive and extraversive tendencies manifested in Jung's personal life became the cornerstone of his understanding of the Freud–Adler conflict and of his own theory of personality. Moreover, his theory of individuation and view of a state of psychic wholeness can be viewed as part of an effort on his part to attain a wholeness within his own inner life. While basically an introvert, he could also be very jovial and entertaining in the company of others. While interested in the mystical and the occult, he could attempt to study these phenomena in a systematic fashion. Introversion and extraversion, thinking and feeling, could perhaps be brought together in some harmonious way.

What is being suggested is that one can consider each personality theorist according to the influence of personal life experiences in the development of his or her theory, not only in the content of the theory but also in the methods each theorist used to study phenomena and in his or her response to challenging the views of others. In many experimental psychologists there is an early history of devotion to gadgets and mechanical devices. Skinner's (1976) autobiography is interesting in this regard. First, those familiar with Skinner's studies of pigeons pecking at discs may be fascinated to read of Skinner's description of how his grandmother would put a seed between her lips so that she could induce her canary to "kiss her, as she called it." He also describes an early interest in a world of animals that could be tamed and trained. A related point is his interest in the control of behavior through positive reinforcement. Here he points out how his other grandmother wielded tremendous power through the dispensation of rewards such as apple pie and maple sugar.

A second issue of interest concerns Skinner's views about emotions or feelings. Skinner recognizes that feelings exist but sees their investigation as useless for a scientific understanding of behavior. Here it is interesting to note that Skinner describes how at the time of the death of his brother he didn't feel very moved and probably felt guilty about not feeling moved. His comment about one of his early poems is also of interest: "When I went back to Hamilton (college) I wrote a poem which, for once, expressed something I really felt and perhaps for that reason was one of my worst" (Skinner, 1976, p. 206). And, what of sexual feelings in particular? As was common in many homes at the time, sex was not openly discussed in Skinner's house. His father hid a set of Havelock Ellis's *Studies in the Psychology of Sex* that he presumably had bought for use in discussing sexual matters with clients in divorce cases. And what of Oedipal issues? Skinner describes how his mother would rub his head and massage his scalp: "It was quite possibly a kind of affection which she no longer gave my father; indeed, she may never have given it, because it would have led in a direction she found distasteful. Once when we were alone and she was rubbing my head, she said that she thought my father was jealous, and she giggled, but it was not a giggling matter" (1976, p. 277). He follows this description of his relationship with his mother and his competition with his father with a description of how at times he would sit motionless in a kind of catatonic stupor and finally indicated that he thought that he should see a psychiatrist. Were such feelings so threatening that they and all other feelings were to be ignored? Is there a relationship to be found between his later views about behaviorism and operant conditioning and these early experiences and his wish to tame and train animals?

The psychobiographical method suggested by Atwood and Tomkins appears to have a great deal of utility in helping us to understand the personal and social forces that affect the development of knowledge and that shape the course of history. At the same time, some caution is to be taken. First, there are dangers in interpretations of relationships. The psychobiographical method involves seeking relationships between theorists' life events and their theories of human behavior. The accounts of life events are taken from biographies and autobiographies. To what extent are these accounts biased by the theories themselves? That is, to what extent does Skinner's drawing attention to his efforts to train animals and to his grandmother's use of apple pie to control behavior reflect his current theoretical position rather than their representing formulative experiences? Is the theorist's life like a Rorschach test in the sense that the psychobiographical perceiver can find in it whatever he or she wishes to see?

The second note of caution concerns the potential for the development of a defeatist, iconoclastic attitude toward personality theory. If all personality theory reflects the personal and social forces operating during the development of the theorist, is it possible to have a scientific theory of personality? Are we not left with personal bias and without hope for a cumulative, time-lasting theory of human behavior? Indeed some psychologists argue that we may only be able to develop laws that will hold for specific historical periods of time, so that changing historical periods may require different sets of laws.

The psychobiographical approach need not, however, be taken to imply such conclusions. To recognize the personal and social element in theory and knowledge does not necessarily mean that all theory and knowledge are only personal. It may be that the personal validity of each personality theorist's theory contributes something toward the cumulative theory of human behavior. If each personality theory contains something of significance toward understanding that individual's history and views concerning the world, then perhaps there is hope for an eventual integration of these various pieces of personal insight. Rather than viewing the theory as reflecting error and bias, we now see it as reflecting truth and insight, though perhaps of a more limited kind than envisioned by the theorist. The task then becomes one of identifying these elements of truth and insight in the various theories and of working toward an integration among them. As with any scientific theory, this is a cumulative process of gradual reshaping and redefinition rather than a final complete picture of things. In sum, the psychobiographical method can help us to be aware of the personal limitations of specific theories without its leading us to conclude that a cumulative theory of personality is impossible.

Another aspect of the psychology of knowledge that is worthy of consideration, one that was briefly described in the account of *The Double Helix*, involves consideration of what it means to people to be engaged in the process of discovery, creation, and the expansion of knowledge. In the book *Passionate Minds* (Wolpert & Richards, 1998), eminent scientists from various disciplines describe the development of their interest in science and the process of scientific discovery. A common theme concerns the excitement and passion associated with the scientific enterprise. One is asked about whether he gets pleasure from science and responds: "Oh, absolutely! I'm absolutely convinced that the pleasure of a real scientific insight—it doesn't have to be a great discovery—is like an orgasm" (p. 12). He also suggests that "the urge to compete is also the fuel, I think, that really leads to many of these achievements" (p. 14). Another describes his love of libraries and the complete isolation from the world. A third describes a group of scientists as voyeurs who "have a splendid feeling, almost a lustful feeling, of excitement when a secret of nature is revealed" (p. 197).

I first became aware of the issue under consideration here when I was working as a clinical psychologist at a university health service and treating students with psychological problems. Many came in with problems related to their studies (e.g., inability to write papers, inability to present their own ideas in class, and inability to do the work in a particular subject). What was striking and puzzling to me was that, except at the extremes, there seemed little relation between the overall psychological health of the student and his or her ability to function academically. Some very disturbed students were able to function extremely well academically while other, basically healthy students were being seriously incapacitated in some aspect of their studies. What became apparent to me was how learning, both in terms of process and content, is hardly a neutral area. For some students, doing the assigned reading or meeting the deadline on a paper represents submission to authority and therefore both are potential targets for rebellious activities. Some could do well in all subjects but one, often a subject a parent valued and insisted that the student take or a subject in which a parent or another member of the family excelled. We are all familiar with how at times siblings will seemingly unwittingly pick out subjects for each to excel in, being careful not to encroach upon one another's territory. One student wrote home to his parents pleading with them to allow him to learn, even if learning meant examining their view of the world and possibly coming to a different conclusion. Another student was surprised and distressed by the comment of a professor that she would like the student's evaluation of the theories being considered. It was shocking to her that her opinion would really count, and distressing, though also exhilarating, to face the task of evaluating figures who previously were idols to her. Finally, one can consider the Peanuts cartoon I saw some time ago where Charlie Brown bemoans the problems of being talented with everyone always expecting so much of you. He concludes that perhaps talent is more of a burden than a valued asset.

The point is that scientists are not neutral about the content or process of their work. This point is brought home in a study by Mitroff (1974) of the functioning of prestigious scientists who studied the lunar rocks during the course of the Apollo space missions. Mitroff focuses on the intense personal character of science and contrasts this view with other descriptions of the impersonal character of science. His study began three months after the landing of Apollo 11 on the moon. It involved extensive interviews with 42 of the most eminent scientists who studied the moon rocks. Each scientist was interviewed intensively four times over a span of three and a half years, an interval during which new discoveries concerning the rocks were being made. The interviews covered a broad range of issues concerning the lunar missions, but the focus was on the nature and function of the commitment of scientists to their pet hypotheses in the face of possibly disconfirming evidence. The rocks were a good focal point for such inquiry since many scientists had strongly committed themselves to a particular position concerning what the rocks and moon would be like. Furthermore, the views of many of the scientists were in direct conflict with one another. Thus, as Mitroff points out, the scientific drama surrounding the Apollo landings had many of the same ingredients described by Watson in *The Double Helix*. In sum, the research provided the opportunity to study the behavior of eminent scientists concerning their pet hypotheses and their responses to the discoveries of other scientists.

Reason and Emotion in Science

The ideal of emotional neutrality. . .is a powerful brake upon emotion anywhere in the instrumental activities of science and most particularly evaluation of the validity of scientific investigation.

Barber, 1952, p. 127

The interviews . . . document the often fierce, sometimes bitter competitive races for discovery and the intense emotions which permeate the doing of science.

Mitroff, 1974, p. 585

I don't know that scientists are any more willing than anyone else to change their minds. If you've worked on something and feel that you see it clearly, you don't like to be told that it is not right.

Cairns, 1998, p. 99

What did Mitroff find as a result of the interviews? His most general finding is stated as follows: "All the interviews exhibit high affective content. They document the often fierce, sometimes bitter, competitive races for discovery and the intense emotions which permeate the doing of science" (1974, p. 585). The status of a theory could hardly be discussed in impersonal or "objective" terms. Sides were taken concerning alternative theoretical views, with groups of scientists serving as personal advocates and defenders for each theoretical position. While not always the case, at times scientists would react simultaneously to the theory and to its proponents, so linked were the two for some of the subjects.

Mitroff reports that these findings were not surprising to him. What was surprising was how open the scientists were in their commitments and the extent to which this commitment affected what they did and how they responded to evidence presented by others. For example, consider the following description of one scientist given by another scientist: "X is so committed to the idea that the moon is Q that you could literally take the moon apart piece by piece, ship it back to Earth, reassemble it in X's backyard and show the whole thing . . . and X would still continue to believe that the moon is Q. X's belief in Q is unshakable. He refuses to listen to reason or to evidence" (1974, p. 586). Was this the description of a poor, lowly regarded scientist? Clearly not. Mitroff notes that the scientists most often perceived by peers as most committed to a particular view were also judged to be the most outstanding and most creative of the scientists in an already distinguished group! Often the scientists seen by their peers as most resistant to change were also described as bold, creative, stimulating, and provocative. Although individual scientists varied in their resistance to change, generally the scientists showed little change in their ideas over the three and a half year period despite the contradictory nature of the positions and the significant accumulation of relevant evidence.

How do the scientists themselves view the passionate commitment that they and their colleagues often express? Mitroff reports that every one of the scientists interviewed felt that the view of an objective, emotionally disinterested scientist was naive. Some were annoyed with such an image; others found it humorous. All, however, saw such an image as simple-minded nonsense, only believed in by the general public or beginning science students. Not only was the actual scientist deeply committed and emotionally involved, but such commitment and involvement were seen as necessary and desirable. One scientist indicated that to come to the right conclusions you must have people arguing all sides of the evidence. Another indicated that without emotional commitment one wouldn't have the energy or drive to press forward despite frustration and failure. A third suggested that you have to "stick your neck out" to get other scientists to listen to you and commitment was a necessary part of being prepared to stick your neck out. Finally, another scientist indicated that science was not really accurately portrayed by journal articles that describe a rational procedure. Instead, science is an intensely personal enterprise. While evidence clearly is a major part of the scientific process, emotional commitments to "favored views" are clearly another part of this process. What is necessary is not indifference but sufficient objectivity to suspend judgment and review the evidence at least occasionally. Since emotion cannot be excluded from the scientific process, the question is how we can understand its role better.

A few other points are worthy of note in the Mitroff study. First, there were clear psychological differences among the scientists in their approach to theory. At one extreme were "speculative thinkers" who "wouldn't hesitate to build a whole theory of the solar system based on no tangible data at all." At the other extreme was the data-bound experimentalist who "wouldn't risk an extrapolation, a leap beyond the data if his life depended on it." The speculative thinkers are positively seen as brilliant and creative, and negatively viewed as rigid and vague. The data-bound experimentalists are positively seen by their peers as impartial and precise, and negatively viewed as dull and unimaginative. In other words, personality factors played a role in the style of approach toward the solution of scientific problems, and the various alternative styles were seen as potentially both positive and negative. In a related vein, the difference between those who favor higher-level, more holistic analyses as opposed to those who favor lower-level, more reductionist analyses is described as follows (Chapter 10): "Basically, some people like reductive analysis into component particles. Others revel in complex wholes. This split is not masculine versus feminine, or science versus art. It is inside every field" (Jolly, 1999, p. 231).

A final point worthy of note concerns the moral and competitive rules associated with scientific activity as described by these scientists. While emotional commitment was fine, distortion and cheating were not. Conscious cheating they felt was not a problem, though in recent years there have been a few reports of faking of results by scientists eager for fame and government funding. What they felt to be much more of a serious problem was the at times unwitting appropriation of another's ideas and presentation of them as one's own. At times this could come about by forgetting an idea read someplace and then "discovering" the idea and presenting it as one's own. Often the issue is even more complicated and subtle. Thus, a scientist may claim that his or her ideas were clearly spelled out in a paper whereas other scientists may feel that there was ambiguity concerning certain issues. For reasons such as these many scientists accept as an unwritten rule the principle that "you don't divulge what you're up to until you're 99% sure that you've got the competition beat in the race to print" (Mitroff, 1974, p. 593).

What are the implications of this study for psychology and our understanding of the development of personality theory? The data clearly support the view of the process of scientific activity as a highly personal and psychologically significant endeavor. Individual personality characteristics not only enter into the choice of problems to be studied but also enter into the way in which these problems are studied. Mitroff suggests that while the balance between the impersonal and the personal, between the objective and the subjective, is part of all scientific activity, it is particularly true of poorly structured fields. This would appear to be true in personality theory today. Because of the lack of a clear structural framework, the personal and subjective take on an even more significant, though not necessarily predominant or destructive, role than might otherwise be the case.

Social and Political Considerations

As studies have shown, sociopolitical biases influence the questions asked, the research methods selected, the interpretation of research results, the peer review proc-

> *ess, judgments about research quality, and decisions*
> *about whether to use research in policy advocacy.*
>
> *Redding, 2001, p. 206*

Until now discussion has focused primarily on the individual scientist—how his or her personality and emotional commitment enter into the work. However, we have also noted that scientific pursuits have a historical context and a political aspect. Discoveries occur within a climate not only of scientific progress but of acceptance of particular views. Beyond the discoveries, the responses of the wider scientific and lay public are expressive of a particular historical period. One often hears that a theory represents "an idea whose time had come" or that "the religious and social views of the time blocked acceptance" of the theory. Discoveries depend not only on data and on creativity, but also on the ability of people to take a particular approach toward phenomena. This approach or view that people take often has an ideological component to it. Where an issue of social significance is concerned, therefore, the data and approach may have serious social and political implications. In the nature-nurture chapter we noted the relationship between positions on this issue and political views, and again the issue was raised earlier in this chapter in relation to work of the cultural anthropologist Margaret Mead.

In this section we will focus on the relationships between Darwin's theory of evolution, Social Darwinism, and psychological views concerning sex and race differences. However, many other illustrations could be given of connections between scientific thought and societal values and beliefs.

Social Darwinism, the Psychology of Sex Differences, and the IQ Controversy

Many scientific discoveries and theories have had a profound impact on social thought and patterns of living. Probably none, however, has had a greater effect than Darwin's publication of *The Origin of the Species* (1859) and his theory of evolution. One eminent historian suggests that though England gave Darwin to the world, it was in the United States that his views received a particularly quick and sympathetic reception (Hofstadter, 1944). Darwin's theory emphasized gradual changes over geological periods, adaptation to the environment, and survival of the fittest. Social Darwinism emphasized gradual change in social and political institutions, the importance of biological factors in differences among human beings, and a laissez-faire (survival of the fittest) economic policy. Those who were politically conservative and supported the existing order saw the environment as a challenge to the adaptive qualities and capabilities of the organism. Individuals in positions of power have been selected by society because of their adaptability to social situations. The individual organism responds to the environment and, in a sense, is manipulated by that environment. Such views are in contrast with liberal views that emphasize an active organism and the potential for radical change. While *biologically determined* does not mean fixed or immutable, Social Darwinism has emphasized the importance of genetic differences to account for later differences in accomplishment and power. Since survival of the fittest is good, and the current social hierarchy reflects such a survival-adaptation process, there is little reason to tamper with the social order.

Is there any evidence of the influence of Darwin, via the social-political philosophy of Social Darwinism, on American psychology? There is convincing evidence that such a relationship can be found in at least two areas: the psychology of sex differences and the heritability of intelligence as reflected in IQ scores. The first area is extremely well developed in a paper by Stephanie Shields (1975) on "Functionalism, Darwinism, and the Psychology of Women." In this paper Shields analyzes interest in the psychology of differences between men and women during the period between 1850 and the 1930s. She notes that during this period research on sex differences was done primarily by men, and women were viewed according to their relationship to the male norm rather than as subjects for study in their own right. Furthermore, she suggests that evolutionary theory was used to buttress a view emphasizing the inherent supremacy of the male and the subordinate role of the female. In the social sciences this focused on the belief that genetic differences could be found between men and women that would account for their differing places in society. Furthermore, since these differences were biological and a product of evolution, there was little point in seeking to influence them.

How were such views related to the study of male-female differences within the social sciences? Shields suggests that this was done through research on three topics: (1) genetic differences between men and women that would be associated with structural differences and then with differences in intelligence and temperament; (2) differences in instincts that are a product of evolution; (3) differences in variability of talent and ability between men and women that might account for selection and placement in positions of power and accomplishment in society. Research on genetically determined structural differences between men and women focused on the size of the brain. According to Shields, the prevailing social view was that women were intellectually inferior to men and therefore "it was left to the men of science to discover the particular physiological determinants of female inadequacy" (1975, p. 740).

Religious and other myths concerning female inferiority were to be given up now in favor of pseudoscientific explanations or scientific myths. Investigations of the brains of men and women promised to substantiate the long-held belief that men were smarter than women. What would constitute such scientific proof? One line of argument ran that since intellectual ability was proportional to the size of the brain, women were clearly inferior since their brains were smaller. How do we know? Well, clearly their heads are smaller. What if we measure actual brain size? Well, there too the evidence suggested that the female brain was smaller than that of the male and, therefore, explained her lesser intellectual ability. The fact that there might be different kinds of intellectual ability and that there was considerable overlap in brain size between men and women, with no clear relationship within a sex between brain size and intelligence, was lost to these scientific thinkers. Furthermore, what of brain size relative to body size as opposed to absolute brain size? If one is to consider brain size alone then there are many species that should be far more intelligent than humans. Isn't the ratio of brain weight to body weight important? Here, according to Shields, the data suggested that women possess a proportionately larger brain than men.

A variety of comparisons were found to be possible, some of which led to a more favorable relationship for men while others led to a more favorable relationship for women. Investigations of differences between men and women in specific parts of the brain, as opposed to the total brain, proved to be little better. Yet, for many the hunt continued with an eye toward finding anatomical differences favoring male superiority and a greater predisposition toward the acceptance of such results than toward the acceptance of results that favored women. Often results that favor the accepted social view are left unchecked and accepted uncritically whereas challenges to such a view are critically dismissed or subjected to every possible methodological criticism.

The Science and Politics of Sex Differences

As much as women want to be good scientists or engineers, they want first and foremost to be womanly companions of men and to be mothers.

Bettelheim, 1965, p. 15

The existence of such an "instinct" would, of course, validate the social norm of female subservience and dependence.

Shields, 1975, p. 750

The second line of research concerning male-female differences involved the concept of instincts, in particular the maternal instinct. Again, the evolutionary point of view emphasized biological differences. Instincts were one expression of such biological thinking. Since there appeared to be differences between men and women, it appeared reasonable to assume that such differences were biologically based in the form of instincts. Whereas the male has more of an aggressive instinct, the female has more of a maternal instinct. The fact that men were in positions of power while women took care of the family was evidence of the role of such instinctual forces. Since such instinctual forces were at work, didn't it make sense to recognize nature and leave each of the sexes to their natural roles? These views were accepted by such prominent American psychologists as William James and Edward Thorndike: "Women in general are thus by original nature submissive to men in general. Submissive behavior is apparently not annoying when assumed as the instinctive response to its natural stimulus. Indeed, it is perhaps a common satisfier" (Thorndike, 1914, p. 34). Shields quotes the psychologist Bruno Bettelheim to the effect that women "first" and "foremost" want to be companions of men and to be mothers, suggesting that such biological-instinctual views remain current in one form or another today: "The existence of such an 'instinct' would, of course, validate the social norm of female subservience and dependence" (Shields, 1975, p. 750).

The third area of research cited by Shields concerns individual differences and the range of biological variability within each sex. Here the Darwinian argument runs that genetic variability is good since it provides the basis for mutation and survival of the fittest. This being the case, one might expect to find greater variability within males than within females. Put differently, one would expect to find a greater range of ability in males than within females. If males were more variable, and variation were the mechanism for evolutionary progress, then clearly males provided the spearhead for the progressive development of the species.

Was there any evidence to support such a view? Havelock Ellis, the noted sexologist, found that there were more men than women in homes for the retarded and more eminent men than women. Therefore, it indeed appeared to be true that males were more variable than females. Arguments began to develop concerning the data and concerning the appropriate measure of variability. As with so many ideological issues, debate focuses on the "scientific issues" rather than recognizing the underlying ideological issue. In this case, data concerning greater male variability were necessary to support the prevailing view that men were naturally more able and intelligent. Such data could then be used to support the view that men should receive better educations than women, which would, of course, serve to enhance their position of power and prestige—which was used as evidence in the first place to support the view of their biological superiority. Since men clearly achieve more than women, they are naturally more gifted and one need not worry about social-environmental barriers to the success of women. Here, again, biological justification was used for enforcement of the social norm of women's subordinate status.

In all, Shields concludes as follows:

> "As a whole, the concept of evolution with its concomitant emphasis on biological determinism provided ample 'scientific' reason for cataloging the 'innate' differences in male and female nature. . . . When issues faded in importance, it was not because they were resolved but because they ceased to serve as viable scientific "myths" in the changing social and scientific milieu. As the times change, so must the myths change. (Shields, 1975, p. 740)"

> As seen in Chapters 5 and 6, in many ways the issue continues to be present with us today.

A parallel to the treatment of the biological basis for male-female sex differences can be found in the treatment of intelligence differences generally and the treatment of racial differences in IQ in particular. Kamin's (1974) review of the history of the IQ concept and the history of IQ testing in America is instructive in this regard. Kamin begins this review with Binet's work in France in 1905. Binet's efforts were directed toward the development of a practical diagnostic instrument that could be used in the prescription of therapeutic efforts with individuals with low scores. The pioneers of the mental testing movement in America associated Binet's test with the concept of "innate intelligence." Kamin suggests that this association between IQ and innate intelligence fits with the sociopolitical views of these pioneers. Thus, Terman, one of these early pioneers, is quoted as follows: "border-line deficiency. . .is very, very common among Spanish-Indian and Mexican families of the Southwest and also among Negroes. Their dullness seems to be racial, or at least inherent in the family stocks from which they come" (Terman, as quoted in Kamin, 1974, p. 6).

During the 1920s these views became associated with the eugenics movement and with significant decisions concerning social action and social policy. The eugenics movement did not need the efforts of psychologists. It had enough lay and scientific proponents to move ahead without such support. It is true, however, that the efforts of psychologists were used by proponents of the eugenics movement and by those who sought to restrict immigration. Citing the many sterilization laws passed in the early 1900s, Kamin suggests that "the belief in the heritability of IQ may thus merely have provided a convenient and 'scientific' rationale for policies and laws which would have been enacted on other grounds" (1974, p. 12). In other words, we again have scientific "facts" being used to support social and political views.

Kamin suggests that the use of such "facts" was even clearer in relation to immigration policy. IQ tests demonstrated that vast numbers of immigrant Jews, Hungarians, Italians, and Russians were feeble-minded. Such data, through the assistance of scientists of the Eugenics Research Association, became generally known in Congress. These scientists proclaimed the belief that they were measuring native or inborn intelligence rather than exposure to American customs or privileged environments. The "race hypothesis" suggested that as the proportion of Nordic blood decreased, the intelligence level decreased in a comparable fashion. After all, the test results had clearly indicated a genuine (i.e., genetic) superiority of the Nordic group. With considerable outrage, Kamin suggests that these activities by psychologists played a role in the Immigration Act of 1924, which imposed quotas designed to restrict immigration of the "biologically inferior" people of southeastern Europe:

> The new law made the country safe for. . .Nordics, but it did little for the safety of Alpines and Mediterraneans. The law, for which the science of mental testing may claim substantial credit, resulted in the deaths of literally hundreds of thousands of victims of the Nazi biological theorists. The victims were denied admission to the United States because the "German quota" was filled, although the quotas of many other Nordic countries were vastly undersubscribed.

(1974, p. 27)

Of all the psychologists criticized by Kamin, probably none comes in for more attack than the British psychologist Sir Cyril Burt. Burt was for many years an extremely influential person in mental testing. In analyzing Burt's data,

Kamin found contradictory data, remarkable inconsistencies that stretched credibility, instances of missing data, unexplained "adjusted assessments" of IQ, procedural ambiguities in testing, and generally evidence of personal bias in the conduct and interpretation of his research. Since Burt's data provided one of the main bulwarks of the hereditarian position, these findings were not trivial. Kamin's questions concerning the scientific and ethical standards of Burt were challenged by Eysenck (1977) as irresponsible accusations and he suggested that whatever errors occurred were due to carelessness rather than fraud. However, a biography written by an admirer of Burt, indeed by the person who delivered the eulogy at his memorial service, concludes that Burt fabricated figures and falsified data (Hearnshaw, 1979). Despite his generally critical and exacting standards for research, Eysenck remains surprisingly tolerant of Burt's "errors" (1981; Maher, 1982). Why Burt should have cheated is related to questions considered earlier in this chapter concerning personal aspects of psychological research. Why his views should have found such broad support and why his errors went unrecognized for so long is related to the issues under consideration here.

The belief in the heritability of IQ may thus merely have provided a convenient and "scientific" rationale for policies and laws which would have been enacted on other grounds.

Kamin, 1974, p. 12

This alleged conformity of political ideology and scientific stance is in fact completely erroneous and historically untenable.

Eysenck, 1982, p. 1288

Is IQ a thing which can be caused by genes, or is it a social construct? If it's a social construct, then we have an interesting problem of the heritability of a social construct.

Lewontin, 1998, p. 105

Kamin suggests that the interpretation of IQ data is never free of policy implications and of ideological overtones. Others similarly point out the relationship between psychology and social concerns in general, and the relationship between the intelligence testing movement and social ideology in particular. As one observer notes, there is a strange transition from the development of a test to solve a social problem (i.e., Binet's test was to be used to ensure the benefits of education to defective children), to the later use of such tests to perpetuate a social problem. Tests were devised to measure intelligence without any clear understanding of what intelligence is. Yet, we manage to take the tests as measures of intelligence and as proof of our understanding of the concept. A society becomes so committed to the test that earlier questions of definition and proof are shunted aside.

> The argument then is that the intelligence test exploded into public acceptability and public use not because of its merits, but because it could be seized on as part of a more fair and more just system of social contracts. The test could be used as part of the system for allocating social opportunity. . . . But the IQ tests of that time had the rather happy property of being a conservative social innovation. They could be perceived as justifying the richness of the rich and the poverty of the poor; they legitimized the existing social order.

> *(White, 1975, p. 12)*

In sum, we have here two dramatic instances in which scientific pursuits seem to be associated with social values and beliefs, in particular the sociopolitical views of Social Darwinism. These views stress the inheritance of genetic differences, survival of the fittest, and the maintenance of the status quo in the social order. Research was conducted and findings reported that tended to substantiate such views. Generally the research was done by individuals with an investment in the privileged position and results reported to others in a similarly privileged position. Unwittingly, the framing of questions, the design of research procedures, and the interpretation of empirical findings may all be biased by and used in support of prevailing social norms. Just as the pursuit of science is not nearly as unemotional and free of commitment as the general public often believes, so the pursuit of science is not nearly as free of social influence as we would like to believe.

Conclusion

In this section we have considered the connection between the scientific enterprise and personal and sociopolitical factors. The issues are complex, of fundamental importance, and highly controversial. Recently an article appeared in the *American Psychologist*, the major professional journal in the field, that highlights the issues involved. The author claimed that "the profession lacks sociopolitical diversity. Most psychologists are politically liberal, and conservatives are vastly underrepresented in the profession. Moreover, when sociopolitical views guide the research, advocacy, or professional practice of psychologists, those views most often are liberal. The lack of political diversity in psychology has unintended negative consequences. . . ." (Redding, 2001, p. 205).

Again, the point is that forces in society and in the profession affect the questions that are asked, how they are studied, by whom, and how the results are interpreted and received. This does not mean that personality theory and research only reflect such social forces. Nor does it suggest that the influence of such forces is equally strong in all aspects of theory and research. Furthermore, in drawing such relationships one must exercise caution. The fact that certain social forces coexist at the time of certain scientific developments does not necessarily mean that these developments occurred because of these social forces. While exercising such caution, however, we should be aware that all scientific progress takes place within a social, political, and economic context. That context may facilitate or impede a variety of scientific achievements. The effects of the social, political, and economic context are probably greatest upon scientific endeavors that most influence the social fabric of the society and upon those sciences that are in their earliest stage of development. Where the questions asked are most relevant to society, where the field or discipline is not highly structured, and where the methods of research to be used are least well defined are all places that social, political, and economic forces most exert their influence. One can see, then, why personality theory and research would be particularly vulnerable to such influences. The questions asked relate directly to our whole view of people and their relationship to society, the field remains somewhat unstructured, and the research methods are varied and changing. The field remains in a state of flux and, while not uniquely affected by social values and concerns, it clearly is open to such effects.

Ethics of the Scientific Enterprise

As we have endeavored to study more important social phenomena, and as we have begun to understand at least some of the principles of behavioral control, questions of ethical concern have become increasingly important. Consider, for example, the following brief descriptions of important research efforts that resulted in considerable controversy.

Milgram's Research on Obedience to Authority

In the 1960s the psychologist Stanley Milgram conducted research on the determinants of obedience to authority. The work received considerable attention—both praise as a research effort (e.g., the 1965 prize for outstanding sociopsychological research awarded by the American Association for the Advancement of Science) and criticism for its treatment of subjects. The issue of concern to Milgram was the factors that determine what a person does when commanded by another person to hurt a third person. The aim of the search was to "study behavior in a strong situation of deep consequence to participants, for the psychological forces operative in powerful and lifelike forms of the conflict may not be brought into play under diluted conditions" (Milgram, 1965, p. 57).

Milgram recruited male adults from the New Haven and Bridgeport (Connecticut) areas. When they arrived at the laboratory, they were told that the research involved the study of the effect of punishment on memory. Each subject was paired with another person who pretended to be a subject but in reality was an accomplice of the experimenter. The subject was told that a teacher and learner were needed. A rigged drawing was then held so that the subject became the "teacher" and the accomplice became the "learner." The learner was then presumably taken to an adjacent room and strapped into an "electric chair." The subject was told that his task was to teach the learner a list of paired associates and to punish him, with an electric shock, whenever error was made. An increase in the intensity of the shock was to be made with each error on the part of the learner. The subject was instructed by the experimenter to keep administering increasing levels of electric shock despite pleas from the learner that the shock was extremely painful.

The Ethics of Milgram's Obedience to Authority Experiment

In view of the effects on subjects, traumatic to a degree which Milgram himself considers nearly unprecedented in socio-psychological experiments, his casual assurance that these tensions were dissipated before the subject left the laboratory is unconvincing. [p. 422] . . . procedures which involve loss of dignity, selfesteem, and trust in rational authority are probably most harmful in the long run.

Baumrind, 1964, p. 423

A person who comes to the laboratory is an active, choosing adult, capable of accepting or rejecting the prescriptions for action addressed to him. Baumrind sees the effect of the experiment as undermining the subject's trust of authority. I see it as a potentially valuable experience insofar as it makes people aware of the problem of indiscriminate submission to authority.

Milgram, 1964, p. 852

Is the situation realistic and what are the results of such realism? The subject used a simulated shock generator with markings on it ranging from "Slight Shock" to "Danger: Severe Shock." The subject was given a sample shock to convince him of the authenticity of the shock instrument. The responses of the accomplice learner-victim were taped and coordinated with the operation of the bogus shock device. Taped responses ranged from grunts and moans, to demands to be released from the experiment, to cries that the pain was unbearable, to insistence that he has quit the experiment and must be freed. Under all conditions the experimenter instructed the actual subject-teacher that he must go on and should treat the learner's refusal to continue as an incorrect response.

The results? As Milgram noted, one might have expected and hoped that subjects would allow their consciences to dictate their behavior and terminate their involvement at an early point. However, a substantial proportion of the participants administered what they thought were extremely painful doses of shock in obedience to the commands of the experimenter. Milgram noted that there were clear signs of tension and emotional strain (e.g., sweating, biting of lips, trembling, stuttering, nervous laughter and smiling, uncontrollable seizures) in many of the subjects as they continued to administer what they thought were increasing levels of intensity of shock. On one occasion a subject experienced such violently convulsive seizures that the experiment had to be called to a stop. After testing almost a thousand adults Milgram concluded that with "numbing regularity" good people would act in cruel ways while engaged in the condition of obedience to authority.

Zimbardo's Prison Experiment

In 1971 Philip Zimbardo conducted research in which subjects assumed the roles of "prisoner" or "guard" for an extended period of time within a mock prison setting on the campus of Stanford University. The goal of the research was to study the social, situational forces that affected the behavior of "guards" and "prisoners" in the psychology of imprisonment. Male college students were selected to participate in a study of prison life in return for which they received a daily wage of 15 dollars for a projected two-week period. Half the subjects were randomly assigned the prison guard role, the other half the prisoner role. All subjects were impressed with the seriousness of the research and were given uniforms appropriate to their guard or prisoner role. Zimbardo reports that conditions in the simulated prison environment were sufficiently realistic and forceful to "elicit intense, personal and often pathological reactions from the majority of the participants" (Zimbardo, 1973, p. 244). The volunteer guards were verbally and physically aggressive and otherwise dehumanizing of the subjects in the prisoner condition. On the other hand, the volunteer prisoners allowed themselves to suffer physical and psychological abuse hour after hour for days: "The projected two-week study had to be prematurely terminated when it became apparent that many of the 'prisoners' were in serious distress and many of the 'guards' were behaving in ways which brutalized and degraded their fellow subjects" (p. 243).

The Zimbardo Prison Experiment

Is the degradation of thirty-two young men justified by the importance of the results of this research? . . . Similar questions are raised by a great many other psychological experiments in which subjects are deceived, frightened, humiliated, or maltreated in some other way.

Savin, 1973, p. 148

> *We are sufficiently convinced that the suffering we ob-
> served, and were responsible for, was stimulus-bound
> and did not extend beyond the confines of the basement
> prison.*
>
> *Zimbardo 1973, p. 249*

The Protection of Subjects and the Conduct of Research

The American Psychological Association's document on ethical principles is clear concerning the issue of harm or injury to subjects: The ethical investigator protects participants from physical and mental discomfort, harm, and danger. If the risk of such consequences exists, the investigator is required to inform the participant of that fact, secure consent before proceeding, and take all possible measures to minimize distress. A research procedure may not be used if it is likely to cause serious and lasting harm to participants. Universities and other research institutions set up research boards to review research projects to ensure that ethical principles are followed and the rights of subjects are protected. In addition, federal government grant agencies have review panels that go over all aspects of the proposed research to make sure that proposals conform to government standards in this regard.

At this point in time it is my guess that Milgram's obedience research and Zimbardo's prison research would not pass institutional or government review boards. At the same time, it is important to recognize that Milgram and Zimbardo defended their research efforts on three counts. First, the behaviors exhibited and stress experienced by the subjects were unanticipated. Milgram expected his subjects to refuse to obey the experimenter after a certain point and Zimbardo did not quite expect his subjects to get so much into the spirit of their roles. Second, no lasting harm was done to subjects and they may have even gained something from participation in the research. Milgram reported that all subjects were given a post experiment treatment in which the experiment was explained, there was a friendly reconciliation with the unharmed "learner," and obedient subjects were assured that their feelings and behaviors were not abnormal. Subjects received a full report of the conclusions of the research. A follow-up questionnaire to subjects showed that 84 percent were glad to have been in the experiment, 15 percent were neutral, and only 1 percent reported negative feelings. Many subjects valued the opportunity to learn something about themselves and about the potential for various kinds of repugnant behavior. Zimbardo similarly claimed that although the subjects did experience physical pain, psychological humiliation, and anxiety, there were no persisting negative reactions and most of the subjects reported that it was a valuable learning experience for them.

Third, Milgram and Zimbardo argued that there were substantial gains in scientific knowledge and public consciousness of critical issues that resulted from their research efforts. Milgram argued that through research efforts such as his own we may hope to avoid catastrophic examples of obedience to authority in the future. Zimbardo noted that his research received publicity in the mass media and forced into public awareness the hell of prison: "In some small way we believe our analysis of the ingredients which create such hells may help to change them" (Zimbardo, 1973, p. 253). A few subjects in the research were so moved by their experiences that they volunteered time to work in local prisons and became advocates for penal reform.

In sum, Milgram and Zimbardo claimed that risk is a part of all research ("Understanding grows because we examine situations in which the end is unknown," Milgram, 1972, p. 113), their research involved no serious or lasting harm to the participants, and the research resulted in benefit to the individuals involved and to society generally. There is much merit to the points they make, and in reading their essays one is impressed with the care they took to examine the issues in their own minds and with their subjects. Efforts were made to protect the subjects from lasting harm. At the same time, the subjects were not informed of the risks beforehand, and one wonders whether there aren't enough daily occurrences of obedience to authority and enough daily occurrences of prison brutality to make real life the focal point of investigation.

Another ethical issue of concern is that of deception. Many psychologists are concerned that there has been such widespread use of deception in psychological research that investigators are losing all credibility in what they tell subjects about the experiment. In fact, some psychologists feel that the problem is so serious and widespread that it is hard to tell who is deceiving whom—are experimenters deceiving subjects about the true purpose of the research or are subjects deceiving experimenters in acting as if they believe what the experimenter tells them?

Deception on the part of the experimenter concerning possible harm or injury to the subject, physical or emotional, clearly is ruled out by ethical guidelines. But what of deception concerning the true nature of the research? Ethical guidelines indicate that deception concerning the purpose of the research should not occur unless it is justified by the study's significant prospective scientific, educational, or applied value and effective nondeceptive alternative procedures are not feasible. In other words, although deception clearly is discouraged, and researchers are encouraged to give participants full information about the nature, results, and conclusions of the research as soon as possible, it is recognized that at times deception may be necessary. This has led to some controversy concerning when deception is necessary and when alternative nondeceptive procedures could be utilized.

The issue of deception was clearly raised in relation to Milgram's research on obedience to authority. The subjects were deceived about the true nature of the research—it was on obedience to authority and not on the effects of punishment on memory—and they were deceived about the effects of their actions, believing the "learner" to be experiencing shock and pain when this was not true. Those who use deception argue that it is necessary in the study of significant problems and in approximating lifelike conditions. The suggestion is made that if subjects know the true purpose of the research they may behave naturally, but they may also fake their responses to comply with what they think the experimenter wants or they may act so as to sabotage the experimenter's goals. In the Milgram research, the argument might be that if subjects knew that the research was on obedience to authority they would respond according to their values and beliefs rather than according to what they would actually do under real conditions. Neither Milgram nor his colleagues expected so many subjects to follow the commands of the experimenter to the extent that they did. Presumably knowledge of the purpose of the research would have led to the observation and conclusion that there was far less obedience to authority than was actually found to be the case.

Psychologists who argue against deception do so on both methodological and ethical grounds. Methodologically they argue that most subjects in any case formulate hypotheses concerning the nature of the research and function in accordance with these hypotheses. Research with college students in particular suggests widespread suspicion and distrust of psychological research and of the ethics of psychological experimenters. Results from experiments have been found to vary considerably according to whether or not the subjects believed the experimenter or felt that they were being deceived. In an atmosphere of mistrust, how can one be sure that one has obtained the cooperation and support of the subject?

In terms of ethical principles, many psychologists argue that often the deception involves information that can be harmful to the subject (e.g., male undergraduates being led to believe that they were homosexually aroused by photographs of men) and that, regardless of the danger of harmful effects, deception involves a violation of the respect due fellow human beings. One psychologist deeply concerned with these questions argues that one must balance the value of the acquisition of scientific knowledge, which may at times necessitate some deception, against the value of being honest with subjects. The greatest concern is expressed with deception where it is used as part of a standard operating procedure and is not examined against the possible use of other methods and the value of the research per se (Kelman, 1968).

Reporting of Results

We come now to perhaps a more subtle ethical question but one of enormous importance. The issue concerns the responsibility of researchers in the reporting of their findings. Ethical guidelines clearly indicate that psychologists are not to fabricate data, are to correct errors that come to their attention, and are to avoid making false or deceptive public statements. In making public statements they are to make sure that these statements are based on the appropriate psychological literature. Such guidelines are valuable but leave considerable room for individual judgment and potential error or abuse.

Consider, for example, a situation where you have evidence that early childhood education projects are of limited benefit unless they are followed up with considerable further educational efforts. Would you be concerned that the media, public, and politicians might pick up on the first part of the message and ignore the second? In other words, would you be concerned that the conclusion would be drawn that early educational efforts, such as Head Start, are a failure? Or, to take another example, suppose you had evidence that a test could predict which individuals would succeed in school or on a job, but the test measured characteristics that one or another group had been prevented from developing. In other words, your "successful" test continued a bias within society. What would you do with your results?

As academicians we believe in freedom of inquiry—individuals should be free to advance knowledge in any area they desire. While we seek to establish ethical principles of method or procedure, no area is held to be taboo from investigation. We also hold dear to the belief that an individual should be free to publish any advance in knowledge. What often is not recognized, however, is that the publication of research findings can have important social implications. It is my belief that the scientist publishing his or her results has an ethical responsibility to be aware of the potential social implications of these findings. It is also the ethical responsibility of the scientist to present the results in a way that promises the least potential for distortion and the greatest opportunity for social good.

This is not a trivial question and may, in fact, be of greater social significance than the issues of deception and harm to subjects. The finding of a lack of relationship between number of years of education and income can mistakenly be taken by some people to mean that education does no good and is useless as a route to economic advancement. The finding of a lack of difference in later years between children who participated in an early education program and those who did not can be taken as evidence that such programs are without value and should be discontinued. Indeed, these findings have been reported and conclusions have been drawn by individuals upon hearing of them. But is it not also possible to conclude that early education programs and continued education can be effective only if they are supported by additional training programs and by the destruction of other barriers to advancement?

During the course of writing this chapter I have been struck with the media picking up a story suggesting that leaving children in daycare facilities leads to aggressive behavior and a story suggesting that gays can shift their sexual orientation. In both cases the data had not been published and others in the field questioned the data and conclusions reached. Yet, apparently the presentations by the authors and by the media ignored both of these important factors. The point here is that the scientist has a responsibility to be aware of how his or her results may be used. I do not think that we can be in the position of avoiding the publication of certain results because they do not fit what our own values hold or what we would like to believe. I also believe that psychologists reporting results with social implications have a responsibility to be guarded in their conclusions, to point out the false conclusions that can be drawn from the results, and to promote the development of further research that will allow for social benefit. Thus, I find myself in agreement with Scarr (1981), who suggests that "there should be no regulation of scientists' rights to think, propose, and conduct ethical investigations on any question" and that "scientists are responsible for the effects of their research reports, particularly to a wide audience" (p. 531). At the same time, it is naive for the researcher to assume that he or she is totally value-free in the phenomena chosen to be investigated or in the way results are reported, and that the consumers of the findings will be equally value-free in the uses to which the results are put.

Summary

This chapter has considered the nature of the scientific enterprise—the personal, social, and political forces that enter into the scientific enterprise and some of the ethical principles that govern it. The emphasis has been on how personality theory and research, as well as all other scientific pursuits, are the products of humans with personal motivations who also reflect the values of their times. In contrast with the view of science as only unemotional, objective, and free of bias, the view has been presented that scientific efforts often are emotional and subject to personal and social bias. The role of personal factors in the development of theory and selection of methods of research has been emphasized. Such influences are present, to a greater or lesser extent, in all psychologists and all scientists. However, it probably is true that, by virtue of its subject matter, personality as a field particularly lends itself to such influence.

The emotional commitment of scientists to their work was illustrated in Watson's book *The Double Helix* and in Mitroff's study of scientists studying rocks found on the moon. Scientific efforts are hardly the cool, unemotional activities that the lay public often believes. These activities are filled with a sense of personal challenge, with rivalry and competition, with politics, and with a deep commitment to one's ideas. Scientists take sides concerning various questions and often perceive the issues in terms of the individuals associated with the different points of view. Theories are held by individuals in the face of disconfirming evidence, demonstrating a considerable resistance to change. This passionate commitment to particular points of view is accepted by scientists as a part of their professional involvement and even valued by some as a necessary part of the creative enterprise. What distinguishes science from other activities is not its neutrality, objectivity, or lack of emotion but rather its ability to use more objective methods in the ultimate evaluation of evidence. In other words, it is the balance between the objective and subjective, the rational and the emotional that distinguishes scientific efforts from other pursuits.

Along with the very clear personal issues that enter into scientific inquiry there are social and political forces that affect the nature of the questions asked, the methods used to address these questions, and the response to the scientific evidence that is gathered. These relationships were discussed in terms of the relation of the social philosophy of Social Darwinism to the study of sex differences and the IQ controversy. Social Darwinism emphasized the importance of genetic differences and environmental selection based on survival of the fittest. Socially and politically it was used as a basis for maintenance of the status quo. In the study of sex differences, Social Darwinism was associated with research on biological differences (e.g., brain size) between men and women, an emphasis on instinctual differences (e.g., the maternal instinct), and differences in variability of talent between men and women (i.e., men are more variable and therefore are more eminent). What is particularly significant about this research is that it started with a preconception and almost exclusively involved men doing the research and interpreting the results. The suggestion made by Shields after reviewing this literature was that underlying the "scientific issue" was an "ideological issue" and therefore the issue was never settled. Instead, the myths changed as social conditions changed.

Similarly, a review of the history of the controversy concerning the heritability of intelligence suggests a strong ideological bias. Kamin points out the social implications of such ideological biases and the role that psychological "facts" can sometimes play in the formation of social policy (e.g., immigration policy). Moreover, of particular significance is Kamin's questioning of the integrity of one of the past leading researchers in the field, Sir Cyril Burt, and the evidence that indeed some results may have been made up to fit the preconceived ideas. While such behavior is rare, it is further testimony to the personal elements that enter into efforts here as well as in other fields. In reviewing the history of research on sex differences and heritability of intelligence, we undoubtedly will want to keep in mind their implications for other current fields of inquiry. In particular, for example, one can consider the implications for research on race and ethnic differences that frequently starts with a specific bias and often involves study of the minority group by members of the majority group. Again, all too often the questions asked reflect the bias of current social myths, and data are interpreted in the light of current social beliefs.

What is one to conclude from these considerations and illustrations? First, one must beware of a defeatist attitude according to which personality theory and research is "nothing but" personal and social bias. To suggest that personal and social forces enter into the enterprise is not to suggest that they represent all there is to the enterprise or even that they dominate the enterprise. Second, one must be careful in drawing relationships between personal-social forces and psychological inquiry. It is possible to draw such relationships on the basis of superficial evidence and the relationships drawn may themselves reflect bias. While being aware of such dangers, we should not shrink from recognizing the role of personal-social forces in psychological inquiry and the implications our findings may have for social policy.

Finally, we considered ethical issues associated with the scientific enterprise—the protection of subjects from harm or injury, the issue of deception in research, and the reporting of results bearing upon social issues in a responsible way. Milgram's research on obedience to authority and Zimbardo's prison research provided illustrative cases of ethical questions that can be raised in the conduct of psychological research. The values of freedom of inquiry and of public presentation of data were emphasized. At the same time, it was suggested that in their public presentations scientists have a responsibility to be aware of how the media and the public may misinterpret or misrepresent what is being reported.

References

Adams, H. E., Wright, L. W., & Lohr, B. A. (1996). Is homophobia associated with homosexual arousal? *Journal of Abnormal Psychology, 105,* 440–445.

Ader, R. (2001). Psychoneuroimmunology. *Current Directions in Psychological Science, 10,* 94–98.

Ainsworth, M. D. S., & Bowlby, J. (1991). An ethological approach to personality development. *American Psychologist, 46,* 333–341.

Alexander, F. (1950). *Psychosomatic medicine.* New York: Norton.

Alexander, F. (1956). *Psychoanalysis and psychotherapy.* New York: Norton.

Alexander, F., & French, T. M. (1946). *Psychoanalytic therapy.* New York: Ronald.

Allport, G. W. (1955). *Becoming: Basic considerations for a psychology of personality.* New Haven: Yale.

Allport, G. W. (1937). *Personality: A psychological interpretation.* New York: Holt, Rinehart & Winston.

Allport, G. W. (1958). What units shall we employ? In G. Lindzey (Ed.), *Assessment of human motives* (pp. 239–260). New York: Holt, Rinehart & Winston.

Andersen, B. L., Cyranowski, J. M., & Aarestad, S. (2000). Beyond artificial, sex–linked distinctions to conceptualize female sexuality: Comment on Baumeister (2000). *Psychological Bulletin, 126,* 380–384.

Anderson, C. A., Lindsay, J. J., & Bushman, B. J. (1999). Research in the psychological laboratory: Truth or triviality? *Current Directions in Psychological Science, 8,* 3–9.

Anderson, P. W. (1972). More is different. *Science, 177,* 393–396.

Andreasen, N. C. (1984). *The broken brain: The biological revolution in psychiatry.* New York: Harper & Row.

Andreasen, N. C. (2001). *Brave new brain: Conquering mental illness in the era of the genome.* New York: Oxford University Press.

Anisman, H., Zaharia, M. D., Meaney, M. J., & Merali, Z. (1998). Do early–life events permanently alter behavioral and hormonal responses to stressors? *International Journal of Developmental Neuroscience, 16,* 149–164.

Arlow, J. A. (1995). Psychoanalysis. In R. Corsini & D. Wedding (Eds.), *Current psychotherapies* (pp. 15–50). Itasca, IL: Peacock.

Asendorpf, J. B., & van Aken, M. A. G. (1999). Resilient, overcontrolled, and undercontrolled personality prototypes in childhood: Replicability, predictive power, and the trait–type issue. *Journal of Personality and Social Psychology, 77,* 815–8432.

Atwood, G. E., & Tomkins, S. S. (1976). On the subjectivity of personality theory. *Journal of the History of the Behavioral Sciences, 12,* 166–177.

Austin, J. T., & Vancouver, J. B. (1996). Goal constructs in psychology: Structure, process, and content. *Psychological Bulletin, 120,* 338–375.

Bailey, J. M., Kirk, K. M., Zhu, G., Dunne, M. P., & Martin, N. G. (2000). Do individual differences in sociosexuality represent genetic or environmentally contingent strategies? Evidence from the Australian twin registry. *Journal of Personality and Social Psychology, 78,* 537–545.

Balay, J., & Shevrin, H. (1988). SPA is subliminal, but is it psychodynamically activating? *American Psychologist, 44,* 1423–1426.

Banaji, M. R. (2001). Ordinary prejudice. *Psychological Science Agenda,* January/February, 9–11.

Bandura, A. (1961). Psychotherapy as a learning process. *Psychological Bulletin, 58,* 143–159.

Bandura, A. (1971). Psychotherapy based upon modeling principles. In A. E. Bergin & S. Garfield (Eds.), *Handbook of psychotherapy and behavior change* (pp. 653–708). New York: Wiley.

Bandura, A. (1982). Self–efficacy mechanism in human agency. *American Psychologist, 37*, 122–147.

Bandura, A. (1986). *Social foundations of thought and action: A social cognitive theory.* Englewood Cliffs, NJ: Prentice Hall.

Bandura, A. (1992). Self–efficacy mechanism in psychological functioning. In R. Schwarzer (Ed.), *Self–efficacy: Thought control of action* (pp. 335–394). Washington, DC: Hemisphere.

Bandura, A. (1997). *Self–efficacy: The exercise of control.* New York: Freeman.

Bandura, A. (1999). Social cognitive theory of personality. In L. A. Pervin & O. P. John (Eds.), *Handbook of personality: Theory and research* (pp. 154–196). New York: Guilford.

Bandura, A. (2001). Social cognitive theory: An agentic perspective. *Annual Review of Psychology, 52*, 1–26.

Barber, B. (1952). *Science and the social order.* New York: Collier.

Bargh, J. A., & Barndollar, K. (1996). Automaticity in action: The unconscious as a repository of chronic goals and motives. In P. M. Gollwitzer & J. A. Bargh (Eds.), *The psychology of action* (pp. 457–481). New York: Guilford.

Bargh, J. A., Chen, M., & Burrows, L. (1996). Automaticity of social behavior: Direct effects of trait construct and stereotype activation on action. *Journal of Personality and Social Psychology, 71*, 230–244.

Bargh, J. A., & Ferguson, M. J. (2000). Beyond behaviorism: On the automaticity of higher mental processes. *Psychological Bulletin, 126*, 925–945.

Bargh, J. A., & Pietromonaco, P. (1982). Automatic information processing and social perception: The influence of trait information presented outside of conscious awareness on impression formation. *Journal of Personality and Social Psychology, 43*, 437–449.

Barkow, J., Cosmides, L. & Tooby, J. (Eds.) (1992). *The adapted mind: Evolutionary psychology and the generation of culture.* New York: Oxford University Press.

Bates, M. (1960). Ecology and evolution. In S. Tax (Ed.), *Evolution after Darwin* (pp. 547–568). Chicago: University of Chicago Press.

Baum, A., & Posluszny, D. M. (1999). Health psychology: Mapping biobehavioral contributions to health and illness. *Annual Review of Psychology, 50*, 137–163.

Baumeister, R. F. (1982). A self–presentational view of social phenomena. *Psychological Bulletin, 91*, 3–26.

Baumeister, R. F. (1998). The self. In D. T. Gilbert, S. T. Fiske, & G. Lindzey (Eds.), *The handbook of social psychology* (pp. 680–740). Boston: McGraw–Hill.

Baumeister, R. F. (1999). On the interface between personality and social psychology. In L. A. Pervin & O. P. John (Eds.), *Handbook of personality: Theory and research* (pp. 367–377). New York: Guilford.

Baumeister, R. F. (2000). Gender differences in erotic plasticity: The female sex drive as socially flexible and responsive. *Psychological Bulletin, 126*, 347–374.

Baumeister, R. F., Dale, K., & Sommer, K. L. (1998). Freudian defense mechanisms and empirical findings in modern social psychology: Reaction formation, projection, displacement, unjdoing, isolation, sublimation, and denial. *Journal of Personality, 66*, 1081–1124.

Baumeister, R. F., & Leary, M. R. (1995). The need to belong: Desire for interpersonal attachments as a fundamental human motivation. *Psychological Bulletin, 117*, 497–529.

Baumrind, D. (1964). Some thoughts on ethics of research. *American Psychologist, 19*, 421–423.

Baumrind, D. (1993). The average expectable environment is not good enough: A response to Scarr. *Child Development, 64*, 1299–1317.

Beck, A. T. (1972). *Depression: Causes and treatment.* Philadelphia: University of Pennsylvania Press.

Beck, A. T. (1993). Cognitive therapy: Past, present, and future. *Journal of Consulting and Clinical Psychology, 61, 194–198.*

Beck, A. T., & Weishaar, M. (1995). Cognitive therapy. In R. Corsini & D. Wedding (Eds.), *Current psychotherapies* (pp. 229–261). Itasca, IL: Peacock.

Bem, S. L. (1998). *An unconventional family.* New Haven: Yale.

Benedict, R. (1934). *Patterns of culture.* Boston: Houghton Mifflin.

Berkman, L. F., Leo–Sumners, L., & Horwitz, R. I. (1992). Emotional support and survival after myocardial infarction. *Annals of Internal Medicine, 117*, 1003–1009.

Berlin, B., & Kay, P. (1969). *Basic color terms: Their universality and their evolution.* Berkeley: University of California Press.

Berne, E. (1964). *Games people play.* New York: Grove Press.

Bettelheim, B. (1965). The commitment required of a woman entering a scientific profession in present–day American society. In J. A. Mattfield and C. G. Van Aken (Eds.), *Women and the scientific professions.* Cambridge, MA: MIT Press.

Beutler, L. E. (2000). David and Goliath. *American Psychologist, 55*, 997–1007.

Block, J. (1971). *Lives through time.* Berkeley, CA: Bancroft.

Block, J. (1977). Advancing the psychology of personality: Paradigmatic shift or improving the quality of research? In D. Magnusson & N. Endler (Eds.), *Personality at the crossroads* (pp. 37–64). Hillsdale, NJ: Erlbaum.

Block, J. (1993). Studying personality the long way. In D. C. Funder, R. D. Parke, C. Tomlinson–Keasey, & K. Widaman (Eds.), *Studying lives through time* (pp. 9–41). Washington, DC: American Psychological Association.

Block, J. (1995). A contrarian view of the five–factor approach to personality description. *Psychological Bulletin, 117, 187–215.*

Block, J., Gjerde, P. F., & Block, J. H. (1991). Personality antecedents of depressive tendencies in 18-year–olds: A prospective study. *Journal of Personality and Social Psychology, 60, 726–738.*

Block, J. H., & Block, J. (1980). The role of ego control and ego resiliency in the organization of behavior. In W. A. Collins (Ed.), *Development of cognitive, affect, and social relations: The Minnesota symposium in child psychology* (pp. 39–101). Hillsdale, NJ: Erlbaum.

Block, J., & Colvin, C. R. (1994). Positive illusions and well–being revisited: Separating fiction from fact. *Psychological Bulletin, 116, 28.*

Boden, J. M., & Baumeister, R. F. (1997). Repressive coping: Distraction using pleasant thoughts and memories. *Journal of Personality and Social Psychology, 73, 45–62.*

Boneau, C. A. (1992). Observations on psychology's past and future. *American Psychologist, 47*, 1586–1596.

Boring, E. G. (1950). *A history of experimental psychology.* New York: Appleton–Century–Crofts.

Borkenau, P., Riemann, R., Angleitner, A., & Spinath, F. M. (2001). Genetic and environmental influences on observed personality: Evidence from the German observational study of adult twins. *Journal of Personality and Social Psychology, 80,* 655–668.

Bouchard, T. J., Jr., Lykken, D. T., McGue, M., Segal, N. L., & Tellegen, A. (1990). Sources of human psychological differences: The Minnesota study of twins reared apart. *Science, 250,* 223–250.

Bouchard, T. J., Jr., & McGue, M. (1981). Familial studies of intelligence: A review. *Science, 212*, 1055–1059.

Bretherton, I. (1992). The origins of attachment theory: John Bowlby and Mary Ainsworth. *Developmental Psychology, 28*, 759–775.

Brewin, C. R. (1989). Cognitive change processes in psychotherapy. *Psychological Review, 96*, 379–394.

Brewin, C. R. (1996). Theoretical foundations of cognitive–behavior therapy for anxiety and depression. *Annual Review of Psychology, 47*, 33–57.

Brown, R. (1976). Reference: In memorial tribute to Eric Lennegerg. *Cognition, 4*, 125–153.

Bruner, J. (1983). *In search of mind.* New York: Harper & Row.

Bruner, J. (1990). *Acts of meaning.* Cambridge: Harvard University Press.

Bruner, J. S. (1992). Another look at New Look 1. *American Psychologist, 47*, 780–783.

Bruner, J. S., & Goodman, C. C. (1947). Value and need as organizing factors in perception. *Journal of Abnormal and Social Psychology, 42*, 33–44.

Burnham, T., & Phelan, J. (2000). *Mean genes.* Cambridge, MA: Perseus.

Buss, A. H. (1997). Evolutionary perspectives on personality traits. In R. Hogan, J. Johnson, & S. Briggs (Eds.), *Handbook of personality psychology* (pp. 345–366). New York: Academic Press.

Buss, A. H., & Plomin, R. (1984). *Temperament: Early developing personality traits.* Hillsdale, NJ: Erlbaum.

Buss, D. M. (1989). Sex differences in human mate preferences: Evolutionary hypotheses tested in 37 cultures. *Behavoriol and Brain Sciences, 12*, 1–49.

Buss, D. M. (1995). Evolutionary psychology: A new paadigm for psychological science. *Psychological Inquiry, 6*, 1–30.

Buss, D. M. (1997). Evolutionary foundations of personality. In R. Hogan, J. Johnson, & S. Briggs (Eds.), *Handbook of personality psychology* (pp. 317–344). New York: Academic Press.

Buss, D. M. (1999). Human nature and individual differences: The evolution of human personality. In L. A. Pervin, O. P. & John (Eds.), *Handbook of personality: Theory and Research* (pp. 31–56). New York: Guilford.

Buss, D. M., Block, J. H., & Block, J. (1980). Preschool activity level: Personality correlates and developmental implications. *Child Development, 51*, 401–408.

Buss, D. M., Larsen, R. J., Westen, D., & Semmelroth, J. (1992). Sex differences in jealousy: Evolution, physiology and psychology. *Psychological Science, 3*, 251–255.

Buss, D. M., Haselton, M. G., Shackelford, T. K., Bleske, A. L., & Wakefield, J. C. (1998). Adaptations, exaptations, and spandrels. *American Psychologist, 53*, 533–548.

Buunk, B. P., Angleitner, A., Oubaid, V., & Buss, D. M. (1996). Sex differences in jealousy in evolutionary and cultural perspective. *Psychological Science, 7*, 359–363.

Cacioppo, J. T. (1999). The case for social psychology in the era of molecular biology. *Keynote address at the Society for Personality and Social Psychology Preconference*, June 3, 1999, Denver, CO.

Cacioppo, J. T., & Berntson, G. G. (1992). Social psychological contributions to the decade of the brain: Doctrine of multilevel analysis. *American Psychologist, 47*, 1019–1028.

Cacioppo, J. T., Berntson, G. G., Sheridan, J. F., & McClintock, M. K. (2000). Multilevel integrative analyses of human behavior: Social neuroscience and the complementing nature of social and biological approaches. *Psychological Buylletin, 126*, 829–843.

Cairns, J. (1998). Not a company man. In L. Wolpert & A. Richards (Eds.), *Passionate minds* (pp. 93–102). New York: Oxford University Press.

Cantor, N. (1990). Social psychology and sociobiology: What can we leave to evolution? *Motivation and Emotion*, 14, 242–254.

Cantor, N., & Kihlsrom J. F. (1982). Cognitive and social Processes in personality. In G. T. Wilson & C. Franks (Eds.), *Contemporary behavior therapy: Conceptual and empirical foundations*. New York: Guilford.

Cantor, N., & Kihlstrom, J. F. (1987). *Personality and social intelligence*. Englewood Cliffs, NJ: Prentice–Hall.

Cantor, N., & Kihlstrom, J. F. (1989). Social intelligence and cognitive assessments of personality. *Advances in Social Cognition, 2*, 1–59.

Cantor, N., & Mischel, W. (1977). Traits as prototypes: Effects on recognition memory. *Journal of Personality and Social Psychology, 35*, 38–48.

Caprara, G. V., & Cervone, D. (2000). *Personality: Determinants, dynamics, and potentials*. New York: Cambridge University Press.

Carroll, J. B. (1997). Psycometrics, intelligence, and public perception. *Intelligence, 24*, 53–78.

Carver, C. S., & Scheier, M. F. (1982). Control theory: A useful conceptual framework for personality, social, and health psychology. *Psychological Bulletin, 92*, 111–135.

Carver, C. S., & Scheier, M. F. (1990). Origins and functions of positive and negative affect: A control–process view. *Psychological Review, 97*, 19–35.

Caspi, A. (1998). Personality development across the life course. In W. Damon (Ed.), *Handbook of child psychology* (vol. 3, pp. 311–388). New York: Wiley.

Caspi, A. (2000). The child is father of the man: Personality correlates from childhood to adulthood. *Journal of Personality and Social Psychology, 78*, 158–172.

Caspi, A., & Roberts, B. (1999). Personality continuity and change across the life course. In L. A. Pervin & O. P. John (Eds.), *Handbook of personality: Theory and research* (pp. 300–326). New York: Guilford.

Caspi, A., & Roberts, B. (2001). Personality development across the life course: The argument for change and continuity. *Psychological Inquiry, 12*, 49–66.

Cattell, R. B. (1959). Foundations of personality measurement theory in multivariate expressions. In B. M. Bass & I. A. Berg (Eds.), *Objective approaches to personality assessment* (pp. 42–65). Princeton, NJ: Van Nostrand.

Cattell, R. B. (1965). *The scientific analysis of personality*. Baltimore: Penguin.

Cattell, R. B. (1979). *Personality and learning theory*. Neew York: Springer.

Cervone, D. (1999). Bottom–up explanation in personality psychology: The case of cross–situational coherence. In D. Cervone & Y. Shoda (Eds.), *The coherence of personality* (pp. 303–341. New York: Guilford.

Chambless, D. L. & Ollendick, T. H. (2001). Empirically supported psychological interventions: Controversies and evidence. *Annual Review of Psychology, 52*, 685–716.

Chen, C., Lee, S., & Stevenson, H. W. (1995). Response style and cross–cultural comparisons of rating scales among East Asian and North American students. *Psychological Science, 6*, 170–175.

Chomsky, N. (1980). *Rules and representations*. New York: Columbia University Press.

Church, A. T. (2000). Culture and personality: Toward an integrated cultural trait psychology. *Journal of Personality, 68*, 651–703.

Church, A. T., Katigbak, M. S., Reyes, J. A. S., & Jensen, S. M. (1999). The structure of affect in a non–western culture: Evidence for cross–cultural comparability. *Journal of Personality, 67*, 505–534.

Church, A. T., & Lonner, W. J. (1998). The cross–cultural perspective in the study of personality. *Journal of Cross–cultural Psychology, 29*, 32–62.

Cloninger, C. R. (1987). A systematic method for clinical description and classification of personality variants. *Archives of General Psychiatry, 44*, 573–588.

Cofer, C. N. (1981). The history of the concept of motivation. *Journal of the History of the Behavioral Sciences, 17,* 48–53.

Cohen, S. (1996). Psychological stress, immunity, and upper respiratory infections. *Currrent Directions in Psychological Science, 5,* 86–90.

Cohen, S., Doyle, W. J., Skoner, D. P., Rabin, B. S., & Gwaltney, J. M. (1997). Social ties and susceptibility to the common cold. *JAMA, 277,* 1940–1944.

Cohen, S., Frank, E., Doyle, W. J., Skoner, D. P., Rabin, B. S., & Gwaltney, J. M. (1998). Types of stressors that increase susceptibility to the common cold. *Health Psychology, 17,* 214–223.

Colapinto, J. (2000). *As nature made him: The boy who was raised as a girl.* New York: Harper Collins.

Collins, W. A., Maccoby, E. E. , Steinberg, L., Hetherington, E. M., & Bornstein, M. H. (2000). Contemporary research on parenting: The case for nature and nurture. *American Psychologist, 55,* 218–232.

Colvin, C. R., & Block, J. (1994). Do positive illusions foster mental health? An examination of the Taylor and Brown formulation. *Psychological Bulletin, 116,* 3–20.

Cosmides, L., & Tooby, J. (2000). Evolutionary psychology and the emotions. In M. Lewis & J.M. Haviland–Jones (Eds.), *Handbook of emotions* (pp. 91–115). New York: Guilford.

Cosmides, L., Tooby, J., & Barkow, J. H. (1992). Introduction: Evolutionary psychology and conceptual integration. In J. H. Barkow, L.Cosmides, & J. Tooby (Eds.), *The adapted mind: Evolutionary psychology and the generation of culture.* New York: Oxford University Press.

Costa, P. T., Jr., & McCrae, R. R. (1988). From catalog to classification: Murray's needs and the five–factor model. *Journal of Personality and Social Psychology, 55,* 258–265.

Costa, P. T., Jr., & McCrae, R. R. (1994). "Set like plaster?" Evidence for the stability of adult personality. In T. Heatherton & J. Weinberger (Eds.), *Can personality change?* (pp. 21–40). Washington, DC: American Psychological Association.

Costa, P. T., Jr., & McCrae, R. R. (1995). Primary traits of Eysenck's P–E–N system: Three– and five–factor solutions. *Journal of Personality and Social Psychology, 69,* 308–317.

Costa, P. T., Jr., & McCrae, R. R. (1997). Longitudinal stability of adudlt personality. In R. Hogan, J. Johnson, & S. Briggs (Eds.), *Handbook of personality psychology* (pp. 269–290). San Diego: Academic Press.

Costa, P. T., Jr., & Widiger, T. A. (Eds.) (1994). *Personality disorders and the five–factor model of personality.* Washington, D.C.: American Psychological Association.

Cousins, S. D. (1989). Culture and self–perception in Japan and the United States. *Journal of Personality and Social Psychology, 56,* 124–131.

Coyne, J. C., & Gotlib, B. H. (1996). The mismeasure of coping by checklist. *Journal of Personality, 64,* 959–991.

Craik, K. H. (1986). Personality research methods: An historical perspective. *Journal of Personality, 54,* 18–50.

Cramer, P. (1991). *The development of defense mechanisms.* New York: Springer–Verlag.

Cramer, P. (2000). Defense mechanisms in psychology today. *American Psychologist, 55,* 637–646.

Crews, F. (1993). The unknown Freud. *New York Review of Books,* November 18, 55–66.

Cronbach, L. J. (1957). The two disciplines of scientific psychology. *American Psychologist, 12,* 671–684.

Cronk, L. (1999). *That complex whole: Culture and the evolution of human behavior.* Boulder, CO: Westview.

Cross, S. E., & Markus, H. R. (1990). The willful self. *Personality and Social Psychology Bulletin, 16,* 726–742.

Damasio, A. R. (1994). *Descartes' error.* New York: Avon.

Darwin, C. (1859). *The origin of the species.* London: Murray.

Darwin, C. (1872). *The expression of the emotions in man and animals.* London: Murray.

Dashiell, J. F. (1939). Some rapprochements in contemporary psychology. *Psychological Bulletin, 36,* 1–24.

Davila, J., Burge, D., & Hammen, C. (1997). Why does attachment style change? *Journal of Personality and Social Psychology, 73,* 826–838.

Davis, P. J., & Schwartz, G. E. (1987). Repression and the inaccessibility of affective memories. *Journal of Personality and Social Psychology, 52,* 155–162.

DeGrandpre, R. S. (1999). Just cause? *The sciences,* March/April, 14–18.

Derakshan, N., & Eysenck, M. W. (1997). Interpretive biases for one's own behavior and physiology in high-trait-anxious individuals and repressors. *Journal of Personality and Social Psychology, 73,* 816–825.

Derlega, Y. J., & Chaikin, A. L. (1975). *Sharing intimacy.* Englewood Cliffs, NJ: Prentice–Hall.

Derrington, A., & Parker, A. (2001). No one way in my mirror. *Cerebrum, 3,* 92–99.

Dickens, W. T., & Flynn, J. R. (2001). Heritability estimates versus large environmental effects: The IQ paradox resolved. *Psychological Review, 108,* 346–369.

Dienstbier, R. (Ed.). (1990). *Nebraska symposium on motivation.* Lincoln: University of Nebraska Press.

Digman, J. M. (1990). Personality structure: Emergence of the five–factor model. *Annual Review of Psychology, 41,* 417–440.

Diven, K. (1937). Certain determinants in the conditioning of anxiety reactions. *Journal of Psychology, 3,* 291–308.

Dobzhansky, T. (1967). On types, genotypes, and the genetic diversity in population. In J. N. Spuhler (Ed.), *Genetic diversity and human behavior* (pp. 1–18). Chicago: Aldine.

Dodge, K. A. (1993). Social–cognitive mechanisms in the development of conduct disorder and depression. *Annual Review of Psychology, 44,* 559–584.

Dodge, K. A. (2000). Conduct disorder. In A. Sameroff, M. Lewis, & S. M. Miller (Eds.), *Handbook of developmental psychopathology* (pp. 447–463). New York: Guilford.

Dollard, J., & Miller, N. E. (1950). *Personality and psychotherapy.* New York: McGraw–Hill.

Donahue, E. M., Robins, R. W., Roberts, R. W., & John, O. P. (1993). The divided self: Concurrent and longitudinal effects of psychological adjustment and self–concept differentiation. *Journal of Personality and Social Psychology, 64,* 834–846.

Duval, S. & Wicklund, R. A. (1972). *A theory of objective self awareness.* New York: Academic.

Dweck, C.S. (1999). *Self–theories: Their role in motivation, personality, and development.* Philadelphia, PA: Psychology Press/Taylor & Francis.

Eagly, A. H., & Wood, W. (1999). The origins of sex differences in human behavior. *American Psychologist, 54,* 408–423.

Ekehammar, B. (1974). Interactionism in personality from a historical perspective. *Psychological Bulletin, 81,* 1026–1048.

Ekman, P. (1992). An argument for basic emotions. *Cognition and Emotion, 6,* 169–200.

Ekman, P. (1993). Facial expression and emotion. *American Psychologist, 48,* 384–392.

Ekman, P. (1994). Strong evidence for universals in facial expressions: A reply to Russell's mistaken critique. *Psychological Bulletin, 115,* 268–287.

Eley, T. C. (1997). General genes: A new theme in developmental psychopathology. *Current Directions in Psychological Science, 6,* 90–95.

Ellenberger, H. F. (1970). *The discovery of the unconscious.* New York: Basic Books.

Elliot, A. J., & Sheldon, K. M. (1997). Avoidance achievement motivation: A personal goals analysis. *Journal of Personality and Social Psychology, 73,* 171–185.

Ellis, A. (1987). The impossibility of achieving consistently good mental health. *American Psychologist, 42,* 364–375.

Ellis, A. (1995). Rational emotive behavior therapy. In R.Corsini & D. Wedding (Eds.), *Current Psychotherapies* (pp. 162–196). Itasca, IL: Peacock.

Ellis, A., & Harper, R. A. (1975). *A new guide to rational living.* North Hollywood, CA: Wilshire.

Emmons, R. A. (1997). Motives and life goals. In R. Hogan, J. Johnson, & S. Briggs (Eds.), *Handbook of personality psychology* (pp. 485–512). New York: Academic Press.

Endler, N. S., & Hunt, J. McV. (1966). Sources of behavioral variance as measures by the S–R Inventory of Anxiousness. *Psychological Bulletin, 65,* 336–346.

Endler, N. S., & Hunt, J. McV. (1968). S–R inventories of hostility and comparisons of the proportions of variance from persons, responses, and situations for hostility and anxiousness. *Journal of Personality and Social Psychology, 9,* 309–315.

Engel, G. L. (1977). The need for a new medical model: A challenge for biomedicine. *Science, 196,* 129–136.

Epstein, S. (1973). The self–concept revisited, or a theory of a theory. *American Psychologist, 28,* 404–416.

Epstein,S. (1977). Traits are alive and well. In D. Magnusson & N. S. Endler (Eds.), *Personality at the crossroads: Current issues in interactional psychology.* Hillsdale, N.J.: Erlbaum.

Epstein, S. (1979). The stability of behavior: I. On predicting most of the people much of the time. *Journal of Personality and Social Psychology, 37,* 1097–1126.

Epstein, S. (1980). The stability of behavior: II. Implications for psychological research. *American Psychologist, 35,* 790–806.

Epstein, S. (1981). The unity principle versus the reality and pleasure principles, or the tale of the scorpion and the frog. In M. D. Lynch, A. Norem–Hebersen, & K. J. Gergen (Eds.), *Self–concept: Advances in theory and research.* Cambridge, MA: Ballenger.

Epstein, S. (1982). The stability of behavior across time and situations. In A. 1. Rabin, J. Aronoff, A. M. Barclay, & R. Zucker (Eds.), *Further explorations in personality.* New York: Wiley.

Epstein, S. (1983). A research paradigm for the study of personality and emotions. In M. M. Page (Ed.), *Personality: Current theory and research* (pp. 91–154). Lincoln: University of Nebraska Press.

Epstein, S. (1996). Recommendations for the future development of personality psychology. *Journal of Research in Personality, 30,* 435–446.

Epstein, S. (1997). This I have larned from over 40 years of pesonality research. *Journal of Personality, 65,* 3–32.

Erdelyi, M. (1984). *Psychoanalysis: Freud's cognitive psychology.* New York: Freeman.

Erdelyi, M. H. (1985). *Psychoanalysis: Freud's cognitive psychology.* New York: Freeman.

Erlenmeyer–Kimling, L. (1972). Gene–environment interactions and the variability of behavior. In L. Ehrman, G. S. Omenn, and E. Caspari (Eds.), *Genetics, environment, and behavior* (pp. 181–208). New York: Academic Press.

Erlenmeyer–Kimling, L., & Jarvik, L. F. (1963). Genetics and intelligence: A review. *Science, 142,* 1477–1479.

Esterson, A. (1993). *Seductive mirage: An exploration of the the work of Sigmund Freud.* New York: Open Court.

Esterson, A. (1998). Jeffrey Masson and Freud's seduction theory: A new fable based on old myths. *History of the Human Sciences, 11,* 1–21.

Eysenck. H. J. (1953). *Uses and abuses of psychology.* London: Penguin.

Eysenck, H. J. (1967). *The biological basis of personality.* New York: C. C. Thomas.

Eysenck, H. J. (1970). *The structure of human personality.* London: Methuen.

Eysenck, H. J. (1977). Personality and factor analysis: A reply to Guilford. *Psychological Bulletin, 84,* 405–411.

Eysenck, H. J. (1981). On the judging of scientific data. *American Psychologist, 36,* 692.

Eysenck, H. J. (1982). *Personality genetics and behavior.* New York: Praeger.

Eysenck, H. J. (1990). Biological dimensions of personality. In L. A. Pervin (Ed.), *Handbook of personality: Theory and research* (pp. 244–276). New York: Guilford.

Eysenck, H. J. (1992). Four ways five factors are not basic. *Personality and Individual Differences, 13,* 667–673.

Fawzy, F. I., Fawzy, N. W., Hyun, C. S., & Elashof, R. (1993). Malignant melanoma: Effects of an early structured psychiatric intervention, coping, and affective state on recurrence and survival six years later. *Archives of General Psychiatry, 9,* 681–689.

Feinberg, T. (2001). *Altered egos: How the brain creates the self.* New York: Oxford University Press.

Festinger, L. (1957). *A theory of cognitive dissonance.* Evanston, IL: Row, Peterson.

Finch, J. F., Panter, A. T., & Caskie, G. I. L. (1999). Two approaches for identifying shared personality dimensions across methods. *Journal of Personality, 67,* 407–438.

Flynn, J. R. (1987). Massive IQ gains in 14 nations: What IQ tests really masure. *Psychological Bulletin, 101,* 171–191.

Flynn, J. R. (1998). IQ gains over time: Toward finding the causes. In U. Neisser (Ed.), *The rising curve: Long–term gains in IQ and related measures* (pp. 25–66). Washington, DC: American Psychological Association.

Folkman, S., Lazarus, R. S., Dunkel–Schetter, C., DeLongis, A., & Gruen, R. (1986). The dynamics of a stressful encounter: Cognitive appraisal, coping, and encounter outcomes. *Journal of Personality and Social Psychology, 50,* 992–1003.

Fong, G. T., & Markus, H. (1982). Self–schemas and judgments about others. *Social Cognition, 1,* 191–204.

Ford, M. E. (1992). *Motivating humans.* Newbury Park, CA: Sage.

Forgas, J. P., & Vargas, P. T. (2000). The effects of mood on social judgment and reasoning. In M. Lewis & J. Haviland (Eds.), *Handbook of emotions* (pp. 350–367). New York: Guilford.

Frank, J. D. (1973). *Persuasion and healing.* Baltimore: Johns Hopkins University Press.

Frank, J. D., & Frank, J. B. (1991). *Persuasion and healing (3rd ed.).* Baltimore: Johns Hopkins University Press.

Freeman, D. (1983). *Margaret Mead and Samoa.* Cambridge: Harvard University Press.

Freud, S. (1895/1966). Project for a scientific psychology. In J.Strachey (Ed.), *The standard edition of the complete psychological works of Sigmund Freud* (Vol. 1, pp. 295–387). London: Hogarth Press.

Freud, S, (1900). *The interpretation of dreams.* London: Hogarth Press.

Freud S. (1915). The unconscious. In J. Strachey (Ed.), *The standard edition of the complete psychological works of Sigmund Freud* (1957, vol. 12, p. 255–266). London: Hogarth.

Freud, S. (1924). *A general introduction to psychoanalysis.* New York: Permabooks (Boni & Liveright Edition).

Funder, D. C. (1980). On seeing ourselves as others see us: Self–other agreement and discrepancy in personality ratings. *Journal of Personality, 48,* 473–493.

Funder, D. C. (1989). Accuracy in personality judgment and the dancing bear. In D. M. Buss & N. Cantor (Eds.), *Personality psychology: Recent trends and emerging directions* (pp. 210–223). New York: Springer–Verlag.

Funder, D. C. (1993). Judgments of personality and personality itself. In K. H. Craik, R. Hogan, & R. N. Wolfe (Eds.), *Fifty years of personality psychology* (pp. 207–214). New York: Plenum.

Funder, D. C. (2001). Personality. *Annual Review of Psychology, 52*, 197–221.

Funder, D. C., & Block, J. (1989). The role of ego-control, ego-resiliency, and IQ in delay of gratification in adolescence. *Journal of Personality and Social Psychology, 57*, 1041–1050.

Funder, D. C., & Colvin, C. R. (1997). Congruence of others' and self-judgments of personality. In R. Hogan, J. Johnson, & S. Briggs (Eds.), *Handbook of personality psychology* (pp. 617–647). Sand Diego: Academic Press.

Funder, D. C., Kolar, D. C., & Blackman, M. C. (1995). Agreement among judges of personality: Interpersonal relations, similarity, and acquaintanceship. *Journal of Personality and Social Psychology, 69*, 656–672.

Galton, F. (1869). *Hereditary genius.* London: Macmillan.

Galton, F. (1876). The history of twins as a criterion of the relative powers of nature and nurture. *Royal Anthropological Institute of Great Britain and Ireland Journal, 6*, 391–406.

Galton, F. (1883). *Inquiries into human faculty and its development.* London: Macmillan.

Garfield, S. L. (1998). Some comments on empirically supported treatments. *Journal of Consulting and Clinical Psychology, 66*, 121–125.

Geertz, C. (1973). *The interpretation of cultures.* New York: Basic Books.

Geertz, C. (1974). From the native's point of view: On the nature of anthropological understanding. In K. Basso & H. Selby (Eds.), *Meaning in anthropology* (pp. 221–237). Albuquerque: Universityof New Mexico Press.

Gergen, K. J. (1982). From self to science: What is there to know? In J. Suls (Ed.), *Psychological perspectives on the self.* Hillsdale, NJ: Erlbaum.

Gergen, K. J., Gulerce, A., Lock, A., & Missra, G. (1996). Psychological science in cultural context. *American Psychologist, 51*, 496–503.

Goffman, E. (1959). *The presentation of self in everyday life.* New York: Doubleday.

Goffman, E. (1971). *Relations in public.* New York: Harper & Row.

Goldberg, L. R. (1990). An alternative "description of personality": The big–five factor personality structure. *Journal of Personality and Social Psychology, 59*, 1216–1229.

Goldberg, L. R. (1993). The structure of phenotypic personality traits. *American Psychologist, 48*, 26–34.

Goldberg, L. R., & Saucier, G. (1995). So what do you propose we use instead? A reply to Block. *Psychological Bulletin, 117*, 221–225.

Goldsmith, T. H. (1991). *The biological roots of human nature.* New York: Oxford University Press.

Gosling, S. D., & John, O. P. (1999). Personality dimensions in nonhuman animals: A cross–species review. *Current Directions in Psychological Science, 8*, 69–75.

Gosling, S. D., John, O. P., Craik, K. H., & Robins, R. W. (1998). Do people know how they behave? Self–reported act frequencies compared with on–line codings by observers. *Journal of Personality and Social Psychology, 74*, 1337–1349.

Gottesman, I. I., & Shields, J. (1972). *Schizophrenia and genetics.* New York: Academic Press.

Gottfredson, L. S. (1997). Mainstream science on intelligence: An editorial with 52 signatories, history, and bibliography. *Intelligence, 24*, 13–24.

Gottfredson, L. S. (2000). Pretending that intelligence doesn't matter. *Cerebrum, 2*, 75–96.

Gottlieb, G. (2000). Environmental and behavioral influences on gene activity. *Current Directions in Psychological Science, 9,* 93–97.

Greenberg, L. S., Elliot, R. K., & Lietaer, G. (1994). Research on experiential psychotherapies. In A. E. Bergin & S. L. Garfield (Eds.), *Handbook of psychotherapy and behavior change* (pp. 509–542). New York: Wiley.

Greenwald, A. G. (1980). The totalitarian ego: Fabrication and revision of personal history. *American Psychologist, 35,* 603–618.

Greenwald, A. G. (1992). Unconscious cognition reclaimed. *American Psychologist, 47,* 766–779.

Greenwald, A. G., & Banaji, M. R. (1995). Implicit social cognition: Attitudes, self–esteem, and stereotypes. *Psychological Review, 102,* 4–27.

Greenwald, A. G., & Farnham, S. D. (2000). Using the implicit association test to measure self–esteem and self–concept. *Journal of Personality and Social Psychology, 79,* 1022–1038.

Greenwald, A. G., McGhee, D. E., & Schwartz, J. L. K. (1998). Measuring individual differences in implicit cogniton: The implicit association test. *Journal of Personality and Social Psychology, 74,* 1464–1480.

Groddeck, G. (1961). *The book of the it.* New York: Vintage. (Original edition 1923.)

Gross, J. L. (1999). Emotion and emotion regulation. In L.A. Pervin & O. P. John (Eds.), *Handbook of personality: Theory and research* (pp. 525–552). New York: Guilford.

Grunbaum, A. (1993). *Validation in the clinical theory of psychoanalysis: A study in the philosophy of psychoanalysis.* Madison, CT: International Universities Press.

Guthrie, E. R. (1935). *The psychology of learning* (2nd ed.). New York: Harper.

Guthrie, E. R. (1952). *The psychology of learning.* New York: Harper.

Hamer, D., & Copeland, P. (1998). *Living with our genes.* New York: Doubleday.

Hardin, C., & Banaji, M. R. (1993). The influence of language on thought. *Social Cognition, 11,* 277–308.

Harris, C. R. (2000). Psychophysiological responses to imagined infidelity: The specific innate modular view of jealousy reconsidered. *Journal of Personality and Social Psychology, 78,* 1082–1091.

Hartshorne, H., & May, M. A. (1928). *Studies in the nature of character: Studies in deceit.* New York: Macmillan.

Hearnshaw, L. S. (1979).*Cyril Burt: Psychologist.* Ithaca, NY: Cornell University Press.

Heider, E. R. (1972). Universals in color naming and memory. *Journal of Experimental Psychology, 93,* 10–20.

Heim, C., Newport, D. J., Heit, S., Graham, Y. P., Wilcox, M., Bonsall, R., Miller, A. H., & Nemeroff, C. B. (2000). Pituitary–adrenal and autonomic responses to stress in women after sexual and physical abuse in childhood. *JAMA, 284,* 592–597.

Heine, S. J., & Lehman, D. R. (1997). The cultural construction of self-enhancement: An examination of group-serving biases. *Journal of Personality and Social Psychology, 72,* 1268–1283.

Heine, S. J., Lehman, D. R., Markus, H. R., & Kitayama, S. (1999). Is there a universal need for positive self–regard? *Psychological Review, 106,* 766–794.

Hejmadi, A., Davidson, R. J., & Rozin, P. (2000). Exploring Hindu emotion expressions: Evidence for accurate recognition by Americans and Indians. *Psychological Science, 11,* 183–187.

Henry, W. P., Strupp, H. H., Schacht, T. E., & Gaston, L. (1994). Psychodynamic approaches. In A. E. Bergin & S. L. Garfield (Eds.), *Handbook of psychotherapy and behavior change* (pp. 467–508). New York: Wiley.

Herrnstein, R. J., & Murray, C. (1994). *The bell curve: Intelligence and class structure in American life.* New York: Free Press.

Hesse, H. (1965). *Siddartha.* New York: New Directions.

Higgins, E. T. (1987). Self–discrepancy: A theory relating self and affect. *Psychological Review, 94,* 319–340.

Higgins, E.T. (1997). Beyond pleasure and pain. *American Psychologist, 52,* 1280–1300.

Higgins, E. T. (1999). Persons and situations: Unique explanatory principles or variability in general principles? In D. Cervone & Y. Shoda (Eds.), *The coherence of personality* (pp. 61–93). New York: Guilford.

Higgins, E.T. (2000). Making a good decision: Value from fit. *American Psychologist, 55,* 1217–1227.

Hilgard, E. R. (1949). Human motives and the concept of self. *American Psychologist, 4,* 374–382.

Hinde, R. A. (1982). Attachment: Some conceptual and biological issues. In C. M. Parkes & J. Stevenson–Hinde (Eds.), *The place of attachment in human behavior* (pp. 60–76). New York: Basic Books.

Hoffman, L. W. (1991). The influence of the family environment on personality: Accounting for sibling differences. *Psychological Bulletin, 110,* 187–203.

Hofstadter, R. (1944). *Social Darwinism in American thought.* Boston: Beacon.

Hogan, J., & Ones, D. S. (1997). Conscientiousness and integrity at work. In R. Hogan, J. Johnson, & S. Briggs (Eds.), *Handbook of personality psychology* (pp. 849–870). San Diego, CA: Academic Press.

Hogan, R. (1982). On adding apples and oranges in personality psychology. *Contemporary Psychology, 27,* 851–852.

Hogan, R. (1991). Personality and personality measurement. In M. D. Dunnette & L. M. Hough (Eds.), *Handbook of industrial and organizational psychology* (2nd ed., Vol. 2, pp. 873–919). Palo Alto, CA: Consulting Psychologists Press.

Hogan, R., & Nicholson, R. A. (1988). The meaning of personality test scores. *American Psychologist, 43,* 621–626.

Hollon, S. D., DeRubeis, R. J., & Evans, M. D. (1987). Causal mediation of change in treatment for depression: Discriminating between nonspecificity and noncausality. *Psychological Bulletin, 102,* 139–149.

Holmes, D. S. (1974). Investigations of repression: Differential recall of material experimentally or naturally associated with ego threat. *Psychological Bulletin, 81,* 632–653.

Holmes, D. S. (1990). The evidence for repression: An examination of sixty years of research. In J. L. Singer (Ed.), *Regression and dissociation: Implications for personality theory, psychopathology and health* (pp. 85–102). Chicago: University of Chicago Press.

Holtzman, P., & Kagan, J. (1995). Whither or wither personality research. In P. E. Short & S. T. Fiske (Eds.), *Personality research, methods, and theory* (pp. 3–12). Mahwah, NJ: Erlbaum.

Horgan, J. (1999). *The undiscovered mind.* New York: Free Press.

Hough, L. M. (1992). The "Big Five" personality variables—construct confusion: Description versus prediction. *Human Performance, 5,* 139–155.

Hough, L. M. (1997). The millennium for personality psychology: New horizons or good old daze. *Applied Psychology International Review, 47,* 233–261.

Hough, L. M., & Oswald, F. L. (2000). Personnel selection: Looking toward the future—remembering the past. *Annual Review of Psychology, 51,* 631–664.

Howard, G. S. (1990). On the construct validity of self–reports: What do the data say? *American Psychologist, 45,* 292–295.

Howes, D. H., & Solomon, R. L. (1950). A critique of vigilance–defense. *Psychological Review, 57,* 229–234.

Hrobjartsson, A., & Gotzsche, P. C. (2001). Is the placebo powerless? *New England Journal of Medicine, 344,* 1594–1601.

Hull, C. L. (1943). *Principles of behavior.* New York: Appleton.

Hyde, J. S., & Durik, A. M. (2000). Gender differences in erotic plasticity—evolutionary or sociocultural forces? Comment on Baumeister (2000). *Psychological Bulletin, 126,* 375–379.

Hyman, S. (1999). Susceptibility and "second hits." In R. Conlan (Ed.), *States of mind* (pp. 24–28). New York: Wiley.

Ichheiser, G. (1943). Misinterpretation of personality in everyday life and the psychologist's frame of reference. *Character and Personality, 12,* 145–152.

Ilardi, S. S., & Craighead, W. E. (1999). Rapid early response, cognitive modification, and nonspecific factors in cognitive behavior therapy for depression: A reply to Tang and DeRubeis. *Clinical Psychology: Science and Practice, 6,* 295–299.

Isen, A. M. (2000). Positive affect and decision making. In M. Lewis & J. Haviland (Eds.), *Handbook of emotions* (p. 417–435). New York: Guilford.

Iyengar, S. S., & Lepper, M. R. (1999). Rethinking the value of choice: A cultural perspective on intrinsic motivation. *Journal of Personality and Social Psychology, 76,* 349–366.

Izard, C. E. (1993). Four systems for emotion activation: Cognitive and noncognitive processes. *Psychological Review, 100,* 68–90.

Izard, C. E. (1994). Innate and universal facial expressions: Evidence from developmental an cross-cultural research. *Psychological Bulletin, 115,* 288–299.

Jackson, J. F. (1993). Human behavioral genetics, Scarr's theory, and her views on interventions: A critical review and commentary on their implications for African American children. *Child Development, 64,* 1318–1332.

Jacobson, N. S., & Christensen, A. (1996). Studying the effectiveness of psychotherapy: How well can clinical trials do the job? *American Psychologist, 51,* 1031–1039.

James, W. (1890). *Principles of psychology.* New York: Holt.

John, O. P. (1990). The "Big Five" factor taxonomy: Dimensions of personality in the natural language and in questionnaires. In L. A. Pervin (Ed.), *Handbook of personality: Theory and research* (pp. 66–100). New York: Guilford.

John, O. P., & Robins, R. W. (1994). Accuracy and bias in self–perception: Individual differences in self–enhancement and the role of narcissism. *Journal of Personality and Social Psychology, 66,* 206–219.

John, O. P., & Srivastava, S. (1999). The Big Five: History, measurement, and development. In L. A. Pervin & O. P. John (Eds.), *Handbook of personality: Theory and research* (pp. 102–138). New York: Guilford.

Jolly, A. (1999). *Lucy's legacy.* Cambridge: Harvard University Press.

Jones, E. (1953). *The life and work of Sigmund Freud,* Vol. 1. New York: Basic Books.

Jones, E.E., Gergen, K. J., & Davis, K. E. (1962). Some reactions to being approved or disapproved as a person. *Psychological Monographs, 76* (Whole No. 521).

Jones, E. E., Gergen, K. J., & Jones, R. G. (1963). Tactics of ingratiation among leaders and subordinates in a status hierarchy. *Psychological Monographs, 77* (Whole No. 566).

Jones, E. E., & Nisbett, R. E. (1971). *The actor and the observer: Divergent perceptions of the causes of behavior.* Morristown, NJ: General Learning Press.

Jones, E. E., & Pittman, T. S. (1982). Toward a general theory of strategic self–presentation. In J. Suls (Ed.), *Psychological perspectives on the self.* Hillsdale, NJ: Erlbaum.

Jones, M. R. (1962). Introduction. *Nebraska Symposium on Motivation, vii–xiii.*

Jourard, S. M. (1971). *Self–disclosure: An experimental analysis of the transparent self.* New York: Wiley.

Kagan, J. (1988). The meanings of personality predicates. *American Psychologist, 43,* 614–620.

Kagan, J. (1994). *Galen's prophecy.* New York: Basic Books.

Kagan, J. (1999). Born to be shy? In R. Conlan (Ed.), *States of mind* (pp. 29–51). New York: Wiley.

Kagan, J. (2001). The need for new constructs. *Psychological Inquiry, 12,* 84–85.

Kagan, J., & Moss, H. A. (1962). *Birth to maturity.* New York: Wiley.

Kallmann, F. J. (1946). The genetic theory of schizophrenia. *American Journal of Psychiatry, 103,* 309–322.

Kamin, J. (1974). *The science and politics of I.Q.* Hillsdale, NJ: Erlbaum.

Kanagawa, C., Cross, S. E., & Markus, H. R. (2001). "Who am I?" The cultural psychology of the conceptual self. *Personality and Social Psychology Bulletin, 27,* 90–103.

Kandel, E. R. (1998). A new intellectual framework for psychiatry. *American Journal of Psychiatry, 155,* 457–469.

Kashima, Y. & Yamaguchi, S. (1999). Introduction to the special issue on self. *Asian Journal of Social Psychology, 2,* 283–287.

Kazdin, A. (1994). Informant variability in the assessment of childhood depression. In W. M. Reynolds & H. F. Johnston (Eds.), *Handbook of depression in children and adolescents* (pp. 249–271). New York: Plenum.

Kelly, G. A. (1955). *The psychology of personal constructs.* New York: Norton.

Kelly, G. A. (1958). Man's construction of his alternatives. In G. Lindzey (Ed.), *Assessment of human motives* (pp. 33–64). New York: Holt, Rinehart & Winston.

Kelman, H. C. (1968). *A time to speak out: On human values and social research.* San Francisco: Jossey–Bass.

Kelman, H. C. (1983). Conversations with Arafat: A social–psychological assessment of the prospects for Israeli–Palestinian peace. *American Psychologist, 38,* 203–216.

Kendrick, K. M., Hinton, M. R., Atkins, K., Haupt, M. A., & Skinner, J. D. (1998). Mothers determine sexual preferences. *Nature, 395,* 229–230.

Kenny, D. A. (1994). *Interpersonal perception.* New York: Guilford.

Kenrick, D. T. (1994). Evolutionary social psychology: From sexual selection to social cognition. *Advances in Experimental Social Psychology, 26,* 75–121.

Kenrick, D. T., & Funder, D. C. (1988). Profiting from controversy: Lessons from the person–situation debate. *American Psychologist, 43,* 23–34.

Kessler, D. (2001). *A question of intent.* New York: Public Affairs.

Kiecolt–Glaser, J. K., & Glaser, R. (2001). Stress and immunity: Age enhances the risks. *Current Directions in Psychological Science, 10,* 18–21.

Kiecolt–Glaser, J. K., Page, G. G., Marucha, P. T., MacCallum, R. C., & Glaser, R. (1998). Psychological influences on surgical recovery: Perspectives from psychoneuroimmunology. *American Psychologist, 53,* 1209–1218.

Kihlstrom, J. F. (1990). The psychological unconscious. In L. A. Pervin (Ed.), *Handbook of personality* (pp. 445–464). New York: Guilford.

Kihlstrom, J. F. (1999). The psychological unconscious. In L. A. Pervin & O. P. John (Eds.), *Handbook of personality: Theory and research* (pp. 424–442). New York: Guilford.

Kihlstrom, J. F., Barnhardt, T. M., & Tataryn, D. J. (1992). The cognitive perspective. In R. F. Bornstein & T. S. Pittman (Eds.), *Perception without awareness* (pp. 17–54). New York: Guilford.

Kimble, G. A. (1984). Psychology's two cultures. *American Psychologist, 39,* 833–839.

Kitayama, S., & Karasawa, M. (1997). Implicit self–esteem in Japan: Name letters and birthday numbers. *Personality and Social Psychology Bulletin, 23,* 736–742.

Kitayama, S., & Markus, H. (Eds.) (1994). *Emotion and culture.* Washington, DC: American Psychological Association.

Kitayama, S., & Markus, H. R. (1999). *Yin* and *yang* of the Japanese self: The cultural psychology of personality coherence. In D. Cervone & Y. Shoda (Eds.), *The coherence of personality* (pp. 242–302). New York: Guilford.

Klein, S. B., & Kihlstrom, J. F. (1998). On bridging the gap between social–personality psychology and neuropsychology. *Personality and Social Psychology Bulletin, 2,* 228–242.

Klinger, E. (1977). *Meaning and void: Inner experience and the incentives in people's lives.* Minneapolis: University of Minnesota Press.

Kluckhohn, C., & Murray, H. A. (1956). Personality formation: The determinants. In C. Kluckhohn, H. A. Murray, & Schneider, D. M. (Eds.), *Personality in nature, society, and culture.* New York: Knopf.

Kluft, R. P. (1997). The argument for the reality of delayed recall of trauma. In P. S. Appelbaum, L. A. Uyehara, & M. R. Ellin (Eds.), *Trauma and memory: Clinical and legal controversies* (pp. 125–174). New York: Oxford University Press.

Kopta, S. M., Lueger, R. J., Saunders, S. M., & Howard, K. I. (1999). Individual psychotherapy outcome and process research: Challenges leading to greater turmoil or positive transition? *Annual Review of Psychology, 50,* 441–469.

Krosnick, J. A., Betz, A. L., Jussim, L. J., & Lynn, A. R. (1992). Subliminal conditioning of attitudes. *Journal of Personality and Social Psychology, 18,* 152–162.

Kunda, Z. (1987). Motivated inference: Self–serving generation and evaluation of causal theories. *Journal of Personality and Social Psychology, 53,* 636–647.

Kunda, A. (1990). The case for motivated reasoning. *Psychological Bulletin, 108,* 480–498.

Laing, R. D. (1960). *The divided self.* Baltimore: Penguin.

Lambert, M. J., & Bergin, A. E. (1994). The effectiveness of psychotherapy. In A. E. Bergin & S. L. Garfield (Eds.), *Handbook of psychotherapy and personality change* (pp. 143–189). New York: Wiley.

Lazarus, R. S. (1993). From psychological stress to the emotions: A history of changing outlooks. *Annual Review of Psychology, 44,* 1–21.

Lazarus, R. S., & McCleary, R. A. (1951). Autonomic discrimination without awareness: A study of subception. *Psychological Review, 58,* 113–122.

Lecky, P. (1945). *Self–consistency: A theory of personality.* New York: Island.

Lehman, D. R., & Taylor, S. E. (1987). Date with an earthquake: Coping with a probable, unpredictable disaster. *Personality and Social Psychology Bulletin, 13,* 546–555.

Lepore, F. E. (2001). Dissecting genius: Einstein's brain and the search for the neural basis of intellect. *Cerebrum, 3,* 11–26.

Levenson, R. W. (1992). Autonomic nervous system differences among emotions. *Psychological Science, 3,* 23–27.

Levenson, R.W., Ekman, P., Heider, K., & Friesen, W. V. (1992). Emotion and autonomic nervous system activity in an Indonesian culture. *Journal of Personality and Social Psychology, 62,* 972–988.

Lewin, K. (1935). *A dynamic theory of personality.* New York: McGraw–Hill.

Lewis, M. (1991). Development, history and other problems of time. *Paper presented at the Jean Piaget Society meeting,* May, Philadelphia, PA.

Lewis, M. (1995). *Unavoidable accidents and chance encounters.* New York: Guilford Press.

Lewis, M. (1997). *Altering fate: Why the past does not predict the future.* New York: Guilford.

Lewis, M. (1999). On the development of personality. In L. A. Pervin & O. P. John (Eds.), *Handbook of personality: Theory and research* (pp. 327–346). New York: Guilford.

Lewis, M. (2000). Models of developmental psychopathology. In A. Sameroff, M. Lewis, * S. Miller (Eds.), *Handbook of developmental* psychopathology (pp. 3–22). New York: Guilford.

Lewis, M. (2001). Issues in the study of personality development. *Psychological Inquiry, 12,* 67–83.

Lewis, M., & Brooks–Gunn, J. (1979). *Social cognition and the acquisition of self.* New York: Plenum.

Lewis, M., Feiring, C., McGuffog, C., & Jaskir, J. (1984). Predicting psychopathology in six year olds from early social relations. *Child Development, 55,* 123–136.

Lewis, M., Rosenthal, S., & Feiring, C. (2001). Attachment over time. *Child Development, 71,* 707–720.

Lewontin, R. (2001). *It ain't necessarily so: The dream of the human genome and other illusions.* New York: New York Review of Books.

Lewontin, R. (1998). Not all in the genes. In L. Wolpert & A.Richards (Eds.), *Passionate minds* (pp. 103–112). New York: Oxford University Press.

Libet, B. (1965). Cortical activation in conscious and unconscious experience. *Perspectives in Biology and Medicine, 9,* 77–86.

Libet, B. (1966). Brain stimulation and the threshold of conscious experience. In J. C. Eccles (Ed.), *Brain and conscious experience* (pp. 165–181). New York: Springer–Verlag.

Lichtman, S. W., Pisarska,K., Berman, E. R., Pestone, M., Dowling, H., Offenbacher, E., Weisel, H., Heshka, S., Matthews, D.W., & Heymsfield, S. B. (1992). Discrepancy between self–reported and actual caloric intake and exercise in obese subjects. *New England Journal of Medicine, 327,* 1893–1898.

Lindzey, G. (1967). Behavior and morphological variation. In J. N. Spuhler (Ed.), *Genetic diversity and human behavior* (pp. 227–240). Chicago: Aldine.

Little, B. R. (1999). Personality and motivation: Personal action and the conative revolution. In L. A. Pervin & O. P. John (Eds.), *Handbook of personality: Theory and research* (pp. 501–524). New York: Guilford.

Locke, E. A., & Latham, G. P. (1990). *A theory of goal setting and task performance.* Englewood Cliffs, NJ: Prentice–Hall.

Locksley, A., & Lennauer, M. (1981). Considerations for a theory of self–influence processes. In N. Cantor & J. F. Kihlstrom (Eds.), *Personality, cognition, and social interaction.* Hillsdale, NJ: Erlbaum.

Loehlin, J. C. (1992). *Genes and environment in personality development.* Newbury Park, CA: Sage.

Loehlin, J. C., McCrae, R. R., Costa, P. T., & John, O. P. (1998). Heritabilities of common and measure–specific components of the Big Five personality factors. *Journal of Research in Personality, 32,* 431–453.

Loftus, E. F. (1992). When a lie becomes memory's truth: Memory distortion after exposure to misinformation. *Current Directions in Psychological Science, 1,* 121–123.

Loftus, E. F. (1997). Creating false memories. *Scientific American, 23,* 243–287.

Loftus, E. F., & Klinger, M. R. (1992). Is the unconscious smart or dumb? *American Psychologist, 47,* 761–765.

Luhrman, T. M. (2000). *Of two minds: The growing disorder in American psychiatry.* New York: Knopf.

Lykken, D. T. (1971). Multiple factor analysis and personality research. *Journal of Experimental Research in Personality, 5,* 161–170.

Lykken, D. T. (1995). *The antisocial personalities.* Mahwah, NJ: Erlbaum.

Maccoby, E. E. (2000). Parenting and its effects on children: On reading and misreading behavior genetics. *Annual Review of Psychology, 51,* 1–27.

MacDonald, D. A. (2000). Spirituality: Description, measurement, and relation to the five factor model of personality. *Journal of Personality, 68,* 153–197.

Magnusson, D. (Ed.). (1988). *Paths through life.* Hillsdale, NJ: Erlbaum.

Magnusson, D. (1990). Personality development from an interactional perspective. In L. A. Pervin (Ed.), *Handbook of personality: Theory and research* (pp. 193–222). New York: Guilford.

Magnusson, D. (1992). Individual development: A longitudinal perspective. *European Journal of Personality, 6,* 119–138.

Magnusson, D. (1999). Holistic interactionism: A perspective for research on personality development. In L. A. Pervin & O. P. John (Eds.), *Handbook of personality: Theory and research* (pp. 219–247). New York: Guilford.

Magnusson, D., & Endler, N. S. (Eds.) (1977). *Personality at the crossroads: Current issues in interactional psychology.* Hillsdale, NJ: Erlbaum.

Maher, B. (1982). Comment on Eysenck's comment. *American Psychologist, 37,* 833.

Maier, S. F., Watkins, L. R., & Fleshner, M. (1994). Psychoneuroimmunology. *American Psychologist, 49,* 1004–1017.

Malatesta, C. Z. (1990). The role of emotions in the development and organization of personality. *Nebraska Symposium on Motivation, 36,* 1–56.

Manuck, S. B., Marsland, A. L. Kaplan, J. R., & Williams, J. K. (1995). The pathogenicity of behavior and its neuroendocrine mediation: An example from coronary artery disease. *Psychosomatic Medicine, 57,* 275–284.

Marcel, A. (1983). Conscious and unconscious perception: Experiments on visual masking and word recognition. *Cognitive Psychology, 15,* 197–237.

Markus, H. (1977). Self–schemata and processing information about the self. *Journal of Personality and Social Psychology, 35,* 63–78.

Markus, H., & Kitayama, S. (1991). Culture and the self: Implications for cognition, emotion, and motivation. *Psychological Review, 98,* 224–253.

Markus, H., Kitayama, S., & Heiman, R. (1996). Culture and basic psychological principles. In E. T. Higgins & A. W. Kruglanski (Eds.), *Social psychology: Handbook of basic principles* (pp. 857–913). New York: Guilford.

Markus, H., & Nurius, P. (1986). Possible selves. *American Psychologist, 41,* 954–969.

Markus, H., & Ruvolo, A. (1989). Possible selves: Personalized representations of goals. In L. A. Pervin (Ed.), *Goal concepts in personality and social psychology* (pp. 211–241). Hillsdale, NJ: Erlbaum.

Markus, H., & Sentis, K. (1982). The self in social information processing. In J. Suls (Ed.), *Psychological perspectives on the self* (pp. 41–70). Hillsdale, NJ: Erlbaum.

Markus, H., & Smith, J. (1981). The influence of self–schemata on the perception of others. In N. Cantor & J. F. Kihlstrom (Eds.), *Personality, cognition, and social interaction.* Hillsdale, NJ: Erlbaum.

Maslow, A. H. (1968). *Toward a psychology of being.* Princeton, NJ: Van Nostrand.

McAdams, D. P. (1992). The five–factor model in personality: A critical appraisal. *Journal of Personality, 60,* 329–361.

McAdams, D. P. (2001). *The person.* New York: Harcourt.

McCartney, K., Harris, M. J., & Bernieri, F. (1990). Growing up and growing apart: A developmental meta–analysis of twin studies. *Psychological Bulletin, 107,* 226–237.

McClelland, D. C. (1951). *Personality.* New York: Sloane.

McClelland, D. C. (1980). Motive dispositions: The merits of operant and respondent measures. *Review of Personality and Social Psychology, 1,* 10–41.

McClelland, D. C., Koestner, R., & Weinberger, J. (1989). How do self–attributed and implicit motives differ? *Psychological Review, 96,* 690–702.

McCrae, R. R., & Costa, P. T., Jr. (1990). *Personality in adulthood.* New York: Guilford.

McCrae, R. R., & Costa, P. T., Jr., (1997). Personality trait structure as a human universal. *American Psychologist, 52*, 509–516.

McCrae, R.R., & Costa, P. T., Jr., (1999). A five–factor theory of personality. In L. A. Pervin & O. P. John (Eds.), *Handbook of personality: Theory and research* (pp. 139–153). New York: Guilford.

McCrae, R. R., Costa, P. T., Ostendorf, F., Angleitner, A., Hrebickova, M., Avia, M. D., Sanz, J., Sanchez–Bernardos, M. L., Kusdil, M. E., Woodfield, R., Saunders, P. R., & Smith, P. B. (2000). Nature over nurture: Temperament, personality, and lifespan development. *Journal of Personality and Social Psychology, 78*, 173–186.

McDougall, W. (1930). Hormic psychology. In C. Murchison (Ed.), *Psychologies of 1930* (pp. 3–36). Worcester, MA: Clark University Press.

McGinnies, E. (1949). Emotionality and perceptual defense. *Psychological Review, 56*, 244–251.

Mead, M. (1928). *Coming of age in Samoa.* New York: William Morrow.

Mead, M. (1935). *Sex and temperament in three primitive societies.* New York: William Morrow.

Mendolia, M., Moore, J., & Tesser, A. (1996). Dispositional and situational determinants of repression. *Journal of Personality and Social Psychology, 70*, 856–867.

Mesquita, B. (2001). Emotions in collectivist and individualist contexts. *Journal of Personality and Social Psychology, 80*, 68–74.

Messick, D. M. (1988). On the limitations of cross–cultural research in social psychology. In M H. Bond (Ed.), *The cross–cultural challenge to social psychology* (pp. 41–47). Newbury Park, CA: Sage.

Milgram, S. (1964). Issues in the study of obedience. *American Psychologist, 19*, 848–852.

Milgram, S. (1965). Some conditions of obedience and disobedience to authority. *Human Relations, 18*, 57–76.

Miller, G. A. (1996). How we think about cognition, emotion, and biology in psychopathology. *Psychophysiology, 33*, 615–628.

Miller, G. A., Galanter, E., & Pribram, K. H. (1960). *Plans and the structure of behavior.* New York: Holt, Rinehart & Winston.

Miller G. A., & Keller, J. (2000). Psychology and neuroscience: Making peace. *Current Directions in Psychological Science, 9*, 212–215.

Miller, J. G. (1984). Culture and the development of everyday social explanation. *Journal of Personality and Social Psychology, 46*, 961–978.

Mischel, W. (1968). *Personality and assessment.* New York: Wiley.

Mischel, W. (1999). Personality coherence and dispositions in a cognitive–affective personality system (CAPS) approach. In D. Cervone & Y. Shoda (Edds.), *The coherence of personality* (pp. 37–60). New York: Guilford.

Mischel, W., & Peake, P. K. (1982). Beyond déjà vu in the search for cross–situational consistency. *Psychological Review, 89*, 730–755.

Mischel, W., & Peake, P. K. (1983). Analyzing the construction of consistency in personality. In M. M. Page (Ed.), *Personality: Current theory and research* (pp. 233–262). Lincoln: University of Nebraska Press.

Mischel, W., & Shoda, Y. (1995). A cognitive–affective system theory of personality: Reconceptualizing the invariances in personality and the role of situations. *Psychological Review, 102*, 246–286.

Mischel, W., & Shoda, Y. (1998). Reconciling processing dynamics and personality dispositions. *Annual Review of Psychology, 49*, 229–258.

Mischel, W., & Shoda, Y. (1999). Integrating dispositions and processing dynamics within a unified theory of personality: The cognitive–affective personality system.

In L. A. Pervin, & O. P. John (Eds.), *Handbook of personality: Theory and research* (pp. 197–218). New York: Guilford.

Mitroff, I. (1974). Norms and counter–norms in a select group of the Apollo moon scientists: A case study of the ambivalence of scientists. *American Sociological Review, 39,* 579–595.

Money, J., & Ehrhardt, A. A. (1972). *Man and woman, boy and girl.* Baltimore: Johns Hopkins University Press.

Morf, C. C., & Rhodewalt, F. (2001). Narcissism: A self–regulatory model. *Psychological Inquiry,* in press.

Morris, J. S., Ohman, A., & Dolan, R. J. (1998). Conscious and unconscious emotional learning in the human amygdala. *Nature, 393,* 467–470.

Morris, M. W., & Peng, K. (1994). Culture and cause: American and Chinese attributions for social and physical events. *Journal of Personality and Social Psychology, 67,* 949–971.

Moskowitz, D. S. (1986). Comparison of self–reports, reports by knowledgeable informants, and behavioral observation data. *Journal of Personality, 54,* 294–317.

Murray, H. A. (1938). *Explorations in personality.* New York: Oxford University Press.

Nathan, P. E., Stuart, S. P., & Dolan, S. L. (2000). Research on psychotherapy efficacy and effectiveness: Between Scylla and Charybdis? *Psychological Bulletin, 126,* 964–981.

Neisser, U. (Ed.) (1998). *The rising curve: Long–term gains in IQ and related measures.* Washington, DC: American Psychological Association.

Neisser, U., Boodoo, G., Bouchard, T. J., Jr., Boykin, A. W., Brody, N., Ceci, S. J., Halpern, D. F., Loehlin, J. C., Perloff, R., Sternberg, R. J., & Urbina, S. (1996). Intelligence: Knowns and unknowns. *American Psychologist, 51,* 77–101.

Newell, A., Shaw, J. C., & Simon, H. A. (1958). Elements of a theory of human problem solving. *Psychological Review, 65,* 151–166.

Newman, L. S., Duff, K. J., & Baumeister, R. F. (1997). A new look at defensive projection: Thought suppression, accessibility, and biased person perception. *Journal of Personality and Social Psychology, 72,* 980–1001.

Newton, T., & Contrada, R. (1992). Repressive coping and verbal–autonomic response dissociation: The influence of social context. *Journal of Personality and Social Psychology, 62,* 159–167.

Newton, T., Haviland, J., & Contrada, R. J. (1996). The face of repressive coping: Social context and the display of hostile expressions and social smiles. *Journal of Nonverbal Behavior, 20,* 3–22.

Nisbett, R. E., Peng, K., Choi, I., & Norenzayan, A. (2001). Culture and systems of thought: Holistic versus analytic cognition. *Psychological Review, 108,* 291–310.

Nisbett, R. E., & Ross, L. (1980). *Human inference: Strategies and shortcomings of social judgment.* Englewood Cliffs, NJ: Prentice Hall.

Norenzayan, A., & Nisbett, R. E. (2000). Culture and causal cognition. *Current Directions in Psychological Science, 9,* 132–135.

O'Connor, T. G., & Plomin, R. (2000). Developmental behavioral genetics. In A. Sameroff, M. Lewis, & S. M. Miller (eds.), *Handbook of developmental psychopathology* (pp. 217–236). New York: Guilford.

Ogilive, D. M. (1987). The undesired self: A neglected variable in personality research. *Journal of Personality and Social Psychology, 52,* 379–385.

Ozer, D. J., & Reise, S. P. (1994). Personality assessment. *Annual Review of Psychology, 45,* 357–388.

Panksepp, J. (2000). Emotions as natural kinds within the mammalian brain. In M. Lewis & J. Haviland (Eds.), *Handbook of emotions* (pp. 137–156). New York: Guilford.

Patton, C. J. (1992). Fear of abandonment and binge eating. *Journal of Nervous and Mental Disease, 180*, 484–490.

Paunonen, S. V., & Jackson, D. N. (2000). What is beyond the big five? Plenty! *Journal of Personality, 68*, 821–835.

Pennebaker, J. W. (1990). *Opening up: The healing powers of confiding in others.* New York: Morrow.

Pennebaker, J. W. (1997). *Opening up: The healing power of expressing emotion.* New York: Guilford.

Pennebaker, J. W. & Graybeal, A. (2001). Patterns of natural language use: Disclosure, personality, and social integration. *Current Directions in Psychological Science, 10*, 90–93.

Pennebaker, J. W., Kiecolt–Glaser, J. K., & Glaser, R. (1988). Disclosure of traumas and immune function: Health implications for psychotherapy. *Journal of Consulting and Clinical Psychology, 56*, 239–245.

Pervin, L. A. (1970). *Personality: Theory and research.* New York: Wiley.

Pervin, L. A. (1976). A free–response description approach to the analysis of person–situation interaction. *Journal of Personality and Social Psychology, 34*, 465–474.

Pervin, L. A. (1981). The relation of situations to behavior. In D. Magnusson (Ed.), *The situation: An interactional perspective.* Hillsdale, NJ: Erlbaum.

Pervin, L. A. (1983). The stasis and flow of behavior: Toward a theory of goals. In M. M. Page (Ed.), *Personality: Current theory and research* (pp. 1–53). Lincoln: University of Nebraska Press.

Pervin, L. A. (1984). *Current controversies and issues in personality.* New York: Wiley.

Pervin, L. A. (Ed.). (1989). *Goal concepts in personality and social psychology.* Hillsdale, NJ: Erlbaum.

Pervin, L. A. (1990). A brief history of modern personality theory. In L. A. Pervin (Ed.), *Handbook of personality: Theory and research* (pp. 3–18). New York: Guilford.

Pervin, L. A. (1991). Goals, plans, and problems in the self–regulation of behavior: The question of volition. In P. R. Pintrich & M. L. Maehr (Eds.), *Advances in motivation and achievement* (pp. 1–20). Greenwich, CT: JAI Press.

Pervin, L. A. (1993). Pattern and organization: Current trends and propsects for the future. In K. Craik, R. Hogan, & R. N. Wolfe (Eds.), *Perspectives in personality* (pp. 69–84). Greenwich, CT: JAI Press.

Pervin, L. A. (1994). A critical analysis of current trait theory. *Psychological Inquiry, 5*, 103–113.

Pervin, L. A. (1996). *The science of personality.* New York: Wiley.

Pervin, L. A. (1999). Epilogue: Constancy and change in personality theory and research. In L. A. Pervin & O. P. John (Eds.), *Handbook of personality: Theory and research* (pp. 689–704). New York: Guilford.

Pervin, L. A., & John, O. P. (2001). *Personality: Theory and research.* New York: Wiley.

Peterson, C., & Park, C. (1998). Learned helplessness and explanatory style. In D. F. Barone, M. Hersen, & V. B. Van Hasselt (Eds.), *Advanced personality* (pp. 287–310). New York: Plenum.

Petrill, S. A. (1997). Molarity versus modularity of cognitive functioning? A behavioral genetic perspective. *Current Directions in Psychological Science, 6*, 96–99.

Pickering, A. D., & Gray, J. A. (1999). The neuroscience of personality. In L. A. Pervin & O. P. John (Eds.), *Handbook of personality: Theory and research* (pp. 277–299). New York: Guilford.

Piedmont, R. L., McCrae, R. R., Riemann, R., & Angleitner, A. (2000). On the invalidity of validity scales: Evidence from self–reports and observer ratings in volunteer samples. *Journal of Personality and Social Psychology, 78*, 582–593.

Plante, T. G. & Sherman, A. C. (Eds.) (2001). *Faith and health.* New York: Guilford.

Plomin, R. (1989). Environment and genes. *American Psychologist, 44*, 105–111.

Plomin, R. (1990). *Nature and nurture.* Pacific Grove, CA: Brooks/Cole.

Plomin, R., & Caspi, A. (1999). Behavioral genetics and personality. In L. A. Pervin & O. P. John (Eds.), *Handbook of personality: Theory and research* (pp. 251–276). New York: Guilford.

Plomin, R., Chipuer, H. M., & Loehlin, J. C. (1990). Behavioral genetics and personality. In L. A. Pervin (Ed.), *Handbook of personality: Theory and Research* (pp. 225–243). New York: Guilford.

Plomin, R., & Crabbe, J. (2000). DNA. *Psychological Bulletin, 126*, 806–828.

Plomin, R., & Daniels, D. (1987). Why are children in the same family so different from each other? *Behavioral and Brain Sciences, 10*, 1–16.

Plomin, R., & Petrill, S. A. (1997). Genetics and intelligence: What's new? *Intelligence, 24*, 53–78.

Polanyi, M. (1958). *Personal knowledge: Towards a post–critical philosophy.* London: Routledge & Kegan Paul.

Powell, R. A., & Boer, D. P. (1994). Did Freud mislead patients to confabulate memories of abuse? *Psychological Reports, 74*, 1283–1298.

Prince, M. (1906). *The dissociation of a personality.* New York: Longmans, Green.

Pyszczynski, T., Greenberg, J., & Solomon, S. (1997). Why do we need what we need? A terror management perspective on the roots of human social motivation. *Psychological Inquiry, 8*, 1–20.

Pyszczynski, T., Greenberg, J., & Solomon, S. (2000). Proximal and distal defense: A new perspective on unconscious motivation. *Current Directions in Psychological Science, 9*, 156–159.

Rachman, S. (1999). Rapid and not–so–rapid responses to cognitive behavioral therapy. *Clinical Psychology: Science and Practice, 6*, 293–294.

Rachman, S. J., & Wilson, G. T. (1980). *The effects of psychological therapy.* New York: Pergamon.

Ramsey, I. T. (Ed.). (1965). *Biology and personality.* Oxford: Blackwell.

Raush, H. L., Diftmann, A. T., & Taylor, T. J. (1959). Person, setting and change in social interaction. *Human Relations, 12*, 361–378.

Redding, R. E. (2001). Sociopolitical diversity in psychology. *American Psychologist, 56*, 205–215.

Reiss, D. (1997). Mechanisms linking genetic and social influences in adolescent development: Beginning a collaborative search. *Current Directions in Psychological Science, 6*, 100–105.

Riemann, R., Angleitner, A., & Strelau, J. (1997). Genetic and environmental influences on personality: A study of twins reared together using the self– and peer report NEO–FFI scales. *Journal of Personality, 65*, 449–476.

Riesman, D. (1950). *The lonely crowd.* Garden City, NY: Doubleday.

Roberts, B. W. (1997). Plaster or plasticity: Are adult work experiences associated with personality change in women? *Journal of Personality, 65*, 205–232.

Roberts, B. W., & Del Vecchio, W. F. (2000). The rank–order consistency of personality traits from childhood to old age: A quantitative review of longitudinal studies. *Psychological Bulletin, 126*, 3–25.

Roberts, B. W., & Robins, R. W. (2000). Broad dispositions, broad aspirations: The intersection of personality traits and major life goals. *Personality and Social Psychology Bulletin, 26*, 1284–1296.

Robins, R. W., & Beer, J. S. (2001). Positive illusions about the self: Short–term benefits and long–term costs. *Journal of Personality and Social Psychology, 80*, 340–352.

Robins, R. W., Fraley, R. C., Roberts, B. W., & Trzesniewski, K. H. (2001). A longitudinal study of personality change in young adulthood. *Journal of Persnality, 69,* 617–640.

Robins, R. W., John, O. P., Caspi, A., Moffitt, T. E., & Stouthamer–Loeber, M. (1996). Resilient, overcontrolled, and undercontrolled boys: Three replicable personality types. *Journal of Personality and Social Psychology, 70,* 157–171.

Robins, R.W., Norem, J. K., & Cheek, J. M. (1999). Naturalizing the self. In L. A. Pervin & O. P. John (Eds.), *Handbook of personality: Theory and research* (pp. 443–477). New York: Guilford.

Rogers, C. R. (1942). *Counseling and psychotherapy.* Boston: Houghton Mifflin.

Rogers, C. R. (1947). Some observations on the organization of personality. *American Psychologist, 2,* 358–368.

Rogers, C. R. (1951). *Client–centered therapy.* Boston: Houghton Mifflin.

Rogers, C. R. (1959). A theory of therapy, personality, and interpersonal relationships as developed in the client–centered framework. In S. Koch (Ed.), *Psychology: A study of science* (pp. 184–256). New York: McGraw–Hill.

Rogers, C. R. (1961). *On becoming a person.* Boston: Houghton Mifflin.

Rolls, E. T. (2000). The brain and emotion. *Behavioral and Brain Sciences, 23,* 177–234.

Rothbart, M. K., Ahadi, S. A., & Evans, D.E. (2000). Temperament and personality: Origins and outcomes. *Journal of Personality and Social Psychology, 78,* 122–135.

Rothbaum, F., Weisz, J., Pott, M., Miyake, K., & Morelli, G. (2000). Attachment and culture. *American Psychologist, 55,* 1093–1104.

Rotter, J. B. (1954). *Social learning and clinical psychology.* Englewood Cliffs, NJ: Prentice Hall.

Rowe, D. C. (1994). *The limits of family influence.* New York: Guilford Press.

Rozin, P., & Fallon, A. E. (1987). A perspective on disgust. *Psychological Review, 94,* 23–41.

Rudman, L. A., & Kilianski, S. E. (2000). Implicit and explicit attitudes toward female authority. *Personality and Psychology Bulletin, 26,* 1315–1328.

Rudman, W. B. (1996). *Combat: Twelve years in the U.S. Senate.* New York: Random House.

Ryan, R. M. (1998). Human psychological needs and the issues of volition, control, and outcome focus. In J. Heckhausen & C. S. Dweck (Eds.), *Motivation and self–regulation across the life span* (pp. 114–133). New York: Cambridge University Press.

Ryan, R. M., & Deci, E. L. (2000). Self–determination theory and the facilitation of intrinsic motivation, social development, and well–being. *American Psychologist, 55,* 68–78.

Salovey, P., Rothman, A. J., Detweiler, J. B., & Steward, W. T. (2000). Emotional states and physical health. *American Psychgologist, 55,* 110–121.

Sapolsky, R. M. (1994). *Why zebras don't get ulcers.* New York: W. H. Freeman.

Saucier, G., & Goldberg, L. R. (1996). Evidence for the Big Five in analyses of familiar English personality adjectives. *European Journal of Personality, 10,* 61–77.

Savin, H. B. (1973). Professors and psychological researchers: Conflicting values in conflicting roles. *Cognition, 2,* 147–149.

Scarr, S. (1981). *Race, social class, and individual differences in IQ.* Hillsdale, NJ: Erlbaum.

Scarr, S. (1992). Developmental theories for the 1990s: Development and individual differences. *Child Development, 63,* 1–19.

Scarr, S., & Weinberg, R. A. (1976). I.Q. test performance of black children adopted by white families. *American Psychologist, 31,* 726–739.

Schacter, D. (1987). Implicit memory: History and current status. *Journal of Experimental Psychology, 13*, 501–518.

Schacter, D. L. (1996). *Searching for memory: The brain, the mind, and the past.* New York: Basic Books.

Schacter, D. L., & Badgaiyan, R. D. (2001). Neuroimaging of priming: New perspectives on implicit and explicit memory. *Current Directions in Psychological Science, 10*, 1–4.

Schafer, R. (1954). *Psychoanalytic interpretation in Rorschach testing.* New York: Grune & Stratton.

Scheier, M. F., Magovern, G. J., Sr., Abbott, R. A., Matthews, K. A., Owens, J. F., Lefebvre, R. C., & Carver, C. S. (1989). Dispositional optimism and recovery from coronary artery bypass surgery: The beneficial effects on physical and psychological well–being. *Journal of Personality and Social Psychology, 57*, 1024–1040.

Scherer, K., & Wallbott, H. G. (1994). Evidence for universality and cultural variation of differential emotional response patterning. *Journal of Personality and Social Psychology, 66*, 310–328.

Schimmack, U., & Hartmann, K. (1997). Differences in the memory representation of emotional episodes: Exploring the cognitive processes in repression. *Journal of Personality and Social Psychology, 73*, 1064–1079.

Schneiderman, N., Antoni, M. H., Saab, P. G., & Ironson, G. (2001). Health psychology: Psychosocial and biobehavioral aspects of chronic disease management. *Annual Review of Psychology, 52*, 555–580.

Schreiber, F. (1973). *Sybil.* New York: Warner Books.

Schwartz, J. E., Neale, J., Marco, C., Shiffman, S.S., & Stone, A. A. (1999). Does trait coping exist? A momentary asessment approach to the evaluation of traits. *Journal of Personality and Social Psychology, 77*, 360–369.

Schwartz, J. M., Stoessel, P. W., Baxter, L. R., Martin, K. M., & Phelps, M. E. (1996). Systematic changes in cerebral glucose metabolic rate after successful behavior modification treatment of obsessive–compulsive disorders. *Archives of General Psychiatry, 53*, 109–113.

Schwarz, N. (1999). Self–reports: How the questions shape the answers. *American Psychologist, 54*, 93–105.

Searle J. R. (2000). A philosopher unriddles the puzzle of consciousness. *Cerebrum, 2*, 44–54.

Sechrest, L. (1986). Modes and methods of personality research. *Journal of Personality, 54*, 318–331.

Sedikides, C., & Skowronski, J. J. (1997). The symbolic self in evolutionary context. *Personality and Social Psychology Review, 1*, 80–102.

Seligman, M. E. P. (1975). *Helplessness.* San Francisco: Freeman.

Seligman, M. E. P. (1995). The effectiveness of psychotherapy: The *Consumer Reports* study. *American Psychologist, 50*, 965–974.

Selye, H. (1956). *The stress of life.* New York: McGraw–Hill.

Seybold, K. S., & Hill, P. C. (2001). The role of religion and spirituality in mental and physical health. *Current Directions in Psychological Science, 10*, 21–24.

Shah, J., & Higgins, E. T. (1997). Expectancy *x* value effects: Regulatory focus as a determinant of magnitude and direction. *Journal of Personality and Social Psychology, 73*, 447–458.

Shedler, J., Mayman, M., & Manis, M. (1993). The illusion of mental health. *American Psychologist, 48*, 1117–1131.

Shields, S. (1975). Functionalism, Darwinism, and the psychology of women: A study in social myth. *American Psychologist, 30*, 739–754.

Shoda, Y., Mischel, W., & Wright, J. C. (1994). Intra–individual stability in the organization and patterning of behavior: Incorporating psychological situations into the idiographic analysis of personality. *Journal of Personality and Social Psychology, 67,*
674–687.

Shore, B. (1996). *Culture in mind: Cognition, culture, and the problem of meaning.* New
York: Oxford University Press.

Shweder, R. A. (1975). How relevant is an individual differences theory of personality?
Journal of Personality, 43, 455–484.

Shweder, R. A. (1982). Fact and artifact in trait perception: The systematic distortion
hypothesis. *Progress in Experimental Personality Research, 11,* 65–100.

Shweder, R. A. (1991). *Thinking through cultures: Expeditions in cultural psychology.*
Cambridge, MA: Harvard University Press.

Shweder, R. A., & Bourne, E. J. (1984). Does the concept of the person vary cross-
culturally? In R. A Shweder & R. A. LeVine (Eds.), *Culture theory: Essays on mind,
self, and emotion* (pp. 158–199). New York: Cambridge University Press.

Shweder, R. A., & Haidt, J. (2000). The cultural psychology of the emotions: Ancient
and new. In M. Lewis & J. Haviland (Eds.), *Handbook of emotions* (pp. 397–414).
New York: Guilford.

Siegler, R. S. (2000). Unconscious insights. *Current Directions in Psychological Science,
9,* 79–83.

Silverman, L. H. (1976). Psychoanalytic theory: The reports of its death are greatly exaggerated. *American Psychologist, 31,* 621–637.

Silverman, L. H. (1982). A comment on two subliminal psychodynamic activation studies. *Journal of Abnormal Psychology, 91,* 126–130.

Silverman, L. H., Ross, D. L., Adler, J. M., & Lustig, D. A. (1978). Simple research
paradigm for demonstrating subliminal psychodynamic activation: Effects of oedipal
stimuli on dart–throwing accuracy in college men. *Journal of Abnormal Psychology,
87,* 341–357.

Silverman, L. H., & Weinberger, J. (1985). Mommy and I are one: Implications for psychotherapy. *American Psychologist, 40,* 1296–1308.

Simpson, J. A. (1999). Attachment theory in modern evolutionary perspective. In J.
Cassidy & P. R. Shaver (Eds.), *Handbook of attachment* (pp. 115–140). New York:
Guilford.

Singelis, T. M. (1994). The measurement of independent and interdependent self-
construals. *Personality and Social Psychology Bulletin, 20,* 580–591.

Skinner, B. F. (1948). *Walden two.* New York: Macmillan.

Skinner, B. F. (1967). Autobiography. In E. G. Boring & G. Lindzey (Eds.), *A history of
psychology in autobiography* (pp. 385–414). New York: Appleton–Century–Crofts.

Skinner, B. F. (1971). *Beyond freedom and dignity.* New York: Knopf.

Skinner, B. F. (1976). *Particulars of my life.* New York: Knopf.

Small, S. A., Zeldin, S., & Savin–Williams, R. C. (1983). In search of personality traits:
A multimethod analysis of naturally occurring prosocial and dominance behavior.
Journal of Personality, 51, 1–16.

Smith, R. E., Leffingwell, T. R., & Ptacek, J. T. (1999). Can people remember how they
coped? Factors associated with discordance between same–day and retrospective reports. *Journal of Personality and Social Psychology, 76.* 1050–1061.

Snyder, M. (1979). Self–monitoring processes. *Advances in Experimental Social Psychology, 12,* 85–128.

Snyder, M., & Campbell, M. H. (1982). Self–monitoring: The self in action. In J. Suls
(Ed.), *Psychological perspectives on the self.* Hillsdale, NJ: Erlbaum.

Spain, J. S., Eaton, L. G., & Funder, D. C. (2000). Perspectives on personality: The relative accuracy of self versus others for the prediction of emotion and behavior. *Journal of Personality, 68,* 837–867.

Spence, D. P. (1982). *Narrative truth and historical truth: Meaning and interpretation in psychoanalysis.* New York: Norton.

Spence, D. P. (1987). *The Freudian metaphor.* New York: Norton.

Spiegel, D., Bloom, J. R., Kraemer, H. C., & Gottheil, E. (1989). Effects of psychosocial treatment on survival of patients with metastatic breast cancer. *Lancet, 128,* 888–891.

Sroufe, L. A., Carlson, E., & Shulman, S. (1993). Individuals in relationships: Development from infancy. In D. C. Funder, R. D. Parke, C. Tomlinson–Keasey, & K. Widaman (Eds.), *Studying lives through time* (pp. 315–342). Washington, DC: American Psychological Association.

Stagner, R. (1937). *Psychology of personality.* New York: McGraw–Hill.

Stone, A. A., Schwartz, J. E., Neale, J. M., Shiffman, S., Marco, C. A., Hickcox, M., Paty, J., Porter, L., & Cruise, L. J. (1998). A comparison of coping assessed by ecological momenary assessment and retrospective recall. *Journal of Personality and Social Psychology, 74,* 1670–1680.

Sulloway, F. J. (1979). *Freud: Biologist of the mind.* New York: Basic Books.

Suomi, S. J. (1999). Attachment in rhesus monkeys. In J. Cassidy & P.R. Shaver (Eds.), *Handbook of attachment* (pp. 181–197). New York: Guilford.

Suomi, S. J. (2000). A biobehavioral perspective on developmental psychopathology. In A. Sameroff, M. Lewis, & S. M. Miller (Eds.), *Handbook of developmental psychopathology* (pp. 237–256). New York: Guilford.

Swann, W. B., Jr. (1997). The trouble with change: Self–verification and allegiance to the self. *Psychological Science, 8,* 177–180.

Swann, W. B., Jr., De la Ronde, C., & Hixon, J. G. (1994). Authenticity and positivity strivings in marriage and courtship. *Journal of Personality and Social Psychology, 66,* 857–869.

Swann, W. B., Jr., & Gill, M. J. (1997). Confidence and accuracy in person perception: Do we know what we think we know about our relationship partners? *Journal of Personality and Social Psychology, 73,* 747–757.

Swann, W. B., Jr., & Read, S. J. (1981). Acquiring self–knowledge: The search for feedback that fits. *Journal of Personality and Social Psychology, 41,* 1119–1128.

Tang, T. Z., & De Rubeis, R. J. (1999a). Reconsidering rapid early response in cognitive behavioral therapy for depression. *Clinical Psychology: Science and Practice, 6,* 283–288.

Tang, T. Z., & De Rubeis, R. J. (1999b). Sudden gains and critical sessions in cognitive–behavioral therapy for depression. *Journal of Consulting and Clinical Psychology, 67,* 894–904.

Taylor, S. E. (1989). *Positive illusions: Creative self–deception and the healthy mind.* New York: Basic Books.

Taylor, S. E. (1999). *Health psychology.* New York: McGraw-Hill.

Taylor, S. E., & Brown, J. D. (1988). Illusion and well–being: Where two roads meet. *Psychological Bulletin, 103,* 193–210.

Taylor, S. E., & Brown, J. D. (1994). Positive illusions and well-being revisited: Separating fact from fiction. *Psychological Bulletin, 116,* 21–27.

Tesser, A. (1988). Toward a self–evaluation model of social behavior. *Advances in Experimental Social Psychology, 21,* 181–227.

Thigpen, C. H., & Cleckley, H. (1954). *The three faces of Eve.* Kingsport, TN: Kingsport Press.

Thomas, A., & Chess, S. (1977). *Temperament and development.* New York: Brunner/Mazel.

Thomas, E. J. (1968). Role theory, personality, and the individual. In E. F. Borgatta & W. Lambert (Eds.), *Handbook of personality theory and research (*pp. 691–727*).* Chicago: Rand McNally.

Thompson, R. A. (1996). Scientific fictions and realities. *Contemporary Psychology, 41,* 168.

Thorndike, E. L. (1914). *Educational psychology.* New York: Teachers College, Columbia University.

Tiffany, S. T. (1990). A cognitive model of drug urges and drug–use behavior: Role of automatic and nonautomatic processes. *Psychological Review, 97,* 147–168.

Tolman, E. C. (1932). *Purposive behavior in animals and men.* New York: Century.

Tomkins, S. S. (1962). Commentary. The ideology of research strategies. In S. Messick & J. Ross (Eds.), *Measurement in personality and cognition* (pp. 285–294). New York: Wiley.

Tomkins, S. S. (1963). *Affect, imagery, consciousness: The negative affects.* New York: Springer.

Tomkins, S. S. (1991). *Affect, imagery, consciousness: Anger and fear.* New York: Springer.

Tooby, J., & Cosmides, L. (1990). On the universality of human nature and the uniqueness of the individual: The role of genetics and adaptation. *Journal of Personality, 58,* 17–68.

Tooby, J., & Cosmides, L. (1992). The psychological foundations of culture. In J. H. Barkow, L. Cosmides, & J. Tooby (Eds.), *The adapted mind: Evolutionary psychology and the generation of culture.* New York: Oxford University Press.

Triandis, H. C. (1989). The self and social behavior in differing cultural contexts. *Psychological Review, 96,* 506–520.

Triandis, H. C. (1995). *Individualism and collectivism.* Boulder, CO: Westview Press.

Trivers, R. (1972). Parental investment and sexual selection. In B. Campbell (Ed.), *Sexual selection and the descent of man: 1871–1971* (pp. 136–179). Chicago: Aldine.

Turkheimer, E. (2000). Three laws of behavior genetics and what they mean. *Current Directions in Psychological Science, 9,* 160–164.

Uchino, B. N., Cacioppo, & Kiecolt–Glaser, J. K. (1996). The relationship between social support and physiological processes: A review with emphasis on underlying mechanisms and implications for health. *Psychological Bulletin, 119,* 488–531.

Uchino, B. N., Uno, D., & Holt–Lunstad, J. (1999). Social support, physiological processes, and health. *Current Directions in Psychological Science, 8,* 145–148.

Vaillant, G. E. (1992). Defense mechanisms: Their assessment in the laboratory and in the clinic. *Contemporary Psychology, 37,* 13–14.

Van Ijzendoorn, M. H., & Sagi, A. (1999). Cross–cultural patterns of attachment. In J. Cassidy & P. R. Shaver (Eds.), *Handbook of attachment* (pp. 713–734). New York: Guilford.

Waddington, C. H. (1957). *The strategy of genes.* New York: Macmillan.

de Waal, F. (2001). *The ape and the sushi master.* New York: Basic Books.

Wagner, R. K. (1997). Intelligence, training, and employment. *American Psychologist, 52,* 1059–1069.

Waller, N. G., & Shaver, P. R. (1994). The importance of nongenetic influences on romantic love styles. *Psychological Science, 5,* 268–274.

Wallerstein, R. S. (1989). The psychotherapy research project of the Menninger Foundation: An overview. *Journal of Consulting and Clinical Psychology, 57,* 195–205.

References   311

Wampold, B. E., Mondin, G. W., Moody, M., Stich, F., Benson, K., & Ahn, H. (1997). A meta–analysis of outcome studies comparing bona fide psychotherapies: Empirically, "All Must Have Prizes." *Psychological Bulletin, 122,* 203–215.

Watson, D., Hubbard, B., & Wiese, D. (2000). Self–other agreement in personality and affectivity: The role of acquaintanceship, trait visibility, and assumed similarity. *Journal of Personality and Social Psychology, 78,* 546–558.

Watson, J. B. (1928). *The ways of behaviorism.* New York: Harper.

Watson, J. B, (1930). *Behaviorism.* Chicago: University of Chicago Press.

Watson, J. D. (1968). *The double helix.* New York: Atheneum.

Weinberg, R. A. (1989). Intellilgence and IQ. *American Psychologist, 44,* 98–104.

Weinberger, D. A., & Davidson, M. N. (1994). Styles of inhibiting emotional expression: Distinguishing repressive coping from impression management. *Journal of Personality, 62,* 587–595.

Weinberger, J. (1992). Validating and demystifying subliminal psychodynamic activation. In R. F. Bornstein & T. S. Pittman (Eds.), *Perception without awareness* (pp. 170–188). New York: Guilford.

Weinberger, J., & Silverman, L. H. (1987). Subliminal psychodynamic activation: A method for studying psychoanalytic dynamic propositions. In R. Hogan & W. Jones (Eds.), *Perspectives in personality: Theory, measurement, and interpersonal dynamics* (pp. 251–287). Greenwich, CT: JAI Press.

Weiner, B. (1993). On sin versus sickness: A theory of perceived responsibility and social motivation. *American Psychologist, 48,* 957–965.

Weiner, B., & Graham, S. (1999). Attribution in personality psychology. In L. A. Pervin & O. P. John (Eds.), *Handbook of personality: Theory and research* (pp. 605–628). New York: Guilford.

Weiner, J. (1999). *Time, love, memory.* New York: Knopf.

Weiskrantz, L. (1986). *Blindsight.* Oxford: Oxford University Press.

Werker, J. F. (1989). Becoming a native listener. *American Scientist, 77,* 54–59.

West, S. G. (1986). Methodological developments in personality research: An introduction. *Journal of Personality, 54,* 1–17.

Westen, D. (1992). The cognitive self and the psychoanalytic self: Can we put ourselves together? *Psychological Inquiry, 3,* 1–13.

Westen, D. (1998). The scientific legacy of Sigmund Freud: Toward a psychodynamically informed psychological science. *Psychological Bulletin, 124,* 333–371.

Westen, D., & Gabbard, G.O. (1999). Psychoanalytic approaches to personality. In L. A. Pervin & O. P. John (Eds.), *Handbook of personality: Theory and research* (pp. 57–101). New York: Guilford.

White, G. M. (1993). Emotions inside out: The anthropology of affect. In M. Lewis & J. Haviland (Eds.), *Handbook of emotions* (pp. 29–40). New York: Guilford.

White, R. W. (1959). Motivation reconsidered: The concept of competence. *Psychological Review, 66,* 297–333.

Widiger, T. A. (1993). The DSM-III-R categorical personality disorder diagnoses: A critique and an alternative. *Psychological Inquiry, 4,* 75–90.

Widiger, T. A., & Sankis, L. M. (2000). Adult psychopathology: Issues and controversies. *Annual Review of Psychology, 51,* 377–404.

Wiener, N. (1948). *Cybernetics.* New York: Wiley.

Wierzbicka, A. (1986). Human emotions: Universal or cullture–specific. *American Anthropologist, 88,* 584–594.

Williams, L. (1994). Recall of childhood trauma: A prospective study of women's memories of child sexual abuse. *Journal of Consulting and Clinical Psychology, 62,* 1167–1176.

Wilson, E. O. (1998). *Consilience.* New York: Knopf.

Wilson, G. T. (1999). Rapid response to cognitive behavior therapy. *Clinical Psychology: Science and Practice, 6,* 289–292.

Wilson, T. D. (1994). The proper protocol: Validity and completeness of verbal reports. *Psychological Science, 5,* 249–252.

Wilson, G. T., & Fairburn, C. G. (1993). Cognitive treatments for eating disorders. *Journal of Consulting and Clinical Psychology, 61,* 261–269.

Winter, D. G. John, O. P., Stewart, A. J., Klohnen, E.C., & Duncan, L. E. (1998). Traits and motives: Toward an integration of two traditions in personality research. *Psychological Review, 105,* 230–250.

Witkin, H. A., Dyk, R. B., Faterson, H. F., Goodenough, D. R., & Karp, S. A. (1962). *Psychological differentiation.* New York: Wiley.

Wolpert, L., & Richards, A. (1998). *Passionate minds.* New York: Oxford University Press.

Wright, L. (1997). *Twins: And what they tell us about who we are.* New York: Wiley.

Wylie, R. C. (1961). *The self concept.* Lincoln: University of Nebraska Press.

Wylie, R. C. (1968). The present status of self theory. In E. F. Borgatta & W. W. Lambert (Eds.), *Handbook of personality theory and research* (pp. 728–787). Chicago: Rand McNally.

Wylie, R. C. (1974). *The self–concept,* rev. ed. Lincoln: University of Nebraska Press.

Yik, M. S, Bond, M. H. & Paulhus, D. L. (1998). Do Chinese self–enhance or self–efface? It's a matter of domain. *Personality and Social Psychology Bulletin, 24,* 399–406.

Zimbardo, P. G. (1973). On the ethics of intervention in human psychological research: With special reference to the Stanford prison experiment. *Cognition, 2,* 243–256.

Zuckerman, M. (1995). Good and bad humors: Biochemical bases of personality and its disorders. *Psychological Science, 6,* 325–332.

Zuckerman, M. (1998). Psychobiological theories of personality. In D. F. Barone, M. Hersen, & V. B. Van Hasselt (Eds.), *Advanced personality* (pp. 123–154). New York: Plenum.

Zuckerman, M., Joireman, J., Kraft, M., & Kuhlman, D. M. (1999). Where do motivational and emotional traits fit within three factor models of personality? *Personality and Individual Differences, 26,* 487–504.